THE GREAT REVERSAL

Ethics and the New Testament

Allen Verhey

WILLIAM B. EERDMANS PUBLISHING COMPANY
GRAND RAPIDS, MICHIGAN

For Phyllis, Tim, Betsy, and Katie

Library of Congress Cataloging in Publication Data

Verhey, Allen.
The great reversal.

1. Ethics in the Bible. 2. Bible. N.T. — Criticism,
interpretation, etc. I. Title.
BS2545.E8V47 1984 241 84-6018
ISBN 0-8028-0004-1

CONTENTS

ACKNOWLEDGMENTS

Writing this book has reminded me of my indebtedness to communities, institutions, teachers, students, colleagues, and family. While I will not name them all — some of them would be embarrassed by such an association with the shortcomings of this book — some acknowledgments must be made and the risk of embarrassing some friends taken. The reader should assume, however, that the shortcomings of the book are the author's responsibility and probably the result of not having paid sufficient attention to the advice and counsel provided me by a number of people.

Calvin Theological Seminary and Yale University provided me with a B.D. and a Ph.D. More than that, they provided outstanding teachers in New Testament and in Christian Ethics and the discipline for my initial attempts at combining these areas. I owe debts of gratitude to all of these teachers; I risk embarrassing Andrew Bandstra, Nils A. Dahl, James Gustafson, David Little, Paul Minear, Henry Stob, James Vander Laan, and Bastiaan Van Elderen by acknowledging my indebtedness to them, but it is a risk I happily take to say "thank you."

Hope College has provided the institutional setting for my teaching and continuing learning. It has provided me with students to teach and with whom to learn. Much of this book has been tried out in one way or another with these students, and for their curiosity, criticism, and patience I am genuinely grateful.

Hope College has also provided me with colleagues who give generously of their time and energy to help each other teach and write better. My colleagues in the Religion Department have read most of this material at one stage or another and have criticized it seriously and playfully even as they have encouraged me in the project. These have earned whatever embarrassment they feel by my gratitude: Elton Bruins, Wayne Boulton, Robert Palma, Dennis Voskuil, and Boyd Wilson. Other friends and colleagues who have read and criticized parts of the manuscript include Jim Ackerman, Chris Hackler, Helen John, S.N.D., Steven Lammers, Larry Mannino, Scott Petersen, Keith Reiter, and David Smith.

Hope College has also supported the project with summer research grants. I was honored to be the recipient of a Hope College Faculty Development grant from the Matthew J. and Anne C. Wilson Trust in the summer of 1980 and to be named the Reimold Fellow in the summer of 1981. For this — and for other less tangible but no less important ways Hope College has supported my work — I am deeply grateful, and I risk mentioning Jack Nyenhuis, Dean for the Arts and Humanities, as a friend and an administrator who has won my biased affection and objective praise.

Some of this material was prepared as lectures for the Fuller Seminary Summer program; for that invitation and for his hospitality then and his encouragement again and again, I thank Lew Smedes. Some of the material was prepared for *Spectrum, '81*, sponsored by the Archdiocese of Detroit; for that invitation and for his criticism and encouragement, I thank Richard Cassidy. Some of this material is revision of previously published material: part of the first chapter and part of the third chapter appeared in *The International Standard Bible Encyclopedia*, revised edition, Vol. II, E–J (Grand Rapids: Eerdmans, 1982), under "Ethics: The Ethic of Jesus" and "Ethics: N.T. Ethics"; parts of the fourth chapter appeared previously as "The Use of Scripture in Ethics," *Religious Studies Review*, 4 (1978), 28–39, and as "Notes on a Controversy about the Bible," *Reformed Journal* (May 1977), pp. 9–12. I thank the publishers for invitations to publish the material and now for their permission to utilize it in this book.

Finally, writing this book has consistently reminded me how important the community I call my family has been to me. For the nurturance and support Richard and Catherine Verhey provided and provide, for the affection and care Phyllis shows and gives, for the patience and joy Tim, Betsy, and Katie learn and teach, I am thankful.

INTRODUCTION

By tradition and vocation Christian churches are communities of moral discourse and discernment.[1] The tradition runs down the centuries and across the divisions of the church. Whenever and wherever Christians have joined together in a gathered community, their intentions have been to discuss and discern their personal and social responsibilities in the light of their shared convictions and common loyalty. This book undertakes to describe one part of that tradition, the moral teachings of the New Testament, and to propose a use of that material in the continuing discourse and discernment of the continuing church.

The tradition reaches back to the earliest Christian communities. The churches addressed in the New Testament evidently talked about and asked their leaders about their individual and social responsibilities. They asked "What should I do?" about sexual intercourse now that the ages have turned, about eating meat that someone with a sensitive conscience found objectionable, about the place women were assuming in worship. They asked "What should we do?" about ordering our community and our worship, about our responsibilities to and for other communities (like the poor in Jerusalem), about disciplining errant members. Such concrete questions,[2] and others like them, were apparently commonplace in the early churches.

They asked, of course, not only about *what* they ought to do but *why* — why they ought to do one thing rather than another and why they ought to do something rather than nothing. Concrete moral questions led inevitably to reason-giving and reason-hearing.[3] Sometimes, admittedly, the reasons were simply appeals to the moral commonplaces of Jewish or Hellenistic culture.[4] Sometimes the reasons involved appeals to the law or the prophets or the writings. Sometimes the reasons appealed to the church's memory of Jesus' life or his teachings or his death on the cross. Sometimes the reasons appealed to ethical principles like love or equity or "one's station and its duties." But always the reasons stood in the service of the church's communal attempt to discern the shape and style of life that is "worthy of the gospel of Christ" (Phil. 1:27). Always the reasons themselves could be tested and defended or discarded by religious convictions about God and his intentions with and for human life, for the whole attempt to discover together what ought to be done and what left undone was motivated and normed by their loyalty to the God who raised Jesus from the dead. It was that common loyalty that made them a *community* of moral discourse and gave them a distinctive moral identity.

The continuing church continues to be a community of moral discourse. This is one of the ways in which the Christian communities of the twentieth century stand in the tradition of the earliest Christian communities. There are other ways, of course—such as worship and therapy and fellowship and education and evangelism. The churches are not only communities of moral discourse; that is not their only function nor their only link to the early church. Nevertheless, moral discourse continues to be a function of the continuing church, and wherever and whenever Christians gather as the church, one intention will be to talk about and pray about their personal and social responsibilities.

The churches function as communities of moral discourse, of course, not only out of a sense of tradition but also out of a sense of vocation. Insofar as they continue to be loyal to the God who raised Jesus from the dead, they continue to be committed to his intentions for human life. That loyalty continues to motivate and illuminate the quest for character and conduct that are "worthy of the gospel of Christ." That common loyalty continues to make the churches *communities* of moral discourse and to give them a distinct moral identity. The tradition and vocation are not totally discrete. The tradition continues under the pressure of the loyalty and mediates the loyalty to our children and to generations yet unborn. Without the tradition, the vocation would not be heard; without the vocation, the tradition would become an object of merely antiquarian interest.

The churches today, of course, face new and different concrete questions. Today members of the Christian community ask "What should I do?" about aged parents kept alive by artificial life-support systems, about unrewarding work on the assembly line, about registration and the draft. Today they jointly ask "What should we do?" about ordering our community in response to the movement for the liberation of women, about our responsibilities to and for other communities, for example, the third-world poor. Such questions, and others like them that are being asked in the church today, were beyond the horizon of the early Christians. And more than just the concrete questions has changed; the context within which the questions are asked and addressed has changed. The churches still ask about authority—but now often in the context of democratic and pluralistic societies. They still ask about law—but now often in the context of "permissive" societies. They still ask about the meaning of love—but now often in the context of a sentimental exploitation of the term. The commonplaces sometimes given as reasons for advice or judgment are no longer the commonplaces of Jewish or Hellenistic culture but the commonplaces of our own place and time. It is surely possible to exaggerate the discontinuities between the first and the twentieth century, but there is no denying that there are important differences. There is no denying that different concrete questions are being asked and that they are being asked from within different ethical contexts. And there is no denying that churches today are called to discern the shape and style of life "worthy of the gospel of Christ" in the twentieth century, not in the first.

That calling conscripts the gifts and talents of the whole church. To discern the will of God in the twentieth century requires the whole diversity of gifts within the church — the special skills, the technical expertise, the gifts of wisdom, creativity, imagination, and experience, the knowledge of people and institutions and of opportunities and obstructions — all illuminating the way to discern what deeds and words are worthy of the gospel in the place and time we are.

Even so, the study of the early churches' discernment and judgment has an especially significant contribution to make to the contemporary churches' communal discernment. To be a community of moral discourse and discernment means, among other things, to stand in a particular moral tradition. And the churches stand in a moral tradition within which the New Testament has an acknowledged primacy. The tradition is surely not limited to the New Testament; it reaches backward to include the Old Testament and forward to our own time as the people of God in diverse times and places have responded to God's claim on them in their own special circumstances. The church has, however, identified the Bible — and especially the New Testament — as the finally normative part of her rich moral tradition. The very process of canonization bears witness to the church's insistence that movements within the continuing tradition be weighed and tested by their coherence with these writings. And with one voice, across the centuries and across her divisions, the church has continued to confess that these writings are her Scripture, her canon, and that they have "authority" for her life and thought.[5]

So, as the churches face changing situations and address new moral problems, they stand self-consciously in a tradition of which the New Testament is a normative part. It is from there that they see and from there that they speak. Therefore, whenever the churches undertake to discuss and discern their responsibilities, the Bible, especially the New Testament — and especially the moral teachings of the New Testament — must be considered relevant and essential to the task. The churches, and all who would undertake moral discourse as a part of the common life of the church, can be served by a study of the moral teachings of the New Testament. They are, after all, committed by their confession and their identity to use Scripture, and especially those New Testament teachings, to illuminate and guide contemporary discernment.

But to describe the kinds of moral judgments found in the New Testament, the patterns of inference used there, and the literary forms within which they are presented there, still leaves open the question of *how* this material bears on contemporary discernment. To say *that* Scripture or the New Testament is "canon" for our decision-making is not yet to say *how* it should function thus. To say that Scripture is an "authority" for the churches' moral discourse and discernment is not yet to say what "authorizes" certain moves in argument from Scripture to contemporary moral claims and not others. Unless this question is answered, the study of the moral teachings of the New Testament will hardly be serviceable to the churches. Indeed, unless this question is at least acknowledged candidly, there will be some danger that we will either consign the ethics of the New Testament to the archivists and museumkeepers along with other antiquated texts and artifacts or relegate the church to the unfruitful role of repeating first-century answers to questions no longer asked. The authority of Scripture, then, forces the question of how Scripture, including the New Testament moral teachings, bears on contemporary moral discourse and discernment in the church — but it does not itself answer that question.

I have undertaken this book, I should say candidly, within the church's confession that Scripture is an authority for her faith and life. Precisely because of that conviction, I find it important to describe the New Testament's moral teachings as honestly and "critically" as possible. And precisely because of that conviction, I consider it important to attend as carefully and self-consciously as possible to the methodological issues involved in any recommendation for the use of that material in contemporary moral discourse. Such is the presumptuous agenda of this work.

The first part of that task is to describe the moral teachings of the New Testament as part of a developing tradition. I begin in Chapter I by examining the ethic of Jesus, not in order to undermine the "authority" of the New Testament itself by reaching behind the text to a different "authority," but rather in order to gain some understanding and appreciation of the origin and impetus of the moral tradition which develops when some respond to the news of his resurrection with the confession that this Jesus is Lord. The examination will also be attentive to the diverse interpretations of Jesus' ethic by Christian ethicists and to the difficulties of "historical Jesus research" identified by the New Testament scholars. But it will not be paralyzed by that diversity and those difficulties. The description of the ethic of Jesus will focus on his use and revision of apocalyptic and rabbinical thought and present his ethic as an ethic of response to the coming reign of God, a response that puts into crisis merely external observance of the law and is given shape and texture by a number of concrete commands.

The second chapter examines the development of a moral tradition within the early church. This chapter analyzes the different forms in which the memory of Jesus' words and deeds were handed down in terms of their contribution to the moral discernment and judgment of the early church. It identifies some of the early collections of these originally independent sayings and stories and observes their special moral interests. It also examines the catechetical tradition, in which the early church assimilated and transformed antecedent moral traditions.

The focus then shifts to the completed works of the New Testament. A common loyalty and common tradition have a great variety of expressions within the New Testament itself. Chapter III shows that the theological convictions and pastoral intentions of the various writers, as well as the unique situations and particular problems of the different audiences, contributed to that variety. The moral tradition which the New Testament receives, and of which it is the normative expression, is diverse and pluralistic, not simple and monolithic. The third chapter undertakes to describe New Testament ethics and to enable an appreciation of both its diversity and its convergence in loyalty to the risen Lord.

The fourth chapter turns to the second part of the agenda for this work, to the question of the relevance of the New Testament to the moral discourse and discernment of the church. It describes some of the recent literature addressed to the methodological problems of moving from Scripture to contemporary moral claims, and it surveys some of the various ways in which contemporary ethicists use Scripture as a source of moral wisdom and as a "canon" for moral judgment. My initial intention is not to "solve the problem" but rather to identify the critical methodological questions, the questions anyone who would be self-conscious about the use of Scripture must be prepared to answer. This survey will also identify a number of resources for relating Scripture and contemporary ethics and will show, occasionally, a developing consensus concerning the use of Scripture in contemporary Christian moral discernment.

After identifying the critical methodological questions, the next undertaking of the fourth chapter is to address those questions in the light of the analysis of New Testament ethics provided in the first part of this book. Those conclusions will provide backing for a modest proposal for the continuing use of Scripture — and specifically of New Testament ethics — to illuminate and guide the Christian life. For the description of New Testament ethics to be serviceable for the moral discernment of the continuing church, such a proposal, however tentative, must candidly state what authorizes certain inferences from Scripture to contemporary moral claims and not others.

The book does not presume to speak the last word in the disciplines of either New Testament studies or Christian ethics. Its greatest ambition is to bridge the gulfs that sometimes separate these disciplines from each other and from the life of the Christian community. I offer it in the hope that it may encourage and enable better New Testament scholars than I not merely to record the moral discourse of the early church but to contribute to the moral discourse of the continuing church. I offer it in the hope that it may encourage and enable better Christian ethicists than I not merely to consider moral issues but to consider them in ways that have self-conscious integrity with the normative part of the tradition in which they stand. And I offer it in the hope that the Christian community may be encouraged and helped to conduct its moral discourse and discernment in ways that stand in creative faithfulness to the New Testament and to the Lord who continues to address his people in it.

Chapter I

THE ETHIC OF JESUS

The church has always turned to the teachings of Jesus for moral guidance. Even before the New Testament was written, the sayings of Jesus circulated in the churches and shaped their moral life and thought. The apostle Paul, writing before the Gospels, certainly knew a tradition that had preserved Jesus' words and appealed to it as normative for moral discernment.[1] The Gospels themselves clearly preserved existing traditions of Jesus' sayings and actively appropriated them, shaped them, and applied them in new contexts. Even as the New Testament takes shape and final form, *The Didache* identifies the teachings of Jesus with "the way of life" and contrasts them to "the way of death."[2] And again and again in her history the church has returned to the sayings of Jesus to discover in them "the way of life" worthy of the gospel. There can be no denying the importance of Jesus' ethic to the moral tradition of the Christian churches.

A. DIVERSITY OF INTERPRETATIONS[3]

But while there can be no denying its importance, neither can there be any hiding the diversity of interpretations of Jesus' ethic within the tradition. Christians have constantly gone to the teachings of Jesus for moral guidance, but what they have found there has been varied indeed. The diversity defies any attempt to provide a comprehensive summary, but some order can be brought to the variety by attending to judgments about the way to construe Jesus' teachings, about their content, and about the mode and range of their application.

Many construe Jesus' teachings as providing moral rules, a new law, which prescribe the conduct appropriate to the new covenant.[4] Many others construe Jesus' ethic as providing ideals or goals to be sought — and perhaps achieved — rather than rules to be obeyed.[5] Others insist that Jesus was concerned not so much with external acts — neither legislating them by a new law

6

nor directing them by a set of ideals — as with the internal dispositions, with the springs of conduct, with the formation of character.[6] And finally, some claim, as Rudolf Bultmann has, that "Jesus teaches no ethics at all"[7] in the sense of offering guidance about what actions ought to be done or left undone or even about what character traits one ought to form. For these interpreters Jesus does not provide a morality, whether of precepts, ideals, or dispositions; rather he reveals a reality to which people must respond, in their moral decisions too.[8]

Those who share a certain judgment about how to construe Jesus' ethic may, nevertheless, differ significantly about the content of Jesus' moral teachings. Among those who construe Jesus' ethic as a new law, Jefferson's version of the "sublime moral code" which stands behind the distorted record of the Gospels is quite different from the prohibition of violence, oaths, private property, and sometimes even marriage that one finds among some Anabaptist writers. And both are distant from the position that Jesus demanded resistance to the Roman occupation.[9] Many have taken the position that the content of the law is simply the love commandment.[10] Among those who agree that Jesus provides ideals, the diversity of judgments about the content of those ideals covers an almost equally wide range. Jesus' ideals have been treated as ascetic,[11] identified with personal moral development and consecration,[12] and understood as the revelation of an ideal social order.[13] Those who take Jesus' ethic to be concerned with the formation of character all agree that Jesus shifted the focus of morality from obedience to external codes to obedience to the heart, to the internalization of certain values; but they do not always agree which dispositions are to be formed. Finally, those who understand Jesus' teachings as the revelation of a reality rather than as the prescription of a morality describe that revealed reality quite differently. One may contrast, for example, the positions of Bultmann and H. R. Niebuhr. For Bultmann the reality is the individual man standing alone before the will of God and called to radical obedience to whatever God commands in the moment, in "the crisis of decision." H. R. Niebuhr agrees that Jesus teaches "no new ethic,"[14] but the reality he reveals is the one God who stands behind the law as Creator, Judge, and Redeemer.

Interpretations of Jesus' ethic also differ on the basis of different judgments about the mode or range of application of that ethic. Christians in the second century already found a double standard within the teachings of Jesus.[15] One standard, incumbent on all Christians, included the love command, the golden rule, and so forth; the second standard, given for those who voluntarily sought a higher and better righteousness, gradually became identified as "evangelical counsels." Luther's rejection of monasticism was also a rejection of this double standard. The ethic of Jesus is valid in its entirety, and it is valid for everyone; but it is, for Luther, valid only for one of two realms, only for private life. There remain for Luther two realms with "two kinds of righteousness," one for personal relations, the ethic of Jesus, and another for social relations.[16] The radical reformation — as well as many others — rejected both monasticism's double standard and Luther's two realms; they insisted that Jesus' teachings are applicable to the whole of life for all who would be Christian.

Recently, the application has been affected by views of Jesus' eschatology. Albert Schweitzer introduced the influential theory that Jesus taught an heroic and rigorous obedience applicable to the brief time he contemplated before the cosmic crisis associated with the dawn of the apocalyptic kingdom; it was an "interim ethic" appropriate and immediately applicable only on the mistaken assumption that the end of the world was imminent.[17] That view of Jesus' eschatology and its implications for the application of Jesus' ethic were disowned by C. H. Dodd. For him the kingdom has already come in Jesus' work and words, so his noneschatological ethic is directly relevant, even if it does not provide rules or even general principles.[18] For Amos Wilder too, the eschatology of Jesus is irrelevant to the application of Jesus' ethic. For although Wilder recognizes the element of futurity in Jesus' teachings, Jesus' references to the future are for him only "formal sanctions" of the ethic whose "fundamental sanctions" are Jesus' teachings concerning the nature of God.[19] Among some radical dispensationalists, Jesus' ethic applies to a future dispensation of the kingdom and only secondarily to the extended interim of this dispensation.[20] For Martin Dibelius also, Jesus' ethic unveils the pure will of God which will govern the future kingdom but which is impossible and irrelevant until that kingdom comes.[21] Some would agree with Dibelius and yet insist that the "impossible" ethic is nevertheless relevant, both to judge our sin and, by means of compromise and approximation, to guide conduct.[22]

Judgments about the relation of Jesus' religious loyalties to his ethic can also affect the range of application. For some, Jesus' ethic, because of its apparent reasonableness, makes claims on the universal human community;[23] but others claim the ethic makes no sense apart from loyalty to Jesus as the Christ or his loyalty to God and thus is an ethic applicable only to the Christian community.

The diversity of interpretations and appropriations of Jesus' ethic is a sign of the importance and richness of Jesus' teachings. Different people with different histories, standing in different concrete contexts, using different tools and skills, have understood and communicated differently what faithfulness to the teachings of Jesus requires. The diversity is hardly surprising and need not be regretted or eliminated; indeed, it is appropriate to celebrate and preserve something of this great variety. Nevertheless, as the church continues to ask what faithfulness to the ethic of Jesus requires, it needs constantly to return to his teachings, not simply to a favorite interpretation of those teachings. At the very least, some weighing and testing of the diverse interpretations against Jesus' teachings themselves is certainly called for. Such a task, however, quickly encounters difficulties.

B. DIFFICULTIES IN DESCRIBING JESUS' ETHIC

The first difficulty is identified by Henry Cadbury as "the peril of modernizing Jesus."[24] Cadbury made the point in his polemic against the social gospel movement, but it is a temptation and difficulty for every interpreter of Jesus' ethic. (Indeed, we may ask whether the rigorous distinction between personal and social morality which Cadbury used to describe the ethic of Jesus is not itself anachronistic and "modernizing.") The point should not be merely that Jesus does not deal with, say, genetic engineering or the use of nuclear energy, but that the mode of moral reflection was not Kantian or utilitarian or idealistic. Positively, the point is that Jesus and his ethic must be understood against the background of first-century Judaism.

The second difficulty is that already within the New Testament, Jesus' ethic is interpreted. We must not forget the nature of the Gospels when we inquire about Jesus' ethic. The premise of the form critics[25] is certainly correct — that the sayings of Jesus and stories about Jesus originally circulated independently and orally. The source critics[26] are certainly right in supposing that these sayings and stories were compiled into collections which became sources for our Gospels. The redaction critics[27] have quite correctly insisted that our Gospels are not merely compilations of sources[28] but unified compositions reflecting the pastoral, theological, and moral intentions of the authors. The Gospels, then, do not merely passively receive and preserve Jesus' ethic as though he were some famous, but dead, rabbi. In their conviction of his resurrection, they actively appropriate the tradition of his sayings and deeds in the confidence that he continues to abide with and speak to his church. Each Gospel shapes and interprets the ethic of Jesus even as it hands it down.

There can be little doubt, for example, that the Sermon on the Mount is Matthew's literary creation, that Matthew has fashioned originally independent sayings into the first great discourse of his Gospel. Matthew's concern that the righteousness of the Christian community exceed the righteousness of the scribes and Pharisees structures the sermon.[29] It is Matthew who selects, organizes, and adapts the sayings of Jesus in the formation of this sermon. It is an inspired and inspiring interpretation of the ethic of Jesus, but it is an interpretation and may not be simply identified with Jesus' ethic (as it often is).

To inquire about Jesus' ethic which stands behind its interpretation and application to new situations by the evangelists is an historical inquiry and thus faces the preliminary question about criteria for making judgments about the historical Jesus (or historical judgments about the ethic of Jesus). To follow the advice of E. Käsemann, that is, to accept as genuine only those traditions "which can be neither derived from Judaism nor attributed to primitive Christianity,"[30] would yield minimal, but quite certain, results. To follow the advice of E. Stauffer, that is, to accept the rule *in dubiis pro tradito,*[31] would yield maximal, but sometimes doubtful, results. Between the extreme positions of Käsemann and Stauffer there are a number of different mediating positions. Closer to Stauffer's insistence on the historical reliability of the tradition is the position of T. W. Manson, who argues that the sayings source, Q, and the "Petrine" sections of Mark are fundamentally eyewitness accounts of the disciples Matthew and Peter, respectively.[32] The Scandinavian scholars H. Riesenfeld and B. Gerhardsson have also defended the historical reliability of the tradition: in their view the tradition is handed down and supervised by a professional class which functioned in ways similar to those of the rabbis.[33] Closer to Käsemann's narrow criterion is J. Jeremias's attempt, on the one hand, to describe certain "laws of transformation" in the developing tradition[34] and, on the other, to describe the Palestinian and Jewish environment of Jesus.[35] He discounts the "tendencies" of the tradition, but though he can use the criterion of discontinuity to good advantage,[36] he is not driven methodologically to disown whatever in Jesus' life and teaching is shared with his Jewish environment. Yet another criterion is "multiple attestation,"[37] which can be used either with respect to the sources or to the forms of literature found within the Gospels. If more than one independent source or more than one of the tradition's literary forms witness to the same characteristic feature of Jesus' life and teaching, then there is warrant for accepting that feature as authentic historically.

We cannot enter into this methodological dispute here, but some observations are apropos. First, there is no place for methodological dogmatism here; different criteria may well be preferred for different purposes. The Käsemann criterion, for example, may be well chosen for the apologetic purpose of showing with the strictest historical scrutiny that the Jesus of history is the basis for and coherent with the Church's proclamation of him as the Christ. Stauffer's criterion, however, seems better chosen for the purpose of edification, of shaping character and identity by the recitation of Jesus' story. Our purpose in this chapter is neither apology nor edification but clarification of the beginnings of the moral tradition of the church. For that purpose the criteria that will serve best are "multiple attestation" and Jeremias's enterprise of drawing lines from Judaism forward to Jesus and from the Christian tradition back to Jesus.[38]

Second, there is no escaping the fact that we know Jesus and his moral teaching only through the memory of his disciples. The initial assumptions of each scholar concerning the early tradition inevitably reveal themselves in any reconstruction of Jesus or his ethic. The criteria offer some check against the arbitrary reconstructions of both those who are initially inclined to suppose that Jesus was either misunderstood or consciously misrepresented in the memory of the disciples[39] and those (like me, I should say candidly) who are inclined to suppose that the church did not create the traditions but preserved them, reproduced them, and shaped them to address new situations. But the criteria do not provide a tidy recipe for "historical objectivity"; they stand guard against arbitrariness, but their use is influenced by one's initial assessments and evaluations.

In line with the preceding observations, I should remark that I do not undertake the reconstruction of Jesus' moral teaching here to be freed from the chains of biblical or ecclesiastical moral authorities,[40] but rather to illuminate the biblical and ecclesiastical moral tradition. We are not attempting to reach "behind" Scripture; rather we are attempting to clarify the beginnings of a tradition that comes to normative expression in the New Testament.

Finally, any reconstruction of moral teachings of the historical Jesus must be coherent with two important and indisputable facts. We may not forget, in the first place, that this Jesus was put to death on a Roman cross. Any description of Jesus' ethic must somehow cohere with that historical datum.[41] It is difficult to imagine, for example, any plot to kill one whose message was "God the Father, and the infinite value of the human soul."[42] We may not forget, in the second place, that a community which recognized in this Jesus their Lord and Christ came into existence and continues to exist. This is not meant, of course, to make the church's confession a substitute for the historical method. The historical method, profane though it is, is the only tool the historian has. With its more or less debatable conclusions, it is no substitute for faith; and neither is faith a substitute for it. Nevertheless, the rise of faith in this Jesus as the Christ, the beginning and continuation of a community which calls him Lord, is an historical datum with which any historical reconstruction of Jesus' life and moral teachings must cohere.

There is no denying the difficulties of the project undertaken in this chapter. But it is wrong to infer from "the peril of modernizing Jesus" that Jesus is irrelevant to the modern age. And it is wrong to infer from the nature of our sources a radical historical skepticism. We must not allow the difficulties to serve as excuses by which to avoid the task of reconstructing the ethic of Jesus. The possibility of historical reconstruction — and the interest in it — is given with the incarnation, for in the incarnation the Word became flesh, not by assuming some general "human nature" but by assuming the concrete and particular reality of Jesus of Nazareth.

C. THE KINGDOM OF GOD AND THE ETHIC OF JESUS

The best starting point for inquiry into the ethic of Jesus is provided by the striking summary of Jesus' teaching which Mark places at the head of his account of Jesus' public ministry: "The time is fulfilled, and the kingdom of God is at hand; repent, and believe in the gospel" (Mk. 1:15). Surely this is Mark's editorial summary of Jesus' teaching rather than a verbatim record of any particular saying of Jesus,[43] but there are few who deny its aptness as a summary. Jesus' proclamation of the kingdom is too well attested in multiple forms and sources to be denied.[44] That Jesus proclaimed the kingdom of God is certain, but what he *meant* by it has been a matter of considerable dispute.

It has been understood in a variety of ways, each of which affects the description of Jesus' ethic.[45] This chapter can neither enter fully into that discussion of "the kingdom of God" nor — because of the question's importance to understanding Jesus' ethic — leave it entirely alone.

1. The Apocalyptic Background

The Jews had always taught that God is king, and they always hoped for the fuller and final establishment of his reign.[46] The covenant itself reminded the people that God is the great sovereign, and their recitals of God's mighty acts witnessed to the establishment of God's reign (e.g., Ex. 15:1-18). The prophets' expectation of that future was based on their conviction that God has already established his reign in the events remembered and recited at the festivals; but for them that future act of God, rather than any past event, will be finally and genuinely decisive. The future will be analogous to God's former work: there will be a new exodus, a new entry into the land, a new David, a new Jerusalem, a new covenant — but the past events are mere tokens of God's future and decisive acts.[47]

This prophetic concentration on the future was the inheritance of the apocalyptic literature.[48] There is in apocalypticism the doctrine of "two ages," a sharp distinction between "this age" and "the age to come." "This age" is under the dominion of sin and death, allied with the powers of darkness but nevertheless running its predetermined course to its eschatological end. This determinism is another characteristic of apocalyptic literature, and it is the assumption behind all those dreams and visions that divide the present age into periods of time leading up to the *eschaton,* the last time, the end. Then God will act to end the old age and begin the new. There is a great gulf between the ages: no historical process links them, and only the act of God can end the reign of sin and death and establish his own complete and unchallenged sovereignty. The apocalyptic expectation combined, therefore, despair about the evil character of this age with the profoundest hope for a new age, an age of God's reign not only over the nations, bringing a reversal of Israel's fortunes, but over the whole cosmos, shattering the rule of sin and death. Little wonder that the beginning of that age would be accompanied by cosmic signs and portents, by resurrection and judgment.

The moral consequences of such beliefs are not at all clear. G. E. Ladd characterizes apocalyptic literature as "ethically passive,"[49] and indeed a great deal of the literature is not marked by any ethical urgency. Their determinism and despair concerning the present age could be — and were, at least sometimes — morally enervating. But other than an occasional flourish of exhortation commending an uncalculating righteousness and love (e.g., especially in The Testaments of the Twelve Patriarchs), there is the persistent and quite rabbinical emphasis on obedience to the law. Apocalypticism's ultimate confidence in God and his future motivated a fierce and sober faithfulness to the law in the midst of this present age. Apocalypticism, therefore, was not alien to the Pharisees or the rabbis of their school, nor to the community of Qumran.[50] The moral consequences of their vision of a new age, an age of God's unchallenged sovereignty and of vindication for the righteous, can only fairly be called "ethical passivity" if faithfulness to the law when sin and death rule can fairly be called "passivity."

It is against this background that Jesus' announcement of "the kingdom of God" is to be understood.[51] Jesus announced to his contemporaries that the promised "age to come," the new age, the age of God's undisputed sovereignty over the whole creation, was "at hand."[52] God was about to act to end the reign of sin and death and to inaugurate his own unchallenged kingdom.

Against that background, interpreting the kingdom as an ideal social order whose coming is contingent on human striving is clearly a misunderstanding. The coming of the kingdom is contingent not on human activity but on the decisive act of God, the apocalyptic, world-shattering, and world-renewing act of God, which brings both final judgment and final salvation. Its coming is not something people can either hasten or delay but something for which they can only pray. And pray they did, both in the Kaddish, the prayer which ended synagogue services with the petitions for the hallowing of God's name and the speedy establishment of his kingdom, and in the prayer Jesus taught his disciples (Lk. 11:2).[53]

Against the background of first-century Jewish apocalyptic, moreover, limiting the kingdom to God's sovereignty in the mysterious region of the soul is equally a misunderstanding; for the coming act of God establishes his sovereignty over the whole cosmos. Jesus nowhere narrows the scope of apocalyptic expectation to the mystical or pious or "existential" surrender of the heart to God. He expects a resurrection, when God will end the reign of death, and a judgment, when God will vindicate the righteous; he expects the destruction and renewal of the world.[54] The kingdom is something people enter, not something that enters people. It is a state of affairs, not a state of mind. Jesus comes with no social program to achieve the kingdom; but the kingdom he announces is no less social than personal. God will establish his sovereignty over all creation.[55]

2. The Revision of Apocalypticism

Jesus comes announcing that the act of God by which he establishes his cosmic sovereignty is "at hand" and, indeed, already making its power felt. The future act is still fundamental in this proclamation, but it is indissolubly related to the present time and to Jesus' own life and ministry. God's sovereignty is not merely future, but already having effect in Jesus' exorcisms and miracles,[56] and even in his ethical teachings.[57] Albert Schweitzer's "consistent eschatology," then, with its single focus on the imminent fture of the kingdom of God and its interpretation of Jesus' moral teaching as "the special ethic of the interval before the coming of the Kingdom (*Interimsethik*),"[58] is a mis-understanding, for it neglects the present effectiveness of God's future act in Jesus. But C. H. Dodd's "realized eschatology,"[59] which emphasizes the present reality of the kingdom to the point of dismissing Jesus' proclamation of the future act of God, is at least equally mistaken. Both the future act of God and its present impact are part of Jesus' teaching concerning the kingdom and of his ethic.[60]

The proclamation of the future act of God remains fundamental, for even in the deeds and words of Jesus it is the future rule of God that makes its power felt. But the present impact of the kingdom is critical, because it forces important revisions of apocalyptic thought. Apocalypticism divided history into "two ages" and fixed a great gulf between them. Jesus bridges the gulf: the future rule of God already begins to be manifest and effective.[61] Apocalypticism saw the present age as unrelentingly evil and, nevertheless, running its predetermined course to its end. So the apocalyptic seer was preoccupied with the discovery of epochs, with the identification of the "signs of the times," the calculation of the end time. But Jesus does not indulge in such speculation and calculation (Lk. 17:20;[62] Mk. 13:22 and par.); he reads no "heavenly book" describing the epochs; he "sees" only "Satan fall like lightning from heaven" (Lk. 10:18;[63] cf. Jn. 12:31). Rather, Jesus emphasizes the suddenness of the end (e.g., Mk. 13:35 and par.; Mt. 24:37-41 par.) and the present impact of God's sovereignty in his own ministry, and he instructs his followers to "watch" (Mk. 13:33,35,37 and par.).

Apocalypticism's determinism and pessimism about this age sometimes rendered human action and exertion fruitless and inconsequential; usually apocalypticism reinforced a sober and fierce obedience to the law. But Jesus brings the future reign of God to bear upon the present. Even his command to "watch" has in the tradition a whole range of ethical cognates (Mk. 14:38; Lk. 12:35-38; 21:34; parables in Mt. about watchfulness, 24:45-25:46).[64] It is implausible that these various traditions all represent the very words of Jesus, but the very variety of the sources and forms suggests that for Jesus the eschatological command "watch" and his moral teachings have a common mother, the coming sovereignty of God and his holy will. This kind of moral alertness is not required where casuistry on the basis of the law neatly and clearly defines what is to be done and what left undone; it is required where anger and lust and pride are condemned with the same seriousness as are murder and adultery. And so they are where the coming sovereignty of God and his holy will make their power felt in Jesus' ministry and teaching. The future sovereignty of God, the future liberation from the dominion of the powers of darkness, already exerts its power in Jesus' "authority," both in his miracles and in his teachings (cf. Mk. 1:21-28). The apocalyptic judgment and salvation begin to take effect as Jesus pronounces the eschatological "woes" and blessings (Lk. 6:20-26; Mt. 5:12; Lk. 11:28,42-52; Mt. 23:13-36). The holy will of God is itself already disclosed in Jesus' words (Mk. 13:31 and par.; cf. Jn. 5:24, etc.). The point is this: while apocalyptic writing provides the background for Jesus' teaching, to reduce Jesus to an apocalyptic seer is also a misunderstanding, for he breaks through the forms and categories and pessimistic determinism of apocalyptic. Surely he is no idealistic optimist announcing a slow but steady progress to a perfect social order, but neither is he an apocalyptic pessimist for whom human action is inconsequential and fruitless. While human action does not establish the kingdom, it is nevertheless again called for, and called for as the eschatologically urgent response to the action of God which is at hand and already making its power felt. That is the first and fundamental thesis with respect to the ethic of Jesus: it is an ethic of response, response to the apocalyptic action of God, which is at hand and already making its power felt.

It becomes crucially important, then, that Jesus describes that action of God differently than apocalyptic literature typically did. He revises the material content of apocalyptic expectation. He still expects the reign of God to bring judgment and salvation, liberation and security. He still expects "a great reversal" of this present age. But the nationalistic hope for Israel's lordship over and revenge against the nations is strikingly absent (e.g., Lk. 4:16ff.).[65] Indeed, the eschatological woes and blessings are promised to (and already pronounced upon) the very people conventionally thought least likely to receive them: the poor, the hungry, those who weep and are despised (Lk. 6:20-22; cf. Mt. 5:1-12; Lk. 16:25). Eschatological woes fall upon the rich and carefree who rejoice in their reputation (Lk. 6:20-26; cf. 16:25) and on the scribes and Pharisees who use religion and their knowledge of the law to assert themselves, their pious reputations, and their financial interests (Mt. 23:13-36; Lk. 11:42-52; cf. Mk. 12:38-40; Lk. 6:32-35; Mt. 6:16-18). The "great reversal" of the kingdom brings a transformation of values. The present order, including its conventional rules of prestige and protocol, pomp and privilege, is called into question by Jesus' announcement of the coming kingdom. The expectation of God's rule is condensed into axioms like "many that are first will be last, and the last first" (Mk. 10:31 and par.; Lk. 13:30; Mk. 9:35-36; Mt. 20:16; also Pap. Oxyrhynchus 654, ar. 3, Gospel of Thomas 4) and "whoever exalts himself will be humbled, and whoever humbles himself will be exalted" (Mt. 23:12; cf. Lk. 14:11; 18:14; Mt. 18:4). In the light of such a transformation of values, the self-assertiveness of nations also falls under judgment, and the national desire for conventional prominence and security is called into question. The "great reversal" makes plain that the apocalyptic seer who dreamed of vengeance and the rabbi who insisted on the first seat in the synagogue (Lk. 11:43; Mk. 12:38-40 par.) alike belong to the present evil age.

The new age, the age of God's undisputed sovereignty, with its transformation of accustomed rules and values, already makes its power felt in Jesus. He is not just a "seer" of the coming kingdom; he is its agent. Blessings already begin to fall on those who were outcasts: "The blind receive their sight, the lame walk, lepers are cleansed, and the deaf hear, the dead are raised up, the poor have good news preached to them" (Lk. 7:22; Mt. 11:5; cf. Lk. 4:16-21; Mt. 10:7-8). He talks openly with women, receives and blesses children, speaks with Samaritans, has table fellowship with publicans and sinners,[66] is known as the "friend of sinners" (Mt. 11:19; Lk. 7:34, etc.). And already those who are entrenched in power, privilege, and their own conventional righteousness begin to be cast out. He persistently returns the challenges of the scribes and Pharisees; he expels the temple merchants who would use religion and law for profit (Mk. 11:15-17). The apocalyptic "great reversal," then, already makes its power felt in Jesus; and Jesus says, "Blessed is he who takes no offense at me" (Lk. 7:23; Mk. 11:6). That is, one's eschatological destiny hinges on the response to the present impact of God's imminent sovereignty in Jesus and his ministry (cf. Mk. 8:38 and par.; Lk. 12:8 and par.). Some are indeed scandalized by this reversal of values, by this challenge to the old order. They have no readiness to repent and so miss the eschatological blessing. But others, particularly among the outcasts and sinners, welcome the kingdom and its proleptic presence in Jesus' ministry. These repent and are blessed.

D. THE ETHIC OF JESUS AND THE SHAPE OF REPENTANCE

The ethic of Jesus is an ethic of response to the coming act of God and its present impact in Jesus himself. The response can be summarized — and was summarized by Mark (1:15) and Matthew (4:17) — as "repentance."[67] Repentance is not merely an uneasy conscience prompted by introspection or meditation on the law. It is surely not merely the external gestures of sackcloth and ashes (Mt. 11:21 and par.) or the pious rituals of fasting (Mt. 6:16-18; Mk. 2:18-22 par.). It is rather a radical and joyful turning. It is to renounce the old securities and the conventional values and joyfully to welcome the reign of God already making its power felt (Mt. 13:44-46, etc). It spells an end to self-assertiveness and self-glorifying and the beginning of the self-forgetfulness that already submits to God's sovereignty and serves the neighbor. Even so and only so does the disciple catch a glimpse of what remains hidden to those outside until the eschatological act of God, the "mystery" of the kingdom (cf. Mk. 4:11). Even so and only so does one enter the kingdom of God (Lk. 13:1-5). What "repentance" means more precisely, what its concrete shape is, can only be discerned in the concrete commands of Jesus that issue from his announcement of the kingdom and from its present impact in his own behavior.

1. Be Last of All[68]

Repentance means to welcome the announcement of a kingdom where "many that are first will be last, and the last first" (Mk. 10:31 and par., etc.) and where "whoever exalts himself will be humbled, and whoever humbles himself will be exalted" (Mt. 23:12, etc.). To welcome that announcement is to allow the present impact of such a kingdom in the ministry of Jesus to transform our values and behavior. So repentance is given shape by obedience to the concrete command of Jesus: "If any would be first, he must be last of all and servant of all" (Mk. 9:35; cf. Mk. 10:43-44 par. Lk. 22:26, Mt. 20:26,27; also 23:11; Jn. 13:12-17).[69]

The concrete command of Jesus is humble service. Such humble service does not assert its own rights and privileges but submits to the coming reign of God and pours itself out for the neighbor's good, especially for the good of the poor and the outcast. The response to this command is also the response to Jesus, who was among them both "as one who serves" (Lk. 22:27; cf. Jn. 13:2-17; Mk. 10:45; Mt. 20:28) and as the one in whom God's kingdom already exerts its power. And the response to Jesus is also the response to the coming kingdom in which the first shall be last and the last first. To welcome the coming of such a kingdom is to welcome Jesus, and to welcome Jesus is joyfully to surrender the rights and privileges of social status and convention and to serve. Humble service, then, is a part of the concrete shape of repentance in view of the coming kingdom and its present effectiveness in Jesus. The juxtaposition of the disposition to be first and the disposition to serve is the juxtaposition of the old age and the new age. The promise to the humble, the warning to the proud, and the command to "be last" both presuppose the futurity of the coming reign of God and make its power felt in the present.[70]

The commandment of humble service takes a number of cognate forms. It extends to matters like not insisting on titles of distinction (Mt. 23:8-10) or the most honorable seats (Lk. 14:7-11; cf. Jas. 2:2-4), and like the duties of hospitality to "the poor, the maimed, the lame, the blind" (Lk. 14:13,21). Perhaps these sayings are not the very words of Jesus, but they surely demonstrate that Jesus' command of humble service was from the very beginning related to the whole of life, including the most mundane of it.

2. Be Not Anxious[71]

We must pay special attention to humble service to the poor. It is a part of the "great reversal" of the coming kingdom that the conventional value and security of wealth is challenged and discarded. The eschatological blessing falls on the poor (Lk. 6:20ff.), judgment on the rich (Lk. 6:24; cf. 16:19-31). And in Jesus' life and teaching that great reversal already begins to take effect. The response to this great reversal is, on the one side, a carefree disposition toward riches. Jesus' concrete instruction is "be not anxious" (Mt. 6:25,31,34; Lk. 12:22; cf. Pap. Oxyrhynchus 655, Gospel of Thomas 36; cf. also Mt. 10:31; Lk. 12:7). The instruction is supported by an appeal to God's care for the birds and lilies, but it is hardly a "commonsense" appeal. Birds and lilies are short-lived and hardly the sort of creatures likely to prevent a conventional mentality's anxiety. The point is that God's care and power extend even to those whose lives are cheap and brief. There is an implicit challenge to this age's standards of value and security. It is an eschatological appeal, joined with "seek first his kingdom" (Mt. 6:33; Lk. 12:31).[72] In the response to the command "be not anxious" is the response to Jesus who had "nowhere to lay his head" (Mt. 8:20; Lk. 9:58) and the response to the coming kingdom of the God whose care extends to those who, by the standards of this age, are neither valuable nor secure. To confront Jesus' command is to confront already now a choice between the present age and the age to come, between serving Mammon or God (Mt. 6:24; Lk. 16:13), between trusting the conventional patterns of privilege, prestige, power, and security or trusting God (Mk. 10:23-25 par.). But to trust riches will soon be shown up as folly (Lk. 12:13-21; cf. Mk. 13:15 and par.; Lk. 17:31), and to be carefree, to "be not anxious," is to lay up "treasures in heaven" (Mt. 6:20; cf. Lk. 12:33; Mk. 10:21 and par., where "treasures in heaven" is related, however, to almsgiving).

3. Give Alms[73]

This carefree attitude toward riches forms in Jesus' followers a disposition, a readiness, to give generously to help the poor. Such action is the other side of the response to the eschatological blessing on the poor. The concrete command is "sell your possessions and give alms" (Lk. 12:33; Mk. 10:21 and par.; cf. Lk. 14:33; Mt. 6:4,20). With such generosity one welcomes the coming kingdom and its present impact in Jesus. Jesus calls for such a response to the great reversal in this command; he is not to be understood as legislating. That the concrete command is not intended as legislation is made clear by the cognate command to lend to the poor (Lk. 6:34-35), which presupposes continuing possession, by the example of Zacchaeus (Lk. 19:1-10), and by the commendation of the costly "waste" of ointment (Mk. 14:3-9; Mt. 26:6-13; Jn. 12:1-8). While the command "sell all your possessions and give alms" is not legislation, it is not for that less stringent or demanding. To help the poor with self-forgetful generosity is to welcome God's coming rule (Lk. 19:9, "Today has salvation come to this house"), and not to is to expose oneself to his judgment (Lk. 16:19-31; Mt. 25:31-36). Such self-forgetful generosity may take abundant concrete forms, of course: feeding the hungry, giving the thirsty drink, practicing hospitality, clothing the naked, visiting the sick and imprisoned (Mt. 25:31-46).[74] And it ought to be observed that almsgiving in the East was not merely encouraging beggary but the predominant form of social help.[75]

Jesus' word "you always have the poor with you" (Mk. 14:7; Mt. 26:11; Jn. 12:8) does not compromise this concern for the poor in his moral teachings. He quotes Deuteronomy 15:11, where it is clear that "the poor will never cease out of the land" only because of the refusal of the community to keep the covenant with its stipulations for the alleviation of poverty (Deut. 15:1-11; cf. Lk. 16:29-31). Jesus rebukes the woman's accusers, but not for their concern for the poor; he rebukes them for presumptuously singling out this woman, for self-righteously judging her when the very presence of the poor judges the whole community. Indeed, her carefree lavishing of ointment on Jesus is her form of welcoming the great reversal of the coming kingdom (cf. the other women who "minister" to Jesus, Lk. 8:3; Mk. 15:41). In Jesus' absence the same obedience to "be not anxious" will lead to generous care for the poor (Mk. 14:7; cf. Mt. 25:40).

The great reversal of the coming kingdom does not make its power felt in a rigorous asceticism. Jesus was not an ascetic; indeed, he was mocked for being "a glutton and a drunkard" (Mt. 11:19 and par.). He does not rush to judgment on the "waste" of ointment. The kingdom makes its power felt in a carefree trust in God rather than in the conventional values and securities of the present age. Repentance, the response to the kingdom, does not take the shape of any rigid legalism. Jesus refuses, for example, to act as an arbiter in the matter of an inheritance (Lk. 12:13,14; cf. Gospel of Thomas 72). Repentance takes the shape, rather, of joyfully welcoming the eschatological blessings on the poor and hungry by practicing generosity toward them.

4. It Shall Not Be Taken from Her[76]

The blessing on the poor and outcast extends to women. Against the background of the conventional depreciation of women in first-century Palestine,[77] Jesus' behavior is indeed a "great reversal." He breaks convention by simply talking publicly with them (Jn. 4:1-26; Mk. 7:24-30, etc.) and by including them among his followers (Lk. 8:1-3, etc.). He commends women (e.g., Mk. 12:41 and par.) and defends women (e.g., Lk. 7:39-40; Mk. 12:40 and par.).

Among all the women, two stand out — the sisters Mary and Martha (Lk. 10:38-42; Jn. 12:1-8). Surely an authentic memory stands behind these separate traditions. In each narrative Martha serves at table (itself a surprising departure from custom when a group of men are present); but Mary's behavior is in each narrative shocking and offensive to conventional protocol regarding women and a challenge to the role assignments of women in first-century Palestine. In John's narrative, she lets down her hair to anoint Jesus' feet (cf. Lk. 7:38), and in Luke's she takes the posture of the pupil, the disciple, sitting at Jesus' feet listening to his teachings. No self-respecting rabbi could or would endure teaching a woman. It is little wonder that women apparently heard him gladly (Lk. 11:27) or that in his passion it was some women who remained faithful to him (Mk. 15:40,41 and par.; Jn. 19:25). The present impact of the coming kingdom was good news to women.

It must be acknowledged that little explicit call for welcoming this aspect of the great reversal can be found in Jesus' sayings.[78] But repentance clearly includes the response to this particular transformation of values and behavior, even if there are no authentic concrete commands preserved which make it explicit. It is not unreasonable to suppose there were such or, perhaps, that they are echoed in Luke's formulation, "Mary has chosen the good portion, which shall not be taken away from her" (Lk. 10:42).[79] To respond to the coming kingdom and its present impact in Jesus is to welcome rather than to resist the good news for women. Her new place in the kingdom may not "be taken from her."

5. Forbid Them Not[80]

The coming kingdom is also good news for children. The disciples' rebuke of the women who brought their children to Jesus was conventional. But Jesus reversed the conventional standards, welcomed the children, and blessed them (Mk. 10:13-16 par.). "Forbid them not, for of such is the kingdom of God" (Mk. 10:14) is a concrete command that challenges both conventional expectations of the kingdom and the customary rules of pomp, protocol, and behavior. To care for, to help, and to love little children is to welcome the coming kingdom and its present impact in Jesus (Mk. 9:36 and par.).

6. Judge Not[81]

Among those blessed in the coming kingdom, finally, are to be numbered the "sinners." Jesus' announcement of the coming kingdom is good news to sinners who repent. To include them in the coming kingdom is scandalous, yet such is the great reversal Jesus announces.[82] And already the coming kingdom makes its impact felt in Jesus. He says, "I came not to call the righteous, but sinners" (Mk. 2:17b and par.; cf. Mt. 21:31; Lk. 19:10). He is notorious as "the friend of sinners" (Mt. 11:19; Lk. 7:34,37,39; 15:2; 19:7); he befriends them, eats with them, and (already!) forgives them (Mk. 2:5 and par.; Lk. 7:48; cf. Jn. 5:21-27). The coming kingdom already makes its power felt among the sinners who repent. There is "joy in heaven over one sinner who repents" (Lk. 15:7,10,32). But the "righteous" who refuse to "repent," who refuse to welcome such a kingdom, who refuse to rejoice in the repentance of sinners, are already judged; and the judgment is the announcement of the coming reversal itself (Mt. 21:31; Lk. 15:7; 18:9-14). The concrete meaning of repentance, of welcoming such a kingdom, is captured in the commands to "judge not" (Mt. 7:1; Lk. 6:37; cf. Mt. 7:24; Lk. 6:41-42; Mk. 4:24) and to "forgive" (Mt. 6:14-15; Mk. 11:25; Mt. 18:21-35; Lk. 17:3,4). One's eschatological destiny hinges on whether or not one welcomes the coming kingdom and its present impact in Jesus by a repentance which conforms to the forgiveness of sinners.[83]

To suggest that this is "works righteousness," however, is a great misunderstanding; the proclamation of the kingdom comes first, and one only gratefully welcomes that coming kingdom when one forgives. One does not earn it. The great reversal is fundamental, and neither the "righteousness" of the scribes and Pharisees nor the disposition to forgive among the repentant gives any claims against God or any reason to boast in oneself or to exclude others from the kingdom.

It is also a misunderstanding to suppose that the prohibition of judging and the requirement of forgiveness leave no place for discernment or mutual admonition. On the contrary, Jesus commands his disciples, "If your brother sins, rebuke him" (Lk. 17:3).[84] But the great reversal transforms such rebukes from attempts to find security in conventional righteousness to finding security in the coming kingdom of God and its present impact in Jesus, who seeks the sinner's good. So, instead of enhancing one's own self-righteousness, such rebukes serve the coming kingdom and the sinner. Jesus' ethic is not antinomian and libertine, but neither is it an ethic of law and casuistry. It is an ethic of response to the coming kingdom of God.

E. THE ETHIC OF JESUS AND THE LAW[85]

Jesus' ethic is fundamentally an ethic of response rather than an ethic of obedience to law. Nevertheless, the question of Jesus' attitude to the law is of obvious importance to any description of his ethic. The question is complicated by the presence of apparent discrepancies in the tradition: some texts seem to disclose an almost rabbinical nomism (e.g., Mk. 1:44; 7:9-10; 10:18-19; 12:28-34; Mt. 5:17-19; 18:16; 23:2-3; Lk. 5:14; 16:27-31) while others seem to call for a radical rejection of law (e.g., Mk. 2:18-3:6; 7:14-23; 10:2-12; Mt. 5:31-32,38-39; Lk. 6:37; 13:10-17; 14:1-6; Jn. 9-10). It is little wonder that some interpretations represent Jesus as an exponent of the law who "exposits" it (sometimes, indeed, reaching "new" depths, penetrating behind the letter to the spiritual principle) and some others represent him as an opponent of the law who abrogates it and disobeys it.[86] The Gospels themselves apparently interpret and communicate the attitude of Jesus to the law differently, relating it to their special themes, intentions, and audiences.[87] But while Mark may emphasize the "rejection" of the law and Matthew the "exposition" of the law, the apparently disparate attitudes of Jesus to the law may be found within both. Before grasping at the catchwords "Hellenists" and "Judaizers" within the development of the tradition, we should ask whether any teaching is susceptible to these different emphases and interpretations.

1. The Rabbinical Background[88]

In first-century Judaism the law (or the Torah) had an unassailable authority. All of life was to be directed by the commandments laid down in the Torah. The biblical Torah, the five books of Moses, was the fundamental authority, supplemented, interpreted, and applied in the oral Torah. This oral Torah — according to the rabbis — also had its origin in God's revelation to Moses at Sinai, but it was not at once committed to writing but passed down orally from Moses to Joshua to the elders to the prophets to a succession of teachers reaching to their own (*P. Aboth* 1.1).[89] Since the biblical Torah contained both precepts and narrative, so in the oral Torah one may distinguish a legal mode (the *Halakah*) from an edifying mode (the *Haggadah*). *Halakah* interprets the commandments of Scripture, carefully following exegetical rules first summarized and described by Hillel.[90] The result was *Halakoth*, specific and authoritative prescriptions and prohibitions which made the biblical law relevant to new and concrete questions of conduct. *Haggadah*, in contrast, is not concerned with questions of proper conduct according to the commandments of the law. Its interpretation of Scripture is less careful methodologically; the narratives are elaborated and stories added for the sake of edifying the community. Within *Haggadah* may be found a great variety: descriptions of the faith of Israel, discussions of the apocalyptic hope, humorous anecdotes, legendary stories, and assorted other material. *Haggadah* is more concerned with identity and character than with conduct, but it both extols the study of the commandments and offers examples and stories of exemplary conduct and character. In this way it supplements *Halakah*, which is acknowledged as more important and authoritative. The professional responsibility of preserving, interpreting, and applying this tradition, written and oral — especially *Halakic*, but also *Haggadic* — belonged to the rabbis. And a serious responsibility it was, for God's revelation at Sinai was considered the foundation of Jewish life and society and eternally valid.[91]

Rabbinical thought, as has been observed, was not altogether alien to apocalyticism. Indeed, one can find in apocalyptic literature the same assumption concerning the eternal validity of the law (e.g., Jub. 3:31; 6:17). Nevertheless, apocalypticism is oriented toward a future act of God which establishes his cosmic sovereignty beyond any challenge. This future act is what is finally and genuinely decisive — not any event of Israel's past, not even Sinai. There is not to be found any polemic against the rabbis or any rejection of the normative status of the law, but the vision and hope of the apocalypticist is something new, something incomparably superior to all previous revelations, something final. Against this background the key to understanding Jesus' teachings about the law is again his proclamation that the kingdom of God is "at hand" and already making its power felt in his ministry and his teachings.

2. Merely Legal Observance in Crisis

In Jesus' teaching, because the kingdom is at hand, merely external and legal observance is put in crisis. The announcement of the imminent sovereignty of God demands a response of the whole person, not merely a conventional righteousness based on observance of *Halakoth*. So, a casuistry that attempts merely to ensure external observance is discredited and condemned, for it leaves the internal dispositions untouched (Mk. 7:15 and par.; Mk. 7:18-23 par.; Mt. 23:25-28 par.).[92] The coming kingdom forces something more radical than *Halakic* application of legal precepts to external behavior, something more penetrating than certain limits on the external expression of one's lust, deceitfulness, vengefulness, avarice, and pride. The coming kingdom demands the response of the whole person, and its proclamation uses the *narratives* of Torah (especially of creation; see Mk. 10:2-12 on marriage and divorce, and Mk. 2:27 and Jn. 5:9,10 on the Sabbath), the prophets and writings, and indeed simply mundane parables to lay claim to and form the whole of character. In Jewish categories, the announcement of the coming kingdom forces a shift of emphasis from *Halakah* to *Haggadah*. In this Jesus upholds the law, but not by casuistry, only by bringing it to its eschatological fruition, so that the intentions of God in the law and the prophets and in creation are fulfilled.[93] Just so, people catch a glimpse of the coming sovereignty of God and his intentions.

3. The Authority of Jesus[94]

The coming kingdom already makes its power felt in Jesus and his ministry. So the will of God is revealed finally not on the basis of ancient authorities but on the basis of the authority of Jesus' own words. Jesus' consciousness of his own authority can hardly be doubted. His deeds express his consciousness of authority.[95] And his words are spoken with authority. His use of "amen" and his use of the emphatic *egō* ("I") testify to his authority.[96] Indeed it was this authority that amazed his hearers, for he spoke "as one having authority, and not as the scribes" (Mk. 1:22 and par.). Here is no pious interpreter of the law; here is rather one who claims to announce the will of God himself. So he sets his own authority, "But I say unto you," over against the authority of the law as the rabbis had used and interpreted it.[97]

The authority of Jesus is connected with the apocalyptic sovereignty of God himself. Already in his ministry the victory over the forces of evil makes itself felt (e.g., the exorcisms); already judgment (e.g., the temple-cleansing) and salvation (e.g., the forgiveness of sins) have effect; and already in his words the apocalyptic revelation of the will of God is unveiled. In the apocalyptic literature the seer knows of some new and superior manifestation of God and his will.[98] But in Jesus this revelation is no longer pseudonymous but straightforwardly identified with Jesus himself; it is no longer merely future but already making its power felt — and its claims. The apocalyptic revelation of the will of God takes place in Jesus' ministry and teaching; there is the shift of the ages already, with the law and the prophets belonging decisively to the former age (Mt. 11:12,13; Lk. 16:16).[99] It is Jesus' words, not the Torah, that provide the foundation for a life able to stand in the judgment of God (Mt. 7:24-27; Lk. 6:47-49).[100]

In all of this, however, Jesus does not destroy the law but fulfills it (Lk. 16:17; Mt. 5:17-18). He brings it to its own eschatological fruition.

4. The Summary of the Law

It is love that fulfills the law.[101] The double love commandment (Mk. 12:28-34 par.)[102] is handed down in the tradition as a controversy saying in which Jesus puts forth his own summary of the law (and reveals that his words fulfill rather than negate the Jewish law). The rabbis themselves had often given summaries of the law by culling out one great commandment (*kelal gadol*), but these summaries were not *Halakah*. The point was not to rank commandments for the sake of eliminating some or giving legal priority to others. Such summaries were "merely" *Haggadah*. But for Jesus legal observance is put in crisis, and the emphasis falls on the total response of the whole person, on the commandment to love. The commandments to love God and the neighbor are, of course, quotations of the Torah (Deut. 6:4; Lev. 19:18) and, it may be noted, they are "not ranked, but listed."[103] But they do allow other commandments to be ranked. In Mark, the low ranking of the sacrificial system is explicit (12:33); Luke makes the same point in his parable of the Good Samaritan, where the priest and Levite do not risk defilement by contact with one who is "half-dead" and hence neglect to "show mercy" (10:30-37). Matthew presents the summary of the law more on the model of the *kelal gadol* of the rabbis ("On these two commandments depend all the law and the prophets," Mt. 22:40, may be compared with Hillel's famous "The rest is commentary. Go and learn it," *b. Shab.* 31a); nevertheless, Matthew too uses love to rank and interpret the laws (cf. Mt. 9:13; 12:7, with their quotation of Hos. 6:6).[104] Some of the controversies arise precisely because Jesus ranks acts of love, within which the coming kingdom of God is already revealed, higher than observance of the Sabbath or purity regulations (e.g., Mk. 3:4 and par.; Mk. 7:1-23 par.; Lk. 14:1-6; Jn. 5:2-18). Love, boundless and uncalculating (as the parable of the Good Samaritan makes clear), is the law for the new age, an age which already begins to make its power felt in Jesus' ministry and teachings. Love is, of course, no mere sentiment; it is a readiness for the concrete action that helps the neighbor. Love is a disposition that drives toward its own concretion in works of love (cf. the conclusion of the parable of the Good Samaritan, Lk. 10:37, "Go and do likewise").

The ethic of Jesus is, nevertheless, hardly an ethic of obedience to law, even the law of love. The love command is not used as a basic principle from which subsidiary rules are deduced. The ethic is rather an ethic of response to the coming kingdom of God and its present impact in Jesus. It is the recognition of what God is doing rather than the love commandment as an ethical principle that consistently shapes Jesus' moral discernment and teaching. And perhaps the clearest instance of that is what happens to Leviticus 19:18 in his teaching.

5. Love Your Enemies[105]

The commandment to love the neighbor had not been judged relevant to enemies, but now Jesus appears announcing that the rule of God is imminent and already making its power felt. And without exegeting the text according to any patterns of rabbinical exegesis, on his own authority he says, "But *I* say to you, Love your enemies" (Mt. 5:44; cf. Lk. 6:27,35). Jesus' authority, of course, does not mean he gives no reasons, no justification. He appeals to the nature of God, who "is kind to the ungrateful and selfish" (Lk. 6:35; cf. Mt. 5:45). Implicit is the imminent rule of this God. To respond to his coming kingdom, to repent, is made concrete in the command to love the enemy. Repentance involves a radical turning from the conventional patterns of reciprocity, of loving those who do us kindnesses (Mt. 5:46; Lk. 6:32) and of seeking the limit of lawful revenge against those who do us harm (Mt. 5:39-40; Lk. 6:29-30).[106] Such reciprocity marks the conventional righteousness of the present age. But the "sons of God" respond to the coming new age by their readiness to love even their enemies. The disposition to love the enemy makes us ready to do good to them, to pray for them, to bless them (Lk. 6:27-28). It even penetrates to commonplace behavior like greeting them on the street (Mt. 5:47), not returning a blow (Mt. 5:36; Lk. 6:29), and lending (Mt. 5:42; Lk. 6:34; the conventional pattern of reciprocity may have its strongest hold when it comes to money). The power of the conventional pattern of reciprocity is only broken by trust in the coming rule of God. So to welcome this saying is to welcome the coming kingdom. Indeed, one's eschatological destiny is chosen as one responds to the present impact of the coming kingdom in Jesus' word. Those who follow the conventional pattern already have their reward, but those who welcome the new age by a repentance and faith which have the shape of uncalculating kindness and unstinting mercy shall receive the eschatological blessing (Lk. 6:35). So Jesus brings the commandment of love to its own eschatological fruition.

It is worth observing that Luke puts the "golden rule" in this context (6:31; cf. Mt. 7:12). The "golden rule" is in itself a formal principle, close to the principle of reciprocity. But its positive form and its connection to the love of enemies keep it from any egotistical calculation and fill it with the content of boundless and uncalculating neighbor-love.

6. Let Your Yes Be Yes[107]

The eschatological pattern of Jesus' attitude toward the law affects other teachings as well. There was a well-developed casuistry with respect to oaths (echoes of which can be heard in Mt. 5:33-37; 23:16-22). But on his own authority Jesus simply demands absolute truthfulness of his followers: "Let what you say be simply 'Yes' or 'No' " (Mt. 5:37; cf. Jas. 5:12). The integrity of one's words should not need the confirmation of oaths: "But I say to you, 'Do not swear at all' " (Mt. 5:34). The external regulations with respect to oaths can simply hide deceit — and indeed be of use to the deceitful one who knows the law (Mt. 23:16-22; Mk. 7:11-13 par.). But Jesus does not legislate here. He does not provide a legal pronouncement that there shall be no oath-taking, for Matthew 23 simply judges the casuistry which makes it possible to swear some oaths "safely" or with impunity and does not condemn oath-taking itself. The controversy over "Corban" demonstrates the same point (Mk. 7:9-13 par.). Jesus does not condemn oaths; he condemns a casuistry (here indeed a legal fiction)[108] that makes it possible to use oaths in vengeful or self-seeking ways rather than in dutiful service to others, indeed, to those one ought especially humbly to serve — one's parents. The emphasis remains on the disposition of truthfulness, on the heart (Mt. 12:34; Lk. 6:45; Mt. 12:18-19). And to be truthful is to welcome the kingdom. Any use of oaths for dissimulation and any departure from the absolute integrity of one's words are to resist the kingdom; they are "from the evil one" (Mt. 5:36). God's coming sovereignty means victory over Beelzebub, the father of lies (Jn. 8:44), and is already at work in Jesus' teaching. So, in confronting Jesus' concrete command, "Let your 'Yes' be 'Yes,' " one confronts the kingdom itself. To welcome the kingdom, to repent, is to accept the demand of absolute trustworthiness of speech. To resist such claims leaves one open to the judgment of God (Mt. 12:37).

The truthfulness Jesus requires is not to be reduced to external conformity between words and the situation. Rather, it has to do with the whole person's response to the coming kingdom, and thus it has to do with seeking the neighbor's good. So truthfulness has its cognates in the prohibition of "careless words" (Mt. 12:36) and in the prohibition of common insults (Mt. 5:22). And so Jesus brings the intention of God in the commandment about false witness to eschatological fruition.

7. Let Not Man Put Asunder[109]

There was a great *Halakic* debate concerning divorce. The rabbis agreed that the relevant Torah was Deuteronomy 24:1-4, but they interpreted and applied it differently.[110] Jesus, on the other hand, brushes aside not only the question of the exegesis of Deuteronomy 24:1-4, but the sacred text itself. This commandment of Torah was given "for your hardness of heart"; it was not so much a law as a "dispensation"; it belongs to the present age and is, since the ages are shifting, no longer the finally decisive thing. Instead, Jesus appeals to the narrative of creation (Gen. 1:27; 2:24) and insists that "what therefore God has joined together, let not man put asunder" (Mk. 10:9 and par.).[111] The present power of the kingdom puts merely legal observance in crisis. Jesus is not interested in "solving" the *Halakic* question; he is not establishing new and extremely rigorous *Halakoth*. He is announcing the kingdom and demanding a response — in marriage as in all other matters — to the fulfillment of God's intentions in the creation. He is not formulating a new moral rule but forming the disposition, the readiness, not to divorce even when the law would permit it.

8. Other Commands and the Law

Everywhere the pattern is the same. Casuistry based on the Sabbath legislation is put aside for the present impact of God's sabbatical and eschatological intentions of relief for the poor: "The sabbath was made for man, and not man for the sabbath" (Mk. 2:27). Casuistry about ritual cleanliness and perhaps the laws themselves are put aside for the fulfillment of God's desire for inward purity (Mk. 7:1-23; Mt. 15:1-20). External observance of even unquestionable stipulations of the law is put in crisis by the kingdom which is at hand and already making its power felt in Jesus' teaching. So on his own authority he commands those who would welcome the kingdom not merely not to kill, but not to be angry and, positively, to be ready always to reconcile (Mt. 5:21-26). And on his own authority he prohibits not merely the external act of adultery but its inner motive, lust (Mt. 5:27-28). Many of these sayings are not attested by multiple sources or multiple forms or by their distinctiveness when compared with Jewish or ecclesiastical teaching; but the pattern is surely authentic. So whatever the judgment on an individual saying is, surely these are instances of the kind of total response that Jesus commanded when he announced the coming of the kingdom and its present effectiveness in his own deeds and words. Surely they are instances of the kinds of concrete commands that gave shape to repentance and that conformed to the eschatological reality of the kingdom. Surely they are instances of the way in which Jesus brought the law to its own eschatological fruition.

9. The Call to Discipleship[112]

The call to discipleship is related to this simultaneous rejection and fruition of the law. The *talmidim* of the rabbis gathered themselves around the teacher and studied the law and its interpretation. They would sit at his feet and listen as the rabbi repeated and commented on the written and oral law. They devoted themselves to the study of Torah. But the disciples responded to Jesus' call to follow him. They devoted themselves *to him,* to the one who spoke with authority. Rather than simply learning the old rules, they heard Jesus' words and were commanded to do them (Lk. 6:47; cf. Mk. 8:34-38). In his words and deeds they caught a glimpse of the coming kingdom, and they struggled to welcome it. To follow him was costly; it meant an end to egotistical calculations and the comfortable old securities (Mt. 8:18-22 par.; Lk. 14:26-33). To follow him became costlier still, of course, when he died.

F. THE POLITICS OF JESUS

He died, of course, on a Roman cross, condemned as a pretender to the Jewish throne.[113] That certain datum has been the starting point for nearly all those who would present Jesus as a Zealot, a political revolutionary committed to the liberation of the land from the Roman yoke.[114] That thesis has been discredited,[115] but it has nevertheless forced an important reconsideration of the politics of Jesus. It is no longer possible naively to suppose that Jesus was simply uninterested or unconcerned about the social and political crises in Palestine during the first century; but it is another and more difficult task to describe Jesus' political stance.

1. The Political Background[116]

One century before Jesus was born, John Hyrcanus, grandson of Mattathias, the patriarch of the Maccabees, had expanded the borders of an independent Jewish kingdom and had established a measure of security and prosperity in Palestine for the Jews. Some of the pious Jews who had first supported the Maccabean struggle for independence and their Hasmonean dynasty, however, had grown disaffected. The community at Qumran apparently began in protest against the Hasmonean use of the title "high priest" even though they were not from the line of Zadok.[117] The worldly ambitions, violence, and luxury of the Hasmoneans, moreover, stood in obvious contrast to the expectations one might have of a high priest. In despair of the leadership in Jerusalem, these pious ones withdrew into the desert[118] and established there a community of strict discipline awaiting the vindication of God, a dissident movement that outlasted the Hasmonean dynasty. When the Romans established the Herodians and ruled indirectly with the help of the Jerusalem aristocracy, the community at Qumran was hardly disposed to reenter Jerusalem. They remained in the wilderness until their destruction by the Romans in A.D. 68. So at the time of Jesus they remained a renewal movement marked by the withdrawal prompted by their despair concerning the political and religious leadership in Jerusalem, by strict observance of the law, and by their expectation of God's vindication of "the sons of light." It was a self-consciously "countercultural" movement.

Other pious Jews who had grown disaffected with the Hasmoneans had remained within Jewish society. The Pharisees also had their origins in the pious reaction to Hyrcanus' lawless assumption of the title "high priest," his worldly ambitions, and his violent means. Indeed, for a time the Pharisees were involved in political intrigue; their vigorous dissent from the policies of Alexander Jannaeus (the son of John Hyrcanus who reigned from 103-76 B.C.) was met with ruthless violence and issued finally in armed conflict. On his deathbed, Alexander urged his wife Salome Alexandra to make peace with the Pharisees, and she did: the Pharisees became for the first time members of the Sanhedrin, the highest judicial body in Jewish society. Within that body and within Jewish society the Pharisees emphasized obedience to the law, both the written and the oral Torah, while patiently waiting for God to intervene on behalf of his people. They initially opposed the Roman takeover in 63 B.C.,[119] but not by force. And they persistently opposed anyone, including Herod and the procurators, who would violate the law. They refused, for example, to swear a loyalty oath or to allow images in the city. But they were content to leave liberation in the hands of God; and meanwhile they accommodated them-selves to Roman rule, refusing only to render to Caesar and his law the sort of obedience due solely to God and his law.[120]

Some of the Pharisees apparently grew discontented with passive disobedience and resignation toward the Romans and joined the cause of the freedom fighters.[121] Judas the Galilean ignited Jewish passion for liberation from the Romans in A.D. 6, after the exile of Herod's son Archelaus, the imposition of direct Roman rule, and an initial census for tax-collecting purposes. Judas upbraided his countrymen "as cowards for consenting to pay tribute to Rome and tolerating mortal masters, after having God for their lord."[122] That radical theocratic vision of Judas called for zealous observance of the law, including the social legislation of the jubilee year,[123] and zealous violence against the Romans and all who submitted to the Roman yoke. Judas was an early victim of the violence, but his story was celebrated among the young, and his cause gained support among the Jews until the Zealots, as they came to be called, were able to push moderation aside and begin the revolutionary struggle of A.D. 66-73.

The Sadducees were not sympathetic toward any of these movements for reform or revolution. Through a policy of accommodation and collaboration they had succeeded in protecting their vested interests in Jerusalem from the time of the Syrian king, Antiochus IV Epiphanes, through the period of independence and the Roman occupation. The ancient Zadokite dynasty of high priests had been horribly compromised under Antiochus IV, when Jason supplanted his brother Onias as high priest by bribery and used the office to promote Hellenism. When the Maccabean revolt was successful and the Hasmoneans, although they were not Zadokites, took over the high priest's office, some of the Zadokite families and other aristocratic families supported them in order to protect their property and position in Jerusalem. The Sadducees had their origins in this circle of priestly and aristocratic families. Their influence declined when Salome Alexandra made her peace with the Pharisees, but even then they remained in the majority on the Sanhedrin. After the Roman occupation, some of them were faithful to the Hasmonean line (and some were executed for this loyalty by Herod) but more prudently calculated that their interests and positions could be best served by cooperating with the Romans. In the office of high priest and in their positions on the Sanhedrin the Sadducees were willing to serve as puppet authorities for the Romans in order to preserve their position, their property, and their control of the temple, including its treasury. They profited considerably from the exchange of pilgrims' money into temple currency. The destruction of Jerusalem and the Temple in A.D. 70 sealed their fate as surely as it did that of the Zealots, whose call for rebellion they had opposed.

These four parties — Essenes, Pharisees, Zealots, and Sadducees — were contending for their policies and positions at the time of Jesus. It was a difficult time, a time of crisis. The glories of an independent kingdom had long since departed. Roman rule had been exercised at first indirectly, and most effectively, through the long reign of Herod the Great. Herod's reign, however, had been marked by both brutality and extravagance. At his death in 4 B.C., he "left behind him an improvished country and a demoralized populace with weakened morality, resigned to misfortune."[124] His realm was divided among his sons, Herod Antipas, Philip, and Archelaus, although a delegation of Jews had made it plain in Rome that they wanted nothing more to do with the Herodians. Herod Antipas ruled in Galilee until A.D. 39 but Archelaus, who ruled Judea and Galilee, had already been deposed by A.D. 6. In his place the Romans installed a series of procurators, the fifth of whom was Pontius Pilate (A.D. 26-36). With this shift to direct Roman rule came the imposition of Roman taxes and the census necessary to taxation. The signs of crisis were suddenly all around in Palestine: the protests of reform movements like those of the Essenes and the Pharisees, the violence of revolutionary movements like that of the Zealots, the criticism of solitary charismatic figures such as John the Baptist, the random acts of violence by *lēistai,* or "robbers" (which were a part, perhaps, not so much of some revolutionary design as a general breakdown of respect for law), and the prevalence of beggars and vagabonds in Jerusalem. It was against the background of this social and political crisis that Jesus conducted the ministry which led him finally to a Roman cross, and it is against this background that the politics of Jesus must be understood.

2. Jesus' Political Posture

Jesus appears announcing that the kingdom of God is at hand. He does not announce it as a political program, as though the coming of the kingdom were contingent on human striving or political decisions. But neither does he announce it as some secret sovereignty over souls. The radically theocratic implications of God's coming sovereignty could hardly be lost or overlooked in the crisis of the times. The coming sovereignty was a cosmic sovereignty, and it demanded total repentance of cities (such as Chorazin and Bethsaida, e.g., Mt. 11:20-24), a whole generation (e.g., Mt. 12:38-42), and of nations (e.g., Mt. 25:32), as well as individuals. A total repentance to a cosmic kingdom is not *merely* political, but it is, nonetheless, certainly political. It may not be reduced to political dispositions and behavior, but it clearly includes them. The promise of theocracy, of God's reign, would quite properly be understood as a promise (or a threat) of an end to the reign of Roman and Herodian rulers.

Even so, there is something quite irenic in Jesus' announcement of the kingdom. Jesus was no Zealot. His rejection of the vengeful use of the *lex talionis* to license, even as it limits, personal retaliation (Mt. 5:38ff.) apparently extends to political dispositions. He rejects at least the vengeful nationalism

LIB USE ONLY

BS
2545
.E8
V47
1984
c.1

AUTHOR (last name first): Verhey, Allen

DATE REQUESTED 1-27-84

15112

TITLE: The Great Reversal: Ethics And the New Testament

EDITION | | VOL

VENDOR: WBEP

LIST PRICE: 13.95

EDITION

YEAR: 1984

NUMBER OF COPIES: 1

PUBLISHER: Wm. B. Eerdmans

LC NUMBER

ACCT

REQUESTED BY: B. Coleman

DT. ORDERED: 10-1-84
H

APPROVED BY
505-0
51-0

COST (15): 11.16 ✓

DT. RECVD (16): 10/9/84

REM (20-29)

WC 82

of much contemporaneous apocalyptic expectation.[125] The "enemy" is to be loved, not destroyed. The Zealot desire for revenge belongs to the old age. Jesus does not proclaim the theocracy as a call to a holy war of national liberation. He does not divide those around him into "children of light" and "children of darkness" and urge or welcome the destruction of the latter (Lk. 9:52-56). On the contrary, he is a friend of Samaritans and tax collectors and other "enemies." When he enters Jerusalem he rides no war horse but an ass; this self-conscious fulfillment of Zechariah 9:9 does not point toward any nationalistic "holy war" but toward "peace to the nations" (Zech. 9:10).[126] It is not merely that single quotation from the prophets, however, that is taken up into the politics of Jesus. The prophets had recognized more clearly than most the ambiguity of power.[127] They did not disown political power, however, because of its ambiguity; instead, the prophets insisted more daringly than most on the accountability of power. The king is neither divinized nor demonized; he is called to account. So, for the prophets, the sign of royalty is humility and submission to God's intention;[128] and the sign of legitimate authority is service of the poor and powerless. So Jesus enters Jerusalem in fulfillment of the prophetic hope for a "humble king." The implication, then, is neither the Zealot prescription of hate and violence nor the pacifist prohibition of political power and coercion. The implication is rather a "great reversal" for political power itself. To welcome the coming kingdom of God and its present effectiveness in this humble king calls for a disposition to construe power as a vocation to humble service (Mk. 10:42-44 par.).

The coming kingdom already made its power felt in Jesus' judgment against the pride of power. He was no Sadducean collaborator either. Herod Antipas, "that fox" (Lk. 13:32),[129] and the Gentile rulers who "lord it over" their subjects (Mk. 10:42) belong to the old age. The temple cleansing (Mk. 11:15-18 par.; Jn. 2:13-17) was surely — even if not solely — a political judgment on the priestly aristocracy. They had used their authority in the temple to make themselves rich at the expense of pious pilgrims and the poor; Jesus drives out the money-changers, whose commerce had enriched the Sadducees. Using Jeremiah 7:11, he even accuses the Sadducees of being the *lēistai,* the robbers (Mk. 11:17). Certainly it was more a prophetic or symbolic action than the programmatic inauguration of a revolution,[130] but even so it was a symbolic action that involved the use of force rather than "personal appeal,"[131] and which already judged the priestly aristocracy. The famous — but notoriously difficult — saying of Jesus about the tribute money, "Render to Caesar the things that are Caesar's, and to God the things that are God's" (Mk. 12:17 and par.), is no Zealot call to arms; but neither is it the sort of compartmentalization of "two realms" that would leave the Herodians, Sadducees, and other collaborators with an easy conscience. In the context of Jesus' proclamation of God's cosmic sovereignty, there can be no question about what things do and do not belong to God. All things will belong to him, the claims of Caesar notwithstanding, and even now Jesus' hearers (in this context the

31

Herodians; not the Zealots, incidentally) are called to welcome that coming sovereignty of God. The collaborators are called to repentance, to political — even if not merely political — repentance.

It is now very difficult to discern the concrete shape of such political repentance. On the one hand, because in announcing the kingdom of God Jesus proclaims a theocracy, it is a political announcement of good news for the poor, for women, for children, for "sinners." This is perhaps clearest in his criticism of wealth and his command to give alms. His judgment on the rich landowners, whose great estates had increased the number of landless tenants (especially during the reign of Herod), may be found in some of his parables (e.g., Lk. 12:16-21; 16:19-31). The peasants had often lost their land to the usurers, having given it up in security. Jesus condemns usury (Lk. 6:34,35) and calls for the remittance of debts (Lk. 6:37; Mt. 18:23-34). The command to "give alms" must be understood in the context of a society in which almsgiving was a predominant form of social assistance. Even when he commended a pious sinner's wasteful use of ointment, he called attention to the community's responsibility to and for the poor (Mk. 14:3-7 par.; Deut. 15:1-11).[132] Politically, the kingdom would bring blessings to the poor.

On the other hand, however, even such criticisms of Jewish society and calls for its reform are utterly unprogrammatic. There is apparently an appreciation that the response to the coming kingdom of God may not be reduced to a political program. The welcome due the kingdom outreaches the grasp of legal sanctions. Truly to welcome God's reign is to serve it freely. Moreover, law and its sanctions focus on external action, but the kingdom of God demands a response of the whole person. And finally, the kingdom outreaches politics in the kinds of actions it prescribes and prohibits. When Jesus commends the behavior of the good Samaritan, for example, he makes a moral point, not a political one. The selfless generosity of the Samaritan deserves high praise, and Jesus prescribes similar behavior when he says, "Go and do likewise" (Lk. 10:37). But he does not urge political sanctions against those who fail so to act. The priest and the Levite deserve blame but not fine or imprisonment; the brigands who robbed and assaulted the man are the ones who deserve the legal punishment. Jesus did not tell the story to make a political point, but he evidently assumes one.[133] Law must always deal with what will inevitably seem to moral people to be "minimal standards," which will always fall short of the self-giving love which the coming kingdom of God enables and requires.

That the response to the coming kingdom of God may not be reduced to a political program, however, does not mean that it is politically irrelevant. The coming kingdom condemns the pride of power and gives direction for the enforcement of "minimal standards," at least concerning who should be especially protected by them. There is no political program in Jesus' teachings, but there is a political posture, a posture that seeks God's intentions for political power. Such a posture seeks peace and judges the Zealot desire for revenge; it seeks justice and judges the Sadducean collaboration in exploitation and extortion; it does not presume that the kingdom of God may be reduced to a political program or to a set of "minimal standards," but it will be prepared to tend to sores in the body politic with remedies considerably less winsome than selfless love in order to protect the poor and powerless, just as Jesus dealt with the extortion in the temple. Such a posture construes power as a vocation to humble service.

G. THE VALIDATION OF JESUS' ETHIC[134]

It is not implausible that this Jesus should be considered dangerous — dangerous enough to require being killed — by those who refused to repent, who refused to welcome the coming kingdom of God and its present impact in Jesus and his words. So they put him to death. And his death placed in jeopardy the implicit claim present in his miracles, his ministry, his teachings, and his entry into and activity in Jerusalem. The one in whom God's future kingdom was already making its power felt seemed powerless in the face of the strength of sin and death. But God raised him. And against the background of apocalyptic (even if its categories are broken by the resurrection of one), the resurrection is the vindication of this one, including his ethic. It verifies his claim to speak with authority. It is the divine stamp of approval on Jesus and his moral teachings. In the resurrection God himself acts to establish his sovereignty over sin and death and to vindicate Jesus' preaching. The evangelist Matthew summarizes it well in his words of the risen Lord (28:18-20): " 'All authority . . . has been given to me. Go therefore and make disciples . . . teaching them to observe all that I have commanded you. . . .' "

Chapter II

THE BEGINNINGS OF A MORAL TRADITION

Because Jesus was raised from the dead, the early church proclaimed him "both Lord and Christ" (Acts 2:36). The resurrection was at once vindication of this Jesus and the prelude of God's final triumph. Moral discernment in the Christian community, therefore, was from the beginning governed by the memory of this Jesus and the expectation of his return. The church, however, beginning in Judea and expanding throughout the Hellenistic world, was quickly constrained to relate to the moral traditions of Judaism and Hellenism. In this chapter I intend to survey the beginnings and early development of the Christian moral tradition. I will focus first on the tradition that preserved and shaped the memory of Jesus' words and deeds and then on the paraenetic tradition that used and modified Jewish and Hellenistic traditions.

A. THE TRADITION OF JESUS' WORDS AND DEEDS

1. The First Tellings of Jesus' Story

From the very beginning, apparently, the announcement of the good news of Jesus' resurrection was accompanied by the demand for repentance.[1] That Jesus was raised from the dead was treated as a fact, but not the sort of fact toward which one could take any attitude he wished. The message was inevitably self-involving. If Jesus was raised from the dead, then personal and communal life had to be reoriented toward him, toward his words and deeds, and toward the parousia, his appearance in glory.

Among those who first proclaimed that he had been raised were some, at least, who remembered him. They had talked with him about life and the meaning of life, sat at his feet listening to his teachings, and heard him debate with the religious leaders. They had walked with him, wondered at the power he revealed in miracles, and eaten with him alongside Pharisees and sinners. And now they remembered these words and deeds and told others. The words Luke attributes to Peter and John following the resurrection catch the beginnings of the tradition neatly: "We cannot but speak of what we have seen and heard" (Acts 4:20). The bearers of this memory evidently appealed to their relationship with Jesus and to his commissioning as the basis of their authority in young communities of believers.[2]

The first tellings of Jesus' story are, of course, lost to us. No doubt they were told with a wealth of detail, but the task of remembering and telling was surely not an archival task. The task was a practical one. The purpose was less to preserve the past than to orient the present to the words and deeds of Jesus and to his appearance. The first tellers were not interested in the past for the past's sake; they were convinced that Jesus was not merely a bygone figure, for he had been raised from the dead. He was not merely some famous — but dead — rabbi, and the pattern for remembering him could not simply preserve his words as though he were.[3] He was the present Christ whose glory would soon be revealed. And as they recounted his deeds, rehearsed his words, and repeated his announcement of the kingdom, they believed that the risen Lord himself reoriented life toward his victory and reordered the cosmos with himself at God's right hand.

One can imagine, for example, a little group of people gathered in their work clothes listening hungrily as Peter retold some episode from Jesus' life, perhaps the healing of his mother-in-law (cf. Mk. 1:29-31). The purpose was not biographical but practical. The focus was not on Peter's mother-in-law, nor on the remarkable occurrence itself, but on the power and messianic authority of Jesus. The story was proclamation: it called for the acknowledgment of Jesus, the establishment of loyalty, and the adoption of identity. Or one can imagine some quarreling people being interrupted by Andrew's story of an earlier quarrel among the disciples and the peace-making intervention of Jesus. Or perhaps someone's fit of temper might have prompted James the son of Zebedee to tell of his own fit of temper and how Jesus lovingly rebuked him. The first tellings did not simply preserve a memory of the past; they made it effective in the present. The purpose of the tellings was not to record some facts but to reorient personal and communal life toward Jesus as the Christ, to give shape to lives awaiting his return.

2. The Oral Tradition

Soon the stories and sayings were being told again — and again. The memory was handed down to those who had not known Jesus when he walked in Galilee and Jerusalem, to preachers and teachers and evangelists who, in leading worship, instructing catechumens, or announcing the good news to unbelievers, exhorted their hearers to life in his name. The oral tradition came to have an authority of its own. The wealth of detail in those first tellings was sacrificed for economy of expression, and certain literary forms became conventional for receiving and relating the memory of Jesus.

a. THE AUTHORITY OF TRADITION

The very fact of "tradition" calls for some explanation. Jesus, after all, had been critical of the tradition, of the *paradosis* (Mk. 7:1-8 par.) handed down among the scribes. In the early church, however, there is a renewal of tradition, a new *paradosis* handed down within the church. There is a remarkable contrast between Jesus' ironic saying to the Pharisees, "You leave the commandment of God, and hold fast the tradition of men" (Mk. 7:8), and Paul's exhortation to "hold to the traditions" (II Thess. 2:15). The justification for the formation and preservation of tradition is the belief that Jesus himself continues to address the believing community through the tradition. Using the technical terminology of tradition, Paul says, "I received from the Lord what I also delivered unto you . . ." (I Cor. 11:23). The "from the Lord" does not rule out the human mediation of tradition, nor does it identify Jesus as the chronological point of origin; it rather identifies "the exalted Lord as the real author of the whole tradition developing itself within the apostolic church."[4] The same point may be made on the basis of John 14:26 and 16:13, where the Spirit, the presence of the exalted Lord, leads the community into the truth by bringing "to your remembrance all that I said to you." The developing tradition is not simply the words of men as contrasted to the "commandment of God"; it is the manner by which the exalted Jesus continues to address his continuing church. Such a tradition naturally is considered authoritative, and it is treated as authoritative.

Consider, for example, Paul's argument in I Corinthians 7: in an obvious reference to Jesus' saying on divorce, Paul says, "To the married I give charge, not I but the Lord, that the wife should not separate from her husband . . . and that the husband should not divorce his wife" (vss. 10,11). Subsequent exhortations carefully distinguish between instructions given with the authority of "a command of the Lord" (1 Cor. 7:25; cf. vs. 12) and Paul's advice. "The Lord" speaks with authority to the Corinthians through the tradition of Jesus' words. The tradition, of course, serves not merely to preserve what Jesus once said, and its authority is not due to the supposition that it contains the *ipsissima verba* of Jesus. Rather, precisely because the risen Lord speaks in this tradition, it is both permitted and required to use and shape the tradition in order to address particular situations Jesus did not encounter. In this case, for example, Jesus had almost certainly dealt only with men seeking to divorce their wives in Jewish society on the basis of Deuteronomy 24:1-4. In Hellenistic society, however, the church confronts the possibility of women seeking divorce, and "the Lord" addresses that situation: "do not separate" (Gk. *mē chōristhēnai*, I Cor. 7:10; cf. Mk. 10:9). On the other hand, there are apparently limits on the creative formation of tradition, for Paul does not present his own advice as a "command of the Lord" even though he claims to be "trustworthy" (I Cor. 7:25) and to "have the Spirit of God" (7:40).[5] The church and her leaders do not merely preserve the tradition nor simply create it; they "bear" it. Apart from this tradition, the church had no enduring moral identity; and apart from the church, the tradition becomes merely antiquarian and quaint. The church is both the locus and the agent of tradition. The tradition is both the activity of handing on the memory of Jesus ("active tradition") and that which is handed on ("passive tradition").[6] The authority of tradition, then, requires both that the memory of Jesus as the Christ be preserved (the passive tradition) and that it be preserved in such a way as to enable the observance of the Lord's command in situations the pre-exalted Christ did not encounter (the active tradition).

b. THE FORMS OF TRADITION

As the memory of Jesus was received and handed down orally, it settled into certain conventional forms.[7] We shall distinguish "apophthegms," "dominical sayings," "miracle stories," "historical stories," and "legends,"[8] and attempt some modest claims concerning the contribution each made to the moral tradition of the early church.

1) The Apophthegms: Morality by Contrast

The apophthegms are brief anecdotes that focus on the climax in a saying of Jesus. The narrative simply provides a framework for the saying. These may be further broken down into "controversy dialogues," "scholastic dialogues," and "biographical apophthegms." In a controversy dialogue, one of Jesus' actions or attitudes provides an occasion for an accusation by one of his opponents, to which he responds with a saying. A scholastic dialogue differs from a controversy dialogue only in that there is no accusation by an opponent; rather, a question from someone seeking knowledge or wisdom provides the context for Jesus' saying.[9] A biographical apophthegm also focuses on a saying of Jesus, but it provides the narrative context simply to make the saying more comprehensible.[10]

Besides identifying these forms, Bultmann attempts to determine their *Sitz im Leben*, their situation (and use) in the life of the early church. In his view, the controversy dialogues and scholastic dialogues had their "proper place . . . in the apologetic and polemic of the Palestinian church,"[11] and the biographical apophthegms served the Palestinian church's task of "edification and discipline."[12] Bultmann's attempt to determine the *Sitz im Leben* of these forms is interesting and plausible but, curiously and ironically, inattentive to the creative use of these traditions and the forms within which they were handed down in the early church. In my view, it is dangerous to circumscribe too rigorously the creative use of the tradition and its forms in the early church. Nevertheless, the peculiar contribution of the apophthegms to the early church's morality can be discerned by combining Bultmann's descriptions. The apophthegms describe and justify the Christian way of life over against Jewish patterns of conduct. They serve both moral and polemical functions, and often both at the same time.

a) The Controversy Dialogues

The controversy dialogues were clearly useful in the church's encounter with Palestinian Judaism, both polemically and apologetically, but they also often bear on the church's morality.

The controversies occasioned by Jesus' healings on the Sabbath, for example, are certainly relevant to the church's polemic against Judaism; but the polemic itself involves issues of moral identity and priorities. The moral identity of the Christian community, in contrast to Judaism, is determined by its loyalty to Jesus, not to the law. That identity, moreover, establishes the priority of "doing good" to observance of Sabbath *Halakoth* (Mk. 3:1-6 par.; cf. Lk. 13:10-17; 14:1-6; Jn. 5:2-18; 7:14-24; 9:14-16). Similarly, the controversy that started when he healed the paralytic is relevant not only apologetically but also morally: it announces Jesus' authority to forgive sins, and it shapes within the church, in contrast to the Palestinian Judaism they encountered, a readiness to welcome repentant sinners instead of judging them (Mk. 2:1-12 par.).[13]

Especially those disputes occasioned by the conduct of Jesus or his disciples must be seen as relevant not only to the early church's polemic but also to its ethic. Jesus justifies the conduct that prompts the controversy over against Jewish patterns of conduct. Jesus plucks corn on the Sabbath (Mk. 2:23-28 par.); he eats with publicans and sinners (Mk. 2:15-17); his disciples eat without scrupulous observance of ritual cleanliness (Mk. 7:1-23). These controversy dialogues secure and defend a Christian morality which, in part at least, stands in contrast to Jewish morality. The task is at once apologetic, or polemical, and exhortatory: in some tellings such controversy dialogues would serve especially to describe and defend the new way of life among the followers of Jesus; in other tellings they would serve to exhort the congregation to continue in such conduct.

b) The Scholastic Dialogues

Some of the scholastic dialogues are even clearer examples of the peculiar contribution of the apophthegms to the church's moral tradition, in their describing and justifying a Christian way of life over against Jewish patterns of conduct. For example, Jesus' saying in response to the rich man's question, "Go, sell what you have, and give to the poor" (Mk. 10:17-22 par.), stands in contrast to the old law (vs. 19). It is not that Jesus disowns the old law, or even that Jesus' command provides a "new law"; but the dialogue is nonetheless relevant both apologetically and morally. Apologetically, it discloses the greater rigor of the Christian tradition, the surpassing righteousness of a morality that makes total claims on a person as well as limiting claims on his conduct; but it could do that effectively only if the purpose of repeating the dialogue was sometimes turned toward shaping character and conduct in the early church.

The response to the question concerning the "great commandment" (Mk. 12:28-34 par.) was surely used to describe and defend the Christian morality over against the Jewish patterns of conduct and also to exhort the Christian community to character and conduct marked by neighbor love. In the scholastic dialogue on divorce (Mk. 10:2-12 par.), the Christian attitude toward marriage and divorce, formed in response to the eschatological fulfillment of the way things were at "the beginning," stands in contrast to the Jewish reliance on the law in their "hardness of heart." The dialogues occasioned by the requests of the sons of Zebedee for places of honor (Mk. 10:35-45 par.) and for violent revenge against inhospitable Samaritans (Lk. 9:51-56) also describe and justify a way of life that stands in polemical contrast to conventional dispositions of the day to seek one's own honor and to seek revenge.

c) The Biographical Apophthegms

The biographical apophthegms are acknowledged by Bultmann to be morally and religiously edifying. According to him, they had their *Sitz im Leben* in the task of preachers "to comfort and admonish the church in her hope."[14] The biographical apophthegms focus less on apologetic defense and polemical contrast and more on the provision of paradigms and exhortations, but in the background typically one can still discern the polemical contrast to conventional patterns of conduct.

Even within those apophthegms that call for general readiness to "follow" Jesus (Mk. 1:16-20 par.; 2:14 and par.; Lk. 9:57-62; Mt. 8:19-22), the vocation demands a total commitment which overrides both prudential calculations and conventional obligations (esp. Lk. 9:57-62). In contrast to conventional family ties, Jesus identifies his brothers and sisters as "whoever does the will of God" (Mk. 3:31-35 par.).

When the apophthegm more specifically encourages particular dispositions, the contrast to conventional morality is almost always subtly present. Jesus' blessing on the children stands in contrast to the more conventional attitude of the disciples, and the narrative provides a paradigm to accompany Jesus' saying and to help form the disposition of sympathy toward children (Mk. 10:13-16 par.). His praise of the widow's gift stands in contrast to more conventional patterns of evaluation and encourages a readiness for sacrificial generosity (Mk. 12:41-44 par.). The story of Zacchaeus contrasts Jesus' behavior to the general disdain for this sinner, and Zacchaeus himself becomes a paradigm of an unconventional generosity born of the liberation from the bondage of wealth, and expressed in a consequent readiness to share what one has (Lk. 19:1-10). The episode with Mary and Martha preserves a challenge to the conventional role assignments for women in first-century Palestine and subtly defends the "part" they have assumed in the early church (Lk.

10:38-42). The story of the ten lepers forms a readiness to receive and welcome "foreigners" like the Samaritan who alone was grateful for God's kindness (Lk. 17:11-19; cf. also Mk. 7:24-31 par.; Mt. 8:5-13 par.).

The contributions of the apophthegms to the church's moral tradition are, then, first, the defense of and call to a morality that stands in contrast to the conventional patterns of behavior in first-century Palestine, and, second, the provision of paradigms to accompany and concretize the saying preserved. These modest claims about the contributions of these forms to the moral tradition of the early church are not intended to circumscribe the creativity of the church into narrow patterns and purposes. The simple apophthegm about Jesus blessing the children, for example, could have been and probably was used in a variety of ways as the situation demanded.[15] Some have argued (and quite plausibly) that the episode was used to address the question whether children of Christian parents should be baptized.[16] The same episode might be relevant to the problem of the status of children where only one parent is a Christian, creating a *prima facie* case for a ruling like Paul's (I Cor. 7:14) that such children are "holy" and acceptable to God. Again the story may have been told in protest against the neglect and abandonment of children in the Roman empire. Or the story, in another telling, may have been used to encourage a childlike faith. We simply do not know the particular *Sitz im Leben* for every recital of the tradition. Each telling was creative as well as preservative. Each telling brought the tradition (in this case the sympathy for children, which was part of the moral tradition borne by the church) to bear on the questions of the moment (in this case questions ranging from the administration of the sacraments to the proper nature of faith to familial and social morality). But with that caveat, the conclusions above may be allowed to stand concerning the discernible contributions of the apophthegms to the Christian moral tradition.

2) The Dominical Sayings

The dominical saying is another form that preserves the sayings of Jesus; the form differs from the apophthegm in that there is no accompanying narrative. They may be further distinguished into "prophetic sayings," "wisdom sayings," "church rules," "I-sayings," and "similitudes" (or parables).[17]

a) Prophetic Sayings: Bearing an Identity

In the prophetic sayings the church remembered and reiterated Jesus' proclamation of the kingdom of God with its call to repentance (e.g., Mk. 9:1 and par.; 13:30; Lk. 17:20-21; 17:23-24 par. Mt. 24:26-27).[18] By remembering and adapting these sayings, the church acknowledged that in Jesus the kingdom has already made its power felt (e.g., Lk. 10:23,24 par. Mt. 13:16,17; Mk. 11:5-6 par.; Lk. 7:22-23; 12:32).[19] And with these sayings they exhorted one another and others to expect the final victory of God (e.g., Lk. 12:35-48; Mk. 13:33-37; and all such exhortations to watchfulness). As they bore this tradition, they bore their identity; they were a community with such a memory and such expectations.

b) Wisdom Sayings: The Eschatological Transformation of a Tradition and Perspective

This identity was given shape and texture through the wisdom sayings. The announcement of the coming kingdom with its call to repentance, the faith that it had already made its power felt in Jesus, and the expectation of God's final victory touched and seized ordinary life by means of the wisdom sayings.

The wisdom sayings are, of course, related to the wisdom tradition of Israel. And there is no denying either the parallels between these sayings and the proverbs of the Old Testament, the Apocrypha, and the rabbis,[20] or the likelihood that wisdom sayings that were useful for moral instruction, edification, and warning were attributed in the tradition to Jesus and treated as dominical.[21] The wisdom tradition grounded and tested its advice in experience. Careful attention to nature and experience allowed the sage to comprehend some basic principles operative in the world beyond the reach of human control; to these principles it is both moral and prudent to conform. But the early church's moral tradition also included the criticism of conventional wisdom (Mt. 11:25 and par. Lk. 10:21),[22] and transformed the wisdom tradition in the confidence that God's cosmic reign had already made its power felt in Jesus.

The wisdom sayings, for all their similarities to Jewish (and sometimes Hellenistic) proverbs, belong within the proclamation of the kingdom announced by Jesus and, according to the faith of the early church, were already operative in the ministry, death, and resurrection of Jesus. The wisdom sayings remain practical, but the experience in which they are grounded and tested is the particular experience of the transcendent power of God already operative in Jesus. It is an eschatological wisdom,[23] intimately related to the prophetic sayings.

The eschatological transformation of conventional wisdom is effected both formally and materially. Formally, the sayings typically are in the future tense, often employing a two-member structure in which the future confronts, judges, and claims the present.[24] Materially, the basis and test of wisdom is what God will do and has already begun to do in Christ. The basic principles operative in the world beyond the reach of human control are the eschatological intentions of God, and they are not known in the distillation of commonplace experiences but in the memory of Jesus' words and deeds. Such an eschatological wisdom is provided for the church in the wisdom sayings.

The "beatitudes" and "woes" are perhaps the clearest example that the "wisdom sayings" are an eschatological wisdom. They announce God's future salvation and judgment and bring that future to bear on the present. They articulate principles operative in the world beyond the reach of human control, principles to which it is prudent and moral to conform. Such wisdom remains practically oriented; it calls for and shapes "fitting" dispositions. Sometimes the beatitudes call for a general disposition to act in ways responsive to the message of and about Jesus (e.g., Lk. 11:28: "Blessed rather are those who hear the word of God and keep it"). And sometimes they shape more specific dispositions to help the poor (Lk. 6:20b), to feed the hungry (Lk. 6:21a), to comfort the grieving (Lk. 6:21b), to be merciful (Mt. 5:7), and to be peace-makers (Mt. 5:9).[25]

The proverbs and maxims also articulate the eschatological principles already operative in the world beyond the reach of human control. They form and inform the perspective of the believing community. Because members of that community experience God's power and way in Jesus Christ, they see God's way everywhere from a different angle, from an eschatological angle, and so they see things differently. They have the perspective of the kingdom, and so their moral perceptions and values are affected. They see already, for example, that "many that are first will be last, and the last first" (Mk. 10:31 and par.; see also Lk. 14:11; 18:14; Mt. 23:12; Mk. 10:42 and par.). This perception changes their disposition toward power and prestige. They will not grab for power or pride themselves in it when they have it; they are freed to use it in the service of the powerless. Their perception of wealth also is affected when they see things from the perspective of the kingdom ("How hard it will be for those who have riches to enter the kingdom of God!" Mk. 10:23 and par.). They are liberated from greed and from trusting in money for security, freed for almsgiving, sharing, and hospitality. They see speech (Mt. 12:34b and par. Lk. 6:45b), care and anxiety (Mt. 6:34b), conventional standards of prestige and pomp (Lk. 16:15b), purity regulations (Mk. 7:15 and par.), marriage (Mk. 10:9 and par. Mt. 19:12), children (Mk. 10:15 and par.), the Sabbath (Mk. 2:27), security (Mt. 8:20 and par.), even the interpretation of the law (Mt. 13:52) and responsibility to the Lord (Lk. 12:47-48) in a new light. It is the light of the kingdom, which cannot be kept hidden (Mt. 5:14-16 par.; Mk. 4:21-23 par.; Mt. 15:14 and par.); it illumines not only their minds but their character and conduct. In all their life they perceive what it means to live in response to and in anticipation of the reign of God.

Beatitudes and maxims, then, articulate an eschatological wisdom. Without being candidly set in the form of exhortations, they are morally relevant, forming and informing a moral perspective and moral dispositions. There are, however, also exhortations within the wisdom sayings. These imperatives are, of course, morally relevant. Even the imperatives, though, assume and invoke an awareness of the eschatological intentions of God already operative in the world. They call for conformity to those eschatological intentions rather than conformity to conventional behavior with its conventional wisdom assumptions. Some of these imperatives demand a discipleship that is set over against conventional obligations and wisdom (Mt. 8:22b and par. Lk. 9:60: "Follow me, and leave the dead to bury their own dead"). Others are urgent calls to a general and total repentance, to welcome the coming kingdom of God (e.g.,

Mt. 7:13ff.; 6:19-21 par. Lk. 12:33-34). Many of the imperatives, however, give specific shape to that discipleship and repentance. There are exhortations to "be servant of all" (Mk. 10:43-44 par.; Mk. 9:35 and par.; Mt. 23:11), to "be not anxious" (Mt. 6:25 and par. Lk. 12:22; Mt. 6:34), to "give to the poor" (Mk. 10:21 and par.; cf. Lk. 12:33; 6:30 and par. Mt. 5:42), to "forgive" (Lk. 17:3-4 par.; Mt. 18:22), to "judge not" (Mt. 7:1 and par. Lk. 6:37), to "love your enemies" (Mt. 5:44 and par. Lk. 6:27), even to "invite the poor, the maimed, the lame, the blind" to a feast (Lk. 14:13), and many others. Such imperatives stand alongside others like to "watch" (Mk. 13:33-37) and to "ask" (Mk. 11:24 and par.; Mt. 7:7 and par. Lk. 11:9) because the imperatives are not primarily concerned with morality per se but with the response to and anticipation of the kingdom.

Insofar as these imperatives are handed down with an accompanying justification, the justification points in the same direction, toward the coming reign of God which has already made its power felt and which is already operating willy-nilly (see, e.g., Lk. 6:35 and par. Mt. 5:44-45; Lk. 12:22-31 and par. Mt. 6:25-33, etc.). However, in these imperatives the ethic of Jesus is remembered not in the form of either a moral code or a systematic ethical treatise, but rather in the form of wisdom. It is an eschatological wisdom that has experienced God's grace and judgment already operative in Jesus Christ and so perceives the world, the older wisdom tradition, and moral conduct and character in a new way. These imperatives are not a new Torah, to be applied casuistically to conduct. They are not the basis of a new Christian *Halakah*. Together with the maxims and beatitudes and "woes," they belong to an eschatological wisdom that makes a distinctive contribution to the early Christian moral tradition, transforming the older wisdom tradition, informing their moral perspective, and conforming character and conduct to the eschatological intentions of God.

c) Legal Sayings: Regulating the Communities

To deny that the wisdom sayings are a new Torah, however, is not to deny that the early church was concerned about the regulation of the community by means of law. The tradition of Jesus' sayings also includes "legal sayings and church rules,"[26] and this form's distinctive contribution is to address the question of law and to regulate the community by means of law.

There are sayings, first, about the Jewish law. As one would expect, these sayings are sometimes more expressive of Jewish Christianity's conviction that the law holds (e.g., Mt. 5:17-19 par. Lk. 16:17; Mt. 23:1,2, etc.) and sometimes more expressive of Hellenistic Christianity's conviction that the law belongs to the old age (e.g., Lk. 16:16; Mt. 11:13; Mk. 7:15 and par., etc.). It is certain that different Christian communities, even as they remembered and preserved the sayings of Jesus about the law, understood and interpreted them differently and, consequently, shaped them and handed them down differently.[27] This plurality of views within the Christian movement about the place of the law confirms the analysis that their common moral identity was not fundamentally based on law but on response to the coming reign of God already experienced in Christ.

There are also sayings, however, that provide for community regulation and thus must be considered "law" in the new community. The most important of these perhaps are those sayings where people are authorized to render judgment in matters of discipline, to "bind and loose."[28] (In Mt. 16:19, such authority is given to Peter; in Mt. 18:18, it is given to the disciples along with the gift of the Holy Spirit.) The authorization to render God's judgment ("in the heavens") justifies the modification and application of wisdom sayings into regulations. In Matthew 18:15-17, for example, an older saying (cf. Lk. 17:3-4) is reformulated into a series of regulations for church discipline. A similar process may be discerned in the saying about divorce: Matthew's addition of "except for unchastity" moves the saying into the realm of regulations and casuistry (Mt. 5:32; 19:9; cf. Mk. 10:11,12). The dominical saying about kindness to children is used to order the community, to call for a policy of leadership where the pastoral care of "minor" members of the community is a first priority (Mt. 18:5-6; cf. Mk. 9:37,41). Similarly, the "great reversal" of conventional leadership can be applied to ordered relationships within the Christian community and regularized into a church rule to guide and judge leadership (Mk. 10:42-45; Mt. 20:25-28; Lk. 22:25-27; Mk. 9:35; Lk. 9:48).

However, the process is not invariably toward regulation. The rules concerning the mission of the disciples (Mk. 6:8-11; Mt. 10:5-15; Lk. 9:1-6; 10:2-12), for example, are not preserved as regulations for the continuing mission of the church.[29] By the time of the Gospels these rules were no longer taken as regulatory for evangelists. These rule-sayings were preserved as justification and exhortation for the churches' missionary activity itself, the forms and rules of which had changed from the time of Jesus. The instructions to the disciples are considered relevant to the early church and to their new and different mission, but they are evidently not applied as a set of regulations. This alone should prevent the attempt to construe even these legal sayings as the basis for a new *Halakah.*[30]

Even as there was a tendency to apply the eschatological wisdom to conduct by way of regulation, the eschatological perspective keeps merely legal observance in a kind of crisis, constantly makes total claims, and re-forms conduct and its regulations in response to the coming reign of God. It is not that the community is constantly collecting and adding rules of conduct to a developing code, but rather that they are constantly reformulating the rules in ways that are faithful both to the new situation and to the reign of God.[31]

d) The I-Sayings:[32] Emphasizing, Moving, and Modeling

The "I-sayings" are the sayings in which Jesus refers to himself in the first person. There can be little doubt that after the resurrection references to Jesus' person and work would multiply also in the tradition of the dominical sayings themselves. Again, however, the issue here is not the authenticity of such sayings but the churches' use of them in their moral discernment and judgment and the contribution they made to the developing moral tradition.

That contribution is threefold. The frequent use of the introductory formula "I say unto you" (e.g., Mt. 5:20, etc.) emphasizes not only the contrast with other moral outlooks but also the stringency and urgency of the saying. For it is, after all, the risen Lord, to whom loyalty is due, who speaks in the churches' memory of Jesus' sayings. The use of "in my name" to qualify actions (e.g., receiving a child, Mk. 9:37) serves in the tradition to provide an explicitly Christian motive for the action. Most significantly, perhaps, some of the "I-sayings" serve not just to introduce or modify other sayings, but to provide a model that can supplement or even replace a maxim or imperative. "I came not to call the righteous, but sinners" (Mk. 2:17), for example, provides a model that helps confirm the disposition to forgive and not to judge. And "I am among you as one who serves" (Lk. 22:27) supplements maxims or exhortations concerning service — almost making them superfluous.

e) The Parables: Shaping Character by Telling Stories

The tradition of dominical sayings also includes the parables,[33] and this attempt to survey the contributions of the dominical sayings to the moral tradition of the early church must include at least some brief references to the parables.

The history of the interpretation of the parables begins in the early church. The early church interpreted the parables before Jülicher demonstrated that allegorizing the parables can lead to distortion and mistaken interpretation.[34] It was quite free to allegorize the parables in order to apply them to their own situation. The parables are allegorized, for example, to make Christological affirmations (e.g., Mt. 24:43-44 par. Lk. 12:39-40),[35] to recite the history of salvation up to the inclusion of the Gentiles (Mk. 12:1-11; Mt. 21:33-44; Lk. 20:9-10),[36] and, more significantly for our inquiry, to exhort Christians to a self-examination about the depth and seriousness of their loyalty to Christ (the interpretation of the parable of the sower, Mk. 4:13-20 par.).[37] That self-examination includes moral examination. The loyalty to Christ is threatened by a lack of courage in the face of "tribulation or persecution" (Mk. 4:17), and by "the cares of the world, and the delight in riches, and the desire for other things" (Mk. 4:19); hearing the word leads properly to "bearing fruit" (Mk. 4:20).

Jülicher interpreted the parables as striking metaphors that inculcated a general moral precept, a position later discredited by Dodd and Jeremias. The early church, of course, interpreted the parables long before the rejection of Jülicher's position by Dodd and Jeremias. It was quite free to attach a lesson to the parable. The parable of the lost sheep, for example, was probably originally intended to defend Jesus' friendship with "sinners." When Matthew uses it in his discourse on rules for discipline within the church, he adds the lesson,

"So it is not the will of my Father who is in heaven that one of these little ones should perish" (Mt. 18:14).[38] The parable is thus interpreted to inculcate a certain pastoral disposition in governance, namely, a concern for the insignificant members of the congregation. Sometimes the "moral" of the parable is an imperative;[39] sometimes it is a maxim of Jesus.[40]

Even when no "moral" is attached, the early church no doubt used and shaped the parables to inform their moral life. They were not interested simply in preserving what Jesus said once, but in hearing what the risen Lord continued to say to his continuing church in and through the tradition. The parable of the great supper (Mt. 22:1-10; Lk. 14:16-24), for example, was very likely first an announcement of the urgency of welcoming the kingdom and a judgment upon the critics of Jesus who refused to repent. In the early church the invitation to the banquet becomes identified with Christian missionary activity, and the parable forms a readiness to engage in that mission, "that my house may be filled" (Lk. 14:23). Both Luke and Matthew demonstrate that the parable could be further modified to shape the moral life of the early church as well. In Luke the parable serves as an exhortation to care for "the poor and maimed and blind and lame" (Lk. 14:21). To his allegorical treatment of the parable Matthew adds the parable of the wedding garment (Mt. 22:11-14) and thus prevents the indiscriminate invitation to "both bad and good" (Mt. 22:10) from being corrupted into an indifference to moral righteousness.[41]

The different moral uses Luke and Matthew made of the parable of the great supper are illustrative of a more pervasive moral use of the parables in the early church. It is impossible, of course, to recover all the ways in which the early church used the parables as morally instructive. Certain moral uses are, nevertheless, quite obvious. Those parables that elicited some moral judgment in the making of another point would surely serve in the early church to reinforce and solidify those moral judgments. The parable of the prodigal son (Lk. 15:11-32), for example, was told originally to vindicate Jesus' proclamation of good news for sinners and to condemn the refusal of his critics to welcome God's reign if it included good news for sinners. But the story assumes and elicits rebukes of the younger son's profligacy and the elder son's stinginess and praise for the father's magnanimity and forgiveness. The sermonic tradition which uses the parable to reinforce those judgments and to strengthen them into dispositions surely began already in the early church. All of the parables that involve the contrast of two types (e.g., the two sons, Mt. 21:28-32; the two servants, Mt. 24:45-51 par. Lk. 12:42-46; the wise and foolish virgins, Mt. 25:1-13; and the Pharisee and the publican, Lk. 18:9-14) elicit such moral judgments and can be used to reinforce and solidify such judgments. The parable of the two servants (Mt. 24:45-51 par. Lk. 12:42-46),[42] to give one more example, originally relied on the moral reaction elicited by the undutiful behavior of the servant entrusted with authority in order to warn Jesus' opponents among the priests and scribes. God's kingdom was "at hand," and when it came he would reveal whether they had abused the authority entrusted to them. In the early church the coming judgment referred to the parousia, and the moral reaction elicited by the servant's behavior became the focus of the parable. It is used to exhort the early Christians, perhaps particularly the leadership, to a watchful stewardship, a stewardship that expects the master's (Gk. *kyrios*) imminent — even if delayed — return, a stewardship that practices justice and self-restraint.

There can be little doubt that each of the parousia parables (e.g., the nocturnal burglar, Mt. 24:43-44 par. Lk. 12:39-40; the ten virgins, Mt. 25:1-13; the doorkeeper, Mk. 13:33-37 par. Lk. 12:35-38, cf. Mt. 24:42; and the talents, Mt. 25:14-30 par. Lk. 19:12-27)[43] served to call the church to a moral earnestness and urgency. The ethic here too was thoroughly eschatological. The church interpreted all of these parables in a Christological sense and used them to exhort the community to watchfulness and to the kinds of character and conduct that cohere with such watchfulness. The specification of the kinds of conduct that cohere with such watchfulness could also be made explicit in these parables. The parable of the last judgment (Mt. 25:31-46) clearly formed watchfulness into dispositions to feed the hungry, give drink to the thirsty, welcome the stranger, clothe the naked, and visit prisoners. The parable of the unmerciful servant (Mt. 18:23-35) also concerned the last judgment and formed watchfulness into a disposition to forgive.

Finally, it is important to call attention to what Bultmann calls "exemplary stories," parables that had an unmistakable hortatory purpose from the very beginning. They include the parables of the Good Samaritan (Lk. 10:30-37), the rich fool (Lk. 12:16-21), the choice of seats at the banquet (Lk. 14:7-11), the rich man and Lazarus (Lk. 16:19-31), and the Pharisee and the publican (Lk. 18:10-14). In each case, the narrative itself is a subtle form of exhortation. The story formed and informed the ethos of the church. In each case, the story did not simply rely on the moral judgments it elicited to make its point. Rather, it taught a reversal of conventional values and judgments: the obligation of love breaks through conventional limits in the parable of the Good Samaritan, both the limits on those to be loved and the limits prudently placed on the obligation to help. The conventional association of wealth, wisdom, security, and blessing is broken down in the parable of the rich fool. The axiom of the kingdom that the humble will be exalted and the proud humbled becomes story in the parable of the choice of seats at the banquet. The eschatological blessing on the poor and woe on the rich becomes narrative in the parable of the rich man and Lazarus. And the surprising and counterconventional expectation of sinners being welcomed into the kingdom while the righteous are shut out assumes narrative form in the parable of the Pharisee and the publican.

Telling and retelling these stories provided ample opportunities for moral reflection and moral education. For example, the Samaritan's behavior is contrasted to the concern of the priest and Levite for ritual cleanliness as they make their way to Jerusalem for their period of service at the temple. The Samaritan begins with simple human compassion (Gk. *esplanchnisthē*), but his compassion leads to behavior far beyond the conventional expressions of helping the neighbor. The responses of Abraham to the pleas of the rich man allow the early church to link God's eschatological intention to bless the poor both with the tradition of "Moses and the prophets" and the resurrection. A community that reads Moses and the prophets as Scripture and believes that Jesus has been raised from the dead may not take up simply any disposition it pleases toward the poor. It is bound and obliged to share that eschatological intention of God to bless the poor.

In each of these stories — and in the parables in general — the church used the tradition of Jesus' parables and adapted it creatively so that the living Lord himself could form and inform his community. Each telling was creative as well as preservative; each telling brought the tradition to bear on the questions of the moment. So the tradition was preserved, and the ethos of the church was formed.

3) The Miracle Stories:[44] Eliciting Loyalty and Confidence

The tradition of Jesus' miracles in the Gospels is clearly not morally didactic. The stories of Jesus' exorcisms, his other healings, and his power over nature are handed down in the early church in order to demonstrate his messianic authority and not his character. They are handed down to confirm the analysis of the eschatological situation, not to confirm their analyses of certain moral problems. But the tradition of Jesus' miracles is by no means morally irrelevant.

The moral relevance of the miracles is not least related to the moral relevance of the messianic authority of Jesus and the eschatological situation which the church believed itself to be in. The miracle tradition and the sayings tradition may be distinguished from one another, but they are not divided from one another in the life of the early church or exiled to different compartments of that life, say, different neatly divided *Sitze im Leben.* There can be little doubt that the miracles were particularly useful to the church's missionary preaching, but their use is not to be restricted to that missionary proclamation. In the evangelists, for example, there is a close link between the authority of the sayings and the authority of the mighty deeds (e.g., Mk. 1:21-28; Mt. 4:23-25; Lk. 4:31-37, and the link in John between the signs and the discourses). The formation of character and conduct in the church took place in the context of the church's loyalty to Jesus and their confidence that God's reign had already made its power felt in him. And that loyalty and confidence are expressed and elicited in the telling and retelling of the miracle stories.

The moral relevance of the miracles may also be seen in the fact that miracles sometimes are reported within the apophthegms. The controversies prompted by healings on the Sabbath (Mk. 3:1-6 par.; Lk. 13:10-17; 14:1-6; Jn. 5:2-18; 7:14-24; 9:14-16) and the healing of the paralytic (Mk. 2:2-12 par.) are morally relevant, as has already been observed above. The biographical apophthegm which relies on the narrative context provided by the healing of the ten lepers (Lk. 17:12-19) makes a point of the contrast between gratitude and ingratitude.

Although it is infrequent in the Gospel narratives, the notice of Jesus' compassion (Mk. 8:2; Lk. 7:13; in Mk. 1:41, "anger" [Gk. *orgistheis*] rather than "pity" [Gk. *esplanchnistheis*] is probably the original reading; also cf. Jn. 12:33-36) should not be overlooked. The miracle-worker is not only powerful and authoritative but compassionate. He heals the sick, does not turn his back on the "unclean" for the sake of his own purity (e.g., Mk. 5:25-34 par.), responds to the pleas of the poor and needy (Mk. 10:46-52 par.), including women (Lk. 7:11-17), Samaritans (Lk. 17:11-19), Gentiles (Mt. 8:5-13 par.), and sinners (Jn. 9). The interest remained focused on Jesus himself as a miracle-worker, but it also shaped the mind of the early church to a similar indiscriminate compassion. That the ministry of Christ brings "good news" to the poor, to women, to outcasts, to children, to sinners, was not forgotten in the miracle stories, and such miracle stories — even while they remain focused on Jesus — made subtle claims on the church's dispositions and conduct.

4) The Stories:[45] Messianic and Moral Submission

The situation is not otherwise with the stories. They focus either on Jesus himself or on the cultic life of the early church.[46] The stories of the baptism by John (Mk. 1:9-11 par.; cf. also Jn. 1:34) and the transfiguration (Mk. 9:2-8 par.) disclose that Jesus is the "Son of God." The stories of the confession of Peter (Mk. 8:27-30 par.; cf. Jn. 6:66-69) and the triumphal entry into Jerusalem (Mk. 11:1-10 par.; cf. Jn. 12:12-15) manifest that Jesus is the Christ. And the passion narrative, of course, concentrates attention on Jesus' death as a messianic pretender and his vindication by God.[47] The institution of the Lord's Supper (Mk. 14:22-25 par.) clearly focuses on the sacramental meal of the church. It is unnecessary to give further examples of the confessional and liturgical focus of these materials. But this tradition can also be put to moral uses within the community.[48]

The story of the temptation, for example, could — in the tradition Mark knew — focus on Jesus' overcoming Satan in a test of strength (Mk. 1:12-13). But in the tradition of Q there is an additional and quite remarkable focus on the temptations themselves (Mt. 4:1-11; Lk. 4:1-12). The claim here is not that the story has been reduced to a moralizing tale cautioning against the physical appetites, the lust for power, and pride; rather, the early church has seen in Jesus' triumph something paradigmatic for its own encounters with temptation. Jesus relies on Scripture, and that itself is paradigmatic; but the devil himself can quote Scripture (Mt. 4:6; Lk. 4:10-11).[49] Jesus wins the real victory when he is humbly submissive to God and his will. He does not use his miraculous powers (or Scripture!) for himself or for display; and he does not sacrifice his integrity even for what is rightfully his. Thus he wins the battle, and thus the Christian community is exhorted to submit humbly to the will of God. The story is important morally and messianically[50] at the same time — and morally because messianically in the early church.

The Gethsemane story (Mk. 14:32-42 par.) is another paradigmatic story, important both messianically and morally. Again Jesus is Messiah and moral exemplar precisely in his humble submission to the will of God. He watches and prays, and he exhorts his disciples to "watch and pray that you may not enter into temptation" (Mk. 14:38). In both the temptation and Gethsemane, the messianic contest with Satan provides a background of intelligibility for early church members and their own temptations. Their life is also part of that contest, a contest between the spirit and the flesh (Mk. 14:38). There are comparable battles to be fought, battles that can be fought with more courage because Christ is the stronger, but battles that nevertheless must be fought with the same kind of humble submission to God's will as they "watch and pray."

The whole passion narrative is relevant both messianically and morally. No doubt the resurrection casts its light on this story, but in the light it sheds, Jesus is Messiah precisely in his humble submission to the will of God. He triumphs precisely in his refusal to use for himself the powers he used for others. He accepts suffering, ignominy, and death for the sake of God's cause in the world. He "came not to be served but to serve, and to give his life a ransom for many" (Mk. 10:45). The moral significance of this includes the use of Jesus as example, model, paradigm, exemplar, and so forth. But it is not exhausted by it: the story of Jesus' passion shapes the moral identity of the early church members, determines their loyalty, affects their perception of the moral struggle, and establishes a disposition to count the other's good more important than one's self-interest.

The moral use of such traditions is manifest also in Matthew's handling of the arrest scene, where he adds a rebuke against the use of the sword (Mt. 26:52). And in both John and Luke, the story of the Last Supper is turned to a hortatory use, in John with the footwashing as an example of humble service (Jn. 13:12-17) and in Luke with Jesus' table service and his sayings about greatness (Lk. 22:24-27). In these ways also the stories form and inform the moral life of the early church, making their own distinctive contribution to its moral tradition.

5) Summary

The survey of the forms of the tradition yields no systematic or comprehensive account of the early church's moral tradition. There are a variety of forms and diverse ways in which they brought the memory of Jesus' words and deeds to bear on the moral life. Nevertheless, amid the great variety, each literary form makes certain distinctive contributions. The apophthegms provide a description and defense of the early church's morality, which stands against the rabbinical and conventional moralities of the first century. The dominical sayings make a variety of contributions. By the prophetic sayings the church remembers and bears a distinctive eschatological and moral identity. By the use of wisdom sayings the church articulates an eschatological wisdom, discerning the eschatological principles already operative in the world beyond the reach of human control and known in the experience of God's power in Jesus Christ. The legal sayings regulate the community in ways that are fitting both to the eschatological situation and to the particular problem within the church. The I-sayings contribute a sense of religious stringency, a religious motive, or a model to moral responsibilities. The parables provide narratives that are both shaped by and give shape to the ethos of the early church; they are used to form and strengthen character. The miracle stories are not morally didactic, but they do express and elicit the ground motive of loyalty to Christ as the one in whom God's transcendent power is already operative and his eschatological intentions already made known. The stories similarly bear the awareness both that Jesus is the Christ, the Messiah, and that their identity, their perception of the moral struggle, and their dispositions should conform to his humble submission.

Moreover, amid the diversity, one can discern a certain coherence in the distinctive contributions of each form. It is Jesus who is remembered: his words and deeds are taken to be normative. He is remembered as the risen Lord who continues to guide and speak to those who would be faithful to him. So the early churches not only passively received but creatively shaped and modified his words and deeds to address new situations they encountered. And they expected him, at his parousia, to win the final victory over the powers of sin and death. This eschatological perspective prevented the tradition, even the regulations within it, from assuming the shape of a code.

This morality is inalienably religious. The tradition's capacity to form the moral life is essentially related to its capacities to claim and nurture certain religious loyalties and to illuminate life and the world from a religious and eschatological perspective. No tidy distinctions between religion and morality, between kerygma and didache, or even between the *Sitze im Leben* of the different forms are discernible in this material.

3. Early Collections

The church repeated the stories and sayings again and again, grouping some of them into small collections for its use. It is difficult, of course, to identify with any certainty sources that were used by the evangelists, but the plausibility of some suggestions makes them noteworthy. The task undertaken in this section is to examine briefly some pre-Marcan collections and more fully examine Q, the important collection used by both Matthew and Luke.

a. PRE-MARCAN COLLECTIONS

Mark, writer of the first Gospel, seems to have already had a number of small collections at his disposal.[51] There are the apophthegms of Mark 2:1-3:6

and of 12:13-37a; there are the two catenae of miracles in Mark 4:35-8:26;[52] there is the "little apocalypse" in Mark 13:5-31[53] and a collection of sayings in Mark 9:35-50. All of this material is reworked by Mark and adapted to the needs of his audience,[54] and it is difficult to be too modest in claims about the ethic underlying these earlier collections or the communities using them. Even so, the very fact that there were such collections is noteworthy. And even modest conclusions are not negligible.

1) Mark 2:1-3:6

The collection of apophthegms in Mark 2:1-3:6 identifies the Christian community as those who are loyal to Jesus, the Son of Man, who has power over sickness and sin and has the authority to forgive sin. It is composed of those who "follow" him. They are, like him, free to fellowship with "sinners" and free to live beyond scrupulous observance of fasts and sabbaths. The collection seems polemical, but it may be directed not against the Jews but against other Christians who would not tolerate flexibility in observance of the law in order to pursue vigorously the urgent mission of the church (see Mk. 2:17 and also the episode concerning the urgent mission of David and "those who were with him" [I Sam. 21:1-6], which is cited [Mk. 2:25,26] in justification of the violation of the Sabbath).

2) Mark 10:1-31

There is an interesting collation of apophthegms in Mark 10:1-31. Eduard Schweizer[55] makes the quite plausible suggestion that the section is based on a catechetical tradition concerning household rules, treating first discipleship in marriage (Mk. 10:1-12), then discipleship concerning children (Mk. 10:13-16), and finally discipleship concerning possessions (Mk. 10:17-31). The *Haustafeln*[56] (or tables of rules for the household) are well known in Stoic and Hellenistic Jewish sources, and, of course, they appear in the New Testament in a variety of places and forms.[57] This form of instruction evidently became an important part of the church's moral education and of its catechesis. Here this form evidently provides the pattern for the collection of materials from the tradition of Jesus' words and deeds, and by means of this collection the tradition is brought to bear on the social roles within which people live. The role obligations themselves, however, are no longer the decisive thing. Rather, radical loyalty to Jesus enables and requires behavior and dispositions that surpass and judge conventional role expectations.

3) Mark 12:13-37

In Mark 12:13-37, there is yet another grouping that probably represents a pre-Marcan collection. The collection is polemically oriented against the Jews and serves to articulate and defend a Christian identity over against a variety of Jewish alternatives. The collection climaxes in the final controversy, in which Jesus takes the initiative in the dialogue (Mk. 12:35-37). There Jesus is represented as citing the important testimony text of early Christian preaching, Psalm 110:1:[58] "The Lord says to my lord, 'Sit at my right hand, till I make your enemies your footstool.'" The enthronement of Jesus provides the background of intelligibility to the affirmation of God's sovereignty over Caesar (Mk. 12:13-17),[59] the expectation of the resurrection (Mk. 12:18-27), and the acknowledgment of obligations to worship the one true God and to love one's neighbor (Mk. 12:28-34).

4) Mark 9:35-50

There is a fascinating collection of sayings in Mark 9:35-50.[60] It is introduced with the words, "And he sat down and called the twelve; and he said to them. . . ." This introduction occurs regularly at the beginning of a series of sayings (e.g., Mk. 4:1; Mt. 5:1; Lk. 4:20; 5:3). Here, however, it seems awkwardly and pointlessly to interrupt the link between the narrative setting (Mk. 9:33-34) and the saying (Mk. 9:35b). The narrative setting is in a house in Capernaum, where Jesus questions the disciples about their dispute concerning who was the greatest. Why, then, have Jesus call them? Why have him sit down to teach the single saying, "If anyone would be first, he must be last of all and the servant of all" (9:35b)? The solution to such puzzles is simple enough on the hypothesis that Mark 9:35-50 is a pre-Marcan collection of sayings. For such a collection the introduction (9:35a) would be natural and appropriate. It is Mark who provides the narrative setting for the first saying of the collection and thereby applies the saying to quarreling church leaders. In the pre-Marcan collection the saying stands without the context of the dispute among the disciples about greatness; it stands rather first in a heterogeneous collection of sayings linked together most often by certain catchwords — "servant"/"child" (Gk. *pais,* 35,36); "in my name" (37,38,39,41); "cause to stumble" (42,43,45,47); "fire" (48,49); "salt" (49,50). The arrangement is mnemonic rather than topical. The collection certainly reaches back to the oral period when such mnemonic aids would be important, and it certainly gathers originally unrelated sayings into an easily taught and remembered group. The collection served a catechetical function, instructing inquirers in the obligations of the followers of Jesus and providing them with an easily remembered set of sayings to form and inform their lives. The collection is heterogeneous, but together the sayings shape dispositions toward mutual service (35b), regard for children (36,37,42,43), tolerance (38,39,50), hospitality (40,41), and moral vigilance and watchfulness (44-49).

b. Q

The most common and satisfying solution to the question of the interrelationship of the Synoptic Gospels is to suppose that Mark and another source, Q (for *Quelle,* source), were utilized by Matthew and Luke. Although the plausibility and necessity of the Q hypothesis has sometimes been challenged,[61] it continues to command the assent of most scholars working with the Gospel materials.[62] The precise extent, vocabulary, and order of Q are probably unrecoverable, since we know it only through the redactions of Matthew and Luke; but the general contours of this early collection may be seen in the material Matthew and Luke have in common, assuming that Luke is generally more faithful to the order and vocabulary of Q.[63]

1) Catechesis, Crisis, or "Christological Cognition"?

Early students of Q were confident that this collection was "intended for use within the Christian community as a manual for instruction in the duties of the Christian life."[64] As such, it was understood as a supplement to the *kērygma* of the cross and resurrection; it was *didachē*, provided as a secondary supplement to the missionary preaching; it was catechesis. A. Harnack, T. W. Manson, M. Dibelius, and V. Taylor all shared this view.[65]

The confident assumption that Q was intended as catechesis was challenged in independent studies by W. D. Davies and H. E. Tödt. Davies attended to Q as background for the Sermon on the Mount.[66] He argued against the conventional position concerning the purpose of Q because, first, in Q there are very few examples of the literary form especially useful in exhortation, the apophthegm; second, the arguments in support of reading Q as exhortation had both misrepresented and misinterpreted a number of sayings and parables; third, there are few parallels between undeniably catechetical materials and Q.[67] Positively, Davies calls attention to the note of eschatological crisis, of impending judgment, that sounds throughout the Q materials. That crisis was announced by John the Baptist and precipitated in Jesus' proclamation of the kingdom. The urgency of that crisis, according to Davies, provided the motive and context for Q's collection and preservation of the sayings of Jesus, not "the normalities of catechetical instruction."[68] The eschatological crisis wrought by Jesus continued to be constituted whenever people were confronted with the radical and revelatory demands of Jesus. In a memorable line Davies says, "In Q crisis and commandment are one."[69] According to Davies, then, Q was itself proclamation, not an addendum to the kerygma; but the proclamation announced a kingdom whose coming put the present in crisis, a kingdom unveiled as bringing and demanding a radical change of values.

H. E. Tödt, working on Q in the midst of his study entitled "Son of Man,"[70] was also constrained to challenge the assumption that Q was catechetical and didactic. He called attention to sections of Q which "cannot be understood as having affinity with a need for exhortation."[71] Positively, for Tödt, the Son of Man Christology provided the clue to Q's purpose and character. The sayings about a suffering Son of Man are conspicuously absent; still more conspicuous by its absence is the passion narrative, the story of the cross and resurrection. The future Son of Man whom Jesus announced had been identified by the community with Jesus himself. This "Christological cognition" took place in the context of continuing fellowship with the risen one and warranted taking up his message again. Q, then, was not a supplement to the kerygma but an alternative way of construing and proclaiming the salvation offered by Jesus. The passion and resurrection are not themselves the saving events to be announced; rather, the cross tends to discredit Jesus, while the resurrection vindicates him and his message, which must be taken up and proclaimed. Thus the motive for Q was not the proclamation of Christ crucified but of Jesus as the Son of Man, the vindicated teacher.

Recent treatments of Q,[72] for all their differences about the genre, provenance, and theological emphasis of Q, have agreed with Tödt and Davies in rejecting the position that Q is catechetical and didactic, a secondary supplement to the kerygma.[73] The same recent studies have also called attention to some emphases in Q that had remained largely overlooked by Davies and Tödt, particularly Q's interest in the wisdom tradition.[74] The following analysis of the ethic of Q builds on Davies' recognition of the role of eschatological crisis, Tödt's recognition of the importance of the Son of Man Christology, and the more recent recognition of the significance of wisdom categories and forms in Q.

The ethic of Q must surely be seen in relationship to its eschatology, and particularly to its identification of Jesus as the coming Son of Man. The conviction that Jesus had been raised led to the expectation of his triumphant manifestation as the Son of Man. The orientation toward a future in which the Son of Man will be revealed is quite unmistakable in Q (Lk. 17:24=Mt. 24:27; Lk. 17:26=Mt. 24:37-39; Lk. 17:28=Mt. 24:37-39; Lk. 11:30=Mt. 12:40; Lk. 12:40=Mt. 24:44; Lk. 12:8-9). The conviction that Jesus had been raised and the expectation that he would return in judgment and glory prompted the community to take up again the ministry of Jesus. They made his way and message their own. To use Tödt's phrase, "Christological cognition" involved moral cognition too. To know Jesus and his eschatological role as Son of Man was the key to understanding one's present responsibilities.

Q's eschatology identifies the present as a time of crisis, for the age hastens to judgment. The note of crisis is introduced immediately with the preaching of John the Baptist (Lk. 3:7-9, 16-17=Mt. 3:7-10, 11-12). The coming wrath makes repentance and the fruits worthy of repentance terribly urgent. And the same note of crisis sounds throughout the preaching of Jesus as well (e.g., Lk. 6:46-49 = Mt. 7:21-27; Lk. 9:57-62 = Mt. 8:18-22; Lk. 10:8-12 = Mt. 10:13-15; Lk. 10:12-15 = Mt. 11:20-24; Lk. 11:19-23 = Mt. 12:27-30; Lk. 11:29-32 = Mt. 12:38-42; Lk. 11:37-52 = Mt. 23:4-36; Lk. 17:22-37 = Mt. 24:17-41; Lk. 19:11-27=Mt. 25:14-30). In the preaching of Jesus, the crisis contains a positive side as well, reflected in his reply to John's inquiry (Lk. 7:18-23=Mt. 11:2-6: "The blind receive their sight, the lame walk, the deaf hear, the dead are raised up, the poor have good news preached to them") and in the eschatological blessings, the beatitudes (Lk. 6:20-23=Mt. 5:3-6, 11-12; Lk. 7:23=Mt. 11:6; Lk. 10:23-24=Mt. 13:16-17; Lk. 12:42-44=Mt. 24:45-47).

This eschatological orientation makes the more remarkable the absence of any apocalyptic speculation; there is nothing like the "little apocalypse" of Mark 13 or the apocalyptic materials in I Thessalonians 4:13ff. or Revelation. The orientation is at the same time both thoroughly eschatological and thoroughly practical.

The practical orientation accounts for Q's interest in wisdom. Conventional wisdom instruction, as has been observed, emphasized the practical and was based on experience. By careful attention to the ways of the world the wise man learned prudence and morality. The wisdom materials in Q, however, are qualified by the thoroughly eschatological orientation of Q.[75] It is an eschatological wisdom: the emphasis still rests on the practical, but it is based on the particular experience of eschatological crisis and blessing. The "Christological cognition," rather than the distillation of past experiences of the ways of the world, enables and demands genuine comprehension of the basic principles that operate in the world beyond human control and to which the wise will conform. The wise person still learns prudence, but it is a prudence in view of the coming kingdom. He still learns morality, but it is a morality of acknowledging Jesus (Lk. 12:8-9=Mt. 10:32-33), of following him (Lk. 9:57-62=Mt. 8:18-22), of seeking his kingdom (Lk. 12:31=Mt. 6:33), of hearing and doing his words (Lk. 6:46-49=Mt. 7:24-27), and of being like the teacher (Lk. 6:40=Mt. 10:24-25).

The basic principles operate in the world willy-nilly, but they can be known by attending to the words and way of Jesus. The call of wisdom, of course, is to adjust and conform to them. Such is the ethic of Q. Typically these basic principles are either expressed in the form of aphorisms or beatitudes which command not only intellectual assent but appropriate behavior (the very distinction would be curious to the wisdom tradition), or they are presupposed in the form of admonitions.

2) The Sayings-Collection within Q: "Moral Cognition"

After the introductory sections of John's preaching (Lk. 3:7-9=Mt. 3:7-10) and Jesus' temptations (Lk. 4:1-13=Mt. 4:1-11), the beatitudes (Lk. 6:20-23=Mt. 5:3-12) introduce a collation of sayings (Lk. 6:27-46=Mt. 5:38-48; 7:12; 7:1-5; 12:36-37; 15:14; 10:24-25; 7:15-20; 12:33-35; 7:21-27) which summarize and express the "moral cognition" of the Q community.

As a conventional wisdom form, beatitudes announce the prudence of conforming to principles operative in the world willy-nilly; in Q's eschatological wisdom that function has not changed, but the principles plainly cannot be known from past experience of the way of the world but from the revelation and experience of an eschatological future. Indeed, there is a reversal of and a challenge to what passes for wisdom and prudence: those blessed are the poor, the hungry, the sad, and those who are despised "on account of the Son of Man." And the beatitude demands not merely intellectual assent but appropriate affective and behavioral response. The "woes" (Lk. 6:24-26: since they are found only in Luke, it is impossible to be certain that they were a part of Q) announce similar principles and call for similar affective and behavioral response.

The sayings that follow the beatitudes make plain what sort of behavioral response is appropriate. "Love your enemies" (Lk. 6:27=Mt. 5:44) stands guard against rejoicing in the woes upon the rich and respectable, while it guides behavior into conformity to the principles articulated in the beatitudes. Loving the enemy is made more concrete in the admonitions that follow: "Do good to those who hate you, bless those who curse you, pray for those who abuse you. To him who strikes you on the cheek, offer the other also; and from him who takes away your cloak do not withhold your coat as well. Give to everyone who begs from you; and of him who takes away your goods do not ask them again" (Lk. 6:27b-30=Mt. 5:39b-42,44b). Such behavior presupposes the beatitudes and the eschatological future announced there. It is wisdom, but an eschatological wisdom; prudence, but prudence based on a "Christological cognition" and its attendant insight into principles beyond the reach of human control. This context spares the "Golden Rule" (Lk. 6:31) from possible misuse as a justification of egotistical calculations of reciprocal benefits. The passage stands as a general directive to do good without calculating possible returns.

Subsequent sayings contrast such wisdom to the way of the world, which is the basis of conventional wisdom (Lk. 6:32-34=Mt. 5:46-47), repeat the admonitions, and insist that this is true wisdom and true prudence (Lk. 6:35=Mt. 5:45). The appeal to experience here is interesting. It is, like conventional wisdom, an appeal to past experience, to the fact that God's sun shines and his rain falls on good and bad alike (Matthew) or to the fact that God is "kind to the ungrateful and selfish" (Luke). Matthew cites the experience, and Luke articulates the principle operating in the world; the exact Q source is beyond our grasp. Nevertheless, it is plain that eschatological wisdom does not disown, in principle, the distillation of past experiences of the way of God in the world but, rather, provides a prism for the discernment of the eschatological way of God already in operation in the world.

There follows the admonition to "be merciful, even as your Father is merciful" (Lk. 6:36).* The quality of mercy is discerned — and experienced — as God's way, and thus it is a requirement of the wise. God's mercy calls for appropriate affective response, which has concrete behavioral correlates. The next sayings admonish the community not to judge or condemn but to give and forgive (Lk. 6:37-38=Mt. 7:1-2). Again, such behavior presupposes a principle operative in the world that is above and beyond human control. It

---

*Mt. 5:48, although it has the same form, identifies a different virtue of God, his being "perfect." Both the preceding context (cf. Lk. 6:35) and, given the likelihood that Luke better preserves Q's order, the following sayings (cf. Lk. 6:37-38) make Luke's "merciful" the quality Q probably called attention to.

is wisdom, but eschatological wisdom; wisdom based on "Christological cognition" and its attendant "moral cognition"; a wisdom found in the way and words of Jesus: "A disciple is not above his teacher, but every one when he is fully taught will be like his teacher" (Lk. 6:40=Mt. 10:24-25). It is prudence, but an eschatological prudence, a prudence that stands in contrast to conventional wisdom, which Jesus compares to the blind leading the blind (Lk. 6:39=Mt. 15:14). The quality of mercy and the admonition not to judge are finally applied within the community with the saying about the log in one's own eye and the speck in the neighbor's eye (Lk. 6:41-42=Mt. 7:3-5). The "moral cognition" that attends "Christological cognition" has no place for moral pride.

The sayings that conclude this collection within Q contrast good and bad trees by their fruits (Lk. 6:43-45=Mt. 7:15-20; cf. Mt. 12:33-35) and wise and foolish builders by the foundation on which they build (Lk. 6:46-49=Mt. 7:21-27; only Matthew explicitly refers to the "wise man" and the "foolish man"). The appeals to agricultural and construction trades are conventional for wisdom. Edwards calls attention to the "correlation of the facts of the building trade with the basic rules or laws one should apply to men."[76] However, those rules — the principles operating in the world — are not known (as conventionally) in the distillation of commonplace experiences but in Jesus and his words. "Everyone who comes to me and hears my words and does them" (Lk. 6:47=Mt. 7:24) is the wise man. Such wisdom is eschatologically prudent, prudent in face of the coming judgment (Lk. 6:48-49=Mt. 7:24-27; see also Mt. 7:19). The conclusion of this collation of sayings within Q emphasizes that the "Christological cognition" involves not merely calling Jesus "Lord" but doing his words (Lk. 6:46=Mt. 7:21). It includes "moral cognition" and moral action. The eschatological wisdom commands not just intellectual assent but appropriate affective and behavioral response.

3) Programmatic Conversations

Such wisdom originates, as we have said, in the community's "Christological cognition." The next section of Q contains three conversations that have a Christological focus. They invite and confirm the acknowledgment of Jesus as having "authority" (Lk. 7:1-10=Mt. 8:5-13, the centurion at Capernaum); as being "the one who is to come" (Lk. 7:18-23=Mt. 11:2-6, the conversation between Jesus and John's disciples); and as being the Son of Man, the agent of wisdom (Lk. 7:24-35=Mt. 11:7-19, Jesus' talk to the crowds concerning John). These conversations are programmatic for Q. The first conversation construes the recognition of legitimate authority as doing what the one in authority says (Lk. 7:8=Mt. 8:9) and recalls the conclusion to the sayings collection examined above (Lk. 6:46,47=Mt. 7:21,24). The second appeals to Jesus' way and words as evidence that he is the one "who is to come" and announces the blessing on the one who "takes no offense" at Jesus (Lk. 7:22-23=Mt. 11:5-6). It foreshadows the next section, the commissioning of and the blessing on Jesus' followers, those who make Jesus' way and words their own (e.g., Lk. 9:1-6=Mt. 10:1,7-11; cf. Mk. 6:6b-13; Lk. 9:57-62=Mt. 8:18; Lk. 10:1-12=Mt. 9:37-38; 10:7-16; Lk. 10:16=Mt. 10:40; Lk. 10:21-24=Mt. 11:25-27; 13:16-17). The third conversation explicitly mentions, for the first time, the rejection of Jesus, foreshadowing the material that will later focus on the opposition to Jesus and his followers (e.g., Lk. 11:29-32=Mt. 12:39-42; Lk. 11:37-54=Mt. 24:4-36; Lk. 12:2-9=Mt. 10:26-33).

4) Taking Up the Way of Jesus

Q's wisdom originates in the community's "Christological cognition," but it consists of taking up the words and way of Jesus again. So they are sent out "to preach the kingdom of God and to heal" (Lk. 9:2; 10:9=Mt. 10:7-8), in sum, to continue the message and work of Jesus (cf. Lk. 7:22=Mt. 11:4,5). This is an urgent and costly task: urgent because of the crisis of the coming judgment (Lk. 10:12-15=Mt. 11:20-24) which they already provisionally and proleptically enact (Lk. 10:8-12=Mt. 10:13-15); costly because of both the expectation of opposition and the assumption of homelessness and poverty (Lk. 9:57-62=Mt. 8:18-22; Lk. 9:3 and Lk. 10:4=Mt. 10:9-10). But it is also a blessed task, blessed because it rests on a cognition of that eschatological truth which is hidden from the conventionally "wise" but revealed graciously to "babes" (Lk. 10:21-24=Mt. 11:25-27; 13:16-17), blessed because it involves them as agents of God (Lk. 10:16=Mt. 10:40: "He who hears you hears me, and he who receives me receives him who sent me"), and blessed because it proceeds with eschatological confidence in God (Lk. 11:1-4=Mt. 6:9-13 [The Lord's Prayer]; Lk. 11:9-13=Mt. 7:7-11).

5) Expecting Opposition

The Beelzebub controversy (Lk. 11:14-23=Mt. 12:22-30) serves as a reminder of the "Christological cognition" (that he is the stronger one, Lk. 11:21-22=Mt. 12:28-29), of the eschatological authority by which he casts out demons (Lk. 11:20=Mt. 12:28), and of the task of taking up his way and words again (Lk. 11:23=Mt. 12:30) — but all in the context of opposition. Q's wisdom originates in the community's "Christological cognition"; it consists in taking up the way and words of Jesus; but it can anticipate no other response than opposition and persecution.

The model according to which Q understands the opposition to Jesus and to their own ministry is provided by the prophets (Lk. 13:34-35=Mt. 23:37-39; see also earlier, Lk. 6:22-23). And the response to opposition consists of prophetic words of judgment and warning (Lk. 11:31-32=Mt: 12:41-42; Lk. 11:39-52=Mt. 23:25-26,23,6-7,27-28,4,29-36; Lk. 12:8-9=Mt. 10:32-33; Lk. 13:22-29=Mt. 7:13-14,22-23; 8:11-12; Lk. 14:24=Mt. 22:8). Some of these judgments and warnings refer to specific practices and dispositions, and hence are helpful in the attempt to understand Q's ethic. The scribes and Pharisees who oppose them are condemned for their scrupulous observance of traditional regulations (cleansing the outside of the cup, Lk. 11:39-41=Mt. 23:25-26; tithing every herb, Lk. 11:42=Mt. 23:23); for their continual adding of traditional requirements (Lk. 11:46=Mt. 23:4); for their self-glorification (Lk. 11:43=Mt. 23:6-7); for their extortion (Lk. 11:39=Mt. 23:25); and for their neglect of justice and mercy (Lk. 11:42=Mt. 23:23). The general point seems to be that their concern with traditional and external *Halakoth* keeps them from perceiving eschatological truth—prompts them, indeed, to oppose it. It is not, however, the case that Q rejects the law; on the contrary, it assumes the abiding validity of the law for this age (Lk. 16:17=Mt. 5:18). Even so, external observance of the tradition is not the standard for final judgment—or, finally, for discernment. The eschatological wisdom rather than the tradition of the scribes and Pharisees enables one to discern the fulfillment of the law.

The opposition they encounter provides the context for the specific admonitions in this section to "fear not" (Lk. 12:4-7=Mt. 10:28-31) and to "be not anxious" (Lk. 12:22-32=Mt. 6:25-34; see also Lk. 12:11-12=Mt. 10:19-20). In each case such a carefree spirit in the face of opposition is prudent and wise in view of the coming judgment. Eschatological wisdom is willing to accept the loss of possessions (Lk. 12:33-34=Mt. 6:19-21; cf. Lk. 16:13=Mt. 6:24), conflicts within the family (Lk. 12:49-53=Mt. 10:34-36; Lk. 14:25-26=Mt. 10:37), and even death (Lk. 14:27=Mt. 10:38) for the sake of taking up the way and words of Jesus. Hoping for recognition from their opposition (Lk. 13:35=Mt. 23:39) and expecting eschatological vindication (but not calculating the date of the Son of Man's day, Lk. 17:22-37=Mt. 24:23,26-27,37-39,17-18; 10:39; 24:40-41,28), the community that collects and takes up the sayings of Jesus in Q wants to be one of "faithful and wise stewards" (Lk. 12:42=Mt. 24:45).

4. Gospel Literature

The tradition of Jesus' words and deeds came to climactic expression in the Gospel literature. The most familiar of the Gospels are, of course, Matthew, Mark, Luke, and John. In these Gospels, moreover, according to the confession of the church, the tradition came to canonical expression. I will examine the ethic of each of these Gospels in the next chapter; for now it must suffice to assert what will be shown later—that each of the Gospels preserves and shapes the tradition in ways that allow the continuing tradition (and the living Lord who continues to speak through it) to address the concrete situation of its original audiences. Faithfully and creatively they use the tradition to announce the gospel and to exhort their audience to live in its light.

It is, however, not only in the canonical Gospels that the tradition finds expression. The apocryphal Gospels also utilize the tradition of Jesus' words and deeds in the service of their own special interests. An adequate account of the apocryphal Gospels would show the docetic tendency in some of these

Gospels, for example, the Gospel of Peter; the ascetic tendency in others, for example, the Gospel of the Egyptians; and the Gnostic tendency in still others, for example, the Gospels in the Nag Hammadi findings, most notably, perhaps, the Gospel of Thomas. In each case the tradition is shaped by the particular theological and moral tendencies of the author, and the consequent Gospel shapes the character and conduct of the audience.[77]

B. THE PARAENETIC TRADITION[78]

Alongside the tradition of Jesus' words and deeds, the early church developed and handed down a paraenetic tradition. The necessity of instructing inquirers about their responsibilities within the believing community provided the most important occasion and impetus for the development of stereotyped materials for instruction and exhortation.

The catechetical tradition may be neither rigidly divided from the memory of Jesus' words and deeds nor simply identified with it. I have observed above that the attempt to describe Q as catechetical fails, but at least two of the pre-Marcan collections (Mk. 9:35-50 and 10:1-31) were judged to be catechetical in intention. Although the catechetical materials below occasionally echo or allude to the sayings of Jesus, they depend on forms and materials from sources other than the church's memory of Jesus' words and deeds.

The church was the heir of the Jewish moral tradition and, as she moved into the Greek world, she encountered the moral traditions of Hellenism. The church had to establish her own identity in relation to this heritage and context, and she had to instruct converts — whether Jewish or Gentile — about their relationship to their former ethic. Those requirements gave rise to a distinctive paraenetic tradition.

There were, of course, within the early church a wide variety of responses to the Jewish heritage and to Hellenistic culture. The variety need not be catalogued, but some awareness of the diversity may provide both a precaution against overstating the unity of the early church's paraenesis and a prerequisite for due appreciation of the measure of agreement one can find in the paraenetic tradition.

Very early within Jewish Christianity there emerged quite different attitudes toward the law and toward the inclusion of Gentiles with their Hellenistic culture. The "right-wing circumcision party" or "Judaizers" insisted on circumcision and the observance of the law (Gal. 2:4,12-14; Acts 15:5). The "Hellenists" (Jewish Christians who apparently spoke Greek and had moved back to Jerusalem) evidently criticized the Jewish law and temple observance (Acts 6:13-14) and devoted themselves early on to the mission among the Gentiles (Acts 8:40). It was the "Hellenists" who inspired and suffered the persecutions wrought out of zeal for the traditions of the fathers (see Gal. 1:14). The Council of Jerusalem (Gal. 2; Acts 15) apparently took yet a different position: that Jewish Christians were required to observe the law but that Gentile converts did not need to be circumcised or to observe the Mosaic law.[79]

Within Gentile Christianity there was certainly no less diversity concerning the church's appropriate relationship to the law and to Hellenistic culture. A few Gentiles were convinced — or at least troubled — by the argument of the right-wing circumcision party that circumcision was the sign of the covenant (Gen. 17) and that the law was its "yoke" (cf. Galatians). But the Hellenists like Philip and Barnabas had had the earliest interest in the Gentile mission and the largest impact; their freedom from the law and from temple observance must have been reflected in many Gentile churches.

We know very little, really, about the early Gentile Christian communities,[80] and it is dangerous to speculate about their morality. There was probably a remarkable diversity. Sympathy with the right-wing circumcision party focused moral concern on the observance of the Mosaic law; sympathy with the position of the Hellenists called for a Christian ethical "occupation" of forms and concepts originally the property of Hellenistic Judaism or Stoicism. Here and there isolated groups probably denied the authority of the Jerusalem community altogether and produced a syncretistic adaptation of Christianity to the mystery religions, neo-Pythagoreanism, and/or Gnosticism. These were typically other-worldly and dualistic construals of the Christian message and yielded either ascetic moralities, which denied the body, or libertine moralities, which denied the significance of what was done in the body.[81]

In the midst of this diversity the wide attestation of common paraenetic traditions is the more remarkable. These traditions can be discerned in parallel exhortations within the New Testament materials, and they may be conveniently identified[82] by certain key words.

1. Abstain

E. G. Selwyn has called attention to a number of parallels between I Thessalonians 4:1-12 and I Peter, and he argues, following P. Carrington, that they both depend on an early Christian "Holiness Code."[83] The parallels can hardly be explained as coincidence, and they are not exact enough to suggest a literary relationship. The most convincing explanation is indeed that there is a common reliance on an early Christian tradition of moral exhortation.[84] This hypothesis is rendered still more plausible by the correlation of this material with "the apostolic decree," attributed by Luke to the Jerusalem Council (Acts 15:20,29; 21:25), and with other verses and phrases and words in New Testament exhortations. Moreover, Paul is quite candid about the fact that this material is not an ad hoc composition but traditional instruction (I Thess. 4:2), and I Peter plainly makes considerable use of traditional materials.

The key word in this tradition is "abstain" (Gk. *apechesthai,* Acts 15:20,29; 21:25; I Thess. 4:3; 5:22; I Pet. 2:11); it appears not only here in the New

Testament but frequently in later Christian exhortation (e.g., Pol. *Phil.* 2:2; 5:3; 6:1,3; 11:1). The tradition required that Gentile converts "abstain" from the pagan immorality in which they formerly lived. They are to "abstain from unchastity" (Gk. *porneia*, I Thess. 4:3; cf. Acts 15:20,29; 21:25), to "abstain from the passions [Gk. *epithymiai*] of the flesh" (I Pet. 2:11; cf. 1:15; I Thess. 4:5). Their immorality is traced to their pagan ignorance of God (I Thess. 4:5), to their own "former ignorance" (I Pet. 1:14; cf. 1:18). Their new life stands in contrast to their former life; they are called to "holiness" (Gk. *hagiasmos*; RSV: "sanctification," I Thess. 4:3; cf. vss. 4,7,8), to "be holy" (I Pet. 1:15-16, citing the Holiness Code, Lev. 19:2). This "holiness" takes shape not only in abstinence but also in positive form, most notably in the "love of the brethren" (I Thess. 4:9; cf. also vs. 10; I Pet. 1:22, probably again related to the Holiness Code, Lev. 19:18). To "abstain" from the former way of life and to "be holy" are related by the tradition to the expectation of God's final victory, to the revelation of Christ as judge and avenger (I Thess. 4:6; I Pet. 1:13,17,20). The tradition also apparently construes such a way of life as testimony to those still in ignorance (I Pet. 2:12; I Thess. 4:12).

This tradition, like the memory of Jesus' words and deeds, was not fixed and final; it was adapted, clearly, for the needs of the audience, shaped on an ad hoc basis to speak relevantly and concretely to the "newborn babes" (I Pet. 2:2) on their way to becoming "obedient children" (I Pet. 1:14) who were being taught then and there. Something of that adaptation can be seen in both I Peter and I Thessalonians: Paul quite concretely focuses on sexual sins,[85] perhaps because the crisis of hope in the Thessalonian church has tempted some to return to pagan sexual practices, whereas I Peter is much more inclusive and general. It is impossible to distinguish very exactly "redaction" from tradition, but the paraenetic tradition is identifiable and its shape discernible. The church had a conventional form for the instruction of converts, to be modified and expanded at each use, which was based on the admonitions to "abstain" from pagan immorality and to "be holy" in view of the expectation of God's final triumph.

2. Children of Light

Another — and in Selwyn's view, related — paraenetic tradition may be discerned in certain other parallels in material in I Thessalonians and I Peter (specifically I Thess. 5:1-9; I Pet. 1:11,13,14; 2:8,9,12; 4:1,2,3,7; 5:8). It is an eschatological tradition that characterizes Christians as "children of light" and exhorts them to conduct befitting their character.[86] The tradition describes Christians with some variation on the idiom of "sons of light" (I Thess. 5:5, Gk. *huioi phōtos*; cf. I Pet. 1:14, "obedient children," Gk. *tekna hypakoēs*; also Eph. 5:8, "children of light," Gk. *tekna phōtos*; Jn. 12:36, "sons of light"). It emphasizes the eschatological contrast between light and darkness (I Thess. 5:4ff.; I Pet. 2:9; also Acts 26:18; Eph. 5:8; Rom. 13:12) and the exhortations to be watchful and sober (I Thess. 5:6,8; I Pet. 1:13; 4:7; 5:8; also I Cor. 16:13; Col. 4:2; Rev. 3:2; Mk. 13:35,37; Mt. 25:13).

One may question[87] some of Selwyn's claims concerning the tradition: that it is clearly a baptismal tradition, that it is necessarily linked with the "abstain" tradition, and that it makes self-conscious use of the sayings of Jesus. But the parallels are nevertheless compelling evidence of a common paraenetic tradition, even if we are more cautious in describing it than Selwyn was. Moreover, Paul himself is quite candid that he is appealing to a tradition the Thessalonian church already knows (I Thess. 5:1-2).

The tradition is certainly indebted to Jewish paraenetic materials, in which the idiom "sons of light" and the contrast between light and darkness were common (as the Dead Sea Scrolls make very plain). Forms of Jewish exhortation became conventional within the early church as well, but now within the certainty that God had acted in Christ and within the expectation of his return.

The expectation of God's final triumph and the present experience of that victory in a provisional and proleptic way affect the identity of converts to the gospel. They are "children of light," they already belong to the new age, and that identity must affect their conduct. There is, however, no triumphalism to either their eschatology or their ethic. The darkness continues, and life in the light involves watchfulness and sobriety in contrast to sleep and drunkenness (I Thess. 5:6-8; I Pet. 5:8; 4:7; also Rom. 13:11-13; I Cor. 15:34; 16:13; Eph. 5:8-14; *Ign. Sm.* 9:1; *Ign. Pol.* 1:3; 2:3; II Clem. 13:1). Such moral vigilance, such self-disciplined alertness, must characterize their conduct as "children of light."

The concrete relevance of watchfulness and sobriety would be explicated on an ad hoc basis as this pattern for exhortation was used in the churches. In I Peter, for example, the watchfulness involved the patient endurance of suffering (5:8). In Romans, on the other hand, sobriety entailed not only refraining from "reveling and drunkenness" and "debauchery and licentiousness," which may have been conventional associations, but also refraining from "quarreling and jealousy," which apparently was concretely relevant to the Roman churches (13:13; cf. 14:1-15:6).

3. Cast Off

A third pattern of instruction may be identified in the parallels that admonish converts to "cast off" or "put off" (Gk. *apothesthai*) their old patterns of conduct and character.[88] The positive correlative is "put on" (Gk. *endysasthe,* Rom. 13:12,14; Col. 3:10,12; Eph. 4:24; I Thess. 5:8; Gal. 3:27). The suggestion[89] that such instruction is related to the disrobing and robing that accompanied immersion in baptism is compelling. A new moral identity is assumed in baptism, an identity in Christ.[90]

That new identity calls for the renunciation—for the "casting off"—of "wickedness" (Gk. *kakia,* I Pet. 2:1; Jas. 1:21; Col. 3:8; Eph. 4:31). Such "wickedness" was associated with the "old nature" (Eph. 4:22), the "former manner of life" (Eph. 4:22); indeed, it could be identified with "the old nature with its practices" (Col. 3:9). The contrast between the "old man" and the "new man" may be Pauline language, but the association of the wickedness to be renounced with the former way of life and the contrast to the new Christian identity are surely part of the tradition.

The baptismal instruction to renounce wickedness was an inclusive and general one in the tradition ("all," Gk. *pas, panta,* appears in I Pet. 2:1; Jas. 1:21; Col. 3:8; Eph. 4:31; Heb. 12:1, and was evidently an established part of the tradition), but the instruction could be made more specific by including a list of vices to be renounced (e.g., I Pet. 2:1; Col. 3:8; Eph. 4:31) and by ad hoc identification of what was to be "cast off." The creative use of the tradition may be seen in Hebrews 12:1, which focuses not on the wickedness that belonged to the former way of life but on whatever hinders us on "the race set before us." That very creativity makes it impossible to identify any particular vices as belonging to the traditional instruction concerning what is to be "cast off," but it is worth noticing that various forms of injustice in speech are regularly emphasized (I Pet. 2:1; Eph. 4:25,29,31; Col. 3:8,9).

Positively, that new identity is expressed in terms of having "put on" Christ (Gal. 3:27, "as many of you as were baptized into Christ have put on Christ"). It may also take the form of an imperative: "But put on the Lord Jesus Christ" (Rom. 13:14), or "put on the new nature, created after the likeness of God in true righteousness and holiness" (Eph. 4:24; cf. Col. 3:9). The new identity is assumed in baptism, but it must be affirmed and lived in the world. The early church knew that in this life their Christian identity would be tried and tested; the temptation to immorality was a constant identity crisis. One would not only have to receive this identity but would have to "win" it in the moral conflicts of life. For those conflicts the baptized received not only instruction but also "the armor of light" (Rom. 13:12) and "the whole armor of God" (Eph. 6:11; also Rom. 13:17), which was also to be "put on."[91] In fact, in place of "put on" (Gk. *endysasthe*), I Peter 4:1 instructs Christians to "arm" themselves (Gk. *hoplisasthe*) with the thought of Christ's sufferings.

Both the "armor" and the character and conduct appropriate to the new identity can be made more specific and concrete by means of lists and catalogues of Christian resources and virtues (e.g., Col. 3:12), but the preacher could also use the tradition creatively and freely, adapting and adding material of particular relevance to the identity crisis facing each church or individual. Examples of this sort of creative utilization of the basic pattern may be found in the book of Ephesians' concern for peace, unity, and love in a divided church and in I Peter's concern for steadfastness and integrity in a persecuted church.

The traditional instruction to "cast off" wickedness may initially seem indistinguishable from the instruction to "abstain," but the two should be distinguished. The instructions themselves are more than linguistically different: "cast off" entails more of a deliberate, active renunciation than does "abstain." More significantly, the positive correlatives are different: "holiness," especially considering its association with the Holiness Code of Leviticus, is different from "putting on" Christ. Separation from Gentile sexual immorality and idolatry is a different emphasis from the renunciation of all evil, especially including injustice in speech. The "abstain" tradition may very well represent the tradition of Jewish Christianity's instruction of Gentile converts (although not, of course, that of the right-wing circumcision party), and "cast off" may reflect a more indigenous Gentile Christian catechetical tradition.[92]

4. The Law of Nonretaliation

Still another pattern of instruction may be discerned in the parallels among I Thessalonians 5:12-22, Romans 12:3-20, and I Peter 3:8-12, 4:7-11, and 5:1-5.[93] The closest verbal parallel states the law of nonretaliation as "Do not return evil for evil" (I Pet. 3:9; cf. Rom. 12:17; I Thess. 5:15). In none of the passages is there any reference to Jesus' criticism of the *lex talionis*; these passages are not indebted to the tradition of Jesus' words and works but to a Christian paraenetic tradition. In each of the passages the prohibition of retaliation is related to a positive requirement: to "bless" (I Pet. 3:9; cf. Rom. 12:14); to "seek to do good [Gk. *agathon*] to one another and to all" (I Thess. 5:15; cf. Rom. 12:9); and to "take thought for what is noble [Gk. *kalos*] in the sight of all" (Rom. 12:17; cf. I Thess. 5:21).[94]

Moreover, in each case the law of nonretaliation stands in the context of a succession of short sentences often using participles with the force of imperatives.[95] Among these exhortations are a number of parallels. There is a call for young Christians to "be at peace" (Gk. *eirēneuete*, I Thess. 5:13; Rom. 12:18 uses the participle; I Pet. 3:8 substitutes Gk. *homophrones*; I Pet. 3:11 cites Ps. 34:15; I Thess. calls for peace "among yourselves"; Romans, for peace "with all"). There are also calls to "be patient" (Gk. *makrothymeite*, I Thess. 5:14; Rom. 12:12 has Gk. *hypomenontes*; see also Col. 3:12; Eph. 4:2); to "rejoice" (Gk. *chairete*, I Thess. 5:16; Rom. 12:12 uses the participle; see also I Pet. 4:13); to "pray" (Gk. *proseuchesthe*, I Thess. 5:17; cf. Rom. 12:12; I Pet. 4:7); to "be aglow with the Spirit" (Rom. 12:9; cf. I Thess. 5:19); to "love one another with brotherly affection" (Gk. *philadelphia*, Rom. 12:10; cf. I Thess. 4:9; I Pet. 3:8; also Rom. 8:9, "Let love [Gk. *agapē*] be genuine [Gk. *anypokritos*]"; I Pet. 1:22, "sincere love of the brethren [Gk. *philadelphia anypokriton*]).

Behind these materials there stands a common paraenetic tradition, a miscellany of general exhortations, which could be and would be expanded and modified as the writers creatively utilized the tradition to address the concrete situation of the hearers. This is evident in I Peter, for instance, where Peter related the tradition to the endurance of persecution. The very miscellaneous character of the tradition makes it impossible to reconstruct it with certainty, but the parallels are compelling, and the creative utilization of the tradition to address concrete problems is clear.

5. Be Subject

Haustafeln or domestic codes[96] — along with related instructions concerning Christian relations to others in the political arena, the church, and the household[97] — appear in a number of passages of the New Testament. In all these passages the key instruction is to "be subject" (Gk. *hypotassesthai,* Col. 3:18; Eph. 5:21,24; I Tim. 2:11; Titus 2:5,9; 3:1; I Pet. 2:13,18; 3:1,5; 5:5; Rom. 13:1). The Christian community is instructed to "be subject to the governing authorities" (Rom. 13:1; also Titus 3:1; I Pet. 2:13; in I Tim. 2:1-3, the duty of prayer takes the place of submission). Slaves are to "be subject" to masters (I Pet. 2:18; Titus 2:9,10; Col. 3:22; and Eph. 6:5 have "be obedient" [Gk. *hypakouete*] rather than "be subject"; I Tim. 6:1 calls for slaves to regard their masters as "worthy of all honor" [Gk. *pasēs timēs axious*]); wives are to "be subject" to their husbands (I Pet. 3:1,5; Col. 3:18; Eph. 5:21,22; Titus 2:5; I Tim. 2:11 uses the substantive "in all submissiveness" rather than the verb); young people are to "be subject" to their elders (I Pet. 5:5; cf. Titus 2:6, where the young are instructed "to control themselves"); children are to "obey" (Gk. *hypakouete*) their parents (Eph. 6:1; Col. 3:20); the Christian community is to "be subject" to those who minister among them (I Cor. 16:16; cf. I Thess. 5:12,13, where the community is instructed to "respect" and "esteem" those who labor among them).

This emphasis on subjection seems to accept and baptize conventional morality with its role assignments. Indeed, Dibelius[98] asserts that it was when the parousia was delayed, when the church was faced with the task of establishing settled communities in a continuing world, that they were forced to adopt the common and conventional moralities of Greek philosophers and Jewish rabbis. To be sure, the emphasis on role responsibilities was certainly parallel to similar house codes in Jewish and Hellenistic morality.[99] However, the early Christian tradition did not simply borrow conventional morality, but transformed it. This claim can be substantiated by calling attention to certain other characteristics of the tradition.

First, the role obligations are *reciprocal.* They are articulated in the context of community rather than in the context of the individual's rational acceptance of his status and role. Reciprocity has wide and diverse attestation in the tradition. Although the house codes do not directly exhort governing authorities, both Romans 13:1-7 and I Peter 2:13-17 emphasize that they have their authority from God and that it is for the protection and well-being of their citizens. Masters are to treat their slaves "justly and fairly" (Gk. *to dikaion kai tēn isotēta,* Col. 4:1; cf. Eph. 6:9); husbands are to "love" their wives (Gk. *agapate,* Col. 3:19; Eph. 5:25,28,33; cf. I Pet. 3:7); parents are to avoid "provoking" or nagging their children (Gk. *mē erethizete,* Col. 3:21; Gk.

mē parorgizete, Eph. 6:4); older members are to be instructed as to their behavior as well as younger members (Titus 2:2,3); leaders in the congregation are to "tend the flock of God" and not to be "domineering" (I Pet. 5:2,3: the word for "domineering" is Gk. *katakyrieuontes;* cf. Mk. 10:42; see also the instructions to church leaders in the Pastoral Epistles). The duties do not all belong to slaves, wives, children — the "lesser" roles; nor do the legitimate expectations all belong to masters, husbands, parents — the "greater" roles. Rather, there is a network of social relationships that makes up a community, and the obligations are reciprocal. The emphasis on role responsibilities in the tradition is hardly innovative; but the emphasis on reciprocity of obligation signals a new chapter in social history by articulating a new life that transforms quite ordinary relationships as well as conquers spectacular evils.

Second, the duty of submission itself is a *mutual* one. Ephesians 5:21 articulates this very clearly: "Be subject to one another out of reverence for Christ." I Peter 5:5 expresses the same thought: "Clothe yourselves, all of you, with humility [Gk. *tapeinophrosynē*] toward one another" (cf. I Pet. 3:8).[100] After Ephesians 6:5-8 instructs the slaves, it instructs the masters to "do the same to them" (Eph. 6:9, *ta auta poieite*). For husbands to "love" their wives is for them to give themselves up for them (Eph. 5:25; cf. Col. 3:19). Leaders are called "ministers" (Gk. *diakonoi*) and called not to be "domineering" (I Pet. 5:3). Perhaps Philippians 2:3 states it best: "In humility count others better than yourselves."

Third, the *background of intelligibility* for these role obligations is provided by Christ. For the Stoic the background of intelligibility was provided by a world-view in which cosmic reason determines what is true. The Stoic accepted and affirmed what was, and thus participated in the cosmic reason. With indifference to circumstances, the Stoic brought his will into harmony with what is. His very acceptance of his role in society was motivated and governed by his aloofness, by his own rational participation in cosmic reason, and by his freedom from passions (Gk. *apatheia*).

The Christian, on the other hand, is not called to be passionless; he or she is called to adopt the passion of Christ. He or she is not called to participate in cosmic reason but in the cross and resurrection of Christ. He or she is not called to noble and aloof individuality but to a mutually submissive community. For the Christian the cross and resurrection of Christ provide a quite different background of intelligibility for these codes. Participation in Christ is the motive and governing principle, which may be seen at every turn. The instruction about mutual submission (Eph. 5:21), "Be subject to one another," is motivated and governed by "reverence for Christ." The model of Christ justifies and motivates the humility that "counts others better" and looks to the interests of others in Philippians 2:3ff. Instructions to slaves (Col. 3:22,23,24; Eph. 6:5,6,7; I Pet. 2:21-23) and masters (Col. 4:1; Eph. 6:9); wives (Col. 3:18; Eph. 5:22,23,24) and husbands (Eph. 5:25,28,29); children (Col. 3:20; Eph. 6:1) and parents (Eph. 6:4); even instructions concerning civil government (I Pet. 3:13) — all are motivated and governed by loyalty to Christ. The frequent additions of "in the Lord" or "for the Lord's sake" are not simply pious irrelevancies. They provide a new and quite different context for the role requirements. It is that background of intelligibility that requires an understanding of the roles as reciprocal requirements and the duty of submission as a mutual duty. In Christ there is fundamental recognition of the unity of slave and free, male and female; in Christ one knows that slave and master stand as equals before one master. Christ himself provides the model of one who did not make the claims that were his to make but humbly served.

Hellenistic Judaism had also used the domestic codes, but for them the background of intelligibility was provided by the law of God. It was not the role itself that determined one's obligations, but the law of God concerning the roles. The roles simply provided a way of categorizing the precepts and narrative materials. The early Christian tradition is indebted to Hellenistic Judaism at this point. I Peter 3:5-6 cites Old Testament examples; Ephesians 6:2 refers to the commandment about honoring parents; I Timothy 2:13-14 refers to Genesis 2 and 3; and Romans 13 makes use of a Hellenistic Jewish tradition based on Old Testament materials.[101] But the Christian tradition puts both the roles and the laws into the context of a new understanding in Christ, which interprets their duties and makes them intelligible.

Christ draws attention neither to one's own noble dignity (as in Stoic codes), nor even to the command of God (as in Jewish codes), but to the *neighbor* and the *neighbor's good*. That is a fourth distinction of this tradition and a fourth transformation of the conventional morality. It directs the husband's attention not to his own place and role but to his wife as neighbor (see esp. Eph. 5:28,33); it directs the master's attention not to his own noble freedom but to the slave as an equal before the one master (see esp. Eph. 6:9).

Finally, we may note a fifth distinction: the Christian tradition evidently put such role obligations in the service of the *mission* of the church (I Pet. 2:11-12,15-16; I Tim. 2:3; 6:1; Titus 2:5; 3:8). Such behavior will win common approval and testify to the power of the gospel to effect the recognizably good.

The tradition itself is unrecoverable. It certainly existed in a variety of forms as the early church utilized and transformed Hellenistic and Jewish sources; but there clearly was a tradition of duties in domestic, ecclesiastical, and civic relationships. The church creatively utilized, modified, and expanded this tradition too, but the tradition's shape and distinctiveness are nevertheless worth observing. The tradition, moreover, is obviously indebted to both the Stoic and Hellenistic Jewish moral traditions. But the "in Christ" is not merely some pious addition;[102] it provides a transforming context. The church could not create *ex nihilo* new role relationships or social structures; but it did not simply leave existing role relationships unmodified either. The reciprocity of responsibilities, the duty of mutual submission, the model of Christ, and the attention to the neighbor all worked to transform the Stoic and Jewish codes.

6. Watch and Stand

On the basis of yet another series of parallels,[103] Selwyn has identified a long and complex tradition that purportedly had its origin and *Sitz im Leben* in the exhortations to endure persecution. The evidence, however, is insufficient to justify Selwyn's reconstruction of a Persecution-Form. Carrington's modest conclusion[104] — that there were smaller traditional units whose key words are "watch" and "stand" respectively — seems more defensible.[105]

The situation that prompted such instruction and continued to provide its context, moreover, may not be narrowly circumscribed as persecution. The *peirasmos,* the trial, sometimes did indeed take the concrete form of persecution, but it took other concrete forms as well. The traditions to be watchful and to stand could be applied creatively to the immediate temptation faced by believers, but the tradition itself remained general enough to include the whole life of the community and its members. The commands rely on and evoke the community's acknowledgment that the times are eschatologically significant. They depend on eschatological reality and remind the hearers that the day of the Lord is at hand. These times are times of moral struggle and vigilance in expectation of God's final triumph.

7. Summary

The paraenetic tradition, compared with the memory of Jesus' words and deeds, seems commonplace and prosaic. The forms regularly utilized within the tradition were conventional ones, lists of virtues and vices, collections of loosely connected pieces of moral advice, antithetical parallelisms, and, of course, the *Haustafeln.* The content, to some extent at least, is also commonplace moral teaching, familiar to both Judaism and Hellenism. The early church utilized and assimilated the moral wisdom of Jew and Gentile; it did not reject it and begin to create a new moral tradition.

The underlying assumptions of the church's tradition, however, when they can be discerned, are the Christological, eschatological, and sacramental affirmations. These assumptions are not inconsistent with the use of common and conventional morality. Christ is the agent of the Creator's will; the end fulfills God's intention from the beginning; in baptism human beings are initiated into Christ and into an eschatological community where the will of the Creator is realized. In Christ, therefore, the natural and human moral wisdom of Jew and Gentile may be utilized and even esteemed (Phil. 4:8). The creation is not itself evil, the Gnostics notwithstanding, and the early church inferred neither asceticism nor the denial of "natural" moral wisdom from the gospel.

If these assumptions allow for and even call for the use of the moral wisdom of Jews and Greeks, they also preclude any simple continuation of that conventional wisdom. The Christological, eschatological, and sacramental affirmations call for the radical reorientation, transformation, and redemption of natural morality. The commonplace paraenetic forms and moral instructions are set in the context of a new and redemptive gospel. The transformation of natural morality, like the redemption of the whole creation, is "in hope" (Rom. 8:19-25); it was not an accomplished reality in the early church, nor is it now. Some discernible marks of the redemptive transformation were left on the *Haustafeln*. The Christological, eschatological, and sacramental affirmations provide a background of intelligibility for other traditions as well. If the traditions could be more fully identified, so too probably could the radical but reconstructive criticism of Jewish and Greek traditions. As it stands, we may assume that the redemptive transformation of moral commonplaces took place in preachers' and evangelists' creative use of these Christian traditions, in their utilizing the traditions in ways that were at once faithful to Christ and relevant to their audience's concrete situation. That this would sometimes take place in a pedestrian fashion in the early church need hardly be denied. But that it occasionally took place in an inspired and radical fashion cannot be denied either, and the evidence for that has been found within the New Testament epistles.

Besides handing down the tradition of Jesus' words and deeds, the early church came to terms with and developed a relationship with the commonplace morality of Jew and Gentile. In the paraenetic tradition that evolved, the early church began the continuing task of assimilating, transforming, and fulfilling the moral wisdom of its time.

Finally, in neither the tradition of Jesus' words and deeds nor in the paraenetic tradition, it should be observed, is the purpose merely moral education. In both the purpose is to encourage and exhort Christians to the new life given and demanded by what God has done in Jesus Christ. Both the creativity and the faithfulness of those who bear the tradition are cause for admiration and wonder. It is thus not surprising that Christians should be exhorted to "stand firm and hold to the traditions" (II Thess. 2:15).

Chapter III

ETHICS IN THE NEW TESTAMENT

The tradition whose beginnings were examined in the previous chapter comes to climactic — and canonical — expression in the writings recognized by the Christian church as the New Testament. These twenty-seven books are acknowledged in the church both as a part of her tradition and as the normative part. The church has never claimed that the New Testament simply fell from heaven; it has always acknowledged that the New Testament itself has a history. It was written by several different human authors, each bringing his own experience and personality to bear on the tradition and the message. It was written to a variety of churches, each facing its own particular problems of faith and conduct. And it was written in a variety of literary forms — letters, evangels, apocalypses, homilies — all affecting, as form does, the meaning. The New Testament is part of the developing tradition. But the church has also claimed that these writings are the normative part of her continuing tradition: here God himself has addressed and continues to address the churches, also morally. The objective of this chapter is to analyze and describe the ethics of the New Testament as a part of the early Christian tradition, recognizing the diversity of authorship, audience, form, and indeed of moral teachings in these books. The next chapter will attend to the ways in which this material has been and should be used as normative for the continuing moral tradition of the churches.

The New Testament, like the tradition of which it is a part, attempts to shape conduct and character into patterns that are "worthy of the gospel of Christ" (Phil. 1:27). The basis and norm for reflection, including moral reflection, is the gospel of Christ. For this reason there is no autonomous morality in the New Testament; New Testament morality is inalienably religious.[1] To isolate the ethics of the New Testament from its religious basis is to distort both. On the one hand, the literature of the New Testament is always oriented toward practical and concrete questions of conduct and character; on the other, it includes no work concerned with the self-conscious and systematic address to questions in ethical theory and no work concerned with providing a comprehensive code. The concern is always rather to bring the gospel of Christ to bear on concrete situations the churches faced. Ethics in the New Testament, therefore, is always both religious and concrete.

The relationship between religious affirmations and concrete moral exhortation is mediated, of course, by the theological and ethical reflections of each of the New Testament writers. The central affirmation, that Jesus had been raised from the dead, could itself be made relevant to concrete decisions in more than one way. The resurrection may be seen and celebrated as the vindication of Jesus of Nazareth, who walked among us, did signs and wonders, and spoke as one having authority. If we take this path, then the memory of Jesus' words and deeds will have a special moral prominence. But we may also see and celebrate the resurrection in relationship to the cross of Christ. If we follow this direction, the moral emphasis will fall on God's saving act which provides justification and liberation. The good, then, is disclosed in the cross of Christ and known in our participation in his death. A third way in which we may see and celebrate the resurrection is as the "first fruits" of the general resurrection, as the "earnest" of God's final victory. In this way the apocalyptic background may move to the foreground and be articulated by "seers" of that future.

We might offer a rough typology[2] along these lines, taking the Synoptic Gospels, the Pauline Epistles, and the book of Revelation as examples of the respective types. But such a typology would need to be supplemented by attention to the ways in which these reflective directions are combined by different authors and skewed by their own pastoral objectives. The authors of the New Testament address different communities with different concrete problems; they have different theological and moral concerns; they are heirs of moral traditions besides the Christian tradition. And even if these authors see those traditions now through the prism of the resurrection, they utilize the wisdom of other traditions in their own ways. The Hebrew scriptures, for example, usually played an important role in the moral discernment and judgment of the early Christian communities, but the precise place and use of the Jewish law was a matter of considerable debate in the early church, and the New Testament authors themselves provide no unified perspective on that critically important ethical question. Other traditions, whether Jewish and rabbinical or Greek and philosophical, were also used and left an impression, both formally and materially, on parts of the New Testament.

The New Testament presents no unitary and monolithic ethic, and we cannot speak of *the* New Testament ethic as though it did. The different situations, objectives, and traditions influenced and shaped the way the gospel of Christ was articulated and the ways in which it was brought to bear on concrete moral questions. The ethics of the New Testament is diverse and pluralistic, not unitary and monolithic. To see and appreciate both the diversity

73

of New Testament ethics and their convergence in loyalty to the risen Lord is the task I undertake here.

The approach is governed by the observation that New Testament ethics is inalienably religious and concrete, and diverse and pluralistic. We shall not begin with topics from moral theology and look for *the* New Testament position,[3] but rather with the books themselves,[4] allowing them their individuality and integrity, attending both to the concrete situation addressed and to the relationship of religious affirmations and concrete moral exhortations.

A. THE SYNOPTIC GOSPELS

The Synoptic Gospels are not the oldest writings in the New Testament; that distinction belongs to the Pauline letters. The tradition of Jesus' words and deeds, which has been the focus of much of our analysis so far, however, comes to expression in these Gospels rather than in Paul, and hence we turn to them first.

1. Mark: An Heroic Morality

Mark was the first "Gospel" to be written. Not only was it written before the Gospels of Matthew and Luke; it is a work in a wholly new genre, and the author of Mark deserves the credit for the creation of this new genre — "Gospel."[5] Of course, in some sense it was inevitable, given the faith that God had acted decisively in the life and ministry, the deeds and words, the crucifixion and resurrection of Jesus of Nazareth. His work and words fairly demanded to be re-presented. Nevertheless, the genre "Gospel" is Mark's achievement, and it has made us all indebted to him.

A "Gospel" is not a *vita;* it is not so much report as proclamation, and not merely proclamation about or concerning Jesus, but a re-presentation of Jesus.[6] Of course, the tradition on which Mark relied was itself proclamation and re-presentation, and Mark stands in continuity with both the assumptions and the content of the tradition. But precisely because he shares the assumption that the living Lord continues to speak and act in the tradition, he is free (and constrained) not merely to receive the tradition passively but to shape and modify it with his community in mind, indeed, to present it in a new genre, a "Gospel."

That he calls his creation a "Gospel" is due on the one hand to the familiarity of the word in the vocabulary of the Christian and on the other — with his community in mind — to the use of "gospel" (Gk. *euangelion*) within the cult of the emperor to refer to the announcements of the birth of an heir to the throne, of the heir's coming of age, of his accession, and so forth. There is an implicit contrast, then, between the kingdom of God and the kingdom of Caesar, between the gospel of Jesus Christ, hidden in mystery and in proclamation, and the gospels of the emperor, apparently in strength and power.

The community that Mark addresses, traditionally and, in my view, correctly identified with the Gentile church in Rome during or shortly after Nero's persecution, confronts the Roman claims to sovereignty and Jewish claims to the authentic covenant with God from a position of powerlessness and estrangement.[7] Mark writes his Gospel to encourage and exhort that community. The Christ he re-presents was himself rejected, betrayed, denied, deserted, condemned, handed over, crucified, and mocked, but also chosen and vindicated by God. And this living Christ himself exhorts the community to follow him.

a. THE CALL TO DISCIPLESHIP

The focus of Mark's exhortation is the call to discipleship[8] (1:16-20; 2:14; 3:13; 8:34; 10:52). Immediately after introducing and summarizing Jesus' proclamation of the gospel, "The time is fulfilled, and the kingdom of God is at hand; repent, and believe in the gospel" (Mk. 1:15), Mark identifies the meaning of repentance and believing in the narrative of the call of the disciples to follow him (Mk. 1:16-20). He has ordered and shaped the traditional materials to bring into prominence the call to discipleship. In the central section of his Gospel, framed by Peter's confession and the transfiguration, Mark places the first prediction of the passion and its sequel, the call to discipleship: "If any man would come after me, let him deny himself and take up his cross and follow me" (Mk. 8:34, addressed to "the multitude" as well as to the disciples). Again, Mark has ordered and shaped the traditional materials to bring into prominence the call to discipleship. The meaning is clear and concretely relevant to Mark's community: to believe the gospel of Christ is to follow him and to follow him is to be willing to suffer with him.

But that was precisely what the disciples could not or would not understand, according to Mark. In each of his three passion predictions, Mark called attention to the failure of the disciples to understand that to believe in him is to follow him and to follow him is to be prepared to suffer with him (8:32; 9:32; 10:32-35). Those failures climax in the Garden of Gethsemane, when the disciples "all forsook him, and fled" (14:50), except for Peter, who followed him to the courtyard of the high priest but then denied him (14:66-72). Peter, of course, as Mark's readers knew, had learned and accepted that to follow Jesus is to suffer with him; he followed Jesus to the cross finally. And Mark encourages and exhorts his readers to a similar discipleship, an heroic discipleship willing to identify with the suffering of Christ, willing to walk the heroic path to martyrdom (10:38,39; 13:9-13).

This heroic morality is essentially eschatological. It is enabled and required by the eschatological command to "watch" (13:33-37). Jesus had begun the great battle against the powers of darkness, and by his patient endurance of suffering he had carried the first stages of that battle to a victorious conclusion (3:23-27, and note Mark's treatment of the temptation, his interest in exorcisms, nature miracles, and, of course, the resurrection: 8:31; 9:9,31; 10:34; 14:28; 16:1-8). The departed Lord will return — and within a generation (13:30; 9:1) — to complete the victory and reveal his glory, but the community does not know "the day or the hour"; they are called to "watch" (13:32-37). Until Christ appears in his glory, the loyalty and perseverance of his disciples are tested by the petty persecutions of Jewish and Roman authorities. They are betrayed by members of their own families, and even put to death (13:9-13). This "night" of testing which lasts until he appears (see 13:35) is parallel to that night in Gethsemane when the disciples failed to "watch."[9] The three exhortations to "watch" (13:33-37) are parallel to the three failures of the disciples to "watch" in Gethsemane (14:32-40). Even as Jesus accepted the will of the Father to drink the cup of his suffering, the disciples, including Peter, slept. But now the command to watch comes to "all" (13:37). Now all are encouraged and exhorted to an heroic discipleship that is prepared to suffer with Jesus in the expectation of his final triumph.

b. THE ATTITUDE TOWARD CIVIL AND RELIGIOUS AUTHORITIES[10]

The community Mark exhorts to heroic discipleship confronts the claims of Roman and Jewish authorities from a position of estrangement and powerlessness. Mark and his community would quite naturally be concerned with the appropriate disposition toward these authorities.

The point of first importance for Mark is to affirm Jesus' authority. Indeed — to call attention again to the way Mark orders his materials — immediately after chronicling the call of the disciples, Mark cites the authority of Jesus (Mk. 1:21-28). He declares that Jesus speaks "as one who had authority, and not as the scribes" (vs. 22), and that he has authority even over demons (vs. 27). Jesus, not the Jewish religious leaders or the Roman officials, has genuine authority. When Jesus cleanses the temple, he is asked by Jewish authorities, "By what authority are you doing these things, or who gave you this authority to do them?" (Mk. 11:28). Jesus refuses to answer their question directly (vs. 33), but the discourse makes plain (as 2:7-10 had already shown) that the authority is God's. Jesus has authority, God's authority, and the authority of Jewish councils and Roman governors is meager by comparison.

Mark portrays the Jewish and Roman authorities in a consistently unfavorable light. The Jewish leaders are consistently trying to entrap Jesus, and the Roman leaders are only too ready to mock, condemn, and execute him when he is "delivered up" to them. Mark mocks the power of "King Herod" even as he records the execution of John the Baptist and foreshadows the deaths of Jesus and of Christians (Mk. 6:14-29). In Mark's Gospel the Herodians and the Pharisees are curious collaborators (3:6; 8:15; 12:13; contrast the parallels): these established authorities are aligned against Jesus. The Herodians, named for the Herods, were the puppet kings of the Romans, collaborators with the Roman establishment. The Pharisees, of course, were the Jewish sect that finally eschewed political involvement and concerned themselves with the maintenance of Jewish piety and purity, with the preservation of an apolitical Jewish authority in the land. Already at the conclusion of the first collection of controversies (Mk. 2:1-3:6), Mark presents a collusion of the Pharisees and the Herodians against Jesus. Peaceful coexistence with the established authorities was never an option for Jesus, for the established authorities were suspicious and jealous of Jesus' authority from the beginning. Jesus' followers, Mark's community, could expect nothing different. No truce had been called, and Jesus warned, "Beware of the leaven of the Pharisees and the leaven of Herod" (8:15).

Jesus' authority calls Mark's community into the uncompromising and uncomfortable status of a counterculture, a new covenant community standing in contrast to both the established religious authorities and the established civil authorities. There is no revolutionary call to arms against civil authority, but no Herodian collaboration or Pharisee withdrawal either. When the Herodians and Pharisees seek to entrap Jesus with the question about taxes (Mk. 12:13-17), his reply is neither collaboration nor the apportioning of rights and obligations to two distinct "realms"; but it is an emphatic assertion of the total claims of God's sovereignty. God's kingdom is "at hand," Caesar's apparent power notwithstanding. Thus Mark poses his "gospel" in contrast to the "gospels" of the imperial cult; it doesn't merely supplement them. The contrast between Mark's community and the civil authorities is to be effective not in revolution but in a new and different understanding and exercise of power within the community. Mark re-presents Jesus as teaching, "You know that those who are supposed to rule over the Gentiles lord it over them, and their great men exercise authority over them. But it shall not be so among you; but whoever would be great among you must be your servant, and whoever would be first among you must be slave of all. For the Son of man also came not to be served but to serve, and to give his life as a ransom for many" (Mk. 10:42-45). It will hardly do to call this "retreat from the world and its problems."[11] It is rather an heroic effort in the midst of opposition to demonstrate and participate in God's reign — even politically.

Jesus denounces the established religious authorities and strips them of their claims to legitimacy. The controversy stories, which make up nearly a fifth of Mark's Gospel, show that opposition to Jesus came not from the common people but from religious leaders with vested interests (e.g., 2:1-3:6). These leaders he denounces as "hypocrites" (7:6,7, citing the Septuagint; 12:15). He shows up the "tradition of the elders" as the "tradition of men" and contrasts it to the "commandment of God" (7:8,9). The temple officials use their authority to enrich themselves by the commerce within the temple court; Jesus, acting on his own authority, cleanses the temple (11:15-18) and denounces the officials as unfaithful stewards (12:1-12). He condemns the scribes for using their position and authority in the service of their own pride and greed (12:38-40).

Mark's interest is not that of an archivist but that of a pastor, for the controversy continues in the relationship of Mark's community to the Jewish religious authorities. Mark re-presents Christ as exhorting the community to an heroic way of life, conducting themselves under the authority of Christ in spite of the accusations and condemnations of the Jewish religious authorities, and in anticipation of his final victory and vindication.

c. LIFE UNDER CHRIST'S AUTHORITY: A MINIMAL ETHIC?

J. L. Houlden calls attention to the "paucity of ethical material" in Mark.[12] He explains the relative scarcity of ethical materials by alleging that Mark has Gnostic tendencies, calling attention especially to his "esoteric apocalypticism."[13] Jack Sanders also claims that Mark's eschatology leaves precious little time for concern either for "the welfare of the world and its inhabitants" or even for "how the Christian was expected to relate to his fellow Christian."[14] Raymond Anderson also calls attention to the relative infrequency of straightforwardly moral instruction, but explains it not in terms of Mark's expectation of the imminent parousia, but rather in terms of the character of the new ethic Mark announces. That is progress, I think. According to Anderson, that ethic is simply the "freedom for a life that is liberated to be responsive in grace." It demands very little direct paraenesis; indeed, it can tolerate very little, for "so long as the disciple is asking for a program regarding what he can do, he is still blind to the ethical way of God's reign."[15]

However, the very assumption that Mark devotes very little of his Gospel to moral teaching needs to be challenged. The focus is, as we have said, on heroic discipleship, but the major premise of discipleship makes the whole narrative a form of moral exhortation. Jesus, who came to serve rather than to be served, who patiently and heroically endured suffering for the sake of God's reign, is paradigmatic in other ways as well. His open sympathy with the ill and helpless, with Gentiles and sinners, his impatience with ostentatious and self-serving piety, his freedom from a legalistic code mentality are all in their own way *morally* instructive. Moreover, the authority of Jesus stands in contrast to the authority of the established leaders in significant, concrete moral exhortation. The decisive norm for Mark, after all, is no longer the precepts of Moses but the Lord and his words (8:38). Mark clearly knows that the morality of Jesus he re-presents takes shape in a wide range of human relationships and responsibilities. Mark applies his eschatological ethic of watchful discipleship to topics besides suffering, and it illumines even the most mundane of them with something of the same moral heroism. Indeed, Mark presents his ethic as a feature of the inevitable and uncompromisable controversy between Jesus (and Mark's community) and the religious and civil authorities; the instruction often comes in the form of controversy stories. The ethic is hardly "minimal."

d. AN ETHIC OF FREEDOM

Whatever else discipleship requires, it evidently provided a significant freedom from scrupulous observance of the regulations of the Jewish authorities, according to Mark. The first set of controversies begins with an assertion of Jesus' authority (specifically, his authority to forgive sins, 2:1-12) and the call to discipleship (of Levi, 2:13-14), the two major foci of Mark's ethic. The following controversies draw attention to the connection between Jesus and his disciples (2:15,16, where the disciples are asked to give an account of Jesus' behavior; 2:18, where Jesus is asked to give an account of the disciples' behavior; 2:23). These and subsequent controversies clearly show that Mark's community has a remarkable freedom from regulations concerning the withdrawal from sinners (2:15-17), fasting (2:18-22), the Sabbath (2:23-3:6), purity (7:1-8), oaths (7:9-13), kosher foods (7:14-23), and the legal permission of divorce (10:2-12). All such regulations belong to the past, not to the eschatological community oriented to watchful discipleship.

The seventh chapter develops this thesis of freedom from regulation: first, in judgments against the religious authorities as "hypocrites" (7:6) whose pettifogging use of the law serves the cause of the proud and greedy rather than the cause of God (Mark gives the Corban oath *as an example*, vs. 13). It further develops the thesis in showing that the regulations of the Torah itself are not exempted from the exercise of Christian freedom: by his gloss on Jesus' words "Thus he declared all foods clean" (7:19), Mark re-presents Jesus as striking out a large number of kosher regulations in Leviticus 11 and Deuteronomy 14. Finally — and positively — Mark makes it plain that the freedom from regulations neither stems from nor flowers in license. The issue is inner purity rather than external purity. In developing this point, Mark uses "a vice list" (7:21-22) which probably had its origin in the catechetical tradition of the church rather than in his memory of Jesus' words. The first six nouns in this list are plural, suggesting *acts* of "fornication, theft, murder, adultery, coveting, wickedness"; the next six are singular, suggesting *traits* of "deceit, licentiousness, envy, slander, pride, foolishness." But Mark focuses neither on acts nor traits as such but on "the heart," the *source* of evil acts and traits. Mark's freedom is not license; it is wholehearted loyalty to God and his Christ, which refuses to be reduced to or bound to external regulations.

The norm is no longer the precepts of Moses but the Lord and his words (8:38). "The commandment of God" still holds, of course (7:8; cf. 10:19), but it is simply not identical with any manipulable code or casuistry, even one based on the law. The law is summarized in the great principles of loving God and the neighbor (Mk. 12:28-34). The position of Furnish that Mark is not interested in Christian ethics here but only in demonstrating Jesus' superiority to his contemporaries as an interpreter of Scripture[16] seems to miss the point because of its ill-considered "either-or." It is ethically relevant precisely because Jesus interprets Scripture without casuistry. Moreover, by providing the *Shema*,

"Hear, O Israel, The Lord our God, the Lord is one" (Deut. 6:4; Mk. 12:29), Mark provides "a non-legal ground for obeying the commandment."[17] The summary of the law does not merely state that these precepts have priority or that (cf. Mt.) the other commandments are essential commentary on these to be learned and obeyed. Rather, it shifts moral discernment to a level where the precepts of the law are insignificant. Moral obligation is no longer determined by external observance of the prescriptions and prohibitions of the law; moral obligation is determined instead by the nature and activity of God and his Christ. Mark's ethic of watchful discipleship provided no code, but it was surely not libertine; it provided a moral posture that was at once less rigid and more demanding than any code, a moral stance that by its readiness for humble service was contrasted to the ethos of both Jewish lawyers and Gentile rulers (10:42-45).

e. RELATIONSHIPS AND RESPONSIBILITIES

This moral posture comes to concrete expression in the re-presentation of Jesus' advice for a variety of human relationships and responsibilities. The tenth chapter is especially instructive. There, in a kind of *Haustafel*, Mark deals with marriage and divorce (10:2-12), children (10:13-16), possessions (10:17-31), and power (10:32-45). But it is not a code. Jesus and his words neither rely on the law nor create a new *Halakah*; he puts the law aside as a reflection of the "hardness of heart" of the Jews (10:5). Instead, Jesus appeals to God's intention at the creation (10:6), to the coming kingdom of God (10:14,15), and to the cost of discipleship (10:21).

With respect to marriage — although Mark later asserts that in the new age there would be no marriage (12:25) — he is neither ascetic nor libertine. Appealing to the creation story, Mark asserts that sexuality is part of God's creation and that it finds its fulfillment in the "one flesh" union of marriage. Thus marriage is also a part of God's creative purpose, and, once entered, should not be broken. "What therefore God has joined together, let not man put asunder" (10:9).[18] This moral advice is not based on the law but on God's actions and intentions. Nor is its force legislative: it states a principle to be honored even when the law would permit divorce, not a new legal precept, for in the private instruction that follows (10:10-12), divorce is assumed while remarriage is prohibited. In the same private instruction, Jesus addresses women as having the same rights and responsibilities as men, quite unlike the law of Deuteronomy 24:1-4 and the rabbinical commentary on that law. Mark recognizes the equality of male and female and their mutual responsibility within marriage. The community that lives under Christ's authority stands in contrast to the religious and civil authorities by its posture toward marriage as a reality that transcends human decisions about it and as a unity that transcends human assertions of rights and privileges. It is affected by the same heroic discipline of watchful service that touches all of discipleship.

Although Mark recognizes that family ties may be severed by identification with the Christian community (10:29), he does not minimize the importance of nurturing children or honoring parents. There are compensations within the community in the new relationships among Christians and in the eschatological hope (10:30; cf. 3:31-35); but there is no denying the costliness of such sacrifices. It is the severest test of all for the moral heroism of the community. Mark reminds his readers that the Jewish authorities with their casuistry fail to protect the honor due to parents (7:9-13, the Corban oath; indeed, it may be part of the experience of Mark's community that the authorities use children as informers against their parents), and he reminds his readers that conventional behavior fails to provide the nurture due to children (9:36-37; 10:13-16).

Mark's community members do not use the law to limit their responsibilities to parents or children; they follow Christ, live under his authority, and watch for a kingdom in which parents are duly honored and children nurtured and blessed (Mk. 10:13-16). Such a moral posture cannot be reduced to a code, but it can touch their mundane life with grace and love.

Mark also recognizes that heroic discipleship may involve the loss of possessions (10:29); but he does not rue this loss as he does the severing of family ties. Again there are compensations both in this age and in the age to come (10:30; cf. 10:21), but here Mark *does* minimize the loss of possessions and the value of wealth. Indeed the rich man (10:17-22), with his professed reliance on the law and his hidden reliance on his possessions, is commanded, "Go, sell what you have, and give to the poor, and you will have treasure in heaven; and come, follow me" (10:21). The rich man "went away sorrowful," for he was in bondage to his possessions. The heroic ethic of discipleship provides a remarkable freedom not only from regulations but also from bondage to possessions. The commandment may not be understood as a new regulation but as the statement of a moral posture that is freed from bondage to possessions for the practice of generosity and hospitality. That posture is not based on the law but on an heroic confidence in God. Possessions cast a spell, however, that continues to threaten the heroic discipleship of Mark's community. In the interpretation of the parable of the sower, it is not just "tribulation or persecution" (4:17) that threaten growth, but "the cares of the world, and the delight in riches, and the desire for other things" (4:19). The posture is concretely modeled in the behavior of Peter's mother-in-law, who "served" them (1:31, the verb is an imperfect), the women who "followed him, and ministered to him" (15:40-41), and the poor widow who gave a penny to the temple treasury (12:41-44), as well as the disciples (10:28[19]). In all such cases, confidence in God and his Christ stands behind the freedom from anxiety and the disposition toward generosity. The heroic ethic of discipleship is willing to endure the loss of possessions for the sake of the gospel and willing to give generously to help the poor and to help the cause.

Finally, we may not forget that Mark teaches an heroic discipleship that acknowledges the authority of Christ and endures the petty persecution of the established religious and civil authorities. Nor may we forget that one way in which this community stands as a counterculture, resisting the influence of the established authorities, is by the new construal of power as service (Mk. 10:42-45). But we must now observe that this ethic does not eliminate positions of authority within the church; it does not disown power, but it understands authority in the church as also under the authority of Christ and in terms of the heroic discipline of following him. Mark provides a narrative setting (9:33-34, the quarrel among the disciples concerning "who was the greatest")[20] for the pre-Marcan collection of sayings in Mark 9:35-50. By this device he applies the first of those sayings, "If anyone would be first, he must be last of all and servant of all," to the quarrel about leadership in his community (probably following Peter's martyrdom). Leaders in the church must follow Christ's path of service and not boast about their position or jealously guard their prerogatives. He makes the same point in the more developed story of Mark 10:35-45. Again there is a quarrel over rank and preeminence; again Jesus enunciates the axiom that whoever would be first must be servant of all (10:43b-44), but now Mark uses the sacramental participation in Christ's death to identify more clearly the path of leadership in this community with the path of martyrdom (10:39), and he explicitly draws upon the model of Christ's death to establish a posture toward power within the community (10:45). This posture, as has been observed, stands in contrast to the Romans' understanding of power (10:42). It is neither based on law nor renderable as legislative regulation. It is part and parcel of Mark's heroic ethic of watchful discipleship, an ethic that provided no code but did provide a moral stance relevant to the concrete questions of Mark's community. In its readiness for humble service and its patient love, this ethic faithfully re-presented the teachings of Jesus to Mark's community and stood in contrast to the ethos of both Jewish lawyers and Gentile rulers.

2. Matthew: A Surpassing Righteousness

The author of Matthew used almost all of Mark's Gospel,[21] but he wrote quite a different Gospel. He re-presents Christ again, now addressing a different audience, a largely Jewish Christian audience, facing different concrete problems, especially the problems of establishing a settled life after having been excluded from the synagogue.[22] The living Christ, by Matthew's rendition, leads the church into a way of life at once distinct from the representatives of the synagogue, the scribes and the Pharisees, and opposed to the antinomianism of some parts of the Christian movement.[23] So, although almost all of Mark's stories and sayings appear again in Matthew (and frequently in the same order and with the same vocabulary), by subtle changes in setting or in wording, or by an addition from Q or other traditional materials, Matthew re-presents Christ in a way that is both faithful to the tradition and relevant to his community. The same changes, however slight in themselves, reveal a significantly different ethic in Matthew from what we found in Mark.

a. THE LAW HOLDS

In opposition to the Christian community's antinomians, those who said the law was abolished by Christ, Matthew insists that the law holds. In Matthew's Gospel this is the teaching of Jesus himself. In a saying found only in Matthew's Gospel (and located in a key position in his Sermon on the Mount), Jesus says that he has not come to abolish or to destroy the law but to "fulfill" it (5:17).[24] In an expansion on that statement utilizing some Q materials, Matthew re-presents Jesus as taking the position that the whole law, down to its very letters, remains in effect, and that even the least of the commandments ought to be taught and done (5:18-19; cf. 23:23). The law holds.[25]

Matthew preserves even the oral law: "The scribes and Pharisees sit on Moses' seat" (Mt. 23:2, a passage found only in Matthew). It is not their teaching function itself but rather their self-righteous elitism and pettifoggery that Jesus excoriates in the remainder of the chapter. He instructs the crowds and the disciples to "observe whatever they tell you but not what they do" (23:3). Matthew is quite clearly opposed to both the scribes and Pharisees on the one hand and to any minimizing of the normative status of the law in the community he addresses on the other. And the possibility that Mark's Gospel would have such a minimizing effect on legal codes is probably one reason for Matthew's revision.

b. THE CONTROVERSY ABOUT THE INTERPRETATION OF THE LAW

The controversies that played so important a role in Mark's Gospel to disclose the new community's freedom from the regulations of the law are consistently modified in Matthew to provide quite a different re-presentation of Christ — a re-presentation designed to uphold the law (against the antinomians within the Christian community) and to describe its proper interpretation (against the scribes and Pharisees).

In the controversy about table fellowship with sinners (Mt. 9:9-13; cf. Mk. 2:13-17) Matthew does not represent Jesus as carefree about the regulations of the law nor as simply acting on his own authority but as the one whose behavior is truly in accordance with Scripture. In Matthew's subtle addition to the story, Jesus appeals to Hosea 6:6 ("I desire mercy and not sacrifice") to justify his association with the irreligious. That subtle addition changes the force of the controversy. The issue is no longer whether the law holds; the issue is rather whether Jesus' behavior and interpretation or the synagogue's "fulfills" it.

Matthew handles the controversies about Sabbath observance similarly (12:1-8; 9:14; cf. Mk. 2:23-28; 3:1-6). He adds legal, *Halakic* arguments to the Marcan materials to show that Jesus was "guiltless" (12:7) and that what he did was "lawful" (12:12).[26] The focus of the controversy is no longer, as in Mark, on Jesus' freedom from legal regulations, but on Jesus' interpretation and application of the law. The law holds, including the Sabbath law (see Matthew's addition in 24:20[27]); that is not the issue between Jesus and the Pharisees. Rather, the issue is how the law is to be interpreted and applied; and once again Jesus interprets the law in the light of Hosea 6:6 (12:7). This divine intention of mercy is what the synagogue is ignorant of (12:7; 9:13), but it is what ought to determine the interpretation and application of the law. The same principle of interpretation is implicit in 12:12, an addition by Matthew: "It is lawful to do good on the sabbath." In Matthew Jesus makes use of a rabbinical rule of inference, the *qal wahomer,* moving from the lesser to the greater in both controversies (12:6, 12); the contrast of interpretations is, therefore, not merely a matter of exegetical rules but a matter of insight into God's intentions with the law.

Matthew modified the controversy about "clean" and "unclean" (15:1-20; cf. Mk. 7:1-23)[28] from the same ethical perspective. He omitted the Marcan interpretation that Jesus "declared all foods clean" (Mk. 7:19), which would abolish a large section of the written laws. The Matthean Christ does not abolish kosher laws but subordinates them to "weightier matters of the law" (cf. Mt. 23:23-28). The focus of the controversy shifts from the law itself to the rabbinical concern about minutiae to the neglect of the essential things. The vice list, which in Mark stands as an alternative to regulations, becomes in Matthew a rendering of the second table of the decalogue (15:19). Matthew's community is not to neglect the minutiae (23:23), but they are to have their priorities properly ordered and to interpret and apply the law in light of those priorities. In another modification of this controversy, Matthew's Jesus calls the scribes and Pharisees "blind guides." He repeats the same stinging rebuke a number of times in chapter 23 (vss. 16,17,19,24,26). It cuts to the heart of the self-understanding of the rabbis: they are blind to the real will of God in the law, and their quibbling interpretations hide it. It is Christ who sees the real intention of God in the law and thus properly interprets and establishes, or "fulfills," it.

Matthew artfully handles Mark's controversy about divorce to cohere with his perspective and to provide *Halakah* for his community (Mt. 19:3-12; cf. Mk. 10:2-12). He reverses the order of Mark: Jesus first takes up the Genesis texts which the Pharisees, significantly, should have "read" (vs. 4), and gives the Marcan conclusion, "What therefore God has joined together, let not man put asunder." At that point the Pharisees cite Deuteronomy 24:1, and Jesus responds, as in Mark, by saying that it is a concession to the hardness of their hearts, but he does not for that reason brush aside either the law or the necessity of interpretation. On the contrary, with his so-called "concession" ("except for unchastity," Mt. 19:9; cf. 5:32) Matthew represents Jesus as providing a legal or *Halakic* interpretation of the law. It is quite like Shammai's ruling, and like his utilizes a rabbinical rule permitting the transposition of the text.[29] Although he utilizes the rabbinical device of transposing the text, the basis for Jesus' interpretations in Matthew is his perception of the real will of God in Scripture.[30] The law holds, and Jesus is its true interpreter.

Finally, it is appropriate to call attention to Matthew's handling of the love commandment (22:34-40; cf. Mk. 12:28-34) in this context, for Matthew not only treats it as a controversy story[31] but modifies it in the interest of the same ethical perspective. Matthew omits the agreement of the scribe: he wants to contrast Jesus and the scribes as interpreters of the law. More importantly, he adds the redactional interpretation, "On these two commandments depend all the law and the prophets" (vs. 40). Matthew's use of "depend" (Gk. *krematai*) corresponds to a rabbinical formula denoting "the exegetical deduction of a *Halakah* from a given portion of scripture."[32] The meaning, then, is that the whole law can be deduced from these commandments[33] — the emphasis, that it holds. Without denying this emphasis, we must not overlook Matthew's care to present the story as a controversy.[34] Matthew presents the love commandment as the "great commandment in the law" (vs. 36; cf. 38). It is here that Jesus finds a clue to the meaning of the whole law.[35] The law holds, and Jesus — in contrast to the Pharisees — is the true interpreter. He is the true interpreter because he sees what God intends in the whole law and uses God's intention with the law to govern his interpretation and application of each part.

c. A SURPASSING RIGHTEOUSNESS: THE SERMON ON THE MOUNT

The author of Matthew generally followed Mark's order, but he self-consciously imposed on it a pattern of five alternating narrative and discourse sections.[36] In the first of these discourses Matthew represents Jesus' ethic as the Sermon on the Mount.[37] The Sermon is Matthew's construction rather than a verbatim record of a lecture by Jesus: he collected, ordered, and edited sayings that he found in Q and in the remainder of the tradition. The Sermon is certainly dependent on the ethic of Jesus, but it is just as certainly not to be identified with it; it is rather the quintessence of Matthew's ethic, made easily accessible for instructing catechumens, as Joachim Jeremias has suggested.[38]

1) The Context

The context in which Matthew places the Sermon must not be overlooked. The first narrative section provides an introduction and summary of Jesus' ministry. Already we hear of Jesus' announcement that the kingdom is at hand and of his summons to respond with repentance (4:17). Already we hear of the call to discipleship (4:18-22), and already we are given a summary of the way the kingdom has made its power felt in his ministry, teaching, and healing (4:23-25). Matthew's order makes it clear that the Sermon is premised on

Jesus' announcement of the kingdom and the anticipatory demonstration of its saving power in his ministry. Moreover, Matthew's Jesus addresses the disciples rather than the crowd (5:1,2). And finally, if Jeremias is right, the instruction is for catechumens who have already acknowledged that God has graciously intervened in Jesus of Nazareth. Such evidence stands as a stumbling block for all who would represent the Sermon on the Mount or Matthew's ethic in general as "works-righteousness." It will be necessary, however, to return to this issue below.

2) The Beatitudes

The Sermon begins with the beatitudes.[39] The beatitudes in Q were an eschatological wisdom announcing the prudence of conforming to principles operating in the world, known not from past experience but from the revelation of an eschatological future. They continue to have that form and function in Matthew. That future has been announced and has already made its power felt in Jesus, and Matthew exhorts his audience to conform to the eschatological way of God. Matthew, however, by subtle changes and additions, "ethicizes" the tradition so that the emphasis falls on the exhortation to develop certain character traits in response to Jesus' proclamation of the kingdom. In the beatitudes that he shares with Luke, he can be seen to interpret the common tradition in the direction of character traits: "Blessed are the poor in spirit" (i.e., the humble,[40] those with a readiness to submit to God and his cause; cf. Lk. 6:20, "poor"); "blessed are those who hunger and thirst for righteousness" (cf. Lk. 6:21a, "hunger"); and even with respect to persecution, "blessed are those who are persecuted *for righteousness' sake*" (cf. Lk. 6:22).[41] With the beatitudes that Matthew adds, these constitute a catalogue of virtues. The additional beatitudes are, moreover, formulated with Matthew's Scripture (our Old Testament) always in view: "Blessed are the meek" (i.e., the humble; cf. Ps. 37:11), "the merciful" (cf. Mic. 6:8), "the pure in heart" (i.e., the sincere, the unhypocritical; cf. Ps. 24:3-4), and "the peacemakers" (cf. Ps. 34:14). The reign of God that Jesus is announcing and already manifesting shapes and requires certain character traits: submissiveness to his reign, humility, the longing for the vindication of the right, mercy, sincerity, and the disposition for peace. Evidently, this is the way Matthew construes the church's role as salt and light, for he puts those images next in the Sermon (Mt. 5:13-16); indeed, this is the way the church itself already manifests the reign of God so that people "give glory to your Father who is in heaven" (5:16).

3) The Theme and Outline

The theme (and the outline) of the sermon — and the focus of Matthew's ethic — may be found in 5:20 (found only in Matthew): "Unless your righteousness exceeds that of the scribes and Pharisees, you will never enter the kingdom of heaven." Matthew's ethic was one of "righteousness" (Gk. *dikaiosynē*, 3:15; 5:6,10,20; 6:1,33; 21:32), a righteousness that does not fall below the standards of the synagogue but rather surpasses them, a righteousness that preserves the law of Moses as a normative standard (5:17-19, and see above) but interprets it in a distinctive and authentic way. The beatitudes, with their catalogue of character traits formed in response to the kingdom, provide an introduction for the whole Sermon and already describe the surpassing righteousness Matthew calls for in 5:20. After this statement of his theme, Matthew describes the surpassing righteousness first in comparison to the righteousness of the scribes (5:21-48), then in comparison to the piety of the Pharisees (6:1-18), and finally, without comparison, as the righteousness nonpareil (6:19-7:27).

4) *Surpassing Scribal Righteousness*

Matthew demanded a righteousness which "exceeds that of the scribes" (5:20). The antitheses of 5:21-48 are at once a judgment on the self-serving and petty interpretations of the scribes (see also ch. 23) and a demonstration of the fulfillment of the law in the surpassing righteousness Jesus required. They do not provide "a new law,"[42] nor do they annul the old one. The law holds, and Jesus fulfills it, bringing it to its own fruition by his perception of the true intention of God in the law.

The antitheses are paradigms of just such a surpassing righteousness. The law forbids murder (5:21), prohibits adultery (5:27), restricts divorce (5:31), condemns swearing falsely (5:33), restricts revenge (5:38), and commands love of (some) neighbors (5:43). Jesus does not sweep these laws away;[43] the law holds. What he does reject is the scribal interpretations that were content with external limits on the expressions of anger, lust, deceit, revenge, and self-centeredness. The scribal righteousness left the moral agent untouched, so that even his observance of the law could be grudging and external. As the true interpreter of the law, Jesus presses beyond external restrictions to God's intentions with the law and claims the whole character of the person for the law-giver. The Christian community's "surpassing righteousness" will be disposed toward reconciliation, not anger; toward purity, not lust; toward faithfulness, not divorce; toward truthfulness, not deceit; toward peace, not revenge; toward uncalculating love, not reciprocity.

Jesus' interpretations here concern character. The character is sometimes described in terms of the ways it breaks into surprising behaviors, such as turning the other cheek or going the second mile. These are indeed signs and symptoms of both the "surpassing righteousness" of the Christian community and of the kingdom. Of course, there is and must be a connection of character and conduct; but Matthew is not providing an external code for conduct here. Perhaps the clearest evidence that he is not is that, if he were, his presentation of Jesus would make him a violator of this code: for Jesus calls the scribes and Pharisees fools (23:17; cf. 5:22) and allows oaths (even as he attacks the pettifoggery surrounding them, 23:16-22; cf. 5:33-37).

5) Surpassing Pharisaical Righteousness

The righteousness of the Christian community was also to exceed the righteousness of the Pharisees (5:20). The contrast is a simple one. The acts of piety of the Pharisees — the almsgiving, prayers, and fasting for which their righteousness was famous — were done, according to Matthew, "to be seen of men" (6:1,2,5,16; 23:5,28). These duties of piety are not to be abandoned by Matthew's community; but the self-righteousness with which they were performed must be.

6) The Righteousness Nonpareil

Finally, Matthew undertook to describe the surpassing righteousness without comparison. To treasure "his kingdom and his righteousness" (6:33) provides and requires freedom from anxiety about earthly treasure (6:19-21)[44] or about food and clothing (6:25-34); calls for repentance and disdains self-righteous severity in judging others (7:1-5); and prompts a life of prayer (7:7-11). The common assumption of these three exhortations is the eschatological assumption that God's reign is at hand and already making its power felt. Conventional securities are challenged by that assumption, judgment belongs to God on that assumption, and prayer rests on that assumption and renders it in the form of petition. Finally, Matthew employs the Golden Rule as a conclusion and summary (7:12, notice the "therefore" [Gk. *oun*] that stands without logical connection to 7:11). With his addition of "for this is the law and the prophets," Matthew points back to 5:17-20 and implicitly claims that the ethic between 5:17 and 7:12 provides the fulfillment, the eschatological fruition of the law and the prophets.[45]

7) Concluding Warnings

A trio of contrasts — the two gates, the two trees, and the two houses (7:13-27) — serves to warn the congregation, finally, that it is not enough to call Jesus "Lord," that it is necessary rather to "do" the surpassing righteousness he announced (7:21). Matthew modifies the gate saying (7:13-14) in the direction of the familiar paraenetic contrast of two ways. Before the image of the tree he sets a specific warning against "false prophets" in the church: these false prophets can be distinguished from genuine Christians by the test of their fruit. And after the saying about trees and their fruit, he returns to the issue of false prophets, who call on the name of the Lord, prophesy in his name, cast out demons, and do other mighty works, but do lawlessness (Gk. *anomian*, 7:22-23). Matthew identifies the false prophets as the lawless, the antinomians, in the church.[46] For all their charismatic gifts, they go wrong in dismissing the law. The law holds.

This renders incredible Sanders' assertion that, because Matthew uses the form "tenets of holy law," he "accepts in an unqualified way the validity of the apocalyptic *lex talionis*, expressed in the form of arbitrary divine tenets, for determining what Christian existence should be."[47] The "tenet of holy law" was a favorite form of early Christian prophecy (even if it did not have its origin in that context), and, insofar as its validity was grounded simply in the ecstatic utterance, it could be arbitrary. But it is precisely such arbitrariness that Matthew finds unacceptable. He uses the form of the tenet of holy law to announce the continuing validity of the Mosaic law (5:19), and he uses the law as it is brought to eschatological fruition by Jesus as a test for the prophecy that occurs within the church — including surely the ecstatic utterance of tenets of holy law. The law is the standard. That is attested by true prophecy (5:19); false prophecy arbitrarily dismisses the law and falls into antinomianism (7:23). The concluding warning uses the contrast of two houses, one with a solid foundation, one with a foundation of sand — an image that was used by the rabbis to describe the law as the foundation for life. In Matthew, to hear and to do the words *of Jesus* is like building with a solid foundation (7:24, the Gk. *mou* is emphatic). The point, however, is not to contrast Jesus' words with the law but to contrast Jesus' interpretation with the scribes' interpretation. To do Jesus' words stands parallel to doing "the will of my Father who is in heaven" (7:21; cf. Lk. 6:46).

d. RULES FOR DISCIPLINE AND DISCERNMENT

Matthew turns Mark's account of Peter's confession into the founding of the church (16:13-20; cf. Mk. 8:27-30)[48] and vests Peter with authority to make judicial rulings and judgments, to "bind" and to "loose" (vs. 18).[49] This authority is vested in the church as a whole gathered in Jesus' name in 18:18-20. He does not spell out Peter's priority in this judicial function, but the fourth discourse (Mt. 18:1-35) does spell out some minimal guidelines for governance — discipline and discernment — in the church.

Set among the exhortations to patient and persevering concern for the "little ones who believe on me" (18:1-14)[50] and to forgive "seventy times seven" (18:21-35) stand the rules for dealing with an offending brother (18:15-20). These rules insist on both the offended individual's responsibility to undertake reconciliation and the church's responsibility of mutual admonition and communal discernment. If the offender adamantly refuses the admonition of the community, given the "evidence of two or three witnesses" (cf. Deut. 19:15), he is cut off from the community. The context protects the element of grace, the patient and forgiving disposition, toward the offender and makes the excommunication a last resort.

The discernment of the church, exercised not only in judgment but in legal rulings which bind and loose, must be undertaken communally and prayerfully (18:19-20). It is in that way that Christ is "in the midst of them" (18:20; cf. 28:20), continuing to teach and lead them even unto the end of the age, when their judgments will be confirmed (18:18).

e. ETHICS AND ESCHATOLOGY: WORKS-RIGHTEOUSNESS?

Matthew's ethic has often been described as "works-righteousness," as a way of salvation.[51] And there is certainly some persuasiveness to this characterization. He sometimes makes "entering the kingdom" (a phrase used more often by Matthew than by any other New Testament author) contingent on doing the righteousness required in the Sermon (5:20; 7:21; but see 21:31). Even forgiveness is contingent on forgiving others (6:14). He consistently emphasizes the rewards (e.g., 6:1,2-4,5,6,16-18; 25:34) and punishments (e.g., 7:23; 13:42,50; 22:13; 24:51; 25:30,41) of the final judgment. (In his treatment of Mk. 8:38, Matthew adds to Mark's description of the coming of the Son of Man in glory: "And then he shall repay every man for what he has done," Mt. 16:27; see also 12:36-37.)

But despite its persuasiveness, the characterization is a deceptive one. It overlooks the fact that the demands themselves are premised on Jesus' announcement of the kingdom and the proleptic demonstration of its saving power in his ministry (see the summary of the first narrative, 4:23-25). Matthew's perspective is thoroughly eschatological: in Jesus the times are fulfilled.[52] The new age, having made its power felt in Jesus' acts of healing and forgiveness and in his resurrection, is certain, and the new age can already mark the life of the community among whom he abides (see the beatitudes, 5:3-12). The risen Lord abides with his community "always, to the close of the age"; that eschatological promise is the context for the exhortation to teach people "to observe all that [Jesus had] commanded" (28:20; cf. 18:20). The message of God's gracious intervention retains its important priority in Matthew's Gospel. That intervention, however, also establishes the validity of his will. There can be no honest joy in the coming of his kingdom without humble submission to his reign — hence the first beatitude, "Blessed are the poor in spirit, for theirs is the kingdom of heaven" (Mt. 5:3).

The present time, then, is a time of testing. It is not, however, testing through *suffering* with Christ, as it is in Mark, but rather through *obedience* to his disclosure of God's kingdom and his righteousness. What is tested is one's response to God's gracious reign. So, in the parable of the unforgiving servant (18:23-35, found only in Matthew), the Lord's forgiveness is both gracious and demanding, the premise both for the exhortation to forgive and the judgment on lack of forgiveness (18:35; cf. 6:15). The servant does not earn his forgiveness; he throws himself on the mercy of God's reign (18:26,27). But God's mercy may not be presumed upon; it demands a response that allows God to form a disposition of forgiveness. God's forgiveness is, therefore, both gift and demand for Matthew, and the present time, the interim before the last judgment, tests the response to God's gift and claims. In the parable of the marriage feast (22:1-14; cf. Lk. 14:15-24), the invitation to the joy of the eschatological banquet is indiscriminately given to "both bad and good";

but with the invitation comes the demand for righteousness, and the guest with no wedding garment is cast out.[53]

In the last discourse of Matthew's Gospel, the apocalyptic discourse (24:1-25:46), the author basically follows Mark 13. He moves the confrontation with the religious and civil authorities (Mk. 13:9-12) into his discourse providing missionary instructions to the disciples (Mt. 10:17-22), and he substitutes the threat of "false prophets" whose wickedness (Gk. *anomia*) leads to a decline of love (Mt. 24:10-12). He then returns to Mark's theme of testing: "But he who endures to the end will be saved" (Mt. 24:13; Mk. 10:13). He has shifted the content of the eschatological testing from the faithful endurance of persecution by the authorities to the faithful perseverance in love and resistance to the antinomians within the Christian community.

At the close of Mark's discourse stands the summons to watch (13:33-37). Matthew also provides such a summons (24:42-44) and explicates it by using a number of parables (24:45-25:46). They all exhort the church to watch, to avoid the temptations of sloth and iniquity during the time before Christ's return in judgment and glory. The exhortations and the whole discourse climax in the final vision of the eschatological judgment (Mt. 25:31-46). Future judgment is the subject of the passage, but the author sounds no note of imminence. Indeed, he is well aware of the delay of the parousia (24:48; 25:5,19). Instead, the author sounds the note of exhortation. He is more concerned with the current ethos of his community than with the final judgment itself. The apocalyptic discourse and this vision do not abandon this life, nor do they treat it as a mere parenthesis. It is a time of urgency, certainly, but of moral urgency. It is a time of testing, surely, but a time of testing that not only calls for triumph over the temptations of sloth and iniquity but provides an occasion to serve "the least" and, in serving them, an occasion for serving Christ himself. That is the final test; it is the basis for the final judgment. And already now Matthew is exhorting his community to live in expectation of and in response to that judgment.

There is here no mention of desert, no claim to a works-righteousness. The surprised question of the saved (25:37-39) stands in opposition to such a reading.[54] The righteousness is not calculating but self-forgetful, responsive to the needs and cares of the neighbor and thus responsive to Christ. Such righteousness is exemplified — but hardly exhausted — in the catalogue of merciful works enumerated here: feeding the hungry, giving drink to the thirsty, practicing hospitality to strangers, clothing the naked, visiting the sick and imprisoned (25:35-36,42-43). Jeremias's position that Matthew is dealing here merely with the question of the criteria according to which the heathen will be judged[55] has nothing to commend it except the assembly of "all the nations" (Gk. *panta ta ethnē*; *ethnē* can mean "heathens"). But the judgment on "all nations" proceeds in such a way that the distinction between Jew and Gentile is immaterial to the judgment; self-forgetful response to the needs of the neighbor is the single criterion of judgment.

The judgment also leaves behind the distinction of Christian and non-Christian, but the parable is addressed to Christians. It stands guard against Matthew's community members' making of faith a final "work," as though they could self-confidently claim entry to the kingdom on the basis of their membership in the community (cf. 13:36-43,47-50; 7:21-23, etc.).

The ethic of Matthew is no calculating works-righteousness; it is rather a response to Jesus' announcement of the kingdom and his summons to a surpassing righteousness. The law holds, but not as a basis for making claims on God's mercy. God's mercy is shown, but it may not be presumed upon. Life responsive to Jesus and expectant of his judgment submits to God's reign. That submission, with its surpassing righteousness, stands in contrast to both the hypocritical self-righteousness of the scribes and Pharisees and the lawlessness of some within the Christian community.

3. Luke-Acts:[56] An Ethic of Care and Respect

The author of Luke,[57] like the author of Matthew, made extensive use of Mark's Gospel, but he modified it and added to it from yet another ethical perspective, a perspective that is distinguished by its solicitude for the poor and oppressed and by its concern for the mutual respect of Jewish and Gentile Christians.

Both distinguishing characteristics are present already in the episode which Luke, by a modification of Mark's order,[58] puts at the very beginning of Jesus' ministry. Jesus' sermon at Nazareth (Lk. 4:16-30; cf. Mk. 6:1-6) becomes the frontispiece and summary of Jesus' ministry, taking the place of Mark's summary of Jesus' preaching (Mk. 1:15, which is omitted by Luke).[59] Jesus went to the synagogue on the Sabbath, "as his custom was" (4:16). There he reads from the prophet Isaiah, "The Spirit of the Lord is upon me, because he has anointed me to preach good news to the poor . . ." (Lk. 4:17-19; Is. 61:1-2), and claims that "today this scripture has been fulfilled in your hearing" (4:21). The quotation of Isaiah 61 stops deliberately short of mentioning "the day of vengeance of our God" (Is. 61:2b), which was expected against the Gentiles. It was evidently this omission that prompted the ensuing discussion with Jesus' reminders of the gracious work of Elijah and Elisha among Gentiles (4:25-27).[60] The form is narrative rather than straightforward exhortation, but there is exhortation here and not so subtle that it is possible to evade it. No one may call this Jesus the "anointed" (i.e., Christ) and be unaffected by his sympathy for the poor and oppressed. No Gentile Christian may call this Jesus "Lord" and repudiate either the Jewish heritage of the gospel or Jewish believers for their Jewish customs. Nor may any Jewish Christian call this Jesus "Lord" and repudiate the inclusion of the Gentiles as Gentiles.

a. SOLICITUDE FOR THE POOR AND OPPRESSED

1) The Poor

From the very beginning, Luke's story of Jesus emphasizes his solidarity with the poor. His parents were poor, offering the sacrifice of the poor (2:24; cf. Lev. 12:6-8); Mary's *Magnificat* (1:46-55) rejoices in God's action to exalt the humble, the hungry, and the poor, and to humble the exalted; the shepherds (2:8-20), not the magi (cf. Mt. 2:1-12), visit Jesus in an animal stall, not in a house (cf. Mt. 2:11).

John the Baptist's preaching includes, in Luke's presentation alone, exhortations to the multitudes to share food and clothing, to the tax collectors not to abuse their power by extortion, and to the soldiers not to abuse their power by pillaging (3:10-14).

In Luke's "Sermon on the Plain" (6:17-49) he makes no attempt to "spiritualize" the beatitudes with their blessings upon the poor and hungry (6:20,21; cf. Mt. 5:3-6), nor to transform them into a catalogue of character traits. With the corresponding "woes" upon the rich (6:24-26), Luke's beatitudes simply announce an eschatological reversal. The announcement of that reversal, however, does call for a response, a response of love and mercy (6:27-42; cf. 6:36 with Mt. 5:48) even toward those who are not expected to reciprocate. The requisite response includes doing good toward one's enemy (6:27), carefree almsgiving (6:30), and lending without expecting a return (6:34,35).

Luke's "travel narrative" (9:51-19:44), a long teaching section set in the form of a narrative of Jesus' journey to Jerusalem,[61] contains a number of hortatory parables on this theme, parables found only in Luke: "The Good Samaritan," which explicates the love commandment in terms of mercy and concludes with Jesus' command, "Go and do likewise" (10:25-37); "The Rich Fool," with its judgment on the wealthy's concern for their own ease (12:13-21); "The Great Supper," with its reminder of God's eschatological blessing on "the poor and maimed and blind and lame" following an exhortation of solicitude toward the same (14:12-24); "The Unrighteous Steward," with its exhortation to generosity and to "make friends . . . by unrighteous mammon" (16:1-13); and "The Rich Man and Lazarus," a parabolic announcement of the eschatological reversal with its blessings on the poor and woes on the ungenerous rich (16:19-31). It includes the story of Zacchaeus, with his choice to do justice and mercy and Jesus' commendation of such a choice (19:1-10), and it includes exhortations to be free from anxiety and to give alms (12:22-34).

The same focus continues in Acts. All the heroes give alms (Acts 3:1-10 — Peter and John; Acts 10:1-4 — Cornelius; Acts 11:27-30; 12:25; 24:17 — Paul). The early church itself "had all things in common . . . and distributed them to all, as any had need" (2:44,45; 4:32-35). The mission encounters resistance because it interferes with the "hope of gain" (16:19; 19:23-25). The only saying of Jesus found in Acts is in Paul's single speech to a Christian audience in

Acts: he cites Jesus' word, "It is more blessed to give than to receive" (20:35), to admonish the Ephesian elders to "help the weak."

It will not do to call this solicitude for the poor merely "a social prejudice"[62] that exercises its influence alongside Luke's theology on the way Luke shapes the narrative, or to hint that it can best be left to one side if we would understand Luke's point. Luke's theology is intimately related to his solicitude for the poor. The "great reversal" theme, first enunciated in the *Magnificat*, emphasized in the inaugural address, and stated in the beatitudes, is displayed in Luke's whole portrait of Christ and is related to the key testimony text, Psalm 118:22 — that the rejected stone has become the cornerstone (Lk. 20:17; Acts 4:11). The "great reversal" was important both morally and Christologically for Luke, and it was important in both ways at the same time. The *Magnificat* was right for Luke. Jesus' ministry was the beginning of the decisive episode of God's raising the humble and humbling the exalted. And the God who exalts the humble exalted Jesus. In the story of the rich man and Lazarus, the rich man asks that one be sent to warn his rich brothers, for "if one goes to them from the dead, they will repent" (16:30).[63] Luke knows, and his audience confesses, that one has indeed been raised from the dead, the very one who preached good news to the poor. The crucified one[64] has been raised, and repentance takes the shape of welcoming the reversal he announced in his words, anticipated in his deeds, and established in his cross and resurrection.

It is true, as Jack T. Sanders says, that "the use of money is picked up as an illustration of something else"[65] in Luke's Gospel. But it does not follow that Luke's interest in money is therefore *merely* illustrative, "as a commonplace and no more than that."[66] The "something else" of which money is, for Luke, illustrative — indeed, sacramental — is one's response to the kingdom which is already established in Christ's ascension. One's use of money is a sign and a symptom of the arrival of the kingdom. When Zacchaeus gives half of his goods to the poor and restores fourfold for his past gougings as a tax collector, it is indeed an illustration of something else, namely that Zacchaeus "received Jesus joyfully" (19:6). Jesus replies, "Today salvation has come to this house" (19:9). Generosity and alms are not *merely* illustrative; they participate in the reality to which they point — the reign of God. When the community in Jerusalem shares a community of goods (Acts 2:44-45; 4:32-37), it is again an illustration of something else, namely the *koinōnia* of the early church (2:42; cf. 4:32a), but it is not *merely* illustrative. That there was "not a needy person among them" is a clear allusion to Deuteronomy 15:4-5, and it discloses that within this community the promises and requirements of the covenant are kept. Here is Israel fulfilled, and the community of goods participates in the reality to which it points. Luke sees the use of money as a manifestation of the disposition of the self to the reign of God.[67] It is not less morally obligatory for that, but the obligation has a special character, an inalienably religious character.

Luke does not legislate in any of this: he gives no legal rulings, and he has no social program. In his account Jesus refuses to adjudicate a dispute about inheritance (Lk. 12:13-14). Jesus' support of enforcement of the sabbatical year (if such is a feature of Luke's account)[68] is not a legislative innovation and is not presented as a law for Luke's communities. Even the communism of the early church is not presented as a legal order, defined by statute and protected by sanction.[69] The sharing was voluntary and spontaneous: "the decisive thing was *koinonia*, not organization."[70] The judgment on Ananias and Sapphira (Acts 5:1-11) was not due to their violation of any law requiring full divestiture, but to their conspiracy in deception against the Spirit (5:3).

Nor does Luke represent Jesus as an ascetic in any of this, as though money is simply "a part of 'this world' " which needs to be rejected along with the rest of it.[71] He represents Jesus as being supported by the generosity and hospitality of wealthy women (8:2,3; 10:38), being a guest at banquets provided by the rich (7:36; 11:37; 14:1), and indeed of being accused of being a "glutton and a drunkard" (7:34).

Luke does not address the question of money with a legal casuistry or in the style of a rigorous asceticism, but rather with a narrative, a story. But to make this story one's own is to own this Jesus, anointed to preach good news to the poor, as the Christ — this Jesus, humbled to the point of death on the cross but exalted to God's right hand as Lord. There is no repentance in Luke that does not practice sympathy toward the poor and outcast, no welcoming the saving act of God in Jesus Christ that does not do justice and kindness, no waiting for his return that does not expect and anticipate God's vindication of the humble poor, no participation in his community that does not give alms or share one's goods or practice hospitality.

2) Women

Women were among the oppressed in the first century. They were numbered among the heathen and illiterate, among sinners and those who knew not the law, among slaves and property by the rabbis. They were not numbered at all when members of the synagogue were counted. Ten adult males were needed for a synagogue; nine men plus all the women of a city could not constitute a synagogue. No self-respecting rabbi would teach a woman the law, or even speak publicly with a woman for longer than necessity demanded.[72] And the situation among the Greeks was little better.[73] Women simply did not count. But in Luke's re-presentation of Jesus' story he adds to the already remarkable number of instances in Mark in which women figure prominently.

It is to Mary, not to Joseph, that the angel appears with the message of Jesus' birth (Lk. 1:26-38; contrast Mt. 1:20). Elizabeth plays as prominent a role as Zechariah does. Anna, the pious old prophetess, stands alongside Simeon welcoming and announcing the arrival of the one in whom ancient promises would be kept (2:36-38). The widow of Zarephath is mentioned alongside the great Naaman as Gentiles to whom God had been gracious in the past (4:25-27). To Mark's healings of women (Lk. 4:38-39=Mk. 1:29-31; Lk. 8:40-56=Mk. 5:21-43) Luke adds still others (7:11-17, a widow's son; 8:2; 13:10-17, a "daughter of Abraham"). In Luke Jesus defends the woman sinner who (scandalously) wipes his feet with her hair (7:36-50). He teaches women (8:1-3; 10:39, Mary; 11:27; 23:27-31, "daughters of Jerusalem") and uses the behavior of women to teach (15:8-10; 18:1-8; 21:1-4). Women accompany Jesus and support him with their gifts (8:1-3). Women follow him to Jerusalem, witness the crucifixion, and witness the empty tomb and the resurrection (23:49,55; 24:1,10,22,23).

Women play an important role in the early church (Acts 1:14). Joel's promise that daughters and sons shall prophesy is fulfilled (Acts 2:17-21; cf. Joel 2:28-32; Acts 21:9; foreshadowed by Anna, Lk. 2:36-38). Women are ministered to—in charity (Acts 6:1) and in teaching (16:16-18)—and they minister, either in charity (like Dorcas, 9:36) and hospitality (like Mary, John Mark's mother, 12:12; or Lydia, 16:14-15) or in teaching (like Priscilla, 18:26).

Cadbury's description of Luke's interest in women as "artistic or domestic or sentimental" is unjustified.[74] His interest is rather governed by his theology of reversal and his consequent concern for the oppressed and despised. The humble Mary is exalted, and her *Magnificat* announces the theme of reversal in ways that can hardly be called "domestic" or "sentimental." Luke, in fact, rejects the domestic sentimentality of a woman who said, "Blessed is the womb that bare you, and the breasts that you sucked" (11:27). In Luke's re-presentation, Jesus tells the woman, "Blessed rather are those who hear the word of God and keep it" (11:28; cf. 8:21). In that reply he rejects the reduction of women to reproductive roles[75] and summons the woman to welcome a kingdom in which women are taught the word of God and treated as agents. In Luke's story of Mary and Martha (10:38-42), Mary has welcomed such a kingdom and assumes a position of equality with the male disciples, sitting at Jesus' feet in the posture of rabbinical students (cf. Acts 22:3), listening to him teach. And when Martha complains, suggesting that Mary return to the conventional and domestic role of helping with the preparation of food, Jesus defends Mary's choice. The contrast is not "the characteristic temperamental differences of the two spinster ladies,"[76] nor is the contrast mundane concerns versus spiritual concerns; the contrast is the conventional role assignments versus Jesus' unconventional treatment of women.

Luke does not provide legal regulations to govern the community in this matter either. He has no social program to achieve equality of opportunity and reward for women. His inalienably religious approach to morality is content to proceed by way of narrative, to retell Jesus' story. Those who make the story their own will be shaped and formed by it; their posture toward women will no longer be determined by conventional role assignments but by Christ's unconventional—and unsentimental—behavior toward them.

3) Sinners

"Sinners" are to be numbered among the outcasts for whom Luke asks solicitude as well. Jesus' infamous friendship with sinners is noted in Mark (e.g., Mk. 2:13-17=Lk. 5:27-32) and in Q (Mt. 11:19=Lk. 7:34); but again Luke's re-presentation of Jesus emphasizes this characteristic by additions. The woman who anoints Jesus' feet is "a sinner" (7:37,39,47); Zacchaeus is "a sinner" (19:7); the thief on the cross is a sinner (23:39-43). Even on the cross — or especially on the cross! — Jesus is sympathetic with sinners. Numbered among the transgressors, he cries out "Father, forgive them; for they know not what they do" (Lk. 23:34). The collection of parables in Luke 15 — the lost sheep (cf. Mt. 18:12-13), the lost coin, and the prodigal son — are all prompted by the complaint of the Pharisees and scribes that Jesus is a friend of sinners (15:1-2). And all three parables have the same theme: the joy in heaven over one sinner who repents (15:7,10,22-24). The parable of the Pharisee and the publican (18:9-14) contrasts the self-righteousness of the Pharisee and the humility of the sinner and judges that the repentant sinner rather than the righteous Pharisee goes home justified. The conclusion of the parable ties it to the theme of the reversal, "for every one who exalts himself will be humbled, but he who humbles himself will be exalted" (18:14).

Through these narratives Luke subtly but powerfully exhorts his community to "judge not" (cf. 6:37-42, where the exhortation is explicit and pointed); to "forgive" (17:3,4); and to "repent" (13:1-5). The straightforward exhortation, however, is relatively infrequent. The story is the morally decisive thing for Luke.

It is little wonder that at the end of Luke's Gospel the risen Lord reminds the disciples of the reversal, as Scripture foretold, "that the Christ should suffer and on the third day rise from the dead" (24:46), or that he instructs them that "repentance and forgiveness of sins should be preached in his name" (24:47, also as Scripture foretold).

b. MUTUAL RESPECT OF JEWISH AND GENTILE CHRISTIANS

"Repentance and forgiveness of sins" is to be preached in Jesus' name "to all nations, beginning from Jerusalem" (24:47; cf. Acts 1:8). That statement is, of course, programmatic for the book of Acts, but it is also typical of Luke's insistence on both the Jewish origins of the gospel and the inclusion of the Gentiles. Once again, the story is morally decisive. For the Gentile Christians who made this story their story, there can be no repudiation of the Jewish heritage or of Jewish believers. And for the Jewish Christians who make this story their story, there can be no repudiation of the Gentile mission or of Gentile believers.

1) The Jewish Heritage

The Jewish origins of the Gospel are plain from the very beginning. Of the Gospels, Luke alone begins in the temple (1:8,9) with Zechariah who, along with his wife Elizabeth, is described as "righteous before God, walking in all the commandments and ordinances of the Lord blameless" (1:6). Luke alone tells us of Jesus' circumcision (2:21; also John's, 1:59), his presentation in the temple "as it is written in the law of the Lord" (2:22-23), and his annual Passover pilgrimage with his parents (2:41-42). In Luke's Gospel Jesus' conducts his ministry almost exclusively among Jews.[77] In his "great omission" of Mark's material (Mk. 6:45-8:26, between Lk. 9:17 and 18), Luke keeps Jesus on Jewish soil, out of Tyre and Sidon, out of the Greek cities of the Decapolis.[78] Luke's re-presentation of Jesus' dealings with the Roman centurion is striking and revealing: in Matthew the centurion comes to Jesus with a request for help; in Luke's version the centurion's access to Jesus is mediated by Jews (7:1-10, esp. 3,4; cf. Mt. 8:5-13). In Luke the resurrection appearances took place in Jerusalem, and the Gospel ends where it had begun, "in the temple," where the disciples went to bless God (24:53).

2) The Restoration of Israel

Israel is divided by the proclamation of the resurrection. Those Jews who do not accept the gospel are purged from Israel; those who do accept the gospel (and there were many, Acts 2:41; 4:4; 5:14; 6:1,7, etc.) constitute a restored Israel. Luke emphasizes that the gospel has its success among faithful and pious Jews (2:41; 6:7; 17:11; 18:8; 21:20), those who attend the temple and observe the law zealously (1:6; 2:46; 3:1; 21:20). Luke's narrative in Acts is not that Israel rejected the gospel and that, because of this rejection, the missionaries turn to the Gentiles. The narrative is rather that Israel is purged by the proclamation of the resurrection, that Jewish believers constitute a restored Israel (Acts 1:6; Lk. 24:21), a rebuilt house of David (Acts 15:16), and that the restoration of Israel is the presupposition of the mission to the Gentiles.[79]

3) The Inclusion of Gentiles

The mission "to all nations" does not begin until Acts — indeed, not until Acts 10, after the restoration of Israel. But from the very beginning of Luke, right alongside the emphasis on the Jewish origins of the Christian movement, there is a foreshadowing of the mission to come. The announcement to the shepherds is that the gospel will be "to all the people" (Lk. 2:10); the song of the devout Simeon, "looking for the consolation of Israel," celebrates God's salvation for "all peoples, a light for revelation to the Gentiles and for glory to thy people Israel" (2:25-32); John the Baptist, citing Isaiah 40 and describing the coming of the Lord, says, "And all flesh shall see the salvation of God" (3:6; cf. 13:29).[80] The centurion's approach to Jesus is mediated by Jews, but he is nevertheless held up as a model of faith (7:9). In the beginning of Acts, long before the Gentile mission begins, Peter quotes the prophet Joel in his Pentecost sermon citing God's declaration that he will pour out his Spirit "upon all flesh" (2:17).

In Luke's narrative of Peter's visit with Cornelius (Acts 9:32-11:18), the real beginning of the Gentile mission, Peter is hardly an eager evangelist: the inclusion of uncircumcised Gentiles is clearly God's decision (15:7), not Peter's idea. By visions, heavenly messages, and the gift of the Spirit, God makes it plain that he "shows no partiality" (10:34; cf. 11:2; 15:9), that "what God has cleansed you must not call common" (10:15; 11:9; cf. 15:9). However, the issue is not yet settled; Paul's mission raises the question of including uncircumcised Gentiles again, and their inclusion is justified — from a Jewish Christian point of view! — at the Council of Jerusalem (Acts 15). Even then the controversy does not cease, but marks the rest of the book of Acts (e.g., 21:19-21; 26:19-23). Luke carefully and repeatedly describes Paul as faithful to the Jewish traditions (22:3-21; 23:6; 24:10-21; 26:4-23). The controversy undoubtedly continued in the Christian communities to whom Luke wrote.

4) Mutual Respect of Jew and Gentile

To those communities to whom Luke wrote, composed of Jewish Christians and Gentile Christians, these features of the narrative were not merely of historical interest but fundamental to their relationship within the churches. They are a narrative expression of a view of salvation history similar in many ways to Paul's in Romans 9-11, and they provide subtle grounding for exhortations like those in Romans 14:1-15:13. The Jewish Christians ought to join Peter in welcoming, not judging, the Gentiles, and in acknowledging, not resisting, God's decision to include them as Gentiles: "What God has cleansed you must not call common" (Acts 10:15; 11:9). The Gentile Christians ought to join the centurion in acknowledging that their access to God's saving power is through the devout Jews, repudiating neither the Jewish heritage of the gospel nor Jewish Christians, and in loving, not despising, the Jews (Lk. 7:5). This mutual respect and unity did not require uniformity. The Jewish Christians were to welcome Gentile Christians *as Gentiles,* demanding neither circumcision nor observance of the Jewish law. The Gentile Christians were to love Jewish Christians *as Jews,* respecting their pious observance of the law.

The story is the morally decisive thing for Luke. To make this story one's own story is to honor the role of Jewish Christians and to affirm the inclusion of Gentile Christians. The story shapes dispositions of mutual respect. That concern, rather than merely the delay of the parousia, prompts Luke to present a history of salvation.

5) The Law in Luke-Acts[81]

Luke's treatment of the law is unique and clearly related to this distinctive concern. The law holds for Jews, including — and especially — Jewish Christians. Certain features of the narrative have already been observed: the pious observance of the law surrounding Jesus' birth and childhood (Lk. 1:6,59; 2:21,22-24,39,41) and the observance of the law in restored Israel (Acts 2:46; 3:1, etc.). Luke's terminology is "conservative and Jewish" when he describes the law:[82] he is the only Gospel writer who calls it, among other honorific terms, "the law of the Lord" (2:23,24,39), "the law of the fathers" (Acts 22:3), and "living oracles" (Acts 7:38). The law remains the law given to Israel in the wilderness (Acts 7:38); it is the mark of Israel's identity as the people of God. It is not altered or discarded in Luke's re-presentation of Jesus. His narrative omits Mark's controversy about ritual cleanliness with its rejection of kosher laws (Mk. 7:1-23). He includes four controversies about the Sabbath (Lk. 6:1-5,6-11; 13:10-17; 14:1-6), but he does not show Jesus as carefree about the law. He exposes the scribes and Pharisees as hypocrites (13:15) for suggesting that Jesus broke the law by rescuing the sick, when they themselves tended their animals on the Sabbath (13:15,16; 14:5); Jesus' accusers are "put to shame" (13:17) and "could not reply" (14:6).

Luke omits Mark's rejection of Deuteronomy 24:1 as the law concerning divorce (see 16:18; cf. Mk. 10:1-12). The law holds (16:17). In Acts the situation is no different. Stephen's speech defends the restored Israel against the charge that "Jesus of Nazareth . . . will change the customs which Moses delivered to us" (6:14). Even after the Jerusalem Council the law holds.[83] Charges that the mission to Gentiles meant the throwing off of Judaic law continued (21:21,28; 28:17; cf. 6:14), but the defense continued to be that the charges were baseless, not that the "epoch" of the law was over.

Luke's interest in the law, however, is not specifically moral: the law is not the standard of morality as much as the standard of Jewishness. Indeed, morality — the duties of love and mercy — is overriding. The priest and the Levite are expected to risk ritual contamination and forfeiture of their service at the temple to show human compassion (Lk. 10:25-37). But to acknowledge the overriding claim of the deed of mercy (10:37) is not to discredit the law; the lawyer is perfectly capable of acknowledging it (see also 6:1-5, 6-11; 13:10-17; 14:1-6).

The law also holds for Gentiles, but in quite a different way. Luke presents the Council of Jerusalem's decision to include Gentiles without requiring them to be circumcised as a legal judgment (Acts 15:19, Gk. krinō). The law simply does not require Gentile observance; to accept God's decision to include them as Gentiles means legally not to require observance of the Jewish law from them. The council, as Luke presents its decision,[84] required only that Gentiles "abstain from what has been sacrificed to idols and from blood and from what is strangled and from unchastity" (Acts 15:29; 21:25; cf. 15:20). These requirements, as Haenchen has shown,[85] are taken from Leviticus 17 and 18, where they are identified as requirements not only of Jews but of the "strangers that sojourn among them" (Lev. 17:8ff., the condemnation of pagan offerings; 17:10ff., the prohibition of eating blood; 17:13ff., the prohibition of Gk. pnikton, eating meat not slaughtered according to Jewish ritual;[86] 18:6ff., the prohibition of marriage to a near relative). Gentiles may be required to observe only those requirements the law itself requires of Gentiles. These are ritual requirements rather than moral requirements;[87] but Luke surely intended to recommend such observance to Gentile Christians, as an expression of respect for the Jewish heritage and the Jewish Christians, at least as a *modus vivendi* to facilitate some degree of fellowship between Jewish and Gentile Christians.

The law does not require Gentiles to be circumcised or to observe the law, and it may not be used to condemn Gentile Christians or to repudiate the Gentile mission. But it holds, even for Gentiles, and Gentile Christians must respect it and the Jewish Christians who observe it. Beyond the law, the moral requirement of them, as of the Jews, is "to repent and turn to God and perform deeds worthy of their repentance" (Acts 26:20). That moral requirement puts Jew and Gentile alike under the same obligation, an obligation that includes solicitude for the poor and mutual respect.

c. ATTITUDE TOWARD GOVERNMENT

Luke-Acts is often read as an apology directed to Roman officials, defending the early Christian movement from Jewish charges against them and claiming the status of *religio licita.* There are, indeed, passages that emphasize the political innocence of Jesus (Lk. 23:2,4,14,22) and of Paul (Acts 18:12-15; 21:37-39; 25:24-27; 26:30-32). Luke may have modified the controversy about tribute (Lk. 20:20-26; cf. Mk. 12:13-17) in the interest of political apology: he omits the reference to the Herodians and seems to focus on the inability of the Jews to find anything in Jesus' answer with which to accuse him before the Romans.

But political apology is, at best, a secondary concern for Luke. In Paul's speeches Luke is much more concerned with defending Paul's Jewish observance than his political innocence.[88] Paul treats the rulers and governors with respect, certainly, but not with the sort of obsequious subservience that marked Tertullus' accusations before Felix (Acts 24:1-8; contrast Paul's defense, 24:10-21). Luke's attitude toward the authorities is too carefree to be styled apologetic. His confidence in God keeps him free to criticize — even ridicule — political officials.

The confidence in God is expressed already in the great Gamaliel's speech (5:33-39), with its advice to Jewish leaders to leave the Christians alone: "For if this plan or undertaking is of men, it will fail; but if it is of God, you will not be able to overthrow them. You may even be found opposing God" (38-39). When the church encounters opposition (4:23-30), it petitions God rather than the political leadership, because God is the "Sovereign Lord" (vs. 24). Luke describes the political rulers by citing Psalm 2: "The kings of the earth set themselves in array, and the rulers were gathered together, against the Lord and against his Anointed" (Acts 4:26; Ps. 2:1-2; Ps. 2:7 is cited in Acts 13:33). Their hopeless conspiracy is doomed, and there is a touch of the Lord's "derision" (Ps. 2:4) in Luke's account of political officials.

In Luke's Gospel, Jesus calls Herod Antipas "that fox" (13:32). Later Luke reports that Herod and Pilate have become friends in their conspiracy against

Jesus, an allusion to Psalm 2 (Lk. 23:12; cf. Acts 4:27, where what was implicit becomes explicit). In Acts 12 Luke derides and condemns the power and pretension of Herod Agrippa: an angel of the Lord delivers Peter from prison in spite of the extraordinary security of his imprisonment; and in the midst of Agrippa's pretensions to deity, another angel strikes him dead "because he did not give God the glory" (12:23). There is a theocratic dimension to politics for Luke. The Lord reigns, and rulers who neglect or deny it do so at risk to themselves (cf. Ps. 2:10-11). Luke ridicules the Philippian magistrates for trying to avoid the public embarrassment of their unlawful treatment of Paul (Acts 16:35-40), Felix for seeking a bribe (24:26), Festus for sending Paul a prisoner to Rome without knowing what charges to indicate (25:27), and other officials for other postures and acts.

But Luke's attitude toward civil authority is not unremittingly critical. He derides corruption, the pretensions of power, incompetence, and, above all, conspiracy against God and his cause. But he praises the proconsul of Cyprus, Sergius Paulus, as "a man of intelligence" and records his conversion (Acts 13:4-12).[89] And Gallio, proconsul of Corinth, sees the issue properly and refuses to be drawn into the dispute (18:12-18). Even so, the gospel's proceeding "unhindered" (the last word of the book of Acts, 28:31) is a result of God's power, not Roman justice.

Luke's confidence in God and his assumption that there is a theocratic dimension to politics stand behind his message to his Christian audience (in Peter's speech to the Sanhedrin), "We must obey God rather than men" (Acts 5:29; cf. 4:19-20; 26:19). The same theocratic assumptions stand behind the boldness with which Luke reminds any Roman official who might read this "apology" (in Paul's reminding Felix) of "justice and self-control and future judgment" (24:25). This is hardly the stuff of conventional apology; it is a bold assertion of the theocratic vision of Psalm 2. In Luke-Acts, solicitude for the poor and oppressed and the mutual respect of Jew and Gentile in the church are not politically irrelevant, even if they are not primarily political.

B. PAUL AND HIS INTERPRETERS

Luke's accounts of Paul's speeches during his trial (Acts 21-28) are less an apology for the Christian movement to Roman officials than an apology for Paul and his mission among the Gentiles to Jewish Christians.[90] Apparently Paul was a controversial figure already in the first century A.D. Indeed, his letters themselves are full of controversy and diatribe with his opponents. And after his death the controversy continued; to some Paul was the greatest heretic,[91] and to others Paul was the greatest apostle. Even among those who laid claim to the Pauline legacy, however, there was controversy about how to understand him and his message.[92] II Peter 3:15-17 already acknowledges that Paul's letters contain some matters that are difficult to understand and warns against those who twist them in the direction of a license for immorality.

Some of Paul's defenders and interpreters wrote letters in his name to protect his legacy from misrepresentation or to address a new situation in the church from what they represented as Paul's perspective. It is no easy task to separate the Pauline letters from the letters of his interpreters. There is almost unanimous agreement that Romans, I and II Corinthians, Galatians, Philippians, I Thessalonians, and Philemon were written by Paul; and there is considerable agreement that the Pastoral Epistles, I and II Timothy and Titus, were written by an interpreter of Paul. But there is considerable disagreement about the authorship of Colossians, Ephesians, and II Thessalonians. It seems best, therefore, to treat the undisputed Pauline letters separately, then Colossians and Ephesians, and finally the Pastoral Epistles.[93]

1. Paul: A New Discernment

a. A PASTORAL ETHIC

Even before the Gospels had put the memory of Jesus' words and deeds into writing, Paul was addressing pastoral letters to his churches. The letters[94] are intimate and personal, relevant to the concrete problems of particular communities, not self-consciously addressed to a larger (or later) audience. But they are not merely a personal correspondence between friends; Paul always wrote as an apostle (e.g., Rom. 1:1; I Cor. 1:1; II Cor. 1:1; Gal. 1:1), and he always wrote to churches (even Philemon was addressed: ". . . to the church in your house," vs. 2). The letters, therefore, are set in the service of Paul's mission, the means[95] by which he was present as an apostle even while he was absent.[96] So he could write with apostolic authority to pronounce judgment in the name of the Lord (I Cor. 5:3-5). But, although he could, he seldom commands; he rather "appeals" to his readers' own judgment (Philem. 8,9; I Cor. 10:15). He uses the language of polite request (Gk. *parakalō*, Rom. 12:1 *et passim*) rather than the language of command and thus conveys to the churches a sense of their own freedom and responsibility in Christ for moral discernment. He respected and cultivated the churches as the communal context of moral discernment and judgment, as "full of goodness, filled with all knowledge, and able to instruct one another" (Rom. 15:14).

The apostolic authority with which Paul wrote was not his own accomplishment, but rather God's gift (Rom. 15:15; cf. 12:3). The communal knowledge and goodness to which he appeals are not the natural endowments of individual members of the church but rather their common participation in Christ. And his exhortations themselves present no "timeless truths" in the style of either a philosopher or a code-maker, but rather the timely and pastoral application of the gospel to the concrete situations faced by the churches. Hence Paul's paraeneses, his moral exhortations, must always be understood in the context of his proclamation of the gospel on the one hand and in the context of the concrete situation encountered by the particular community he addressed on the other.[97]

b. INDICATIVE AND IMPERATIVE

As an apostle and pastor Paul was always proclaiming the gospel, "the power of God for salvation to everyone who has faith" (Rom. 1:16). The proclamation takes shape sometimes in the indicative mood (e.g., I Cor. 5:7b, "You really are unleavened") and sometimes in the imperative mood (e.g., I Cor. 5:7a, "Cleanse out the old leaven"). Frequently statements in the indicative have hortatory force: they function as subtle imperatives (e.g., Rom. 5:1-5[98]). The opening prayers of thanksgiving in Paul's letters all have a subtle paraenetic function.[99] Paul uses Gk. *parakalō* and *paraklēsis* to mean both the "comfort" or "encouragement" of the gospel (e.g., I Cor. 1:4-7) and exhortation or moral instruction. So in Philippians 2 the "encouragement (Gk. *paraklēsis*) in Christ" finally comes to expression in the exhortation, "Have this mind among yourselves, which is yours in Christ Jesus" (vs. 5).[100] "The word *paraklēsis* itself embraces the twin aspects of Paul's preaching: the gift of God's love in Christ and the consequent demand of God upon men."[101] There is clearly, in Paul's thought, an intimate relationship between the indicative and the imperative.

Both moods are appropriate—indeed integral—to the proclamation of the gospel, because the power of God, for Paul, is intentional and active. God is not some passive deity who watches his law-abiding creation run; he is actively at work in it to accomplish his will. God intends the good, and his power stands opposed to what is evil.[102] The relationship of indicative and imperative, then, must be understood in terms of Paul's conviction that in the crucified and risen Christ God has acted and is acting eschatologically. In Christ God has acted to end the old age and to begin the new age of the undisputed sovereignty of his transcendent power. However, the old age still continues; the powers of sin and death have not yet laid down their arms. They have been conquered but not vanquished; and they are, therefore, not yet ineffectual, not even against the believer. The power of God, however, stands in fundamental opposition to the powers of this age. And the one who receives the gospel, the power of God, is freed from their dominion to stand under the lordship of Christ. That "standing" is now always both gift and demand, both indicative and imperative (compare Rom. 5:2 with I Cor. 10:12; 16:13).

There is, to be sure, an important priority to the indicative in Paul's thought, as his insistence on "justification by grace" makes clear (e.g., Rom. 3:21-30; cf. I Cor. 4:7). But the priority must not be understood in terms of the establishment of an ideal or principle that needs to be "actualized" or "realized" later and separately in decisions about character and conduct, for there is also an important "finality" to the indicative, as Paul's persistent references to the promised future make equally clear (e.g., Phil. 3:20,21; Rom. 13:11-14). The indicative mood has an important priority and finality in the proclamation of the gospel, but the imperative is by no means merely an addendum to the indicative or even exactly an inference drawn from the indicative. Participation in Christ's cross and resurrection (the important priority of the indicative) and anticipation of the new age of God's unchallenged sovereignty (the important finality of the indicative) are *constituted* here and now by obedience to God's will (the imperative).

The juxtaposition of indicative and imperative is possible, then — and indeed indispensable — precisely because of the present coexistence of the old age and the age to come. The indicative describes the eschatological salvation of which Christians in the Spirit have the "first fruits" (Rom. 8:23) and "guarantee" (II Cor. 5:5). But the imperative acknowledges that Christians are still threatened by the powers of the old age, though their doom is sure, and therefore that they are responsible for holding fast to the life that is given them in Christ against the powers of sin and death. "If we live by the Spirit, let us also walk by the Spirit" (Gal. 5:25).[103]

The relation of indicative and imperative in the proclamation of the gospel may also be seen in the Pauline use of "sentences of holy law."[104] To give one example of such a form, Paul says in I Corinthians 3:17, "If any one destroys God's temple, God will destroy him." The assumption of the form is the gospel, the active and intentional power of God. He intends the good and stands — and will stand — in judgment on what is evil. The "sentences of holy law" anticipate the final judgment. It is not true that the final judgment is contingent on obedience to a set of independent imperatives; it is rather true that the final judgment is anticipated in the formation of "law," of imperatives. To anticipate, the indicative of the future judgment (and of the new life) is constituted by the formation of and obedience to imperatives.

These sentences of holy law may not be styled "arbitrary . . . and altogether to be explained from his belief in imminent eschatological divine judgment."[105] The imminence of judgment is less critical than the anticipation of judgment, the assumption that the judgment is already making its power felt. And, although the emphasis of the form is surely anticipation, it is usually set in a context of participation in what God is already doing. So in I Corinthians 3:16 Paul asks, "Do you not know that you are God's temple and that God's Spirit dwells in you?" The rhetorical question presumes that his readers are familiar with and assent to the idea that God intends to build an eschatological temple, a community of people in whom the Spirit dwells. To participate in that indicative is constituted by obedience to imperatives not to tear down or divide "the temple"; in that context "the sentence of holy law" in 3:17 is hardly arbitrary or altogether to be explained from Paul's belief in imminent divine judgment. Anticipation of the judgment and the new life is related to participation in the power of God already made effective in Christ's cross and resurrection and in the provision of his Spirit. And both anticipation and participation are here and now constituted by obedience to the power of God articulated as imperatives.

c. A NEW DISCERNMENT

The new age has begun, and there is to be a corresponding change in discernment. So Paul admonished the Romans, "Do not be conformed to this world [RSV margin: age; Gk. *aiōni*] but be transformed by the renewal of your mind, that you may prove [or discern, Gk. *dokimazō*] what is the will of God, what is good and acceptable and perfect" (Rom. 12:2). Participation in the new age has as one component a renewed mind, capable of and called to a new discernment of God's will. For Paul, the Christian's discernment ought to be radically affected by God's eschatological action in Jesus Christ.

Discernment is a complex human phenomenon, of course, involving different elements in different people in different proportions; but all human discernment involves at least the self-understanding of the moral agent, the perspective on the situation at hand, and certain rules or principles to help one discern and to defend one's discernment.[106] The renewal of the mind and the new discernment Paul calls for do not eliminate these elements of discernment but affect them. The self-understanding of moral agents, their perspective on the situation at hand, and even the principles and rules appealed to are transformed by the renewal of their mind, by their participation in Christ and in a new age.

1) Moral Identity

The self-understanding of moral agents is to be determined by their incorporation into Christ. They are identified with Christ and his cross (Gal. 2:20). These texts are not concerned with a "mystical union" but with a moral identity.[107] So the Gentile Christians "live no longer for themselves but for him who for their sake died and was raised" (II Cor. 5:15). They "must consider" themselves "dead to sin and alive to God in Christ Jesus" (Rom. 6:11). They "belong" to Christ (I Cor. 6:19b-20) and freely offer themselves as "living sacrifices" (Rom. 12:1). The Jewish Christians are also called to a new self-understanding; by their participation in Christ and his cross they are "discharged from the law, dead to that which held us captive, so that we serve not under the old written code but in the new life of the Spirit" (Rom. 7:6). Their former self-understanding (Rom. 2:17-20) with its old discernment (vs. 18) belongs to the old age just as surely as Gentile unrighteousness belongs to the old age. Proper attention to the self-understanding of the believer in Paul would demand a book rather than a paragraph,[108] but enough has been said to suggest the importance of this new moral identity for moral discernment in Paul. Those who are "in Christ" or "with Christ," who "belong to Christ," "offer" their whole lives to God (Rom. 12:1). Their moral identity is determined by their loyalty and commitment to God in Christ, and their loyalty to God's cause and intentions shapes their discernment. They will intend and strive to live in ways that are consistent with such self-understanding.

2) *Eschatological Perspective*

The perspective on the situation has also been affected by God's eschatological act. Paul's communities know that there is a "new creation," that "the old has passed away" and "the new has come" (II Cor. 5:17), but also that there is a continuing conflict between the power of God and the "powers" (Rom. 8:38), and they look for the day on which "the creation itself will be set free from its bondage to decay" (Rom. 8:21). This eschatological perspective shapes the way they see all events and situations; everything is illumined from this perspective: "We regard no one from a human point of view [Gk. *kata sarka*]" (II Cor. 5:16).[109]

The perspective required a delicate balance, and Paul's own emphasis was relative to his audience and their situation.[110] To the Galatians, who were tempted to submit again to the yoke of the law, Paul emphasizes that Christ had already established a new age, that "the fullness of time" (Gal. 4:4) had come, and that "neither circumcision counts for anything, nor uncircumcision, but a new creation" (Gal. 6:15). To the Corinthians, however, where the confidence of some enthusiasts led sometimes to libertinism (I Cor. 5:1,2; 6:12), sometimes to asceticism (I Cor. 7:1), and always to elitism (I Cor. 1-4,12-14), Paul consistently emphasizes the "not yet" character of our existence, the future judgment (I Cor. 5:3-5), the continuing "temptation to immorality" (I Cor. 7:2), and the coming resurrection (I Cor. 6:14; 15:12-58). Discernment always involves an analysis of the situation in proper eschatological perspective, blinded neither to the ways God's power is already effective in the world and in a particular situation nor to the ways the powers of sin and death assert their doomed reign.

3) *Fundamental Values*

This Christological and eschatological perspective on the self and the world could be articulated by Paul in terms of some fundamental values, which in turn inform the moral identity of the self and illumine the ways the power of God is at work in the world. Paul does not first carefully define and defend these values and then deductively and casuistically apply them to concrete cases; his discernment is more like the expression of the character and community formed by Christ in his Spirit in a world still "groaning in travail" (Rom. 8:22). Paul provides no systematic ethic, but it would be wrong to describe his ethic as ad hoc exhortations or as "situation ethics,"[111] for there are articulated values, statements of principle, and indeed appeals to moral wisdom taken from a number of sources. Discernment as personal and historical response to what God has done, is doing, and will do in Christ certainly involves rational discrimination for Paul.

Perhaps the most fundamental of the Christian values for Paul's discernment is freedom.[112] "For freedom Christ has set us free; stand fast therefore, and do not submit again to a yoke of slavery" (Gal. 5:1; cf. II Cor. 3:17, "Now the Lord is the Spirit, and where the Spirit of the Lord is, there is freedom"). Freedom is a mark of the new age. The old age is marked by bondage — bondage to sin and death, bondage to the law. The Christian, however, is to understand himself as free in Christ. This is freedom from bondage to sin and death surely, but it is also always freedom from the law (Gal. 5:2-4), and not only from the curse of the law but from the divisions established in and by the law, especially the division between Jew and Gentile, circumcised and uncircumcised (Gal. 5:5; 3:28). This gift and value took concrete shape when Paul insisted that the Galatians not yield to those who would compel them to be circumcised and to keep the law, when he judged the Corinthians free from scruples about food offered to idols (I Cor. 8:4-8; 10:25-26), and when he proclaimed to the Romans "the glorious liberty of the children of God" (Rom. 8:21) that allowed Jewish and Gentile Christians their Jewish and Gentile identities as long as they were subsumed under the Christian identity (Rom. 14:1-9).

If freedom is the most fundamental value, love is the most important.[113] They are related to each other because they are both related to God's eschatological action in the cross and resurrection. Christ frees us from our bondage to the powers of the old age to an eschatological existence whose distinguishing characteristic is love (I Cor. 13:8-13; Rom. 5:5; also Gal. 5:22-23, where love stands first in Paul's list of the "fruit of the Spirit"). The liberation God wins and grants in Christ is not license or independence but the freedom to love. As Paul says in Galatians 5:13, "Do not use your freedom as an opportunity for the flesh, but through love be servants of one another." He qualifies the Corinthian freedom-slogan by the important value of love: " 'All things are lawful for me,' but not all things are helpful" (I Cor. 6:12; cf. 10:23,24). Faith, by which we receive the liberation God has wrought, acts "through love" (Gal. 5:6). Indeed, love is a *sine qua non* for the new discernment: "It is my prayer," Paul says, "that your love may abound more and more, with knowledge and all discernment, so that you may approve what is excellent" (Phil. 1:9-10; cf. I Cor. 8:1-2). Love is the "fulfillment" of the law (Rom. 13:8-10; Gal. 5:14). This gift and value took concrete shape when Paul called for unity, peace, and love and prohibited mutual recrimination in churches composed of Jew and Gentile (Rom. 14:1-15:6; cf. Gal. 5:6), when he admonished some enthusiasts in Corinth against an elitism based on their spiritual gifts (I Cor. 12-14), when he encouraged the Corinthians to give generously to the collection for the poor in Jerusalem (II Cor. 8:8,24), and when he advised Philemon about his relationship with Onesimus (Philem. 7,16). Love drives toward concrete expression everywhere; just as God's love came to concrete expression in the crucifixion suffered for sinners (Rom. 5:8), so the Christian's love — God's love "poured into our hearts through the Holy Spirit" (Rom. 5:5) — can only be appropriately described in terms of its works (I Cor. 13:4-7).[114]

Paul's discernment involves the expression of Christian identity, the analysis of the situation in light of the eschatological perspective, and the concrete application of the fundamental principles of freedom and love. But it does not either abandon the rules and moral wisdom it finds around it or create new rules for conduct and guidelines for character. Love's discernment makes use of other sources, especially the teachings of Jesus, the Church's catechetical tradition, the Jewish law, and "natural" moral standards.[115]

4) *Utilizing and Modifying Concrete Moral Wisdom*

a) *The Tradition of Jesus' Words and Deeds*

The tradition Paul received and handed down certainly included a collection of Jesus' sayings, and he did occasionally make use of these in moral argument.[116] Moreover, when he did use them, he clearly considered them authoritative, for he took care to distinguish them from his own opinion (I Cor. 7:12,15). Still, they are surprisingly seldom used; the collection of Jesus' sayings did not apparently play a leading role in Paul's ethic, and surely did not provide "the basis for a kind of Christian Halakah."[117] Paul's discernment begins with the Christ event, not the tradition of Jesus' words and deeds.[118] Such a tradition is never, however, discounted or deliberately abandoned. It belongs to the tradition of the churches and forms part of the communal context within which discernment takes place for Paul.

b) *The Paraenetic Tradition*

The communities Paul addresses are also familiar with the paraenetic tradition of the church, and Paul uses it in his exhortations too. Once again, however, the tradition does not play the central role in Paul's discernment. Paul writes as an apostle, not as a sage collecting and commending a miscellany of moral wisdom that can stand on its own to guide discernment. The paraenetic tradition in the church, as we have seen, was itself[119] not fixed and final, and Paul utilizes it and modifies it to make it serve the Pauline discernment.

It is impossible to distinguish very exactly Paul's "redaction" from the tradition, but it is fair to say that Paul's use of the paraenetic tradition is shaped both by his concern about concrete situations in the churches[120] and by his moral concern with identity, perspective, and the fundamental principles of freedom and love. For example, in Galatians 5:22-23 Paul catalogues qualities of character in a fashion surely indebted to the "virtue lists" of the Christian paraenetic tradition. But he sets this catalogue in the context of describing the Christian's moral identity (Gal. 5:24, "those who belong to Christ"), in an eschatologically charged atmosphere of the struggle between the Spirit and the flesh, between our participation in the new age and our susceptibility to the powers of the old age (Gal. 5:16-21, 24-25; 6:8-9), and as part of an exhortation to a life of freedom (5:1,13,18) and love (5:13-14). Paul presents his catalogue itself as "the fruit of the Spirit" (5:22). Thus he does not regard them as individual "virtues" to be achieved by human effort (and note that he quite self-consciously avoids calling them "works" — cf. vs. 19, "works of the flesh"). He regards them collectively as the mark of eschatological existence, the "fruit" of the "first fruits" of the new age (Rom. 8:23). He regards them as the mark of the identity of those who "live by the Spirit" (5:25). The catalogue places "love" at its head, and in view of the singular, "fruit," the other traits of character explicate the concrete meaning of love (cf. I Cor. 13:4-7). Finally, in an addition obviously related to the Galatian polemic, Paul adds, "Against such there is no law" (5:23). Love's discernment is free from the law, but it "fulfills" it (5:14). It "fulfills" it, but in a way that renders it obsolete as a code. In sum, Paul shapes and modifies the paraenetic tradition in the interest of making it serve love's discernment of God's will for the Galatian church.

c) *The Jewish Scriptures*[121]

Paul frequently cites the Jewish scriptures in the context of moral exhortation, but he never uses them as a code to determine conduct. He cites the Prophets and Writings more often than the Torah, and when he does appeal to the Torah, it is more often to narratives than to statutes.

Reliance on the law as a code to determine conduct belonged for Paul to the old discernment (II Cor. 3; Rom. 2:17-24). Paul acknowledged that the "law" and the "commandment" are "holy and just and good" (Rom. 7:12), but he insisted that the law is not eternal, but secondary, added after the promise (Rom. 4:10; Gal. 3:17). Moreover, in the old age it was co-opted by the powers of sin and death; it is even "the power of sin" (I Cor. 15:56). It led to sins being "counted" (Rom. 5:13), and it provided an "opportunity" for sin (Rom. 7:8,10); it was a "custodian until Christ came" (Gal. 3:24-26). Then the promise is kept, and Christ is "the end of the law" (Rom. 10:4; cf. Gal. 3:25). With Christ we have died to the law (Rom. 7:4; Gal. 2:19) and are "discharged from the law . . . so that we serve not under the old written code but in the new life of the Spirit" (Rom. 7:6). The fault was not with the law itself, of course, but with "the flesh," with people's susceptibility to the powers of sin and death (Rom. 8:3). The promise is fulfilled in Jesus Christ, that in him "the just requirement of the law might be fulfilled in us" (Rom. 8:4; see Rom. 13:8-10). But there is no going back to the boasting self-righteousness, to the condemnations, to the old written code. There is no building up again that which divided Jew from Gentile (Gal. 2:18). So when Paul uses the Jewish scriptures, he makes them serviceable to the new discernment. The moral identity of the Christian, the eschatological perspective, and the fundamental values of freedom and love provided criteria for the use of the law. He does not use the scriptures as a code to determine God's will casuistically; he uses them in the light of the new discernment as narrative, promise, and moral wisdom to illuminate and persuade his readers with respect to the gift and claim of the new life in Christ.

d) *"Natural" Moral Wisdom*[122]

Paul also used the "natural" moral wisdom of the Hellenistic street preachers and philosophers. Even pagans, after all, live in God's creation and can know something of God and his law (Rom. 1:19; 2:14-16). So Paul could and did use Hellenistic concepts such as "conscience" (Gk. *syneidēsis*), contentment (Gk. *autarkeia*), freedom (Gk. *eleutheria*); Hellenistic terminology for certain moral qualities (especially in Phil. 4:8); Hellenistic forms of moral instruction (especially the "diatribe";[123] e.g., I Cor. 6:12-20); and the Hellenistic appeal to nature as a moral teacher (e.g., I Cor. 11:14). He can even pick up the Hellenistic emphasis on role responsibilities in response to the Corinthian enthusiasts at Corinth who claimed to be already fully in the new age and so no longer in this world with its callings and states (I Cor. 7:17-24). In all of this, however, the new discernment remains finally normative. Paul's use of moral commonplaces was not inconsistent with his eschatological and Christological emphasis, for it was his conviction that the new creation is the fulfillment of the original will of God the Creator. That will is not altogether unknown within his creation, even though it is subjected to bondage. Familiar standards could be assimilated, but also modified, in ways governed by the moral identity in Christ, the eschatological perspective, and the fundamental values of love and freedom.

The transformation of Stoic "contentment" is an example of the way natural morality is both assimilated and criticized by the new discernment. Epictetus[124] describes the true Stoic as one who is "sick and happy, in danger and happy, dying and happy, in exile and happy, in disgrace and happy." That sounds very much like Paul's "I have learned, in whatever state I am, therein to be content" (Phil. 4:11). Paul assimilated the Stoic emphasis on contentment but gave it an altogether different background of intelligibility and meaning. To the Stoic the world was fundamentally rational, governed by a divine *logos*. Once a person recognized the world as rational, as a rational agent he could and would will whatever happened, and thus could also accept it with equanimity. Only the passions would interfere with such contentment (and the contentment was often named Gk. *apatheia*). For Paul, however, this age is aligned with sin and death, the new age with God's reign. The Christian participates in God's reign not merely as a rational agent, but as a whole person. The Christian is not called to put an end to passion, but to share the passion of Christ (Paul never uses *apatheia* to refer to contentment). For the Stoic, contentment comes through participation in reason and through submission of the passions to reason. For Paul contentment comes by participation in the cross and resurrection of Christ and by submission of the whole person to God's power. It is little wonder that Paul goes on to say, "I can do all things in him who strengthens me" (Phil. 4:13).

5) Summary

Paul provides no theory of discernment, no analysis of the elements of decision making, but the pattern is clear. Discernment is always done in view of God's eschatological action in Jesus Christ, his gift and demand of a new life. God's act establishes a new identity, a new perspective on the world and situations within it, and certain fundamental characteristics of eschatological existence — such as freedom and love. This new discernment, however, has not created new moral directives for conduct and character. Both Paul and his readers belong to historical communities with moral resources and traditions. The new discernment does not discredit these resources and traditions — especially when the historical community is the people of God — but brings them under the criticism and the transforming power of the new life claimed in Christ for Christians. The new discernment has selected, assimilated, and transformed Christian, Jewish, and Hellenistic moral wisdom in order to discern the particular conduct and character that was demanded or permitted at a particular time. These sources of wisdom were never normative for Paul in the same way that God's action in Jesus Christ was; the new discernment always stops short of identifying itself with moral rules as though it could ever be reduced to a code; but it never stops short of formulating them, articulating the claims of the gospel, respecting moral traditions, and addressing concrete situations.

6) Addendum on "The Law of Christ"

This interesting phrase in Galatians 6:2 has been subject to quite different interpretations. On the one hand, C. H. Dodd[125] and especially W. D. Davies[126] have identified "the law of Christ" with a collection of the sayings of Jesus which Paul uses as authoritative moral guidance, indeed, as "a New Torah"[127] — even, for Davies, "the basis for a kind of Christian Halakah."[128]

Against that interpretation Furnish has correctly insisted that Paul's appeals to Jesus' teachings are surprisingly infrequent, that the surrounding exhortations in Galatians 5 and 6 are neither citations of the Lord's words nor given in elucidation of the phrase "law of Christ," and finally that the point of the context, that life in the Spirit inherently makes moral claims on the Galatians without imposing an external law, is overlooked — even contradicted — by such an interpretation.[129] Having rejected this option, Furnish adopts the other major tradition of interpretation, that the "law of Christ" is the law of love, where love is the "fulfilling of the one law which has already been given."[130]

The "law of Christ" certainly includes love, but it should not be reduced to this principle, no matter how fundamental it is. The broader context of Galatians treats the law as a principle of identity rather than simply as a collection of commandments. It separates those who are Jews from "Gentile sinners" (2:15). As a principle of identity, the law is discredited; for the law itself discloses that all are sinners (2:16, citing Ps. 143:2; 2:19), and in Christ both Jew and Gentile are made righteous (2:16) and one (3:28). So here in Galatians 6:2 it is best to understand "law of Christ" as a principle of identity and not simply as a commandment, even the commandment to love. It is the Christian identity to which the context points: "those who belong to Christ" and "live by the Spirit" (5:25) are reminded that their identity is not only gift but also claim in the phrase "law of Christ." To articulate the identity as a law and a claim coheres, of course, with Paul's eschatological perspective; it will necessarily refer to the fundamental values of freedom and love, and it will assimilate rules and wisdom from many traditions, including the sayings of Jesus. "The law of Christ," then, may be taken as shorthand for what has been described as Paul's "new discernment."[131]

d. CONCRETE PROBLEMS

Paul exercised that new discernment in terms of the concrete problems that he and the churches of his mission faced. An examination of his moral teachings concerning these concrete problems will demonstrate both the Pauline pattern of discernment and the pastoral character of his ethic.

1) Jew and Gentile

Among the most difficult problems was the relationship between Jews and Gentiles in the church. For the Galatians and Romans, this problem seems to have been, in different ways, the occasion for Paul's epistle. In Galatia some were insisting that Gentile converts needed to become Jews, to be circumcised and to observe the law of Moses, in order to fully become Christians. In Rome some Jewish Christians condemned the Gentiles for their lawlessness, and some Gentile Christians scorned and despised the Jews for their scruples.[132] This issue was a continuing crisis in Paul's ministry. The unity and equality of Jew and Gentile was for him closely related to "the truth of the gospel" (Gal. 2:4,14) and to the "obedience of faith" (Rom. 1:5; 16:26).

Paul's discernment began with Christians' identity in Christ: they are "one in Christ Jesus," "there is neither Jew nor Greek" (Gal. 3:28; cf. I Cor. 12:13). In Christ's cross Gentiles have died to sin (Rom. 6:1-11) and Jews have died to the law (Rom. 7:1-6). Jew and Gentile are equally "justified by his grace as a gift . . . to be received by faith" (Rom. 3:24-30; cf. Gal. 3:6-14). Indeed, Paul's talk of justification by faith is never addressed to the introspective question of the individual, "How can I get right with God?" but always to the social question of the early Christian communities, "How are Jew and Gentile to relate to one another?"[133] Justification by faith rather than by the works of the law establishes a social reality in which "there is no distinction" (Rom. 3:22; 10:12).

This unity and equality was an eschatological reality, to be sure, and Paul never denies that the Jewish Christians are Jews or that the Gentile Christians are Gentiles. He never demands that Jews stop observing the law or that Gentiles start living like Jews; in fact, he repudiates such demands (Gal. 2:14). That eschatological reality, however, must shape the social reality of the church in the present. Jews need not live like Gentiles, but they may not condemn and repudiate them either; Gentiles need not be circumcised or live like Jews, but they may not despise and scorn them either (Rom. 14-15).[134]

The announcement of the gospel that formed a new identity and provided a new perspective called for freedom and love, a harmonious pluralism within the church marked by respect and love for those who were and remained different. Paul enjoined them to "welcome one another, therefore, as Christ has welcomed you, for the glory of God" (15:7; cf. also 14:1).

The eschatological unity of Jew and Gentile also already comes to expression in the collection.[135] At the Council of Jerusalem, Paul and Barnabas had promised to "remember the poor" (Gal. 2:10) in Jerusalem. The fulfillment of his promise, a collection among the Gentile churches accepted by the Jerusalem church, would ratify the unity of Gentile and Jewish Christians. In giving the gifts, the Gentiles would acknowledge their indebtedness to the Jews (Rom. 15:27; II Cor. 9:12); and in receiving them the Jewish Christians would acknowledge the "surpassing grace of God" among the Gentiles (II Cor. 9:13-14). The enmity between Jew and Gentile will thus be overcome and a single community — although still composed of Jews and Gentiles — will give "thanks to God for his inexpressible gift" (II Cor. 9:15).

2) Slave and Free

There is also an eschatological unity between slave and free (Gal. 3:28; I Cor. 12:13). Nor did that unity demand uniformity: slave and free remained what they were just as Jew and Gentile did. But Paul brings the relationship between slave and free under the criticizing and transforming light of his new discernment.

In Christ the social distinction is trivialized. The one "who was called in the Lord as a slave is a freedman of the Lord. Likewise he who was free when called is a slave of Christ" (I Cor. 7:22). The social order of slavery is superseded, "for the form of this world is passing away" (I Cor. 7:31). But the eschatological perspective of Paul cautions against the enthusiasm of some members of the Corinthian congregation. Their claim to live already fully and without remainder in the new age is a pretentious one. The form of this world is not yet simply past, and the new discernment does not call for disowning one's role but for contentment with God in one's role (I Cor. 7:17,20). The argument does not hinge on an assumption of imminence; it hinges, rather, on the denial of the Corinthian enthusiasts' claim to be already fully participating in the new age. In the "not yet" character of our existence, equality of slave and free does not create a whole new set of social standards and role assignments. Neither Paul nor the enthusiasts can snap their fingers and produce a whole new social system. But the new age — the equality of slave and free — is not irrelevant for all that. The new identity, the eschatological perspective, the fundamental principles of love and justice, and the special principle of the equality of slave and free enable and require new relationships in the midst of old roles.

Paul's advice to slaves who have the opportunity to gain their freedom (I Cor. 7:21) is notoriously ambiguous.[136] Does Paul tell the slave to "avail yourself of the opportunity" for freedom (I Cor. 7:21b) or "make use of your present condition instead" (I Cor. 7:21, RSV margin)? Whichever it is, Paul's fundamental point is that "in the Lord" there is no slave or free.

The little letter to Philemon — and to the house church of which he is a part — [137] is a masterfully crafted address to the concrete issue of slavery in the church.[138] Paul does not command; he appeals to Philemon to exercise a new discernment (8,9,14). The conventional legal response is not to be the final norm for Philemon's discernment, although Paul himself obeys the law by returning a runaway slave. The discernment rests on a new identity given in Christ: Philemon is to see Onesimus "no longer as a slave but . . . as a beloved brother . . . both in the flesh and in the Lord" (16). Onesimus is not simply to be reinstated into a network of role relationships left unchanged. Paul does not say, "Philemon, in the Lord you and Onesimus are one, but of course in the flesh nothing has changed." He does not separate the unity, equality, peace "in the Lord" from the "real world" of Philemon and Onesimus. The unity is eschatological, but it is not docetic; it must have some "fleshly" expression.

Just exactly what form the "fleshly" expression of their unity and fraternity in Christ was to take Paul leaves to Philemon's new discernment. Paul does not explicitly demand emancipation, but he plainly does expect Onesimus to be freed to do the work of the Lord with Paul (13,14; vs. 20 is a pun: Paul says, "I want some benefit [Gk. *onaimēn*] from you in the Lord"). It is left to Philemon's new discernment — but not as a private matter. The discernment takes place in the context of a church that functions as a community of moral discourse, a community in which, moreover, slaves and masters have an equal share in discernment.

Paul does not condemn the institution of slavery outright, but he makes the direction of the discernment plain. The new identity and the principles of love, freedom, unity, and fraternity finally shatter the social structures of slavery.

3) Male and Female

Paul also sees an eschatological unity of male and female (Gal. 3:28). Again this unity does not require uniformity; male and female remain what they are. The distinction can be traced, after all, not only to the law but to the original creation (I Cor. 11:8,9; Gal. 3:28, however, uses the very language of Gen. 1:27 [Gk. *arsen kai thēly*] to say "there is no 'male and female' ").[139] The unity, however, does shape the new life in Christ according to Paul's discernment. Paul considers Prisca his "fellow-worker" (Rom. 16:3-5; cf. I Cor. 16:19; Acts 18:2,18,26), and he calls Phoebe the "deacon" his "helper" (Rom. 16:1).[140] He recalls that Euodia and Syntyche "labored side by side with me in the gospel" (Phil. 4:2), and he mentions or greets a number of other women who evidently had important roles in his churches (see esp. Rom. 16:6,7,12,15).

Nevertheless, in I Corinthians Paul insists that, when women prophesy and pray, they be veiled (11:3-16) and, moreover, that they "be silent"

(14:33b-35). The passages are difficult to reconcile with each other and more difficult still to reconcile with Paul's practice or with his eschatological perception that in Christ there is no male and female. The advice in I Cor. 11,[141] it must be observed, far from prohibiting the full and equal participation of women in the life of the church, assumes that they pray and prophesy at the same time that it instructs them about the necessity of being veiled. Paul clearly raises the concrete question of the veil because some Corinthian women had cast down their veils and asserted their independence of their husbands and of conventional proprieties. Among those Corinthian enthusiasts who claimed to participate already and fully in the new age on the basis of their spiritual gifts were some women, evidently, who in the exercise of their spiritual gifts and in their protestations of independence disturbed the peace and order of the church and home. Paul would have been quite unsympathetic with their eschatology and with their concept of freedom. In a wide variety of appeals — to the law, to rabbinical teachings, to church customs, and to nature — Paul attempts to convince the church not to tolerate the excesses of these women. He makes it plain that he does not disagree with the principle of the unity and equality of men and women "in the Lord" (11:10,11), but he also makes plain that the new discernment leads not to the assertion of independence but to mutual submission: "In the Lord woman is not independent of man nor man of woman" (11:11).

The curious advice to women in I Corinthians 14:33b-35 has been taken by many to be a non-Pauline interpolation.[142] These arguments are not unsubstantial, but I do not find them fully convincing either. Furnish claims that these verses disrupt the flow of Paul's argument.[143] But Paul is advising the church about concrete abuses of the spiritual gifts, especially speaking in tongues in worship, and his advice here speaks to the same point. To "speak" in this context very likely refers to speaking in tongues (Gk. *lalein,* 14:34b,36; cf. 14:2,4,5,6,9,13,16,23,27,39). The command to be silent can also be understood in terms of the context: the same word (Gk. *sigaō*) is used earlier with respect to prophecy and tongue-speaking (14:28,30), and in both cases it is clearly not an absolute command but relative to certain concrete abuses of the gifts. Finally, the command to the women to "be subordinate" (RSV 14:34, Gk. *hypotassesthōsan*) should be understood in the light of vs. 32, "the spirits of prophets are subject [Gk. *hypotassetai*] to prophets," a subtle exhortation to the prophets to exercise self-control. The law that Paul appeals to here may very well be a Roman law in Corinth which, in response to the excesses of the ecstatic women at the festivals of Dionysus, prohibited ecstatic utterance and the loss of self-control by Corinthian women.[144] The force of this advice to women, therefore, is not to establish an eternal principle or the element of a timeless code, but to exercise the new discernment concerning a concrete problem in the Corinthians' worship. The principles are mutual edification (14:12) and peace (14:33). Such discernment called for an end to the abuse of tongue-speaking by some women "enthusiasts" who disowned this world and its role responsibilities, who exercised neither self-control nor mutual subjection.

Paul does not proclaim a woman's year any more than he calls for a slave revolt, but he does not simply baptize existing social roles and institutions in either case.[145] Paul neither disowns such existing relationships (as the enthusiasts did) nor does he accept them as the final norm; he assimilates, qualifies, and transforms them in the light of a new discernment. The new identity in Christ yields its first fruits in the important place of women in Paul's ministry and in his churches, and it challenges and judges any attempt to construe freedom as independence (or license, see I Cor. 6:12; 10:23) rather than in the light of Christ as freedom to serve.

4) Sex and Marriage

Nowhere does Paul express the eschatological unity of male and female quite so clearly as he does in his instructions concerning marriage in I Corinthians. On this subject also, Paul's pastoral discernment is pressed and challenged by the enthusiasts at Corinth, who claim that they already fully live in the new age of the Spirit.

Some of these enthusiasts drew the inference that, because they were already really living in the new age of the Spirit, what they did in the body was a matter of indifference (I Cor. 6:12-21). Some even boasted about their sexual libertinism (5:1-2). Against these people Paul insists that they—and their bodies—belong to Christ (6:13,19-20) and are united to Christ (6:17). He reminds them of Christ's resurrection and—against their eschatological assumptions—insists that God "will also raise us up by his power" (6:14). He acknowledges the truth of their slogan "all things are lawful,"[146] but he protects it against libertine constructions by reminding them that Christian freedom is freedom to love ("but not all things are helpful," 6:12) and by instructing them that libertinism is nothing but a form of slavery to the flesh ("but I will not be enslaved by anything," 6:12). The new discernment does not countenance sexual immorality.

Others among the enthusiasts at Corinth had drawn quite a different conclusion: they thought that because they already lived fully in the new age, their lives were to be ascetic; so they refrained from sexual intercourse. "It is well for a man not to touch a woman" is a Corinthian slogan which Paul, while not rejecting it, immediately qualifies (I Cor. 7:1,2). On their side, Paul affirms that celibacy is a sign of the new age and that in the new age marriage is no longer a duty. But against them Paul insists on the "not yet" character of our existence, recognizes the temptation to immorality (7:2), and refuses to make celibacy a duty either. Both celibacy and marriage are "gifts" (Gk. *charisma*, 7:7); but neither is a duty.

Even though Paul affirms celibacy as a sign of the new age, he consistently insists that they view even their celibacy in the perspective of the "not yet" character of our existence. Paul agrees that it is a sign of the new age—he can even say that to refrain from marriage is "better"—but the grounds for his preference are never that the celibate one thereby lives in the new age. The new discernment approves the preference for celibacy but not the eschatological assumptions of the enthusiasts. Paul recommends celibacy as an eminently practical choice given the "not yet" character of our existence (7:26-35). His point rests less on the imminence of the parousia than on the quality of our eschatological existence.

Marriage is no longer a duty, but a gift; and it too participates in both the "already" and the "not yet" character of our existence. The grounds for marriage no longer give priority to (or even include) the duty of procreation, for the Messiah has come and the ages have turned. To permit marriage as a "remedy for concupiscence" clearly recognizes the continuing effectiveness of the powers of the old age.[147] But the Pauline understanding of marriage is also decisively influenced by the eschatological unity and equality of male and female. The Pauline discernment does not discredit or discard marriage as a "one-flesh" union (Gen. 2:24; I Cor. 6:16). Marriage has its own eschatological fruition in the full mutuality and equality of the relationship, including the sexual aspect of that relationship (I Cor. 7:3-4). It was hardly surprising to the first-century Christians that Paul says the husband "rules over" his wife's body (I Cor. 7:4a); but it was quite surprising—indeed shocking—that Paul says the wife "rules over" her husband's body (I Cor. 7:4b). The mutual rule and mutual submission of marriage partners is a concrete consequence of the new discernment concerning sexuality.[148] The eschatological unity of male and female does not permit libertinism or require celibacy; it allows and transforms the marriage relationship, bringing the one-flesh union of sexuality to fulfillment in authentic mutuality.

The eschatological situation permits and qualifies both celibacy and marriage: now either one can be consecrated to God. In this eschatological situation the Corinthians who are married are not released from their marital responsibilities, even if those responsibilities are transformed in the light of Paul's new discernment. Paul advises against divorce in this same context. The church's disposition toward divorce is still to be shaped by Jesus' word on the matter (I Cor. 7:10; cf. Mk. 10:5-9). But Paul does not utilize the saying as the basis for *Halakah*, for legal rulings. He acknowledges the reality of divorce in the church in a parenthetical remark (7:11a), and, faced with the concrete problem of whether marriage to an unbeliever can be dissolved, he exercises his own discernment (7:12-16). On the basis of the one-flesh understanding of marriage, the couple is holy if one of the partners is: the believer "consecrates" the union. Therefore, Paul advises the believer not to initiate divorce; but if the unbeliever initiates the divorce, his advice is to permit it, "for God has called us to peace" (I Cor. 7:15).

5) Rich and Poor

Perhaps the most striking thing about Paul's moral teachings concerning wealth and poverty is that, in contrast to the tradition of Jesus preserved in the Synoptic Gospels, Paul says so very little about them — and never anything quite so radical as "Go, sell what you have, and give to the poor" (Mk. 10:21).

There are warnings against "covetousness" (Rom. 1:29; cf. I Cor. 5:10; 6:10), to be sure; but these warnings occur in the context of lists of vices and seem an almost inescapable part of the tradition rather than Paul's focus or interest. He does not condemn wealth or exhort Christians to obey Jesus' strong words about renouncing wealth. He does exhort them to work diligently in order to provide for themselves and to "be dependent on nobody" (I Thess. 4:11,12; cf. II Thess. 3:10-12). The principle seems to be the Stoic one of autarchy (Gk. *autarkeia*, II Cor. 9:8; Phil. 4:11).[149] Each one, in order to maintain his independence, must have enough to care for his needs and to be "content" with what he has. Paul's teachings seem a good deal closer to the middle-class respectability of Stoic morality than to the tradition of Jesus.

Paul's exhortations, however, stand in the context of a different discernment from that of the Stoics. The root of Stoic contentment was willing whatever happened; that was the way one participated in the great reason that was at work in the world. The root of Paul's contentment is the eschatological act of God in Jesus Christ. The Christian finds identity there rather than in the cosmic reason, and that identity enables and requires participation in the eschatological cause of God. Paul's eschatological perspective allows him to discern the relative insignificance of property and money (e.g., Phil. 4:5,6, where "have no anxiety about anything" follows directly upon "the Lord is at hand"; also I Cor. 6:2, where he calls court cases concerning money "trivial"), without disowning economic responsibilities like the "loafers" at Thessalonica (I Thess. 4:11,12; 5:14; cf. II Thess. 3:6-12). Such is the root of Paul's exhortation to be independent. Paul never says that "in Christ there is neither rich nor poor," but the pattern is nevertheless present. He does not call for uniformity here either, or for a common purse. But when — even at the Lord's Supper — groups formed along social class lines, Paul clearly rebukes the rich for their behavior: they "despise the church of God and humiliate those who have nothing" (I Cor. 11:22). It is precisely that lack of regard for the poor among them that Paul refers to as partaking "in an unworthy manner" (11:27) and not "discerning the body" (11:29), and appropriately so, for the cup and the bread are signs of our common participation (Gk. *koinōnia*, I Cor. 10:16) in Christ so that "we who are many are one body" (I Cor. 10:17).

If the sacrament can be violated by the rich's lack of concern for poor, it is also the case that generosity and hospitality are "nearly sacramental"[150] themselves (Phil. 4:18), a material sign of a spiritual grace. The unity and equality of rich and poor come to concrete expression when the rich "practice hospitality" (Rom. 12:13; cf. 16:23) or contribute liberally (Rom. 12:8; cf. Philem. 4-7) or do acts of mercy cheerfully (Rom. 12:8), or share with their teachers (Gal. 6:6; cf. Phil. 1:5; 4:14-20). Paul does not exhort the rich to sell all and give it to the poor or to the common purse; but he evidently expects them to use their wealth in freedom and love in the service of the church.

Paul's shows his new discernment concerning wealth most clearly perhaps in his exhortations concerning the collection. We have already called attention to the collection as instrumental in establishing the unity of Jewish and Gentile Christians (Rom. 15:25-31; II Cor. 9:11-15). But in exhorting the Gentile Christians to give to this collection for the poor in Jerusalem, Paul reveals the pattern of his discernment of responsibilities with money.[151] He does not command them (II Cor. 8:8); he appeals to their identity, their life in the grace of Christ (II Cor. 8:9), to their eschatological confidence in God (II Cor. 9:6-10), to the fundamental principles of love (II Cor. 8:8,24) and freedom (II Cor. 9:7). This new discernment makes fundamental claims on their character and dispositions (their "readiness" to give, II Cor. 8:12), and such transformed dispositions drive them to concrete expressions in action. The claims on action are not strictly patterned after the self-sacrifice of Christ; Paul does not exhort the Corinthians to give everything away so that "others should be eased and you burdened" (II Cor. 8:13). Rather, he articulates the concrete meaning of love in terms of the principle of equality (Gk. *isotēs,* II Cor. 8:13,14). He further articulates that principle in the distributive principle, which supplies the needs of some from the abundance of others (II Cor. 8:13). He corroborates the argument by appealing to Exodus 16:18, God's provision of manna for the Israelites: hoarding was futile, daily needs were met, and God had to be trusted to provide. Moreover, manna is a familiar eschatological symbol: the economic pattern marked by equality, sharing, freedom from hoarding, and dependence on God participates already in that eschatological reality symbolized by manna.

6) Love and Politics

The new discernment is also exercised in Paul's advice concerning political authorities. Romans 13:1-7, of course, is the *locus classicus* of Paul's view of the state. Unfortunately, it has often been wrenched from its historical and literary context and read as requiring uncritical obedience to the state, no matter how unjust and pernicious the regime. Historically, it is important to observe that the passage was written when there was still considerable hope that the young Nero would conduct himself with justice and humanity. The passage has literary affinities with the advice current in Hellenistic Judaism concerning the state.[152] Paul would seem to be instructing the Roman churches, especially the Jewish churches there, to keep to the tradition that had formed their political posture. Paul's advice is quite at home within the wisdom of Hellenistic Judaism when he argues that rulers are appointed by God (13:1-2),[153] that their legitimate function is to protect the innocent, promote the good, and punish the evil (13:3-4), and that those who desire a well-ordered community life ought to render the authorities appropriate taxes and honor (13:5-7). But Paul posits that advice, that moral wisdom, in a new context, a transforming context. It is part of his call for a new discernment (Rom. 12:1,2), and he sets before it and behind it reminders of the eschatological situation (12:2; 13:11-12) and of the duty to love (12:9; 13:8). Submission to government is set in the context of the more urgent duty to love our neighbor while we await God's justice. To love our neighbor in a world still marked by greed and injustice *requires* political responsibility, it does not *disown* it. However, if our neighbor is threatened by the greed and injustice of a tyrant, the new discernment's political responsibility would acknowledge the priority of the neighbor's claims.

When Christians bring suit against each other, however, as they did in Corinth (I Cor. 6:1-8), it signals for Paul a failure to live the kind of life that ought to mark their character and community. It is a violation of their eschatological identity in Christ, for they, the saints, are to judge the world (6:2) and the angels (6:3). It is a "defeat" (6:7) and puts the lie to the presumptuous claims of the Corinthian enthusiasts. Paul judges and condemns such suits under the fundamental principle of sacrificial love: "Why not rather suffer wrong?" (6:7).

Love's politics, then, do not insist on one's own rights. They are willing rather to "suffer wrong" (I Cor. 6:7). But they do insist on government, on protection for the neighbor in a world still marked by injustice and greed (Rom. 13:1-7). The gospel does provide and require a new political discernment.

7) Conclusion

In each of these concrete cases Paul's pattern of discernment is operative. God's eschatological act in Jesus Christ provides a moral identity and a perspective on the world, and it establishes certain fundamental values, but it does not create new rules or roles or institutions. To deal with concrete cases, the new life in Christ assimilates and transforms different traditional sources of moral wisdom. Thus the renewal of their minds enables Christians to discern the will of God (Rom. 12:1-2).

2. Colossians and Ephesians

The authenticity of these Epistles is so much debated that it is best to treat them separately.[154] The issues are complex, and the question is likely to remain unresolved. But whether they were written by Paul or by a Pauline interpreter utilizing traditional liturgical and hortatory materials, the letters exercise a Pauline discernment concerning new crises facing the church.

a. COLOSSIANS: HERESY AND MORALITY

The crisis facing the Colossians was created by a Jewish Gnosticism that was willing and eager to assimilate the Christian message to its own religious teachings.[155] The assumptions of this heresy were that God is holy and unapproachable, that people are imprisoned in earthly desires and cut off from God by their bodies, and that between God and people live the angelic powers, the *plērōma*. These powers are mediators between God and people, and so it becomes necessary to placate them, which is accomplished by a rigid observance of the law (for the angels gave the law) and by a rigorous asceticism.

The spiritually elite who claimed such esoteric *gnōsis* were quite willing to incorporate Christ as one of the powers.

In response, the author of Colossians denounces such views as "empty deceit" and as the "traditions of men" (2:8). He insists that God has "triumphed" over the powers in Christ (2:15). In Christ alone "all the fullness [Gk. *plērōma*] of God was pleased to dwell" (1:19) — and, moreover, to dwell "bodily" (2:9). Christ alone mediates between God and people, and those who are in Christ need not seek "wisdom and knowledge" anywhere else (2:3). The Colossian Christians are identified in their faith (2:12) and in their baptism (2:11) with this Christ, whose preeminence over the powers they acknowledge in their own hymn (1:15-20);[156] they "have come to fullness of life in him, who is the head of all rule and authority" (2:10). They violate that Christian identity if they now submit to those powers over whom they — in Christ — are already victorious. To submit to circumcision (2:11) or to the "legal demands" of the law (2:14) or to the ascetic regulations (2:20-22) is to deny one's identity in Christ. To allow the spiritually elite in Colossae to judge them on questions of food, drink, and festivals (2:16), or to insist on "self-abasement and worship of angels" (2:18) or on an ascetic "severity to the body" (2:23), is to refuse to live in the new age. Christians belong to Christ (2:20): they have died with him, and their life is "hid with Christ in God" (3:3). They may seem powerless against the "beguiling speech" (2:4) of these spiritually elite, but they can expect eschatological vindication, for "when Christ who is our life appears, then you also will appear with him in glory" (3:4).

The Christian identity provides a perspective on the world that is no less eschatological in Colossians than in the unchallenged letters (cf. also 2:17,23; 3:6,25; 4:2).[157] The emphasis certainly falls on the "already," but it is only and precisely because the Colossian Christians are tempted to submit again to the powers of the old age that the author emphasizes that Christ has "already" achieved lordship over the powers, that their power was "already" broken, and that the Christian church "already" participates in his victory. He never denies the "not yet" character of our existence. The Pauline eschatological perspective is an assumption of the intimate relation between indicative and imperative in Paul; both that perspective and the intimate relation of indicative and imperative remain in effect in Colossians: "As you have received Christ Jesus the Lord, so live in him" (Col. 2:6).[158]

I agree with Sanders that "the main theme of Colossians is the opposition to 'heresy,' "[159] but I am baffled by his inference, "Thus, there is in Colossians no inner coherence between theology and ethics."[160] The eschatological identity in Christ is inconsistent with the rigorous observance of the law and ascetic regulations, with the ethic of the Jewish Gnostics. The Christian identity is coherent with — indeed, is insistent upon — an ethic of freedom (2:8-23).

The other fundamental principle of Pauline discernment is love, and in Colossians it is also "a vital, indeed the pivotal aspect of the new life in Christ."[161] Already in the thanksgiving section, there is a subtle exhortation to (as well as thanksgiving for) "love in the Spirit" (1:8). Paul's labors have intended that the Colossian Christians be "knit together in love" (2:2, Gk. *symbibazō*). In 2:19 it is by holding fast to Christ the Head that the whole body is "knit together (Gk. *symbibazō*) through its . . . ligaments" (Gk. *syndesmoi*). And in 3:14 the author exhorts the Colossians, "Above all these put on love, which binds everything together" (Gk. *syndesmon,* "the ligament"). These parallels are hardly accidental, and they testify to the relationship of identity in Christ and the gift and duty of love.

The paraenesis itself is traditional, utilizing especially the baptismal instruction to "put off" old patterns of conduct and character and to "put on" the new nature (Col. 3:5-14), the *Haustafel* (3:18-4:1), and the traditional exhortation to watch (Col. 4:2,3). The traditional paraenesis is set in the context of the Pauline discernment and is not left untouched by it. Perhaps the clearest example of the effect of this context is that the word *tapeinophrosynē*, used in Colossians 2:18 and 23 to describe the "humility" or "self-abasement" (RSV) of the spiritually elite, soon recurs in Colossians 3:12 in a list of character traits to be "put on" (RSV: "lowliness"). *Tapeinophrosynē* or "humility" may belong to either the old or the new age, to the "flesh" (2:23) or to the "new nature" (3:10). The "humility" of the spiritually elite is really a device of religious pride, an attempt to make some claim on God or achieve some favorable comparison with the neighbor; it lets go of the head and destroys the unity of the new community (2:18-19). The Christian virtue makes no claim on God but submits to the reign of God, makes no claim against the neighbor but is part of the disposition to love (3:14).[162]

The *Haustafel* is traditional, and we need not repeat here the comments from an earlier chapter about the tradition.[163] It may be simply observed again, however, that the role obligations are reciprocal, that the duty of love and service is mutual, that the background of intelligibility is provided by Christ, and that attention is drawn not to one's own noble dignity (as in Stoic codes) or to the command of God (as in Jewish codes) but to the neighbor and the neighbor's good. The Christians in Colossae are instructed again that integrity with their confession does not entail leaving this world with its role assignments. They are to fill and fulfill their roles in ways that serve Christ and the neighbor. The most carefully qualified role instructions concern slaves and masters (3:22-4:1). The eschatological standing of equality before one Master who will judge impartially (3:24-4:1)[164] qualifies and transforms existing role relations; it does not destroy them and create new social structures.

b. EPHESIANS: *PAX DEI*

The crisis facing the Ephesians was very likely created by the antipathy between Jew and Gentile surrounding the Jewish Rebellion of A.D. 66.[165] This antipathy had deep roots and periodically broke out in repression or rebellion; the enmity was always there. Moreover, the antagonism was supported "ideologically." It was a "holy enmity" on both sides: to the Jew, the Roman or Greek was an idolater; to the Roman or Greek, the Jew was an atheist, refusing to acknowledge the gods or the divine authority of Caesar. The Jewish Rebellion broke out in A.D. 66, and the war that followed was no polite reassertion of Roman domination. It was a blood bath. Moreover, the animosity of war spilled over throughout the empire in anti-Jewish riots in Alexandria, Caesarea, and Antioch.[166] This political situation must not be underestimated, for it threatened the accomplishments of Paul's mission, and the unity of Jew and Gentile that he preached was in jeopardy again. This crisis prompted the encyclical epistle known as Ephesians. Whether written by Paul (and dating it to the Jewish Rebellion would suggest that it was not) or by a faithful and creative interpeter of Paul, the letter reminds Jewish Christians of their new unity with Gentiles and reminds Gentile Christians that they have made the Jewish heritage their own. They are to discover their identity not in the racial and political animosities of their time but in Christ.

> He is our peace, who has made us both one, and has broken down the dividing wall of hostility, by abolishing in his flesh the law of commandments and ordinances, that he might create in himself one new man in place of two, so making peace, and might reconcile us both to God in one body through the cross, thereby bringing the hostility to an end (Eph. 2:14-16).[167]

Out of Jew and Gentile a new humanity has been created in Christ, namely, the church. There Jew ("we") and Gentile ("you") both exist for "the praise of his glory" (1:12,14; cf. 1:6). The Pauline formula "by grace have you been saved through faith" (2:8; cf. 2:6) once again points to a social reality rather than addressing an introspective conscience. Gentiles ("you") and Jews ("we") were both sinners, "children of wrath" (2:1-3), and both are saved by grace (2:4-9). Jew and Gentile are "fellow citizens" (2:19).

This identity—with its gift and demand of reconciliation between Jew and Gentile during the crisis of political and racial hostility—is developed theologically also in terms of Christ's victory over "the principalities and powers" (1:20-23; 3:10; 6:12).[168] This concept of the powers was not an invention of the author of this Epistle: not only does it appear in the acknowledged Pauline letters (Rom. 8:30-39; I Cor. 2:8; 15:24-26) and in Colossians (1:16; 2:15), but it was familiar to both the Jewish and Gentile heritage.[169] In both heritages the powers are spiritual beings that influence life on earth, particularly politically. They "stand behind" political rulers and ideologies. The emphasis on principalities and powers and "spiritual rulers" in Ephesians does not occur because the Epistle is more "spiritual" than the others, but because it is more "political."[170] Ephesians explicates the significance of the resurrection not only in terms of resurrection from the dead but also as resurrection to sovereignty over the powers (1:20-21). And by their participation in him Christians partake in the same sovereignty (2:6). Christians are "above" the political animosity and racial enmity that mark the times. The eschatological perspective is alert to the fact that the powers assert themselves against the lordship of Christ — however hopelessly finally — and alert to the struggle in which they themselves are therefore involved (6:12). The church, one new humanity of Jew and Gentile, is the first effect of Christ's reconciling activity and the tool for his continuing activity. It is the author's prayer (and subtle exhortation) "that through the church the manifold wisdom of God may now be made known to the principalities and powers in the heavenly places" (Eph. 3:10).

The principle developed in response to the crisis of the war is "peace." While the *pax Romana* crumbles, the author announces the good news and the requirements of the *pax Dei*. The indicative of God's eschatological action in raising Christ to sovereignty over the powers, thus creating "one new man in place of two, so making peace" (Eph. 2:15; cf. also 2:14,17), is rendered as an imperative in the exhortation that the churches should be "eager to maintain the unity of the Spirit in the bond [Gk. *syndesmon*] of peace" (4:3; cf. the whole opening paraenesis, 4:1-16). This exhortation is related to Colossians 3:14, where love is the bond (Gk. *syndesmon*). If Ephesians is by a later Pauline interpreter, the exhortation may be understood as an exegesis of the Colossians passage. The fundamental principle of love is made more relevant and concrete by developing it in terms of "peace." Love is not absent from the Epistle by any means; in fact, it is clearly a fundamental principle. In a general exhortation, the author instructs them, "Be imitators of God, as beloved children" (5:1). The way in which they are to imitate God is already identified in the phrase "as beloved children"; but earlier as well, God's love has been observed (1:5,6), and it is made explicit in the commandment that follows: "Walk in love, as Christ loved us and gave himself up for us" (5:2; cf. 3:17,19; 4:2,15; 5:25,28,33). But the fundamental principle gives way to what is for Ephesians its most important implication, "peace." In the catalogue of Christian armor, where we expect to find "love," we find instead "the gospel of peace" (5:15; cf. 2:17). In the benediction, finally, itself a subtle exhortation, "peace" is joined with "love" as the blessing of God (6:23).

The remaining paraenesis is traditional, clearly related to the Colossian materials, utilizing the same traditional forms and a good deal of the same material. There is again the baptismal instruction to "put off" the old nature and to "put on" the new nature (Eph. 4:22-32; cf. Col. 3:5-14); there is again the *Haustafel* (Eph. 5:21-6:9; cf. Col. 3:18-4:1); there is again the traditional exhortation to stand and watch (Eph. 6:13-20; cf. Col. 4:2,3); there is, in addition, use of the "children of light" tradition (Eph. 5:7-12). Most of this is quite traditional in content as well as in form. However, the treatment of the *Haustafel* is interesting. I need not repeat the observations about the *Haustafeln* in general, but I should observe that the Ephesian *Haustafel* emphasizes the obligation of mutual subjection. That requirement is placed as its head (5:21), and it provides a context for the whole teaching.

The relationship of husband and wife, particularly, is more carefully and theologically qualified here than in Colossians. The analogy of the relationship between Christ and his church to the relationship between husband and wife is a beautiful one but, like all analogies, dangerous if one tries to extend it beyond its intention. Clearly both husband and wife are under Christ — and equally under Christ. The opening instruction to "be subject to one another out of reverence for Christ" should make that clear. The analogy does not intend to say the husband is the "Lord" or "Savior" of the wife. It points instead to the husband's service and love. The meaning of headship is defined in this context by the command to husbands, "Love your wives, as Christ loved the church and gave himself up for her" (Eph. 5:25; cf. 5:28-30,33). The author of Ephesians does not disown the traditional authority of the husband, but he transforms it by this analogy to Christ's authority over his church. The authority of the husband is not what is being taught here; that is assumed in the conventional role assignments of the times. But that authority is put into the context of mutual subjection, reciprocal obligations, loyalty to Christ, and the fundamental obligation to love the neighbor, including and especially the neighbor who is one's wife.

The relationship between slave and master gets very similar instructions in Ephesians to those in Colossians. The slave is first of all and essentially to submit to Christ; he is a "slave of Christ" (6:6). Secondarily (and not essentially) he submits to his earthly master, not disowning his role assignment but transforming it into a free and special form of the service Christ gave and requires. The author tells the earthly master to "do the same to them" (6:9), to render his servants service; and he reminds him of a heavenly Master with whom "there is no partiality" (6:9) and before whom he and his slaves stand as equals. The *Haustafel* of Ephesians stands as far from the conventional understanding of roles as the peace of God stands from the conventional hostility between Jew and Gentile.

3. The Pastoral Epistles: Sound Doctrine and Morality

The Pastoral Epistles were probably not written by Paul;[171] but whether by Paul or a devoted student, the spirit of the ethic here is indisputably more pedestrian and prosaic. To be sure, the gospel is defended against the attacks of heresy, but in the process it becomes a deposit entrusted to Paul (I Tim. 1:11), which he in turn entrusts to Timothy (1:18), charging him to guard it (6:20) and to entrust it to "faithful men who will be able to teach others also" (II Tim. 2:2). The gospel gradually has become identified with "sound doctrine" (I Tim. 1:10; cf. 4:6; 6:3; II Tim. 1:13; 4:3; Titus 1:9,13; 2:1,2,10, etc.[172]). Hence also the frequency of captions like "The saying is sure and worthy of full acceptance" (I Tim. 1:15; cf. 3:1; 4:9; II Tim. 2:11; Titus 3:8).

The particular heresy opposed here seems to have been a Jewish Gnostic form of Christianity. Their Jewish character may be seen in reference to "teachers of the Law" (I Tim. 1:7), "Jewish myths" (Titus 1:14), "quarrels over the law" (Titus 3:9), and "the circumcision party" (Titus 1:10). The Gnostic character can be seen in their asceticism, grounded in Gnostic dualism (I Tim. 4:1-5), in their holding "that the resurrection is past already" (II Tim. 2:18; cf. II Tim. 4:8; Titus 2:11-14), and in their libertine trends (I Tim. 1:19; I take Titus 1:15a, "To the pure all things are pure," to be a slogan of the Jewish Gnostics, possibly based on Rom. 14:14, which the author does not reject but immediately qualifies).

It is against these heretics that the Pastorals emphasized "sound doctrine" and sound morality, and in that context it was surely necessary to define — however prosaically — and to defend — in however pedestrian a fashion — sound Pauline doctrine and morality. Against the ascetic morality inferred by some from the Gnostic premise of dualism, that is, against those "who forbid marriage and enjoin abstinence from foods," it was necessary to affirm that "everything created by God is good, and nothing is to be rejected if it is received with thanksgiving" (I Tim. 4:3,4). Marriage is not only permitted, it is a standard requirement for church officials (I Tim. 3:2,12; Titus 1:6). Even wine is protected from the asceticism of the heretics (I Tim. 5:23): the author's advice is to be temperate, not ascetic (I Tim. 3:2; cf. 3:3,8,11; Titus 1:7; 2:3). Against the speculative use of the Jewish heritage by these heretics, the Pastorals insist that "the law is good, if any one uses it lawfully" (I Tim. 1:8) even while they reject "Jewish myths" (Titus 1:14), "stupid controversies, genealogies, dissensions, and quarrels over the law" (Titus 3:9; cf. I Tim. 1:4). They call the use of Scripture among these heretics "unprofitable and futile" (Titus 3:9), but they affirm Scripture itself as "profitable for teaching, for reproof, for correction, and for training in righteousness" (II Tim. 3:16).

Against the libertine inferences drawn by some of these heretics, the Pastorals appeal to the law (I Tim. 1:8), to the vice lists (I Tim. 1:9,10; 6:4,5; II Tim. 3:2-5), and to the *Haustafeln* in order to insist on submission by women (I Tim. 2:8-15) and slaves (I Tim. 6:1,2). Even the interest in the established hierarchy of the church may be a response to a tendency toward insubordination among the libertines.

This resistance to Jewish Gnostic perversions of the Christian ethic is commendable, of course, but it is accomplished with condemnations rather than with any Pauline discernment. Sound doctrine and sound morality are a matched set for the Pastorals (e.g., I Tim. 1:5,19; 3:9; Titus 2:1-9), but any relationship between the two seems extrinsic. It is typical of the Pastorals that the vice list of I Timothy 1:8-10 concludes, "and whatever else is contrary to sound doctrine," without any indication of the kinds of inferences that join doctrine and morality (cf. Titus 1:1-7).

Sound doctrine can be determined by the Pauline tradition to be properly handled in the succession of teachers. The creedal formulations and hymns one finds in the Pastorals, of course, are particularly relevant to the controversy with the Gnostic heretics: for example, that there is one God (I Tim. 2:5, against the cosmological dualism of the Gnostics), that the one mediator between God and men is the man Christ Jesus (I Tim. 2:5, against their speculations concerning the *plērōma* and against their docetic Christology), that Christ joined this world and the spiritual world (I Tim. 3:16, against the docetic Christology and cosmological dualism of the gnostics[173]), that we await the appearing of the Lord in glory (Titus 2:13; II Tim. 4:8, against the Gnostic position that the resurrection is already past).

The "aim" of religion is not "knowledge" (*gnōsis*), but "righteousness, godliness, faith, love, steadfastness, gentleness" (I Tim. 6:11; cf. 6:4). The gospel of God trains us "to live sober, upright, and godly lives in this world" (Titus 3:12). That there is a connection between orthodoxy and morality is assumed but hardly demonstrated in the Pastorals. Sound morality apparently can be determined by the traditional moral commonplaces that any but the heretics would accept. The gospel exercised little critical and transformative power on the sources of moral wisdom that are assimilated and used in the Pastorals. The virtues and vices listed[174] (I Tim. 1:9,10; 3:2-3; II Tim. 3:2-5; Titus 1:7-8, etc.) are largely commonplaces for that time. The position on the law simply affirms it against the libertines and protects it against Gnostic and speculative interpretations (I Tim. 1:8). Most strikingly and troublesomely, the conventional use of *Haustafeln* stresses the submission of women (I Tim. 2:9-15; Titus 2:3-5)[175] and slaves (I Tim. 6:1-2; Titus 2:9) without being balanced by appeals for mutual submission. The exhortations to pray for (I Tim. 2:2) and to be submissive to (Titus 3:1) rulers are commonplace to Hellenistic Judaism and are not transformed here by being set in the context of loving the neighbor in a still selfish world (cf. Rom. 13:1-7). The treatment of riches is also traditional (I Tim. 6:6-10; vss. 7 and 10 especially reflect moral commonplaces, being virtually proverbs of the time), but the final exhortation (I Tim. 6:17-19) uses the eschatological perspective both to stand against asceticism and to demand that the rich be "rich in good deeds, liberal and generous." Orthodoxy and morality are a matched set, but the determination of what is good and right depends more on the common moral assumptions of his readers than on any "new discernment." Perhaps precisely because of the necessity to resist Gnostic ascetic and libertine tendencies, it was important soberly to reinforce mundane obligations as taught in the law and acknowledged in this world.

The acceptance and assimilation of the common moral assumptions of the readers determines as well the special ethical vocabulary of the Pastorals, which is so close to the vocabulary of Greek ethics. The most telling example may well be "godliness" (Gk. *eusebeia*). The word is the Pastorals' favorite term to describe the way of life they require.[176] Such "godliness" is considered virtually of one piece with holding fast to the teachings handed down in the Pauline tradition through the succession of teachers (I Tim. 6:3). Orthodoxy and morality are a matched set; the teaching "accords with godliness" (I Tim. 6:3; Titus 1:1). Indeed, "godliness" can be used as a synonym for the tradition (I Tim. 3:16). Elsewhere it is a summary of the way of life required (I Tim.

4:7; II Tim. 3:12). Frequently it is associated with other virtues or contrasted with vices, which vices are attributed to the heretics. It stands, for example, closely linked with other telling descriptions of the Christian life in I Timothy 2:2: "a quiet and peaceable life, godly and respectful in every way." That prosaic description of the Christian life, moreover, is identified as "good" and "acceptable in the sight of God our Savior" (I Tim. 2:3). It is linked with a series of other virtues which, in quite un-Pauline fashion, the author exhorts his reader to "aim at": "righteousness, godliness, faith, love, steadfastness, gentleness" (I Tim. 6:11). Again it is tellingly linked with living righteously (Gk. *dikaiōs*) and moderately (Gk. *sōphponōs*, another favorite Greek concept in the Pastorals; Titus 2:12). "Godliness" comes to concrete expression in "contentment," the mastery of self which is the "gain" of godliness and quite inconsistent with the heretics' desire for wealth (I Tim. 6:5,6; cf. 4:8); it is practiced by supporting one's aged parents (I Tim. 5:4, in obedience to the law surely; contrast II Cor. 12:14). The eschatological situation is never quite forgotten (see I Tim. 4:7-8; Titus 1:1-2; 2:12-13), but the ethic of the Pastorals is settling into the world, establishing itself over against the world-denial of the heretics, whether in the form of asceticism or libertinism. The ethic is moderate, not heroic. The key to "godliness" and to the ethic of the Pastorals is moderation and sober good sense, avoiding enthusiastic foolishness.

C. THE CATHOLIC EPISTLES AND HEBREWS

Seven letters, James, I and II Peter, I, II, and III John, and Jude,[177] are often called the "Catholic Epistles" because they are not addressed to a particular audience but to a wider public. Hebrews can be counted among them for that very reason. Perhaps Paul's letters had already been collected and circulated (II Peter at least knows such a collection), and so the epistle has become a literary form in the early church. These letters are generally concerned with preserving the authentic Christian tradition against the threat of heretics on the one hand and with encouraging the Christian community in the midst of persecution on the other. The Christian moral tradition is also handled within this context, and in ways sometimes quite distinctive.

1. Hebrews: New Covenantal Exhortation

Hebrews describes itself as a "word of exhortation" (Gk. *logos paraklēseōs*, 13:22), and so it is. The sustained and involved theological arguments are punctuated and climaxed by vibrant exhortations to acknowledge the truth and act on it (2:1-4; 3:7-4:13; 5:11-6:12; 10:19-39; 12:1-13:19). The author, whoever he or she[178] may be, is not interested in theological or exegetical elegance for its own sake, but for the sake of showing his/her readers their great privilege and the immeasurable loss that would be theirs if they were to let the passage of time — whether in hardship or in ease — weary them in their "struggle against sin" (12:4). Words of warning are repeated again and again (2:1; 3:6; 4:11; 5:11; 6:4-12; 10:23,29,32-39; 12:4-17,25-29). The readers must "pay the closer attention to what we have heard, lest we drift away from it" (2:1). Indeed, one exhortation is to engage in mutual exhortation daily that no one be "hardened by the deceitfulness of sin" (3:13; cf. 10:23-25).

a. THE NEW COVENANT

The theological basis for this "word of exhortation" is the covenant, more explicitly, the "second" covenant (8:7), which is "new" (8:8,13; 9:15; 12:24) and "better" (7:22; 8:6) than the former covenant. The old covenant is judged a failure and "obsolete" (8:13). But just as the old covenant was established by God, so the new covenant is established by God (8:8-9). Just as the old covenant contained stipulations and laws, so the new covenant provides the context for the requirements placed on a covenantal people, which are, however, no longer in the form of a written code (8:10; 10:16). And just as the covenant contained blessings and curses, so the new covenant includes blessings and the threat of judgment (e.g., 10:26-31,35-36). The difference is that the old covenant failed to accomplish God's intention; it failed to create a people who would do his will; its stipulations and sacrifices did not and could not "perfect the conscience of the worshipper" (9:9-10). The new covenant is "better," indeed "eternal" (13:20), precisely because it is based on God effectively and "once for all" dealing with sins[179] in the new and "perfect high priest Jesus Christ" (7:26-28; 9:11-14,23-28; 10:10-18). His offering of himself in the covenant, in contrast to the ritual sacrifices of the old covenant, did deal effectively with sins and could "purify" the believer's conscience and enable him to "serve the living God" (9:14; cf. 10:8-10). In place of the offerings of the old covenant required in the law, then, the author of Hebrews invites his/her readers to "offer to God acceptable worship, with reverence and awe" (12:28). Such worship may not be reduced to ritual or code, but it is the requirement of the new covenant no less seriously than those offerings abolished by Christ were requirements of the old covenant, written in the law. In the benediction, it is the author's prayer that the God who raised the crucified Christ from the dead and thus made "eternal covenant" may equip his/her readers that they "may do his will" (13:20-21). God may be trusted to keep covenant, and the exhortation is given to Christians that they keep covenant also.

b. KEEPING COVENANT

Cultic observance, priestly duties, temple service are all simply things of the past; the division of sacred and profane is done away. Instead, the new worship occurs when the Son intercedes with the Father (7:25) and when his people "continually offer up a sacrifice of praise to God" (13:15). The author, of course, is not opposed to meeting together; indeed, he/she is opposed to the "neglecting" of regular meetings (10:25); but the purpose of such meetings is not to observe some ritual but "to stir one another to love and good works" (10:24). Such is the stuff of the continuous sacrifice of praise offered by God's new covenanted people.

There is, I must acknowledge, very little concrete instruction in Hebrews. The concern is less to help the church discern what they ought to do than to exhort the church to do what it knows it ought to: the problem is not knowing what to do but doing what it knows. The Christian moral tradition has already formed the consciences of these people; the task the author undertakes is to exhort them against inattention to what they know (2:1), against disobedience (4:11), against becoming dull of hearing (5:11), against being "sluggish" (6:12).

The mode of discernment in Hebrews, therefore, can only be a matter of speculation. However, the old law seems not to have played a role in their discernment of what they ought to do. The old law, with its ritual observances and other stipulations, apparently simply belongs to the past. It "was valid" and "declared by angels" (2:2), but now one greater than the angels (1:4) has come. With the change in the priesthood comes a change in the law as well (7:12). Gentiles — and apparently Jewish Christians too — need not observe the law. The law is treated usually either as predictive (e.g., Heb. 8:8-12, the fulfillment of Jer. 31:31-34; Heb. 12:26, the promise of the fulfillment of Haggai 2:6) or as symbolic — in however shadowy a way — of the new covenant realities[180] (e.g., Heb. 9:9a). Hebrews never treats the law as a moral code or guide. This is not to say that the law is without moral significance for the author. He/she uses the law as a shadowy symbol of God's just and unfailing punishment of vice and disobedience (2:2-3; 4:5,11; 12:16-17) and of his gracious and unfailing reward of virtue and faithfulness (6:11-15; 11:4-12:2). Such a use of the law makes it serviceable to the author's task of exhortation, but it is not the basis for the author's discernment.

Apparently, discernment relies mainly on the Christian traditional paraenesis, which is used in chapter 13.[181] The paraenetic tradition, however, and the discernment that used it are set in the context of response to the new covenant, a response of gratitude and worship in all of life (13:15-16).

The thirteenth chapter does not identify and address concrete crises in the life and fellowship of those Christians addressed in this epistle. Indeed the admonition is, "Let brotherly love *continue*" (13:1, italics mine). The admonition to "remember those who are in prison" (13:3) recalls the earlier commendation for their "compassion on the prisoners" (10:34a). Similarly, the admonition to contentment (13:5-6) recalls the commendation of their "joyful" acceptance of the plundering of their property, "since you knew that you yourselves had a better possession and an abiding one" (10:34b). But if it is wrong to suppose that the admonitions of chapter 13 address particular crises, it is nevertheless fair to say that the author selects these admonitions as particularly urgent paradigms of new covenant life.

The weakening of faith and resolve, which the author admonishes against so persistently in general terms, threatens to weaken the covenant bonds that unite Christians with each other as well as with the Lord, and therefore the plea to "let brotherly love continue" (13:1) is particularly urgent. Concrete applications of "brotherly love" include hospitality to strangers (13:2), a sympathetic identification with prisoners and all who suffer (13:3), respect for marriage (13:4), and contentment (13:5-6). Love requires chastity and contentment; it is inconsistent with covetousness of either the neighbor's spouse or the neighbor's goods.

The challenge provided by "diverse and strange teachings" (13:9) makes particularly urgent the advice to remember their former leaders, to imitate their faith (13:7), and to obey and submit to their current leaders (13:17).

These duties are paradigms of the response of gratitude and praise that keeping covenant requires. All such duties are summarized in 13:16, where they are identified as the "sacrifices" appropriate to the new covenant: "Do not neglect to do good and to share what you have, for such sacrifices are pleasing to God." All of life is worship: "holy unto the Lord" is written on the common and mundane.

c. THE DISCIPLINE OF GOD

The old covenant included blessings and curses; God was constantly responding to the responses to his covenant. The author of Hebrews consistently draws attention to the same reality in the new covenant (e.g., 2:2-4; 4:1-11). The sufferings the community endures, however, are not considered retributive and certainly not vengeful; they are a fatherly discipline exercised for the perfecting of his children (12:5-11). The readers are to learn from the sufferings of Christ not to "grow weary or fainthearted" (12:3). Christ himself, the Son, was made perfect and learned obedience through suffering (2:10; 5:8). Thus he is the great high priest, able to sympathize with our suffering but without sin (4:14-5:10). We can bear suffering, then, in the confidence that God's fatherly care intends our good, that Jesus, "the pioneer and perfecter of our faith" (12:2), can sympathize with us and make intercession for us, and that we may learn through suffering (12:11).

The discipline, of course, can sometimes sound the note of judgment. To refuse the discipline of the Father is not a matter to be taken lightly. The author warns against apostasy and deliberate sin with rigorous severity (6:4-6; cf. also 10:26-31; 12:16-17). Tertullian[182] and others have understood Hebrews to be introducing a system of penitential discipline into the church within which there is no possibility of a second repentance. But the author makes neither a dogmatic point nor a ruling for canon law; he/she is engaged in pastoral exhortation, and is warning his/her audience about the urgency of continuing steadfast in the faith. The author is neither telling the leaders what rules to follow in dealing with those who have fallen away nor telling the apostates that there is no hope; he/she is writing to the "beloved" (6:9) that they may endure and "receive what is promised" (10:36).

2. James: Moral Miscellany

The "letter" of James is really a "paraenesis," a didactic text that collects moral instructions, often — as here — into a miscellany without a single focus.[183] It is as such that it must be read and understood, but as such it defies systematization and summarization. The moral instructions themselves are eclectic and draw from a variety of sources, including Greek morality, the wisdom literature of Hellenistic Judaism, the law and the prophets, and the sayings of Jesus.[184]

James' interest is not a theological one: he does not undertake to provide either a theological basis for morality or a theological transformation of morality. He is a pedagogue, not a theologian. But he certainly writes as a Christian. He identifies himself as "a servant of God and of the Lord Jesus Christ" (1:1; cf. 2:1) and reminds his readers of "the coming of the Lord" (5:7-8). He uses the memory of Jesus' words quite extensively,[185] and the expectation of Jesus' return grounds the exhortation to patience and marks the whole paraenesis with urgency and stringency.[186] If there is any theological basis to be discerned in James, it seems to be the memory of Jesus' proclamation of a "great reversal." James 2:5 plainly articulates such a reversal of the kingdom; James 4:6-10 warns that the proud will be humbled and the humble exalted, and calls for repentance; and James 5:1 announces woes upon the rich. But more than the occasional explicit citation of axioms of the great reversal, the whole ethos of James — the animosity toward "the world" (4:4), the warnings against judgment (2:13; 4:12), the calls for humble submission to God (4:10) and for readiness to help (2:14-16) — is an ethos of the poor, of the *anawim,* who look for God's vindication and a great reversal.[187]

a. "JUSTIFIED BY WORKS"

James is perhaps best known for its polemic against "justification by faith alone" (Jas. 2:14-26). The relationship of James' polemic to Paul's is controversial, to be sure,[188] but there can be little doubt that James' remarks presuppose the activity of Paul and his announcement of "justification by faith apart from works of the law" (Rom. 3:28). Dibelius[189] has made that clear. Dibelius stops short, however, of suggesting that James' polemic is addressed against Paul himself. That step is taken — and adroitly — by Jack Sanders, who argues not only on the basis of the common use of the Abraham example and explicitly Genesis 15:6 (which can be explained on the basis of the widespread use of Abraham as an example of faith in Jewish paraenesis),[190] but more critically on the basis of the linguistic parallels and contrasts between James 2:24 and Romans 3:28.[191] Sanders' conclusion is inescapable: James "seeks deliberately to counter Romans 3f."[192]

But one must ask why. James is hardly interested in defending a different theology of justification or a new concept of faith. Indeed, he acknowledges the important priority of God's gracious action (1:17-18). He is interested only in undercutting the opportunity to rationalize one's avoidance of obvious duty (2:14-17, the duty of caring for the needy). It is not Pauline theology that he opposes as much as the use of Pauline slogans and of the Pauline letters to justify libertine conduct (cf. II Pet. 3:14-17).[193] Such a use of Pauline materials is, of course, a misunderstanding and misrepresentation of Paul (witness I Corinthians). And if James had stood within the Pauline tradition in the churches, he undoubtedly would have attempted to demonstrate that such an understanding and use of Paul was inappropriate. But he does not stand in the Pauline circle, and so he polemicizes not against the misuse of a slogan but against the slogan itself. James, like Paul himself, wanted a faith that acts (2:22; cf. Gal. 5:6; see also Jas. 1:22-25; cf. Mt. 7:24-27). A faith that does not issue in deeds is for Paul inconceivable, for James reprehensible. For Paul faith exists as obedience; the indicative can also be announced as an imperative. For James the relationship of faith and obedience, of indicative and imperative, has been rendered problematic by the claims of certain putative Paulinists, and his solution is to insist on works along with faith. To accuse James of synergism, however, presupposes a theological interest that he did not have.[194]

b. THE LAW

James posed the issue of the relationship of faith and works without any reference to the law. Indeed, "works of the law" in Romans 3:28 becomes simply "works" in James 2:24. His polemic against the Pauline slogan is not given as much in defense of the law as in defense of practical and concrete helpfulness (2:15-16). There is no defense of circumcision or other ritual obligations of the law in James; his silence on such questions would seem to announce his lack of interest in such regulations of the law. Indeed, he thoroughly relativizes such regulations by insisting on the overriding religious (Gk. thrēskos, 1:26; thrēskeia, 1:27) significance of morality, explicitly controlling one's tongue, practicing kindness toward orphans and widows, and moral purity (1:26-27).[195]

This is not to say that "the law" is unimportant for James. Quite the contrary, he uses the term ten times in his instructions (1:25; 2:8,9,10,11,12; 4:11, four times), and often with a qualifying phrase (1:25; 2:8,12). Of special importance is James' reference to the law as the "perfect law of freedom" (RSV: "the perfect law, the law of liberty," 1:25; cf. 2:12). Here too James uses tradition; if he had created this concept, it would have been necessary to clarify and define it. His audience knows the concept, probably bred from Diaspora Judaism out of Stoic concepts (cf. the parallel expression "the implanted word," Gk. logos, of 1:21) by Hellenistic Jewish Christians.[196] The "perfect law of freedom" is the moral law; it is not identical with the letter of the law of Moses, but it includes the spiritual and ethical interpretation of that law.

James uses this tradition as part of his response to the putative Paulinists and their false understanding of "freedom," but he does not thereby adopt a "right-wing circumcision party" position with respect to the law. It is the interesting position of Dan Via, Jr., that James "wants to break through legalism."[197] But legalism is not the problem of James' audience: they had already decided against the right-wing circumcision party and adopted a more cosmopolitan attitude toward the Jewish law. The problem is rather the false understanding of faith and freedom that was emerging with reputed Pauline backing. In his address to that problem, James makes use of the tradition concerning the law already found among his audience.

James presupposes the same understanding of the law when he appeals to the love commandment to judge the favoritism shown to the rich in the assembly (5:8). He refers to the love commandment as the "the royal law,"[198] but he does not reduce the law to or identify it with the love commandment; otherwise, the argument of 5:10 would make no sense.[199] Instead, the love commandment is *primus inter pares* in the law. The law includes the whole of morality, and nothing but morality. The argument that "whoever keeps the whole law but fails in one point has become guilty of all of it" (5:10)[200] is clearly indebted to the Jewish tradition, but James uses it quite innocently of any rabbinical defense of the "lesser commandments" (contrast Gal. 5:3). The examples he cites are moral ones — adultery and murder (2:11); he does not include ritual or cultic obligations. The argument presupposes not a pharisaical understanding of the law but the conviction that morality is of one piece, and James uses it against any who would consider themselves "moral" while they practice partiality toward the rich. If James' understanding of the law was rabbinical, one might expect to see the simple citation of, say, Leviticus 19:15 in this context rather than the sort of argument he gives. The love commandment, the royal law, the first among equals in morality, entails impartiality;[201] so one may not show favoritism to the rich without violating the whole of morality, the "whole law."

The law for James is certainly normative, but it cannot simply be identified with the 613 commandments of the Torah nor with the single commandment of love. It is morality as morality is known through Scripture and "wisdom" and borne in the traditional paraenesis that James draws upon and hands down.

c. CONCRETE INSTRUCTION

It is impossible to identify any single theme of James' paraenesis, but there is an unmistakable focus on sympathy for the poor, along with the accompanying rebuke of the rich. That this is a special interest of James may be seen in his repeating such expressions of sympathy and rebuke (1:9-11; 2:1-7; 5:1-6), in his use of proper conduct toward the poor and needy as illustration of the relationship of faith and works (2:15-16),[202] and in his relating "impartiality" to the "royal law," the love commandment (2:8,9; cf. 2:1).

In such instructions, although there continues to be a variety of sources for the paraenesis, the memory of Jesus' words and the expectation of his final triumph are especially vivid. The great reversal still challenges the conventional reliance upon wealth (1:9-11; 4:13-5:3); and it still demands the responses of welcoming the poor (2:2-4), of impartiality (2:1,9) and justice (5:4), and of concrete charity (1:27; 2:15-17). The reign of God establishes a new social reality in which those who are lowly according to the world's standards are exalted and those who are exalted according to the world's standards — the rich — are humbled. This new social reality is an eschatological one, to be sure, but it already has and must have some effect in the communities James addresses. If there is any cause for boasting, it is surely not in the arrogant security the world's standards provide (4:13-16), but in that new social reality (1:9-11). James calls on the whole community to accept that reign, to "humble yourselves before the Lord" (4:10).

Another focus of James' admonitions concerns the use of the tongue (1:19,26; 3:1-12; 4:11; 5:9,12). There are echoes here of instructions and metaphors found in Jesus' sayings, Hellenistic Judaism, and Stoicism; the eclecticism of James' paraenesis is unmistakable.[203] James compares the tongue to a flame that can set ablaze a whole forest (3:5). Anyone who can control his tongue is capable of controlling his whole life (using the images of the horse's bit and the ship's rudder, 3:3-4). But the tongue is a recalcitrant little bit of flesh, untamable (3:7-8). The tongue reveals our double-mindedness, for with it we bless God and curse persons who are made in the image of God (3:9). It is clear that this should not be, but it is reinforced in another series of illustrations taken from nature (3:11-12). It is hardly possible and probably unfruitful to identify the closest parallels to these instructions — whether the sayings of Jesus, Jewish paraenesis, or Stoic morality. James simply utilizes traditional paraenesis here for the sake of moral persuasiveness, not for the sake of providing specifically Christian admonitions or motives. Even where the reliance on the tradition of Jesus' words is clear (5:12; cf. Mt. 5:33-37), the author provides it as paraenesis without citing it as a word of the Lord. Such morality does not require religious backing. The demands of truthfulness and the prohibitions of slander do not depend on any specifically Christian grounds for their justification. Even so, the context within which such demands and prohibitions are handed down and acted on is eschatologically charged. A struggle between God and the reign of evil occurs every time we open our mouths and let loose our tongues (3:6-8); and "behold, the Judge is standing at the doors" (5:9; cf. 5:12). The morality may be commonplace, but James gives it an eschatological urgency and stringency.

The present time is a time of testing, of "various trials" (1:2). James makes that point first of all. "Trials" (Gk. *peirasmoi*) can mean either afflictions or tests; in either case it is characteristic of our eschatological situation. The one who endures trial "will receive the crown of life" (1:12, where *peirasmos* probably meant "affliction" in the tradition James draws upon, but may refer to "test" for James). This eschatological situation does not provide excuses but rather makes more urgent the vigilance against evil desire (1:13-15). Already James' readers may — and must — rely on God (1:16-17; note the interest in prayer, 1:5-8; 4:3,8; 5:13-18) and submit to him (4:7). The tests of such reliance and submission are moral ones: bridling the tongue, concrete deeds of charity, and moral purity or integrity.

3. I Peter[204]: Owning One's Baptism

Some have identified I Peter (or its source) with a baptismal homily.[205] Such an identification overstates the case, but the baptismal allusions are clear[206] and leave their mark on the ethic of this Epistle.

The readers are "newborn babes" (2:2): they have been "born anew to a living hope through the resurrection of Jesus Christ from the dead" (1:3; cf. 1:23). This is cause for great joy (1:6,8); but it is also reason to "be sober, set your hope fully upon the grace that is coming to you at the revelation of Jesus Christ" (1:13). This jubilation and sobriety presuppose the eschatological situation between the resurrection of Jesus Christ (1:3) and the revelation of Jesus Christ (1:13). Such an eschatological perspective corresponds to Paul's and, like his, issues in moral instructions where indicative and imperative stand in intimate relationship.

Peter exhorts the "newborn" to be "obedient children," not to be "conformed to the passions of your former ignorance" (1:14). They have "purified" themselves "for a sincere love of the brethren" (1:22a), and he exhorts them to "love one another earnestly from the heart" (1:22b). The new moral identity they have in baptism can be expressed both in the indicative mood and in the imperative mood. Peter describes them as "ransomed from the futile ways inherited from your fathers" (1:18), and he exhorts them to "abstain from the passions of the flesh which wage war against your soul" (2:11). The sober attention to the imperative does not diminish the joy, but it does acknowledge that Christians are still threatened by "the passions of the flesh," though their doom is sure, and therefore are still responsible for holding fast to the new life that is given them in Christ.

Peter describes the new identity they are given in baptism in many different ways, all of them subtle exhortations as well. They are "sanctified by the Spirit for obedience to Jesus Christ" (1:2); they are incorporated into Christ, the "living stone," and like living stones themselves are to be "built into a spiritual house" (2:4-5); they are "a chosen race, a royal priesthood, a holy nation, God's own people" (2:9,10); they are "aliens and exiles" (2:11); "freemen" and "servants of God" (2:16).

The eschatological perspective is pronounced. Peter exhorts them to hope (1:13; cf. 1:4,5,20), warns them of the judgment (1:17; 4:17), and reminds them that the end is "at hand" (4:7). They live in the last days — days of testing and crisis before the final triumph of God — and they are to live them in mutual love and quiet confidence.

The eschatological perspective on morality is perhaps nowhere better seen than in I Peter's emphasis on "glory" (Gk. *doxa*) and its equivalents.[207] In general, and in I Peter particularly, the word has eschatological associations. The prophets predicted "the sufferings of Christ and the subsequent glory" (1:11); in raising Jesus from the dead, God "gave him glory" (1:21); and his glory will be revealed at the last day (4:13; 5:1).[208] It is to this glory that believers are "called" (5:10), and even now it is possible provisionally and proleptically to share in that glory, to partake "in the glory that is to be revealed" (5:1). That sort of existence is now both gift and demand. The demand comes in the form of the exhortations to love one another, to practice hospitality, and to use God's gifts for one another "that in everything God may be glorified through Jesus Christ" (4:11). And the demand also comes in the form of the exhortations now to rejoice to "share Christ's sufferings" (4:13; cf. 4:16), "because the spirit of glory and of God rests upon you" (4:14). The eschatological existence is doxological existence for I Peter, and doxological existence encompasses the moral life.

The requirement of love is certainly a basic principle for I Peter (1:22; 2:17; 3:8; 4:8): it is related both to the identity of Christians and to their eschatological situation. The baptismal admonition of 1:22,23 takes up the statements of identity in the greeting and opening prayer (1:2-5). They are "sanctified by the Spirit of God for obedience to Jesus Christ" (1:2). The admonition begins, "Having purified your souls by your obedience to the truth for a sincere love of the brethren . . ." (1:22). The participle "having purified" (Gk. *hēgnikotes*, from *hagnizō*) takes up the "sanctified" (Gk. *hagiasmoi*), and "obedience" takes up the "obedience" of 1:2; but the thought is advanced in each case. Their sanctification is effected by the Spirit (1:2), to be sure, but not without their own obedience. It is both gift and demand. Moreover, "obedience to Jesus Christ" is further specified as "obedience to the truth" (as an equivalent of obedience to the gospel). And such sanctification and obedience take concrete shape in sincere love for the brethren. Faith exists as obedience, and obedience exists as love no less for Peter than for Paul. The eschatological situation is identified in 4:7a in terms of the nearing end, and it is used to introduce a series of admonitions that climax in a doxology (4:11). As one would expect, there is the traditional admonition to be "sane and sober" (4:7b), but the imperative set "above all" is "love for one another" (4:8). The allusion to Proverbs 10:12 in "love covers a multitude of sins" (4:8) must be explained in terms of the eschatological context: that if love is at work within the church, God's judgment will be marked by his own mercy and love.[209] The works of love within the community are exemplified in ungrudging hospitality (4:9) and in "stewardship" of God's varied gifts in service to one another (4:10,11).[210] Such acts of love already glorify God (4:11). They demonstrate a new order and evoke praise; they already participate in the doxological and eschatological existence to which Christians are called.

I Peter does not emphasize the principle of freedom, so important to Paul. He mentions it (2:16a, "live as free men"), but only to dissociate it from license (2:16b, "yet without using your freedom as a pretext for evil") and to associate it with submission to God (2:16c, "but live as servants of God"). The Christian is freed to "do right" (2:14,15,20; 3:6,17; 4:19). Peter does not spell out the meaning of "doing right" in terms of the Mosaic law but in terms of the Christian paraenetic tradition[211] and in terms of what is universally acknowledged as responsible conduct. Indeed, to be freed for the service of God is to be freed to "be subject for the Lord's sake to every human institution" (2:13). It is God's will that Christians should live lives beyond any possible reproach. Such lives will silence their detractors and be serviceable to the missionary enterprise of the church (2:15; cf. 2:12; 3:1-2,16).

This is the context for the *Haustafel* of I Peter. He does not forget the eschatological situation (2:11-12), but his concern governing the use of the traditional paraenesis is more clearly simply "good conduct," "doing right," for the sake of the advancement of the church's cause. Even so, we can see the transformation of conventional role responsibilities here. The traditional exhortation to be subject to civil authorities (2:13-16) is here balanced on one side by the exhortation to freedom (2:16). Peter's readers are not merely subjects; indeed, they are "aliens" and "exiles" (2:11). Their submission is a free submission, not a constrained one. It is balanced on the other side by the recognition of God's greater authority (2:13,16,17). And finally, Peter puts the obligation to "honor the emperor" in the context of a series of other obligations, obligations that may override duties to the emperor: "Honor all men. Love the brotherhood."

The exhortation to slaves to be submissive (2:18-25) is not balanced by any exhortation to masters to recognize one impartial master in heaven (but see 1:17 and 2:23). However, it becomes Peter's occasion for introducing the important theme of Christ's suffering as an example (2:21-23) as well as an atonement (2:24-25). The slave who participates in Christ's sufferings as a gift is expected to follow the model of nonretaliation and patient endurance of unjust treatment. "To this you have been called" (2:21) patently does not refer to the "calling" or "vocation" of slavery but rather to the participation in Christ's suffering; the role of slave is simply the place where that higher calling is fulfilled. And just as Christ's suffering led to his vindication and glory, so slaves may, like Jesus, "trust to him who judges justly" (2:23; cf. 1:17). Finally, it should be observed that this advice is not given to slaves alone; rather, it is repeated as an admonition to all (cf. 3:9 with 2:21-23).

The exhortation to wives (3:1-6)[212] is given a missionary motive (3:1-2) and is balanced by a reciprocal exhortation to husbands "likewise" to treat "the weaker sex" with consideration and honor as "joint heirs."[213] The recognition of the status of women as "joint heirs" (cf. Num. 27:1-11; 36:1-12) subtly challenges and relativizes the otherwise conventional role assignments and, indeed, the denigrating designation of women still found here. The spiritual equality of women with men does not create new role expectations, but it does at least produce a creative tension between the conventional dispositions toward women and Christian ones, a tension that would not honor any attempt to turn these exhortations into an iron and eternal code.

"Finally," Peter makes mutual submission and the patient endurance of unjust suffering the duty of all (3:8-9). Love of the brethren and love of the enemy are to mark the community in the midst of its endurance of persecution.[214] The same point is made in the ecclesiastical code. The "younger" are to be subject to "the elders" (5:5), but that exhortation is balanced by the earlier exhortation to the elders not to "domineer" but to be examples themselves (5:3) by following Christ's example surely. Moreover, these exhortations, too, lead up to the requirement of mutual submission, of "humility toward one another" (5:5; cf. also the rule for the exercise of gifts "for one another," 4:10-11).

Peter does not disown the civic, domestic, and ecclesiastical relationships. He accepts them as the context within which one's relationship with Christ and his patient love can have effect while one waits for Christ's revelation in glory. Thus they are subtly but constantly transformed and reformed by being brought into association with the Christian moral identity and perspective. It is in terms of one's baptism, finally, one's dying with Christ and living in hope, that I Peter understands the moral life, emphasizing a new moral identity, an eschatological perspective, the duties of mutual love and nonretaliation, and encompassing civic, domestic, and ecclesiastical relationships.

4. II Peter and Jude

These two Epistles resemble one another in many ways: vocabulary, phrasing, order, and also in their theological and moral concerns.[215] They both ardently defend orthodoxy and morality against the heretics who "promise freedom" (II Pet. 2:19) but "pervert the grace of God into licentiousness" (Jude 4; cf. II Pet. 2:2), who "scoff" at the promise of Christ's return (II Pet. 3:3-4; cf. Jude 18).

Both Epistles are content to defend the tradition of the church by accusing the heretics of all kinds of misconduct. Both use the Old Testament to provide examples — mostly the same ones — of God's rigorous judgment against sinners.[216] Both claim that the abandonment of orthodoxy and morality renders these heretics "creatures of instinct" (II Pet. 2:12; Jude 10). The selfish and drunken behavior of these heretics at the Christian fellowship meal draws a special rebuke in both (Jude 12; II Pet. 2:13).

Jude seems addressed to some special crisis in the church (Jude 4 identifies "some" who have gained admission to the church). II Peter comes later, probably used Jude, and enlisted Peter's authority against those who were using Paul to justify their libertine behavior (see II Pet. 3:15-17).

II Peter's "redaction" of Jude discloses a couple of new moral concerns. We have mentioned the reference to the misuse of Paul's letters (3:15-17), but this is part of a broader concern about the individualistic reading of Scripture in general, which probably stands in the service of the heretics' antinomianism (3:16; 1:20,21). II Peter is also more concerned than is Jude with the delay of the parousia, and adds arguments in defense of the certainty of the Lord's return (3:8-10). He shares with Jude the confidence that God's judgment is sure, and that hope gives urgency to "lives of holiness and godliness" (3:11). But here II Peter adds a new note: such lives can actually "hasten [Gk. *speudō*] the coming of the day of God" (3:12). The rule of God is moral, not mechanical. God delays for the sake of providing time for repentance; he will respond to the response of people who live in "holiness and godliness" expecting him.

II Peter's redaction also adds a carefully wrought catalogue of virtues (1:5-8). God has given "all things that pertain to life and godliness" (1:3), and his gift demands our "every effort" (1:5; cf. 1:10). The list of virtues his readers are to cultivate begins with faith and ends with love. To their faith they are to add "virtue" (Gk. *aretē*, a classic term of Greek ethics used in the New Testament only in II Peter — notably also in 1:3b to refer to Christ's moral excellence, to which believers are "called" — and in Phil. 4:8). To faith and that virtue or moral excellence should be added "knowledge" (Gk. *gnōsis*),[217] which here probably refers to discernment of God's will (as in Phil. 1:9; Heb. 5:14). Then "self-control" (Gk. *enkrateia*) and "steadfastness" (Gk. *hypomonē*) are to be added; such self-discipline in matters relating to the senses and such endurance of suffering had already been key virtues in Greek morality for centuries. "Godliness" (Gk. *eusebeia*) is next on the list. We have observed that this Greek virtue was also a favorite of the Pastoral Epistles; in II Peter it occurs in 1:3,6,7; 2:9, 3:11; moreover, Peter describes the heretics as "ungodly" (Gk. *asebeis*). Finally and climactically, "brotherly affection" (Gk. *philadelphia*) and "love" (Gk. *agapē*) complete the program of Christian moral development this catalogue provides. The list is interesting because of both the prominence of Hellenistic vocabulary to describe the Christian life and the concern for moral development by the nurturing and supplementing of virtues. Peter certainly does not forget the basis of such a life in the gift of God, but the notes of progress and achievement in virtuous character are surely more Greek than Pauline. I should also observe, finally, that the list has one eye on the licentious immorality of the heretics and thus is an implicit rebuke of their lack of such virtues (cf. 1:9). Even so, it stands as a positive statement — assimilating a number of Greek virtues — of the requirements of Christian character and of an effective and fruitful Christian life (1:8).

D. THE JOHANNINE LITERATURE

The distinctive writings that bear the name of John in the New Testament include a Gospel, three Epistles, and an Apocalypse.[218] This literature contains certain common themes, which makes it legitimate to speak of a Johannine circle; but in many ways — including in their ethics — they are nearly as distinct from one another as they are from the remainder of the canon.

1. John's Gospel: Life in His Name

a. THE JEWISH BACKGROUND

John's Gospel differs from the Synoptic tradition in a variety of ways.[219] One distinctive feature of John's Gospel is the frequent use of "the Jews" as the opponents of Jesus (nearly seventy times). This has led some to accuse John of anti-Semitism. But John's Gospel never draws a contrast between "the Jews" and "the Gentiles" (indeed Gk. *ta ethnē* never occurs in the Gospel).[220] The contrast is rather between "the Jews" and "the Jews who had believed" (8:31; 2:23; 4:39, etc.). Indeed, only one Gentile — Pilate — figures in the narrative, and he makes it plain that he is an outsider (18:35).[221] Nowhere does John give the heritage of the Jews to the Gentiles,[222] and nowhere does he hold up a Gentile as an example of faith.[223] If he criticizes "the Jews," he criticizes them from within Judaism (e.g., 5:45-47; 7:19-24). Far from being anti-Semitic, John's Gospel competes with Matthew for the distinction of being the most Jewish of our Gospels. Where John does mention "Greeks" (Gk. *Hellēnes*, 7:35; 12:20), he is clearly referring to Greek-speaking Jews of the Diaspora, the group John is probably addressing.[224] The crisis John addresses is understood as a crisis within Judaism, specifically the crisis of the Jewish response to Jesus, their Messiah, a crisis already enacted in Judea and Galilee, then being repeated among Jews of the Diaspora. John's Jewish kin were confronted with a choice between light and darkness, between truth and falsehood, between life and death. They were making the choice in their response to their Messiah.

John's ethic must also be understood against this Jewish background. The law of Moses apparently still stands: "The law was given through Moses" (1:17a). It is true that this law stands as a preliminary to the "grace and truth" (the "steadfast love and faithfulness"; cf. Heb. *ḥesed* and *emeth*, e.g., Ex. 34:6) fully revealed in Jesus Christ (1:17b). It is true that the great Nicodemus, with his knowledge of the law, still must be "born anew" (3:3). The crisis was real; and the law by itself provided no protection against it. But John never discards or discredits the law. Indeed, the refusal to come to Jesus is a refusal to accept the testimony of Scripture (5:39-40) or to keep the law (7:19). It is Moses who will accuse those who refuse to accept Jesus as the eschatological prophet (5:45-47; cf. 4:19; 6:14; 7:40; 9:17; cf. Deut. 18:15).[225] The law stands.

As the eschatological prophet, Jesus renders final judgment about what the law requires. All judgment, including the eschatological judgment, belongs to him (5:21-29; 9:39; 3:17-21). As eschatological prophet, he settles the old dispute between Jews and Samaritans about whether the law requires worship in Jerusalem or Gerizim by discarding localized worship in favor of "worship in spirit and in truth" (4:19-24). He subordinates Sabbath observance to his work of healing (5:9b-18; 7:22-24; 9:13-34). In all of this, however, Moses remains an authority; but his authority is not to be used independently of Jesus or in judgment against Jesus (cf. also 5:39-47). Nowhere does John discredit the law — even circumcision (7:22) — or discard it.

If John thought that the crisis within Judaism bore upon the observance of the law, his readers would undoubtedly have heard more about it; but, as the Gospel stands, we can only assume that the law was to guide conduct in ways that were familiar to the synagogues and to the Christian conventicles within them (or recently exiled from them, 9:22; 12:42; 16:2) which John addresses. (It is also noteworthy that John does not provide Jesus' sayings concerning divorce, possessions, the state, and so forth. If he knows these traditions, he is evidently satisfied with their observance among the Christians.)

b. LIFE AND LOVE

The focus of John's moral concern in his Gospel is not the law or its messianic interpretation; the focus is rather Christ and the "life in his name" (20:31; 10:10; 12:50, etc.). "Life in his name" is inalienably a life formed and informed by love. Christ is the great revelation of God's love for the world (3:16). "The Father loves the Son" (3:35; 5:20; cf. 10:17; 15:9; 17:23,24,26); Jesus "abides" in the Father's love and does his commandments (15:10); Jesus "loves his own" (13:1; cf. 13:34; 14:21; 15:9,12); he instructs them to "abide in my love" (15:9) and to "keep my commandments" (15:10; cf. 14:15,21); and his commandment is "that you love one another as I have loved you" (15:12; 13:34; 15:17).[226]

John calls this a "new" commandment (13:34). The commandment, of course, is hardly novel, but it is "new" precisely because of the new situation Jesus had inaugurated. The new and true life Jesus gives is constituted by obedience to this commandment. The basis is not Scripture but Christ's own love, signed in the addition, "as I have loved you." The context makes the same point. Having announced that the hour for Jesus' glorification had come (13:1; cf. 12:23; 17:1), John provides his distinctive account of the Last Supper. Jesus washes the disciples' feet (13:1-11) and then instructs them to "wash one another's feet" (13:12-17). Jesus is exemplar (13:15) and teacher (13:13,14), but both his example and his instruction are set in the context of his glorification, of his vindication as the one in whom the Father acts in love. Christ, who makes the Father's love known, serves the disciples in love, and they are therefore obliged by what they have been given. Then, following the prophecy of the betrayal, John reiterates the theme of Jesus' glorification (13:31) to set the context for the "new commandment" (13:34). The new commandment rests on a new reality; the new imperative is based on a new indicative, the love of God in Christ and the love of Christ in his own.

John's narrative of the cross, unique and arresting in its description of

Jesus' crucifixion as his glorification (13:14; 8:28; 12:32,34), is related to this new commandment (e.g., 15:13; 10:17,18). Jesus does not go to the cross as a victim, humiliated and powerless; he is "lifted up" on the cross. This leaves its mark on John's narrative: there is no Gethsemane agony (cf. 12:27); Jesus instructs Judas to do his deed (13:27); at the arrest scene Jesus is clearly in control (18:4-11); he even carries his own cross (19:17). Such a narrative turns our conventional judgments of glory upside down and inside out. We behold his glory, "glory as of the only begotten of the Father" — on the cross in his self-sacrificing love! And this is the glory that Jesus shares with those who follow him (17:22) as indicative and imperative. They too are lifted up to be servants, exalted in self-giving love. There is indeed a "new" commandment born of the Christological and eschatological reality that John perceives and reports.

In contrast to the Synoptic tradition, the commandment in John's Gospel always refers to love for "one another," never to love for the neighbor or the enemy. Many have taken this to be a regrettable narrowing of the scope of love,[227] and it is undeniable that the commandment to love in John focuses on relations within the community. But a focus is not necessarily a restriction. The argument that John *restricts* love to members of the community is finally an argument from silence. John does not explicitly demand that we love our neighbors or our enemies, but neither does he — in contrast to Qumran[228] — demand that we hate those outside the community. The focus on love within the community follows from John's interest in the unity of the Father and the Son and the unity of the Son and the community in a hostile world. "For John, unity is a mark and quality of the heavenly realm in the same way in which truth, light, and life are the quality and mark of the heavenly realm."[229] In the community one may and must abide in Christ's love; there one may and must enact the concrete service that marks the new life. However, although John focuses on love within the community, he "does not mark any frontier."[230] Indeed, if there is any frontier at all, it is the mission to the whole world. "God so loved the world that he gave his only Son" (3:16).[231] Just as the Father has sent Christ into the world, so Christ sends his followers into the world (17:18; 20:21). The mission of the Father's love toward the world begins and continues with self-sacrificing love,[232] but it marks its success by mutual love, and that is John's focus both in proclamation and in exhortation. By the mutual love of the community, indeed, "the world may believe" (17:20-26). John's distinctive treatment of the love commandment does not license hatred of the enemy or of the neighbor; rather, it focuses on the fulfillment of God's love within the community. Love — even God's love, even *agapē* — seeks a response, an answering love. It seeks mutual love, and where it finds it, the heavenly realm is entered.

2. The Epistles of John: Knowing Love

The Epistles that bear John's name — like the Pastoral Epistles, II Peter, and Jude — are occasioned by the need to defend sound doctrine and morality against false teachers. But these Epistles make their defense in ways clearly oriented to the Johannine perspective.

John is probably citing and condemning the claims of the opponents in the series of contrasts at the beginning of the first Epistle that begin with the words "If we say . . ." (1:6,8,10) or "He who says . . ." (2:4,6,9). If so, the opponents claim to be in fellowship with God (1:6), to "abide in him" (2:6), to be "enlightened" (2:9) — indeed, to have some special *gnōsis* (2:4) — and to be without sin (1:8,10). It is evident from John's direct address to their positions (2:18-27; 4:1-6; 5:5-8; II Jn. 7-9) that they deny that the human, fleshly Jesus is the Christ. The opponents, then, may be identified as Christians influenced by Gnosticism. Their Gnostic dualism is unable to comprehend or appreciate the tradition that believes the human, embodied, and crucified Jesus is the Christ, so they honor Christ as a purely spiritual being. In him they claim already to exist fully in the Spirit, to have attained a spiritual perfection (1:8-10) and the capacity to do without the old commandments. They are — or claim to be — the spiritually elite, and their elitism leads them to withdraw from the community (2:19).

The response of these Epistles does not accuse them of libertine and licentious behavior (cf. Jude). It does not simply repeat and insist on traditional affirmations of faith and conventional standards of behavior. It calls for a reorientation to the life made manifest bodily to the eyes and hands (1:1-4) and thus, given the Johannine perspective, for brotherly love (e.g., I Jn. 2:9-11; 3:11,14-18,23; 4:7-12,16-21; II Jn. 5-6).

In opposition to the eschatology of the opponents, the author of I John reminds his readers of the "not yet," that "it is the last hour" (2:18), that temptations still threaten (2:15-17), that Christ's coming and judgment are still to be expected (2:28-3:3; 4:17). But the critical eschatological judgment has to do with the "already": "We know that we have passed out of death into life, because we love the brethren. He who does not love remains in death" (I Jn. 3:14). It is love that marks the new life, and the elitists who withdraw from the community only disclose by their withdrawal that they "are not of us" (2:19), that they do not share in the new life.

In opposing the perfectionism of the opponents, the author of I John realistically calls for the honest and humble confession of sins (1:8,10)[233] and practically calls for putting words, especially the claims to know and love God, into practice (*passim.* but especially 1:6; 2:4,9; 3:17,18; 4:8,20,21).

In opposing the antinomianism of the opponents, the author of I John emphasizes the importance of keeping the commandments of God. In 2:3,4, for example, to "know" God is inalienably related to keeping his commandments (cf. 3:22,24; 5:2,3; II Jn. 6). Not unlike in his Gospel's silent acceptance of the law, John never identifies "the commandments" here, except to say, "This is his commandment, that we should believe in the name of his Son Jesus Christ and love one another, just as he has commanded us" (3:23; cf. 4:21; II Jn. 6). "Commandments" and "commandment" often stand together, as though the author were reflecting on the relationship between the one and the many commandments. Moreover, the author insists that the new commandment (2:8, notice the eschatological associations) is not at all novel; it is really an old commandment (2:7; II Jn. 5). The new commandment stands in continuity not only with the beginning of Christian preaching and with Jesus' proclamation (2:7,24 and II Jn. 5,6 are probably to be taken in this sense) but also with God's intention from the very beginning, so that the devil's sin (3:8) and Cain's (3:11,12) are precisely their violation of the unity and love that mark the heavenly reign of God. Love is the primal will of God, the original and fundamental commandment, now fulfilled — or, to use a Johannine term, "perfected" (2:5; 4:12,17) — in Christ and in his community. The commandments are not discarded or discredited by the new reality or the new commandment; they are "kept" (2:3,4; 3:22-24; 5:3; II Jn. 5,6). Against the antinomians, then, the author of these Epistles insists on the inalienable relationship of the commandment of brotherly love to the other commandments. Even so, he does not accuse them of wantonly licentious behavior but of their violation of brotherly love.

Sound doctrine and sound morality are as indivisible here as in the Pastorals or in Jude, but here the connection between theological affirmation and moral exhortation is not merely presumed but exercised. The one commandment can be identified as "we should believe in the name of his Son Jesus Christ and love one another" (I Jn. 3:23).[234] To believe in this Jesus is to stand under the obligation to love. The relationship is clear again when his real death on the cross is the way in which "we know love" and in which the obligation to love the brethren is grounded (3:16; cf. 4:1-3,9-10). Or one need only consider the moral implications of the affirmation that "God is love" (4:8,16). The faith that God sent Jesus in the flesh, that Jesus died on the cross, and that he offers new life in the Spirit, expresses itself in love.

The scope of love in John's Epistles, just as in his Gospel, is primarily focused on the community, but again this focus should not be understood as a restriction. Indeed Bultmann says that in 2:9, 3:15, and 4:20, " 'Brother' means . . . not especially the Christian comrade in the faith, but one's fellowman, the 'neighbor.' "[235] Bultmann asserts too much here: "brother" clearly means member of the community in I John 3:13 and III John 3,5,10; and "to love the brother" is apparently used interchangeably with "to love each other" (cf. I Jn. 3:10,11,14,15,16,17,23; 4:7,11,12,20,21; see also 5:1,2).[236] But if claiming with Bultmann that "brother" does not mean "especially the Christian comrade in the faith" is asserting too much, claiming that only members of the community are to be loved is asserting too little. The missionary frontier is still present (I Jn. 2:1,2; 4:14).[237] If we know love from the death of Christ (3:16), and if Christ's death is not for us only but for the whole world (2:1,2), then it would be quite unreasonable for the author to *restrict* love to members of the community. Moreover, the reference to Cain and Abel (3:11-12) presupposes a broader application than just to the Christian community. And finally, the contrasts between love as a mark of existence in the light and hate as a mark of existence in the darkness (2:9,10) — and between love as a mark of the new life and hate as a mark of death (3:14) — lose their power if love is strictly *inter nos*, restricted to an inner circle. Thus, although he focuses on the community as a place where love must be put into practice, the author does not (and would not) deny that the whole world is the place where God's love is active and where the Christian's love must also be practiced.

3. The Revelation to John: Patient Endurence

Revelation (Gk. *apokalypsis*, 1:1) must surely be classified as apocalyptic literature. Such literature originated from Jewish and later from Christian circles between 200 B.C. and A.D. 100. These writings share elements of literary form and content. Formally, apocalyptic literature is concerned with the "unveiling" of the secrets of the end time; it is esoteric, usually visions or dreams of a seer in which the secrets of the world are made known to a select group; it always makes great use of symbols, usually including numerical symbols. Materially, apocalyptic literature shares the apocalyptic religious perspective.[238] Apocalyptic literature was not written, however, for the sake of entertainment or for the sake of divining the future. It was written to protest against oppressors and to console the oppressed. The context of most apocalyptic literature — and for Revelation — is a group's experience of alienation and oppression. Revelation was not intended — and it must not be read — to provide a basis for computing the date of the end or for calculating from an aloof and neutral position the next movement in the inevitable and determined course of world history. It was intended to provide consolation and encouragement to the churches in Asia Minor that found themselves powerless victims of the emperor's vicious injustice and persecution.[239] Revelation calls for watchfulness, not computation — for courage, not calculation.

The apocalyptic character of Revelation is unmistakable; however, we must not overlook that the apocalypse quite self-consciously adopts the letter format (note the epistolary salutation in 1:4-8 and the epistolary closing in 22:21). This confirms the judgment that Revelation is intended as concrete pastoral encouragement and exhortation to the churches in Asia Minor.

True to the literary form he has chosen, however, John's exhortation does not take the shape of moral admonitions and advice. Rather, the author constructs a symbolic universe to make intelligible both their faith that Christ is Lord and their daily experiences of injustice and suffering at the hands of Caesar. Such a symbolic universe with its intelligibility structure makes plausible and meaningful the "patient endurance" that Revelation calls for. The rock on which his universe is built, and on which he would have his readers build their lives, is the confidence that God has acted, is acting, and will act eschatologically in Jesus Christ (cf. 1:3-8). The material for his construction comes largely from the holy war tradition of Jewish prophets and seers with its roots in the ancient Near Eastern combat mythology.[240]

There are sovereignties in conflict:[241] on the one side are God, his Christ, and those who worship them; on the other are Satan, his vice regents, the beasts and "the kings of the earth," and those who prostrate themselves before them. The victory has been won by Christ, but Satan and his minions still battle and threaten Christ's people on earth. That, very briefly, is the background of intelligibility for their suffering and their obligations.

The seer is imprisoned on the island of Patmos, an exiled rebel, keen to be a part of the battle, anxious about the churches on the mainland where some try to avoid the conflict, accommodating Caesar and the standards of this age. "On the Lord's day" (1:10), the day the victory of Christ is celebrated, he sees and communicates his apocalyptic visions and his pastoral exhortation and encouragement. He and his audience share and are called to share with Jesus "the tribulation and the kingdom and the patient endurance" (1:9).

a. THE SEVEN LETTERS

The seven letters to the churches (2:1-3:22)[242] are the best clue to the focus of Revelation's exhortations. They are introduced by a magnificent vision of the living and reigning — though slain — Christ (1:10-20); it is he who finally addresses the churches. From the very beginning John identifies the basis for the commendations, censures, and commands to follow as the resurrection of the crucified Christ. Christ's authority was established by God's vindication and accepted by the church in their worship of him. After being introduced by the identical command to write "to the angel of the church in . . ." (2:1,8,12,18; 3:1,7,14), each letter identifies the speaker again and, although a great variety of images is used, each identification of the speaker acknowledges the unlimited lordship of Christ. There follows in each case (2:2,9,13,19; 3:1,8,15) a report of Christ's discernment of the church's character and conduct, his verdict on them, and his commandment to them. Revelation emphasizes the "works" of the churches. Especially commended is "patient endurance"; especially censured is any lack of loyalty to the cause; especially commanded is repentance and faithfulness. In each case these commendations, censures, and commands bear concretely on that particular congregation's life. The patient endurance that John commends and calls for takes the shape not only of continuing in the confession in the midst of the persecution by the emperor (2:3,10,13; 3:10), but also enduring the harassment of the Jewish synagogues which had cast them out (2:9; 3:9), resisting the false teachers (2:2,6,14,15,20), continuing in their earnest devotion to God (2:4; 3:15,16) and in their love and service of each other (2:19), and resisting the temptations to immorality (2:14,20; 3:4) and the seductions of ease (2:9; 3:17). The letters each close with a promise of a share in Christ's victory if they continue in the struggle (2:7,11,17,26-28; 3:5,12,21; the images of victory return in the last two chapters of Revelation). The conflict of sovereignties is not *a cosmic drama which one may view*[243] as though the seer is engaged in spectator sport; it is an eschatological battle for which one must enlist.

"Patient endurance" in these letters stands opposed to the policies and practices of certain false teachers, whom Revelation metaphorically calls "Nicolaitans," "Balaam," and "Jezebel."[244] Elizabeth Schüssler Fiorenza's analysis of these groups[245] is very helpful. Like the libertines in Corinth who argued that one may eat meat sacrificed to idols because idols have no real existence (I Cor. 8:4; cf. Rev. 2:14,20), these false teachers claimed that one may participate in the imperial cult because Caesar's claim to divinity was "nothing more than a constitutional fiction to promote political loyalty to Rome."[246] On that basis accommodation is possible and, indeed, desirable given the advice of the apostles to honor the emperor (Rom. 13:1-7; I Pet. 2:17). But John will not tolerate any such attempt at compromise; the conflict of sovereignties makes it treasonous. The freedom of patient endurance is not a freedom to accommodate the claims of Domitian and so to live comfortably, but a freedom from conventional standards of prosperity and power (Rev. 2:9; 3:8,17), a freedom to accept poverty and powerlessness in faithful loyalty to Christ and in the expectation of his final triumph and blessing, a freedom to resist the totalitarian and religious claims of Rome.

b. THE COUNTER-EMPIRE

The remainder of the book is a series of apocalyptic visions developing the promise to the churches of a share in Christ's victory and the basis of the exhortation to patient endurance.

The victory is already assured in the vision of the enthronement of the Lamb that was slain (chs. 4-5). The language of the vision is both political and liturgical. Heaven is portrayed less as a temple than as a throne room. Instead of acclaiming Domitian as "worthy" and as "Lord and God,"[247] the heavenly court/choir gives its praise to God and to his Christ, and they are joined by more and more until "every creature" (5:13) gives praise to the Lamb. That a slain lamb is counted worthy to reign stands in obvious contrast to the conventional and imperial understanding of power, but the Lamb is "the Lion of the tribe of Judah, the root of David" (5:5), and he has won the victory. By his death he has redeemed people from all nations to be "a kingdom and priests to our God, and they shall reign on earth" (5:10). The church already participates in the hymnic acclaim given the Lamb in its worship. More than that, it understands itself as already God's empire, God's kingdom — in Domitian's empire a counter-empire. They acknowledge Christ rather than the Caesar as Lord; their hymns are political as well as liturgical. They are heralds of God's reign and a token of its realization; they are the voice for now of the whole creation, of all that is abused and oppressed by the false sovereign, of all that will be liberated by the Lamb who was slain. The promise that they shall reign stands under the standard of the Lamb who was slain, not of Domitian's pomp and privilege. Their reign may thus, like his, paradoxically be found through their death but at least through "patient endurance."

The lion that is a lamb opens the seven seals (chs. 6-8), and the seer sees first the four horsemen (6:1-8), four "aspects of Roman power and rule."[248] military expansionism, civil strife and war, inflation which robs the poor of sustenance, and death. The fifth seal (6:9-11) unveils another aspect of Roman rule in its image of the martyrs who cry out to the Lord for judgment and vindication. The sixth seal (6:12-17) discloses the beginning of that judgment, and, after a little while, the seventh seal (7:1-8:1) reveals its completion in the protection, salvation, and vindication of the counter-empire, God's kingdom drawn "from every nation" (7:9). The salvation wrought by God is an answer not only to the plea of the martyrs for vindication (6:10), but also to the damage and harm of the four horsemen (6:1-8); for the victory God wins brings in its train not strife and hunger and death but complete well-being (7:15-17).

The judgment, of course, has its wrathful side as well, gruesomely described in the visions of the trumpets (8:2-11:18): God's very goodness requires severity, and the conflict of sovereignties is a war, after all. But, in spite of the repulsiveness of the plagues (8:2-9:21), it is noteworthy that they are intended to bring repentance (9:20,21). They are horror stories, indeed, but horror stories not so much of vengeance as of sovereignty, intended to prompt not merely fright but repentance. The path of the imperial cult, of idolatry, murder, sorcery, immorality, and theft (9:20), acknowledged sins all but subtly pervading life under Satan's sovereignty, leads not to power but to death. The way of patient endurance leads not to powerlessness but to life. The seventh and climactic trumpet (11:15-18) announces the sovereignty of God and of his Christ (11:15, "The kingdom of the world has become the kingdom of our Lord and of his Christ, and he shall reign for ever and ever") and makes it very clear that his wrath is a response to the raging of the nations (11:18). God destroys "the destroyers of the earth"; he protects and saves the earth, not only the "prophets and saints" but all who repent and "fear [his] name" (11:18).

The eschatological holy war dominates the visions in the central section of Revelation (11:19-16:20). Satan is defeated in heaven at the exaltation of Christ and thrown down to the earth (12:7-12). There he continues the battle, raging against those who would worship God and his Christ. He summons first a beast from the sea (13:1-10) and then a beast from the land (13:11-18). Without attempting to identify these beasts exactly, we can clearly see that they use political (13:5-7) and economic (13:16-17) power to persecute and oppress. Both, moreover, are related to the imperial cult (13:4,12-15). Satan's battle initiative in summoning the imperial power with its totalitarian and religious claims calls for "endurance" (13:10) and "wisdom" (13:18). The seer thus unveils the real cause and issue of the daily suffering of their communities and exhorts them to be loyal to the sovereignty of the Lamb. And he promises them the victory in his vision of the Lamb on Mt. Zion before the throne of God (14:1-5).[249] The message of good news is announced to the whole world

(14:6,7), and accompanying it is the message of judgment on Rome/Babylon (14:8) and on the imperial cult (14:9-11). Here is another call to endurance (14:12), identified as keeping the commandments of God and the faith of Jesus,[250] and another hymn of praise (15:3-4), by which the church already acknowledges and shares in Christ's victory.

The vision of Babylon/Rome and her fall (17:1-19:10) portrays the great splendor of Rome, at which even the seer "marveled" (17:6). Her flaunting of wealth and power, however, does not hide her immorality and idolatry, her oppression and murder, and, therefore, God's judgment is unveiled (18:1-8, 21-24). The fall of Babylon/Rome is lamented by those who are powerful and wealthy according to her standards and with her aid ("the kings of the earth," 18:9-10; "the merchants," 18:11-17a;[251] and "the shipmasters," 18:17b-19). The certainty of Babylon's fall and the Lord's victory, however, is cause for celebration and exhortation among God's people. They "rejoice" (18:20) and already join in the heavenly "hallelujah" (19:1,3,6) even as they heed the call for a spiritual exodus (18:4, "Come out of her, my people"). The exodus required is from the demonic values, the pride of power (18:3,9-10) and the greed (18:3,11-19), that marked Rome's life and justified her doom. Such a spiritual exodus could be undertaken only in the assurance of the victory of the Lamb that was slain, who judges justly and makes war for righteousness (19:11), the "King of kings and Lord of lords" (19:16). Such a spiritual exodus could be undertaken only in the expectation of a new world and a new city, a "holy city, new Jerusalem" (21:2), where God dwells and reigns and blesses and where his creation and his people flourish. Such a spiritual exodus requires and enables "patient endurance."

"Patient endurance" is not passivity. To be sure, this resistance movement, this counter-empire, does not take arms to achieve power. They do not plot a coup to seize economic and political control. But even in the style of their resistance, they are to give testimony to the victory of the Lamb that was slain and to the transformation of economic and political power wrought by him. They are to defend the Lord's claim to an earth corrupted and abused by its alliance with Satan and the emperor. They are to live courageously and faithfully, resisting the pollutions of the cult of the emperor, including its murder, fornication, sorcery, idolatry, and especially its lie that Caesar is Lord (cf. the vice lists in 21:8; 22:15; 9:20,21). All of life is to be lived under the sovereignty of the true lord. "Patient endurance" is not a "retreat from the ethical dimension"[252] but the introduction to it, for conventional, legal, and prudential standards are all overridden by what one really ought to do — submit to the rule of God. The prophet by his visions and the churches by their counter-empire existence bear witness to that rule and are tokens of its realization for the whole earth.

Revelation remembers Jesus and expects his final triumph in a context of persecution and oppression. For all its distinctiveness, it shares the common moral perspective of the New Testament: from the past of Christ's life and death and resurrection and from the future of his final triumph it surveys and assesses the peculiar responsibilities and opportunities of its particular current situation. Moreover, by returning, in however distinctive a fashion, to the apocalyptic announcement of God's reign and the great reversal it brings, it brings us back again to the message of Jesus and so provides a fitting conclusion to our analysis of New Testament ethics.

*   *   *

"In many and various ways God spoke of old to our fathers" (Heb. 11:1). That line, of course, refers to the Hebrew scriptures as fragmentary and preliminary revelations preceding the final and decisive revelation in God's Son. But the Greek scriptures too, reflecting on that final and decisive revelation and using it to illumine and guide the church through diverse moral problems, we have observed, are "many and various." Many authors, addressing various communities, different forms of literature, and diverse concrete problems, have left their mark on the moral teachings of the New Testament. The ethics of the New Testament was part of a developing moral tradition in the churches, a tradition that was founded on one (rejected) stone but which, nevertheless, did not become monolithic. To fashion the great variety of New Testament ethics into one massive, undifferentiated whole is impossible and impoverishing. These writings — in all their variety and relativity to particular situations — not only were a part of a developing moral tradition but also are a part, the normative part, of a continuing moral tradition. The church acknowledges that in these writings God himself has addressed and continues to address the churches about many things, including morality. The church acknowledges the authority of these writings for their own moral discernment and judgment. The ways in which that authority may and should be understood, the ways in which New Testament ethics may and should be brought to bear on contemporary Christian ethics, are the concern of the next chapter.

Chapter IV

A CONTINUING TRADITION

In II Timothy 3:16, an early Paulinist confidently declared that Scripture is "profitable for teaching, for reproof, for correction, and for training in righteousness." That declaration has been echoed down the centuries and across the divisions of the Christian church—and with reference to the New Testament as well as the Hebrew scriptures. The Christian churches have always considered it a part of their calling to teach, to reprove, to correct, and to train in righteousness, and they have always considered Scripture "profitable" to that task. They have looked to Scripture as a source of moral wisdom and as canon, as a moral authority.[1] With virtually one voice the churches have acknowledged that Scripture is an authority for their moral discernment and judgment.[2] And Christian ethicists—at least those who consider their work part of the common life of the Christian community—have shared that affirmation.

That one voice, however, suddenly becomes many voices as soon as Scripture is actually *used* as an authority. To say that the New Testament (or Scripture in general) is an authority for morality is to invoke its use in discernment and judgment in certain ways, but it is not to prescribe what those "certain ways" are. To affirm the authority of Scripture does not yet settle the question of how Scripture should be used or what authorizes certain moves in argument "from the Bible to the modern world."[3] That distinction between the authority of Scripture and the authorizations for its use in argument is the first step toward methodological candor and clarity concerning the use of Scripture.[4] Of course, unless one acknowledges with the church the authority of Scripture, the question of how it should be used—of authorizations for certain moves in argument from Scripture to moral claims—will seem trivial and irrelevant. But to acknowledge the authority of Scripture does not settle the question of authorizations: it only makes it an urgent question for the believing communities.

In this final chapter we must address that urgent question. An initial survey of some of the literature that has focused on the methodological issues involved in moving from Scripture to moral claims will serve to identify some of the principal methodological questions that must be asked and answered by anyone who would be candid and careful about the use of Scripture. These questions in turn will provide the framework for a survey of recent recommendations, whether explicit or implicit, for the use of Scripture. Thus a great variety of recommendations and resources will come into view, along with the methodological and practical consequences of answers to these questions. Without attempting to force the great variety of voices into a prearranged harmony, I will try to allow the happy note of an occasional consensus to sound. This survey will also enable us to formulate certain recommendations, not yet for the use of Scripture, but for the making and defending of such recommendations. Finally, this chapter will attempt to defend and illustrate my own proposal for the use of Scripture within the church.

A. BRINGING ORDER TO DIVERSITY: SOME CRITICAL METHODOLOGICAL STUDIES

Clarity and candor about the use of Scripture in moral discernment and judgment have been served by some useful descriptive work which both shows the diversity of appeals to Scripture and brings some order to it. That the patterns for providing order differ is itself instructive, suggesting different methodological issues.

1. James M. Gustafson: Modes of Ethics

In an instructive essay,[5] James M. Gustafson brings order to the diversity in the use of Scripture by attending especially to the mode of ethics within which Scripture is taken as authoritative. He begins by making a basic distinction between a "moral use" and a "theological use" of Scripture in Christian ethics. Advocates of the moral use take Scripture to be the source of a morality that is authoritative for discernment and judgment. Advocates of the theological use take Scripture to be the source of the knowledge of God which shapes and guides our response to him. Within the moral use, Gustafson further distinguishes a moral law model, a moral ideal model, an analogical model, and a great variety model.

The moral law model takes Scripture to be the revelation of a moral law, of certain rules or principles to be obeyed. The moral ideal model takes Scripture to be the source of moral ideals, of certain goals to be striven for. The analogical model takes Scripture to be the source of moral precedents. One can discern God's judgment for a contemporary situation in the precedent provided by his recorded judgment in some similar biblical situations. The great variety model (which Gustafson favors) takes Scripture to be a witness to a great variety of values and norms through a great variety of literary forms.

This model refuses to reduce the forms of moral instruction in Scripture to a single form or the moral themes in Scripture to a single theme. Scripture, on this model, "informs" the agent or "illuminates" the situation, but it is not sufficient to authorize any particular judgment; Scripture is limited to providing corroborative evidence.

The relationship of these uses of Scripture to different modes of ethics is patent. Those for whom "responsibility" is the basic category for moral reflection tend to use Scripture theologically. Deontologists, for whom "law" is the basic category, tend to use Scripture as moral law. Where the mode of ethics is teleological — where the basic category is "end" or "goal" — Scripture is construed as a source of moral ideals. And where precedent and analogies are central to ethical reflection, Scripture is used as a source of analogies.

The assumptions concerning the appropriate mode of moral reflection, however, while they are important, are not altogether determinative of the use of Scripture. Within the theological use of Scripture, for example, there are diverse views concerning which biblical themes are central and essential to the contemporary discernment of who God is and "what he is doing." And that variety, of course, both reflects judgments about the message of Scripture and is reflected in the variety of themes that are taken as central and essential to the contemporary prescription of the appropriate human response to God and his work. Within the moral law model there is a variety of answers to the questions of the content of the law and of the mode of applying it to contemporary life. Within the moral ideal model there are various ways of identifying and applying biblical ideals for contemporary discernment and judgment. The analogical model requires the selection of biblical situations which are to count as precedents. And the great variety model, as Gustafson acknowledges, requires some "generalization . . . in order to bring some priorities of biblical morality into focus."[6] Within each of the models, then, the options multiply as moralists face the questions of the material content the Bible provides and how it is to be applied. It is at this point that Gustafson's essay is methodologically very perceptive, for his focus on the mode of ethics reveals rather than hides the importance of other significant methodological questions — such as the nature of Scripture, the message of Scripture, and the relationship of biblical materials to other sources of moral insight.[7]

2. Edward Leroy Long, Jr.: Levels of Moral Discourse

Edward Leroy Long, Jr., in an article[8] published before Gustafson's and usually overshadowed by Gustafson's, identifies the basic options for the use of Scripture as three: Scripture may be used as a source of concrete prescriptions or of more general principles or of knowledge of the God to whom we are related and to whom we respond. The similarity of these options to some of Gustafson's models is more apparent than real, for the pattern Long uses to bring order to the variety is not provided by different modes of ethics but by what Henry David Aiken would call "the levels of moral discourse."⁹ For some, Scripture provides the normative moral rules that may be appealed to when they face concrete moral questions, when the question is, what should I do? To authorize the use of Scripture at this level (Aiken's "moral-rule level"), Long classifies as the "prescriptive use." For others, however, an appeal to Scripture is not authorized at the moral-rule level; rather, Scripture provides more general ethical principles or ideals that are normative at the "ethical level," when the rules themselves are being tested and judged. Authorizing the use of Scripture at the "ethical level" Long classifies as the "ideal-principle use." Still others would refuse to authorize the use of Scripture at either the moral or the ethical levels, to provide either moral rules or ethical principles. For this third group, Scripture provides knowledge of God and calls us to respond to him. The use of Scripture is authorized in this view only at what Aiken would call the "post-ethical level," where the question is, why be moral? and where the answers can inform and influence ethical principles and moral rules but not supply them. Long classifies this third kind of authorization as the "relational use."

Long is content to describe these three basic options. He is aware that there are sometimes vast differences between two representatives of the same classification, but he does not attend to the reasons for those differences nor to the reasons to prefer one option to another. If he had, other important methodological issues would have come into view. Nonetheless, he has identified an important question: the level of moral discourse at which it is appropriate to inquire of Scripture.

3. Wolfgang Schweitzer: The Nature and Message of Scripture

For the World Council of Churches' Symposium on "The Biblical Authority for the Churches' Social and Political Message Today," Wolfgang Schweitzer prepared a survey of ways in which that authority was understood.¹⁰ The grid adopted by Schweitzer to give order to the diversity was formed by answers to the question, "What is the connection in the Bible between the Word of God and the human word?"¹¹ The survey presents a number of different answers to that question, and each answer is reflected in certain views of the place and use of Scripture to illuminate and guide the churches' address to social and political problems.

Schweitzer's first option relies on ecclesiastical authority to interpret Scripture, to determine the Word of God in Scripture. This position makes the churches' identity and/or interests the real authority and the authorization for the use of some parts of Scripture and not others. The second option, fundamentalism, identifies the human words of Scripture with the Word of God. Accordingly, for fundamentalism Christian ethics is virtually identical with biblical ethics, at least with the systematization and harmonization of the biblical ethical materials. The third option, liberal theology, selects from among the human words of Scripture those to be regarded as the Word of God on the basis of antecedent values and principles. Here the antecedent values and principles are finally normative, and appeals to Scripture are licensed and limited by their coherence with a moral wisdom known from other sources. Schweitzer considers these three answers inadequate either to the churches' experience of the Word of God in Scripture or to the historical critics' demonstration of the humanity of the documents. The alternative Schweitzer recommends refuses to either identify or separate altogether the human words and the Word of God; rather, it identifies the Word of God with the "whole message" of the human words of Scripture. Such a view of the nature of Scripture is reflected in the refusal to attempt a "direct application of isolated Biblical passages"[12]; the use of Scripture must rather be an application of the biblical message, and every particular appeal to Scripture must cohere with the biblical message. But what is the "whole message" of Scripture? Answers to that question, too, have certain implications for the use of Scripture, as Schweitzer points out as he continues his survey. One answer to the question of the message of Scripture would identify the Word of God with the religious significance of the history reported and interpreted in human words. This position may use Scripture as a source of precedents and/or of a morally relevant perspective on history through, for example, the patterns of justice and mercy or promise and fulfillment (depending on what the religious significance of history is taken to be). Another answer identifies the message of Scripture with the kerygma, which evokes the self-understanding expressed in human (and "mythological") words. Here Scripture may be used to enable and require an existential decision; clearly, it may not be used as the source of an inauthentic security, whether found in the past with its rules or in the future with its ideals. The final position surveyed by Schweitzer identifies the whole message of Scripture with Christ, who is witnessed to by all the human words of Scripture. This position will test any and every appeal to Scripture by whatever is taken to be the moral significance of Christ.[13]

Schweitzer's survey is not intended to be exhaustive or impartial, but it does provide a pattern to the diversity of authorizations for the use of Scripture in ethics, and it does demonstrate the methodological importance of the questions concerning the nature and message of Scripture.[14]

4. Identifying the Critical Questions

Other writers have been less concerned with describing the diversity than with simply identifying the methodologically important questions.

C. Freeman Sleeper[15] has identified the critically important questions as "what we see," or the question of the "sources," "how we see," or the question of "perspective," and "how we express what we saw," or the question of "communication." Charles E. Curran,[16] after emphasizing both the contributions of biblical studies to Roman Catholic moral theology and some limitations on the use of biblical materials, draws attention to the methodological importance of the question of the relationship of biblical materials to nonbiblical sources of moral insight.

My own work[17] has confirmed the methodological importance of these questions. Drawing on Aiken's analysis of the levels of moral discourse[18] and utilizing Toulmin's categories of nonformal logic,[19] I have attempted to describe the morphology of appeals to Scripture in Christian ethics. Walter Rauschenbusch, the eminent American social gospel writer, has provided the case study, and Carl F. H. Henry, who reawakened American fundamentalism's social conscience, has provided the test. Both affirm the authority of Scripture, but they find quite different authorizations for the use of Scripture in moral argument. After identifying the authorizations, or (in Toulmin's categories) the "warrants," used in moving from Scripture to moral claims, I have examined the arguments in which those authorizations or "warrants" were themselves the claims. In such arguments the relevance of certain sets of data was not questioned — specifically, judgments about the message of Scripture, the nature of Scripture, and the questions appropriate to ask of Scripture were assumed to be relevant. The judgments themselves, of course, could be questioned and become the claims of still other arguments. On the other hand, the relevance of "natural morality," of moral certainties independent of biblical revelation, was not assumed. Rauschenbusch *argues* both that such certainties agree with Scripture when Scripture is read in the ways he proposes and that such an agreement is relevant to his defense of his authorizations. Carl Henry makes no such arguments; indeed, he will not allow "natural morality" such control over the use of Scripture. Both Rauschenbusch and Henry, however, acknowledge that any proposal for the use of Scripture is subject to the tests of consistency and nonidiosyncrasy. They defend their own authorizations as requiring no inconsistency in the use of Scripture and as coherent with the best understanding of Scripture in the Christian tradition and community. Finally, in arguments where they make claims about the nature of Scripture, the message of Scripture, or the questions appropriate to Scripture, both Rauschenbusch and Henry make important appeals to their own experience of the authority of Scripture and attempt to evoke similar experiences in their readers.

To propose certain authorizations for the use of Scripture in ethics is of a piece with inviting people to construe the Christian life in a certain way. That certainly demands nothing less than good argumentation, but, of equal certainty, it involves something more than good argumentation. We must acknowledge that particular authorizations for the use of Scripture are justified not at the end of an argument as much as in the midst of life, where an experience of the authority of Scripture can make Scripture vivid and alive and can illuminate and unify the moral life in particular ways.

This survey of studies that describe or explain the diverse use of Scripture in ethics enables one to identify some of the principal methodological questions that must be asked and answered by anyone who would be candid and careful about the use of Scripture. They are: 1) What are these writings? This is the question of the sources, of the nature of Scripture. 2) What questions are appropriate to Scripture? This is the question of perspective, of the mode of ethics from which we ask questions of Scripture and of the level of moral discourse at which we look to Scripture as normative. 3) What does one understand when one understands them? This is the question of the message of Scripture, the "wholeness" of Scripture, roughly equivalent to Sleeper's question of "communication." And 4) What is the relationship of biblical materials to other sources of moral wisdom? This is the question of the relevance of nonbiblical sources of moral insight. In addition to these questions, we may note that consistency and nonidiosyncrasy provide formal criteria for any recommendation. Self-conscious reflection about authorizations for particular uses of Scripture will surely have to attend to these four questions.

B. A SURVEY OF RECENT RECOMMENDATIONS

Both to confirm the methodological importance of these four questions and to carry forward the important descriptive work of Gustafson, Long, Schweitzer, and others, I will use these four questions as a framework for surveying various recent proposals for the use of Scripture in ethics.

1. What Are These Writings?

The most obvious example of the relevance of answers to this question is simply the use of different canons. Judaism, of course, does not accept the New Testament as its Scripture. So appeals to Scripture are clearly limited to writings recognized and accepted as canonical within the community. The question and responses to it are, of course, much more complex than that. David Kelsey[20] has insisted that doctrines about Scripture are "second-order" in character, that, whereas the "authority of Scripture" is simply given with the concept of "church," doctrines about Scripture are invoked in order to explain and justify a particular use of Scripture established on other grounds. Even if doctrines about Scripture are "second-order," however, they still establish expectations for the way Scripture will function in argument.

Within the Jewish community, for example, one of the important debates concerning the use of Scripture concerns the eighth principle of Maimonides, *Torah min hashamayim* ("The Torah is from heaven"). For orthodox thinkers like Immanuel Jacobowitz, this principle is as close to the essence of Judaism as the principle of monotheism. Orthodoxy's insistence on this principle identifies the words of Torah with the words of God and, consequently, receives as normative any rule or law found in Torah, recognizing "the equal sanctity of all parts of the Torah and its laws."[21] Other Jewish thinkers quite candidly reject that principle and select only some words or concepts or images as authoritative.[22] Without suggesting that the issue is settled, we can observe that there does seem to be a developing consensus around what Louis Jacobs. calls "the middle way."[23] The "middle way" attempts to affirm Maimonides' eighth principle while also recognizing the human origin of the words of Torah. The result is usually an emphasis on the biblical law coupled with an emphasis on the dynamic growth and change of *mitzvoth* (regulations) through inter-pretation and application within the community.[24]

We find a similar debate within the Christian community. On the one hand, fundamentalists like Harold Lindsell insist that the words of the Bible are simply identical with the words of God.[25] Lindsell's rigid and fragile view of inerrancy insists that laws or rules found in Scripture must be received as normative.[26] Of course, there are other inference licenses *implicitly* at work that effectively deny the "equal sanctity" of all the laws found in the Bible, but Lindsell does not attend to them.[27] On the other extreme is the work of Jack Sanders,[28] whose recommendation for the continuing use of the New Testament quite candidly demands a selection of those concepts and teachings which the modern and moral person can accept, so that we are "freed from bondage to that tradition."[29] Between these extremes there seems to be a developing consensus, identified by Birch and Rasmussen as the "important two part consensus" that "Christian ethics is not synonymous with biblical ethics" and that "for Christian ethics the Bible is somehow normative."[30] This consensus rejects both the identification of the human words of Scripture with the Word of God (sometimes found among the heirs of fundamentalism), and the separation and division of the human words from the divine Word (some-times found among the heirs of liberalism). It acknowledges the union of the divine Word and the human words in a Chalcedonian fashion,[31] without iden-tifying, confusing, separating, or dividing them.

2. What Questions Are Appropriate?

The methodological importance of this question was clearly and decisively demonstrated by Rudolf Bultmann. Bultmann, of course, proposed a particular question, the existential question, as appropriate to the text as well as showing that some question is always put to the text.[32] However one judges Bultmann's recommendation about what question to ask, we are all indebted to him for so clearly showing that some question is unavoidably asked, that some as-sumption is always made concerning the questions to which Scripture speaks with authority.

Any self-conscious recommendation for the use of Scripture in ethics will have to make a judgment concerning both the *level* of moral discourse at which appropriate inquiry is made and the *type* of question that may appropriately be asked. And our analysis must deal with both, attending first to the level, then to the type, and finally to the relevance of views of the person as a moral agent in these judgments.

With respect to the level of moral discourse at which inquiry is appropriate. Aiken's categories are helpful in describing the diversity of practice. And again Jewish discussions are parallel and illuminating. Jacobowitz[33] and Blidstein[34] look for answers on the moral level, where the question is, what ought I to do? Jacobowitz even defends the primacy of the "letter" over the "spirit" of the law: "The practical regulations governing Jewish conduct define our theology, our philosophy, our ethics, and our attitude vis-à-vis any intrinsically abstract subject or problem."[35] Solomon Freehof's *responsa* use the legal materials more loosely as "our guidance but not our governance."[36] Sometimes his use seems quite subjective, without any self-conscious methodology; but in at least one article[37] Freehof makes clear his distillation of certain principles from law and custom which are in turn used to defend, challenge, or reform moral rules, including those found in Scripture. Here, then, the focus is on the ethical level, where the question is, how shall I decide what moral rules are right? For Freehof and similar Jewish thinkers, of course, the moral rules defended or criticized are themselves biblical or *Halakic*, but their continuing authority depends on their consistency with the ethical principles distilled from Scripture. Other Jewish thinkers use scriptural data to claim neither moral rules nor ethical principles, but to develop a perspective which justifies and shapes the moral quest itself. These thinkers judge that the appropriate level at which to ask questions of Scripture is the post-ethical level, where the question is, why be moral? Thus Hans Jonas uses Scripture to develop a perspective on man and nature that he contrasts to what he takes to be the contemporary perspective.[38] Martin Buber's radical insistence that the post-ethical level is the appropriate one for inquiry of Scripture leads to a refusal to use Scripture as a source of laws or principles.[39]

Christian ethicists also differ about the level at which it is appropriate to inquire of Scripture. The biblicism of Lindsell allows inquiry at the moral level, of course, but other thinkers who distinguish the tasks of biblical ethics and Christian ethics also defend the legitimacy of inquiry at the moral level. Brevard Childs, for example, describes a reflective process for seeking biblical warrants at the decision-making level.[40] Richard Mouw seems to claim the appropriateness of inquiry at the moral level in his defense of an ethic of obedience to divine commands against the charges of being infantile, despotic, irrational, or stultifying.[41] And James Childress defends a law-model approach to the ethics of Scripture.[42]

James Sellars, on the other hand, is quite candid in insisting that inquiry at the moral level is inappropriate: "Scripture we take to be *constitutive* for major dogmatic or theological themes, *criteriological* for ethical reflection, but *invalid* for morality as such."[43] Those many moralists who appeal to Scripture to defend love as the basic ethical principle agree about the appropriateness of inquiries at the ethical level.[44] Decisions about the mode of applying this principle may affect the use of Scripture at the moral level; that is, they may authorize an appeal to moral rules in Scripture that are taken to be consistent with love or constitutive of love. But love is not the only plausible biblical response to inquiries at this level.[45]

Other Christian ethicists assume or argue that the appropriate level at which to inquire of Scripture is the post-ethical level. H. R. Niebuhr, for example, says that Jesus gives us no new ethics, neither principles nor rules, but rather reveals the lawgiver to whom we are responsible. This revelation, without providing rules or principles, makes the law more stringent, extends and intensifies it, forces a revolutionary transvaluation of it, and converts it from a coercive imperative to a free response.[46] Rudolf Bultmann insists that the only appropriate question is the question of self-understanding, and that the biblical answer is radical obedience apart from rules or principles or ideals, even those found in Scripture.[47] The examples could be multiplied both of those who *recommend* that inquiries be made at this level[48] and those who actually *use* Scripture primarily or exclusively at this level.[49]

There is diversity also with respect to the *kind* of question that is judged appropriate. This diversity reflects some enduring disputes in ethics, one of which is whether considerations of duty or of goal are more basic. Wolfhart Pannenberg,[50] Reumann and Lazareth,[51] and William Baird[52] agree that inquiries are appropriate at the ethical level but not at the moral level. Yet their questions differ. Pannenberg asks, "How shall we decide what is good?" and moves from the eschatological teachings of Jesus to a statement of the kingdom of God as a social ideal. The resemblance of that question and answer to the American social gospel is clear, and Pannenberg only insists on distinguishing his own eschatology and ethics from the "superficial optimism" of liberalism.[53] Reumann and Lazareth ask, "How shall we decide what is right?" and discover the biblical reply of righteousness and justice. Baird asks for precedents and thus abstracts certain principles, both teleological and deontological, from Paul's response to the urban culture of Corinth and takes them to be authoritative for the churches' response to analogous problems in contemporary cities.[54]

Another enduring dispute reflected in differing judgments about the kind of question appropriate is the distinction and relationship between individual and political morality. Roger Mehl[55] thinks social and political questions are inappropriate to the New Testament and suggests that they can be addressed only by a set of analogical inferences from Jesus' personal and apolitical kingdom ethic. But John Yoder and Jürgen Moltmann disagree. Yoder inquires of the New Testament for a "particular social-political-ethical option."[56] Moltmann insists that the appropriate question, the "question of theodicy, the question of suffering in expectation of God's just world," today takes a political and social form.[57] (It may be observed that, although Yoder and Moltmann agree that the political question is appropriate, they ask it at different *levels* of moral discourse.)

These judgments about the level at which inquiry is appropriate and about the kind of question asked are related to judgments about the nature of Scripture, the authority of other sources, the message of Scripture, and the person as a moral agent. The relevance of judgments about the person as a moral agent deserves attention. Using H. Richard Niebuhr's categories,[58] "man-the-citizen" who accepts the authority of Scripture will think it appropriate to ask for laws or "constitutional" principles; "man-the-artisan" will judge the appropriate question to be about ideals and ends; and "man-the-answerer" will ask for a perspective on the things that are happening to him and for images to discern the action of God in those things, for the story that gives us moral identity.[59] In a fine article, James Childress complains that recent reflection about the use of Scripture has typically overemphasized "responsibility" and underemphasized rational deliberation and justification as features of moral agency. But the relevance of judgments about persons outreaches Niebuhr's synecdoches.[60]

C. Freeman Sleeper argues against Bultmann[61] and Funk[62] and for his own recommendation at least partly on the basis of the inadequacy of the existentialist view of the self. Sleeper claims that the perspective from which questions get asked must be more appreciative both of the interaction of self and society (against Bultmann) and of the importance of "act" as well as "speech" to our self-knowledge (against Funk). Max L. Stackhouse[63] tellingly contrasts Rauschenbusch's and Bultmann's use of Scripture in terms of their different understandings of how the historicity of the self influences decision making. Theological anthropology is no less relevant. Mouw's defense of the use of Scripture at the moral level argues that "sin has affected human capacity for moral deliberation to the degree that we are desperately in need of divine guidance."[64] Jacques Ellul[65] also appeals to the category of sin, but for Ellul morality is itself part of the fallen order, part of the pride of persons who think themselves wise and refuse to rest in God's free decision. Thus, to ask Scripture for rules or principles or ideals or analogies — for a morality — is to ask an inappropriate and sinful question. Because of Ellul's dialectical position, however, the "impossible" Christian ethic is nevertheless "necessary," and his methodological point is waived in practice; it serves only as a caution against the moral pride in biblicism and as a protection for the free decision of God in particular circumstances. In practice, the commands and narratives of Scripture are used to mark "the continuity of the revelation" within which decisions must find their place.[66]

This survey of responses to the questions about the *level* and *kind* of question appropriate to Scripture has not identified any consensus, but it has at least demonstrated the importance of these questions to the use of Scripture. It has shown, moreover, the relevance of judgments concerning the person as a moral agent to the explanation and justification both of responses to those questions and of recommendations for the use of Scripture.

Without now arguing for a particular view of the person as a moral agent, we may base certain limiting suggestions on the respect due the reason-hearing and reason-giving capacity of the moral agent. The reason-giving capacity does not necessarily demand that biblical moral rules or commands be omitted, but it does demand that they be connected with more general biblical principles and perspectives. Reason-giving capacity does not necessarily imply that a sensitive conscience may not "intuit" God's action in the world, but it does imply that the conscience be made sensitive not only by some nonmoral images of God but also by the kinds of reasons and justifications that stand behind biblical moral claims.

3. What Does One Understand When One Understand These Writings?

The question of the wholeness or message of Scripture is not a new one, nor are recent recommendations the first to emphasize its methodological significance. St. Augustine candidly insisted that any movement from Scripture to moral claims is licensed if and only if it is consistent with the double love commandment, which he identified as the message of Scripture.[67]

The World Council's attempt to find a biblical foundation for social criticism and construction depended on the judgment that "the primary message of the Bible concerns God's gracious and redemptive activity for the saving of sinful man that he might create in Jesus Christ a people for himself."[68] This "activity" has its "center and goal" in Jesus Christ. Hendrik Kraemer's contribution to the World Council's attempt to develop "a purely biblical social ethic" insists that "Christ is the center of the biblical message in its entirety."[69] But then, of course, Christological judgments become relevant methodologically. Kraemer understands Christ as "the entering of the eternal, living God into time," and that bears on the methodological issue in the consequent "tension of the transhistorical and historical character of the biblical message."[70] The transhistorical character prohibits system making or casuistry, based on Scripture; but the historical character enables us to find behind and in the narratives and concrete regulations a direction or perspective that will take a different embodiment in our own historical situation.[71] Amos Wilder's critique of Kraemer[72] concerns both the way Kraemer has identified the message of Scripture and his mode of applying that message. The two are not unrelated. Wilder prefers a "trinitarian" rendering of the message of Scripture; partly on that basis he rejects Kraemer's mode of applying the kerygma, which tended to abstraction, isolation from the actualities of life then and now, and the exclusion of a legitimate casuistry.

Gustavo Gutiérrez[73] understands "liberation" to be the meaning of Scripture. The critical Christological judgment here is that Christ is the complete savior, the total liberator. The generalization that liberation is the message of Scripture backs a use of these writings that takes the Exodus experience as paradigmatic, both for God's intentions and for human participation in human liberation. This view licenses other moves from Scripture to moral claims if and only if they are consistent with the central theme of liberation. There are, of course, many others besides Gutiérrez who take Scripture as a narrative focused on the Exodus and Jesus Christ. For all of these Scripture provides a history of complete salvation oriented toward the future in which a contemporary praxis of liberation can participate. Some of these are other third-world theologians;[74] some are black;[75] some are women;[76] and some are even white males from developed countries.[77] Within black theology, J. Deotis Roberts[78] stakes out a position in opposition to the liberation theology of Cone. He insists that Cone has not understood the whole message of Scripture, which involves reconciliation as well as liberation. Partly on that basis, Roberts disagrees with Cone's mode of applying "liberation" in his unreserved endorsement of "black power."

John Yoder concludes his fascinating book by insisting that "a social style characterized by the creation of a new community and the rejection of violence of any kind is a theme of New Testament proclamation, from beginning to end, from right to left."[79] This provides backing for his moves from Scripture to moral claims throughout the book. The Christological judgment here focuses on the historical Jesus as teacher and pattern; this Jesus is what one understands when one understands the New Testament. And movements in argument can be tested by their consistency with that understanding. Richard Mouw, in a Reformed response to Yoder and others in the Anabaptist tradition, summarizes the biblical message in terms of creation, fall, redemption, and the future age.[80] That summary provides backing for Mouw's own use of Scripture and his criterion to test other uses of Scripture. It is in terms of that more trinitarian summary that Mouw expresses his appreciative reservations about Yoder's work; and, also in those terms, accuses William Stringfellow's[81] identification of government with Babylon of being inattentive to the themes of creation, preservation, and redemption as they bear on politics. Mouw differs with Yoder on the message of Scripture but resembles him in the place he gives Scripture in applying those understandings at the ethical and the moral levels of discourse. Mouw is close to H. R. Niebuhr's judgments about the message of Scripture but very different from him in the use of Scripture at the ethical and moral levels. That difference is due to different judgments about Scripture, man as a moral agent, and the relevance of other sources of moral wisdom.

The examples could be multiplied. James Sellars[82] is self-conscious about the methodological importance of his proposal that the "wholeness" of Scripture is its portrayal of the divine promise for man and its fulfillment. Sellars also claims the Christological key — where the emphasis falls on Christ as pattern for human wholeness. Colin Morris's use of Scripture[83] depends on his judgment that one understands "revolution" when one understands Scripture; his Christological focus is on the "historical Jesus" discovered by S. G. F. Brandon.[84] In contrast, James Douglas[85] has insisted that the biblical message of "revolution" included intrinsically the means of nonviolence.

Some theologians have challenged either the possibility or the necessity of a judgment about the wholeness of Scripture. For some conservative Protestants, such a judgment represents an attempt to escape the authority of all Scripture. Carl F. H. Henry, for example, insists that Scripture's moral propositions themselves form "a unitary whole."[86] Frank analysis of Henry's movement from Scripture to moral claims, however, demonstrates the crucial importance of Henry's judgment that forensic atonement is the message of Scripture.[87] Brevard Childs describes "the crisis in biblical theology" as at least in part due to a breakdown in the movement's consensus about the message of Scripture. But he refuses to recommend any new understanding of the whole to fill the vacuum; instead, he recommends the whole Scripture as a control for the use of any part. If we attend to the whole canon, we will put a check on the rationalizing use of Scripture and we will discern "the continuity of the one covenant God's directing and leading his people according to his will."[88]

James Gustafson suggests that Scripture witnesses to a great variety of values, norms, principles, and perspectives in different kinds of literature, and that this variety is not reducible to a single theme. But Gustafson himself acknowledges that "some efforts at generalization are necessary in order to bring some priorities of biblical morality into focus."[89] Birch and Rasmussen develop the emphasis of Childs and Gustafson in the context of their helpful analyses of the modes of ethics, the church as communal context, and the relevance of nonbiblical sources. But again it may be asked whether some judgment about the wholeness of Scripture is not necessary, particularly since they state that a moral decision that violates the biblically based identity of the church "is suspect even though it might be claiming biblical support."[90] If that is going to be anything more than a purely formal principle, and if the church's sense of identity is going to remain open to criticism and reform by the Word of God, then it is essential to risk a proposal about what one understands when one understands Scripture.[91]

Without now risking a proposal for construing the wholeness of Scripture, I would like to offer certain limiting recommendations for methodological proposals in view of this survey. First, judgments about the wholeness of Scripture are methodologically necessary; moral discourse would be served by candor about these judgments. Second, these judgments rest not so much on an exegetical demonstration as they do on the experience of the authority of Scripture in the context of one's own moral struggles as well as the believing community and its moral tradition. Third, these judgments about the message may not be substituted for the writings themselves. They may only be fashioned and exercised in the midst of reverently listening to the canonical text within the believing community.

4. What Is the Relevance of Other Sources?

Judgments about the nature of Scripture, the questions appropriate to Scripture, and the message of Scripture are generally acknowledged as relevant to the idea that certain warrants for moving from scriptural data to claims ought to be adopted. But there is no such shared acknowledgment of the relevance of other sources. Some writers issue a theological veto of "natural" morality, and this renders other sources irrelevant to the recommendation and use of authorizations for moving from Scripture to moral claims. At the other extreme some insist on the autonomy of morality and establish consistency with other sources of moral wisdom as the basic authorization for appeals to Scripture. Between these extremes of a theological veto and a wholly autonomous morality are many theologians who call for some form of dialogue between Scripture and other sources.

The theological veto of natural morality and of philosophical ethics was typical of neo-orthodoxy.[92] This position of neo-orthodoxy was influential on World Council discussions: Visser 't Hooft called for an "ethic of inspiration" based on the Bible alone, and among those who responded to the call was Kraemer.[93] Jacques Ellul[94] is probably the most important contemporary representative of this neo-orthodox veto on natural morality and moral philosophy. Some of these thinkers are content with a biblically informed perspective or a biblically sensitized conscience that can intuit the work and will of God from within the *koinōnia*;[95] others provide a good deal larger place for Scripture in discerning concretely the will of God; none, however, would appeal to moral philosophy or natural morality to test their authorizations or to help apply a biblical perspective.

Neo-orthodoxy was not the first to take this position, of course. It was typical of the Anabaptist tradition, of which John Yoder is a contemporary representative,[96] and of orthodox Judaism, of which Jacobowitz is an example.[97] Here the rejection results in a refusal to acknowledge possible challenge to a biblical moral rule (whether located in the sayings of Jesus or the Torah) from moral philosophy or "natural" morality.

The other extreme, the insistence on the autonomy of morality and the use of Scripture only insofar as it is consistent with other sources, is seldom proposed seriously by Christian or Jewish moralists. But Jack T. Sanders suggests that his work relieves us of the "temptation" to look to the Bible if we wish to develop coherent ethical positions. "We are freed from bondage to that position, and we are able to propose that tradition and precedent must not be allowed to stand in the way of what is humane and right."[98] This position surrenders control of decisions to other sources than those that are intimately related to the religious community's moral identity.[99]

Between these extremes may be found a whole spectrum of positions recommending some form of dialogue between Scripture and natural morality.[100] Of course, the dialogue is understood and undertaken in various ways. Sometimes Scripture's part in the dialogue is to challenge and disrupt conventional moral certainties and securities. Sometimes Scripture's role is to confirm and collaborate moral decisions reached on the basis of other sources. Sometimes Scripture's role is to supplement or transform natural moral wisdom. Sometimes other sources challenge and disrupt a conventional understanding and use of Scripture and force a new examination of what Scripture requires. It is difficult, of course, to be perfectly clear and candid about this dialogue.[101] Nevertheless, among those who call for dialogue between Scripture and other sources, a consensus seems to be developing that, with respect to the question of moral identity, Scripture must have the last word and that that biblically based identity must limit, corroborate, and transform appeals to natural morality as well as govern appeals to Scripture about questions of conduct.

5. Conclusion

This survey has not presumed to identify "the correct" use of Scripture. My intentions have been much more modest than that. It has brought into view a great variety of resources; it has identified an occasional consensus; and, above all, it has confirmed the methodological significance of the questions about the nature of Scripture, the questions appropriate to Scripture, the message of Scripture, and the relevance of nonbiblical sources.

Beyond such modest accomplishments, however, the survey has also suggested the plausibility of some general guidelines concerning the use of Scripture in Christian moral discourse and discernment. The recognition of the authority of Scripture is not optional for members of the believing communities. It is a necessary affirmation for those who would construe their moral reflection as part of the continuing life of the Christian community. There is no "Christian ethics" that would deny the authority of Scripture, for apart from Scripture the Christian church has no enduring identity. It must be recognized, however, that even those claims made on the basis of Scripture are quite human claims, arrived at by means of quite human authorizations. There is no excuse for the religious arrogance of thinking we have the absolute view, the final word — God's Word concerning some hard case — simply because we can appeal to Scripture. It is precisely that profession of the authority of Scripture (with the confession of our tendencies to self-deception and rationalization) that commits us to self-conscious and self-critical reflection about the authorizations we use to move from Scripture to moral claims. Such reflection will attend to the questions we have identified above and to the theological, anthropological, and ethical data relevant to answering them. Those questions are not answered, nor is the task of self-critical reflection about authorizations undertaken, simply by reaffirming "the authority of Scripture."

With respect to the question about the nature of Scripture, we have already suggested the methodological importance of the "Chalcedonian" unity of the divine Word and human words of Scripture. With respect to the question of the appropriate question to bring to Scripture, we have already suggested the methodological importance of respect for the moral agent as a giver and hearer of reasons. With respect to the question of the message of Scripture, we have already suggested that, while such judgments are critically important, they may not be substituted for Scripture itself, and they must be fashioned and exercised only in the midst of reverently listening to *the whole canon within the believing community.* [102] With respect to the relevance of nonbiblical moral resources. we have already suggested that proposals may neither reject natural morality nor allow it "the last word." Moreover, we have earlier observed and now repeat two formal criteria: an unwillingness and/or an inability to be consistent with one's recommendation for the use of Scripture counts against it; and the recommendation may not be idiosyncratic, but rather must bear some positive relationship to the ways in which at least some Christian traditions and communities have heard Scripture speak to their moral life.

These general guidelines still leave room for a variety of recommendations, but they do provide a much-needed check against a rationalizing use of Scripture. against a use of Scripture that hides or sanctifies our own sloth and pride. The variety itself need not be rued, for it can keep us from presumption and contentment in our own decisions about the use of Scripture and keep us attentive to the whole Scripture and to the whole believing community in our concern with and for the world.

C. A MODEST PROPOSAL

These general guidelines do not prescribe a particular use of Scripture; they do not establish a certain set of authorizations as the right set; but they do prepare the way to make such a recommendation both intelligently and modestly. The task undertaken here is to address the questions identified as methodologically important. Beginning in each case with what we have identified as a consensus, we will attempt to develop it in terms of what we have seen of the New Testament moral teachings themselves.

1. What Are These Writings?

a) THE CHALCEDONIAN CONSENSUS

The consensus here identified as the Chalcedonian consensus is that the Bible is the Word of God *and* the words of men. The Bible did not fall directly from heaven. Islam may make that claim for the Koran. but Christians do not make such claims for the Bible. The Bible is not a translation of secret writings on golden tablets. Mormons may make such claims for the Book of Mormon, but Christians make no such claim for their Scripture. We do claim that the Bible is the Word of God. but we also acknowledge — and affirm — that it is the words of men.

It is, after all, as human words that the New Testament presents itself to the reader. There is in it no attempt to deny or hide the human authorship of the little works it includes or the historical particularity of the audiences and situations it addresses. To disown the historical particularity of these materials is to render unlikely either an appropriate understanding of this literature or an appropriate use of this Scripture. Still, when we understand and appropriate these writings as human, the church reminds us, we understand and appropriate the Word of God.

The conjunction of the divine and human has always been difficult to be precise about — whether the conjunction is relevant to the church's confession about Jesus of Nazareth or the sacraments or the Bible. In the case of Jesus of Nazareth, for example, the church finally contented itself at the Council of Chalcedon (A.D. 451) by constructing four dikes against heresy. Chalcedon did not make a positive statement but a series of limiting ones about this conjunction of the divine and human. The conjunction is made *asynchytōs, atreptōs, adiairetōs*, and *achōristōs*: that is, the conjunction that the Bible is both the Word of God and human words must not confuse the two natures, transmute the one into the other, divide them into separate categories, or contrast them according to area or function.

Chalcedon's dikes may be erected today against the floodwaters of both liberalism and fundamentalism. The error of fundamentalism has typically been to *identify* and *confuse* the human words with the Word of God; the error of liberalism has typically been to *divide* the two and to *contrast* the human words with the divine Word. A Chalcedonian perspective will appreciate fundamentalism's concern for faithfulness to Scripture and liberalism's concern for creative attention to contemporary issues, but it will disown both fundamentalism's identification of the human words of Scripture with the Word of God and liberalism's contrast of the human words of Scripture to the Word of God. It will disown not only these judgments about the nature of Scripture but also the authorizations for the use of Scripture that rest on them.

The fundamentalist's identification of the human words of Scripture with the Word of God has sometimes backed an identification of biblical ethics with Christian ethics. The authorization, candidly stated, would be this: if a rule or command or any moral teaching is found in Scripture, then an identical rule or command or a moral teaching is normative for the church today. (There is usually some condition of rebuttal — such as, unless the rule or command or teaching is intended to be only a temporary obligation rather than a perpetual obligation.) In this view, the tasks for Christian ethics are to harmonize and systematize the biblical rules and commands and moral teachings and to apply them to cases as a contemporary code.

Liberalism's contrast of the human words of Scripture with the divine Word has sometimes backed the "liberation" of Christian ethics from the human words of Scripture. Where there remains a concern for biblical authority, the authorization, candidly stated, is this: if a rule or command or moral teaching found in Scripture is the Word of God rather than merely human words, then it is normative for the church (or for everyone). In this view, the tasks remaining for Christian ethics are to identify the Word of God found within Scripture (say, the social idealism of Jesus or the law of love or the

teaching of freedom from the law or whatever) and to articulate it in a contemporary way. One does not undertake the task of identifying the Word of
God, moreover, by attending carefully to the human words of Scripture but
by attending carefully to contemporary needs and problems, to the Spirit of
God in the age. (Ironically, the fundamentalist's "condition of rebuttal," with
its undeveloped distinction between temporary and perpetual obligations, can
allow and even require a similar selectivity of what is finally normative.)

The Chalcedonian perspective would authorize neither the mere repetition
of biblical morality as a normative code nor the selective identification of some
part of Scripture as the Word of God within Scripture. The authorization for
the use of Scripture must necessarily be more complex than that, more attentive to the humanity of Scripture on the one hand and to the divine inspiration
of Scripture on the other. The Chalcedonian perspective, however, does not
entail any particular positive authorization for moving from Scripture to contemporary moral claims. The candid development of that must await a reply
to the remaining questions. Even so, it is possible to build on the Chalcedonian
consensus by calling attention to some of what we have observed about the
nature of these writings.

b. PART OF A CONTINUING TRADITION: CONTINUITY AND CHANGE

The New Testament, as our analysis has made clear, is part of a tradition.
The church, in canonizing these writings, has acknowledged that they are the
normative part; but in formulating authorizations for the use of these writings,
we may not neglect their character as part of a continuing tradition. One
feature of the New Testament and the continuing tradition is that tradition
enables and requires both continuity and change. Indeed, one may say with
James Mackey that "change and continuity are two facets of the same process,
the process we call tradition. So much so that continuity can only be main-
tained by continual development, and development or change is only such (and
not simply replacement) because of continuity. Tradition means continuity and
change, both together and both equally."[103]

The New Testament itself represents a part of the tradition at once continuing its traditions and changing them. Moreover, it did not develop simply
in one way or in one direction. It developed in diverse ways, each of which
has its source in Jesus Christ, who was recognized as the historical beginning
of the tradition and as the risen Lord who was constantly operating within it.
This observation calls for an exegetical interest in the ways New Testament
authors utilized their traditions that were at once faithful to the Christian
tradition and creatively responding to new situations, interpreting tradition
and appropriating it with new understanding and power in new situations.
And it calls for authorizations that sacrifice neither continuity to change (or
"relevance") nor change to continuity — authorizations that combine faithful-

ness and creativity in addressing contemporary issues from within the Christian community and tradition.

The fault with fundamentalism, from this perspective, is that it constantly runs the risk of permitting the tradition to fossilize, to petrify. The fault with liberalism, on the other hand, is that it constantly runs the risk of cutting itself off from the tradition. The sort of authorization that is called for enables and requires both faithfulness and creativity, both continuity and development.

An illustration may be helpful, and the domestic codes, the *Haustafeln*, provide an illuminating one. To the fundamentalist these codes are identified with the boundless and eternal Word of God, and their authorization permits and requires the fundamentalist to repeat them as normative for the contemporary church as well: wives and slaves ought to be subject. Thus they sacrifice change for continuity, and the tradition petrifies. To the liberal, on the other hand, these codes are in contrast to the Word of God as merely human words, as regressive compromises with Hellenistic or rabbinical morality and thus as nonnormative for the contemporary church. The Chalcedonian perspective will neither identify these codes with the Word of God and simply repeat them today nor contrast them with the Word of God and disown their authority for the church today. Rather, it will recognize that the continuity and change in those traditions, the ways in which existing traditions and role responsibilities were challenged, assimilated, and transformed in ways at once creative and faithful to the Christian tradition will be normatively instructive for the continuing Christian community and tradition. Those traditions, it will be recalled, have brought existing role assignments under the critical and redemptive power of the moral person's recognition of Christ as Lord and his consequent interest in his neighbor's welfare and integrity and his freedom from conventional standards of status and power to serve the neighbor.

c. INTENTIONAL AND PURPOSEFUL

We can build on the Chalcedonian perspective in yet another way. To join the divine and human in Chalcedonian fashion permits one to neither disown nor disparage the humanity of these writings: God's Word is neither to be identified with these human words nor to be contrasted to them. To affirm the real humanity of these words should make us particularly attentive to the context-relative intent of these words, both exegetically and morally. Exegetically, we must look for the intention behind the time-bound words relative to the particular context in which they were first given; and morally, we must continue to view the world *from* these same intentions, that is, we must allow them to form and inform our perspective. For example, Matthew's *Halakic* treatment of the sayings of Jesus about divorce is neither to be repeated as a moral rule or *Halakoth* governing judgments about divorce today, nor is it simply to be disowned. It is to be interpreted and understood in terms of Matthew's purpose, audience, and setting. God's Word is neither to be identified with the human words of Matthew nor contrasted to them. Instead, in and through Matthew's time-bound and context-relative words we can discern the intention to appropriate and apply the disposition toward marriage found in the tradition of Jesus' words for his Jewish-Christian community. He does this creatively and faithfully. The faithful and creative use of Matthew as a part — a normative part — of the tradition will neither simply repeat his words as a rule for all Christian communities for all times nor disown them. Rather, the creative and faithful use of Matthew will share his intention but allow it to form and inform our perspective on marriage and divorce, appropriate it, and apply it in ways and words bound to our time rather than the first century and relative to our place rather than Jewish Christianity in confrontation with the Jewish synagogue.

There is an analogue to this use of intention in both legal reasoning and moral reasoning. In legal reasoning, the intention of the statute both permits and enables the judge to decide when to make exceptions, when and how to modify the statute, and, indeed, when to discard it. "It is a familiar canon of construction that a thing which is within the intention of the makers of a statute is as much within the statute as if it were within the letter; and a thing which is within the letter of the statute is not within the statute unless it be within the intention of the makers."[104] In moral reasoning, there are analogous reasons or intentions behind moral rules and ethical principles that help to determine the application of principles and the scope and modification of moral rules. Just so, it seems to me, the intention of the human words of Scripture enables and requires judgments about how to apply and modify the human words themselves — the rules, codes, judgments, exhortations, and so forth — relative to the concrete times and places of the original authors. This authorization might be stated candidly as this: "Only if the use of a passage is coherent with its intention is that use in moral argument authorized." Of course, identifying the author's intention is no easy task. It is not, for example, simply identical with the "meaning then," for Matthew evidently meant to provide *Halakoth* for his community. Identifying the intention of a legal statute or of a moral rule is not an easy task either; in spite of such difficulty, however, the task is an important one if both continuity and change are to be allowed and in ways that join faithfulness and creativity.

The Chalcedonian consensus on the nature of these writings provides precious little concrete, positive guidance about authorizations for the use of Scripture in the moral life of the church today. However, it has warranted certain limiting remarks about the use of Scripture and forced us to distance ourselves from two kinds of proposals. We have attempted to build on that consensus by observing that the New Testament is part of the tradition — the normative part. Authorizations for the use of Scripture in contemporary moral discernment, therefore, whatever they may be concretely, must enable both continuity and change; they must enable creative faithfulness — or faithful creativity — in the use of Scripture. Finally, still building on the Chalcedonian consensus, affirming the humanity of the words of Scripture has led us to concentrate on the purposefulness of these words, on the intent that stands behind their context-relative expression, and to authorize those moves in argument from Scripture to moral claims that are consistent with the intention of the author. Such observations, however, still fall short of a candid and concrete recommendation for the use of Scripture. They invite further reflection concerning the other methodologically significant questions rather than rendering such reflection inconsequential.

2. What Questions Are Appropriate to Scripture?

As we have seen, any self-conscious recommendation for the use of Scripture in ethics will have to make a judgment both concerning the *level* of moral discourse at which appropriate questions are asked and concerning the *kinds* of questions that may appropriately be asked. Moreover, we have observed the methodological importance of judgments concerning the person as a moral agent to the explanations and justifications of responses to these questions. Short of identifying any consensus on these questions, I have suggested the methodological significance of the respect due the moral agent, especially the moral agent's capacity to hear and give moral reasons.

a. WHAT KIND OF QUESTION IS APPROPRIATE?

Regarding the *kinds* of inquiries that are appropriate to bring to Scripture, we may first build on the Chalcedonian consensus again. The reader will recall that the Chalcedonian perspective refuses to allow a contrast between the divine Word and the human words of Scripture in terms of area. It would disallow the position that Scripture speaks with authority about religion but only quaintly about morality — or the position that it speaks as the veritable Word of God in response to religious or moral inquiries but only as human words in response to, say, natural, historical, or political questions. The presumption must be, therefore, that moral questions as well as religious questions are appropriate to Scripture. And that presumption rests not only on the Chalcedonian perspective of the nature of these writings, but on the intention of all the New Testament writings, as we have seen, to exhort, encourage, and admonish congregations in the midst of concrete moral questions.

1) Some Inappropriate Kinds of Questions

That is not to say, however, that every type or level of moral inquiry is appropriate to Scripture any more than the presumption that Scripture speaks with authority about nature implies that Scripture answers *all* questions about nature with authority. The Bible is concerned about nature, but not in the manner some twentieth-century natural scientist would be. In countless expressions of awe and wonder, the Bible presents nature as the arena of

God's activity as Creator, Provider, and Redeemer. But if someone asks about the shape of the universe and, reading Genesis 1:6-8, claims that Scripture reveals that an expanse called "Heaven" divides "the waters above" from "the waters below" the earth — the fault lies with the question put to Scripture and not with Scripture itself. The fault with the question is not that it is a question about nature, however, but that it is not the kind of question about nature to which we may expect Scripture to speak with any authority.

Again, the Bible stakes its case on history, but it is quite unconcerned about minute circumstantial accuracy. "If Christ has not been raised, then our preaching is in vain and your faith is in vain" (I Cor. 15:14). All four Gospels recount the discovery of the empty tomb; but when they do, they are not concerned about giving the kind of report an "objective observer" might give or wish to be given. So if we ask whether Mary Magdalene was alone when she visited the tomb or was accompanied by other women, whether there was one angel or two or "a young man" at the tomb, whether the women tell the disciples to go to Galilee or remind them of what Jesus had said in Galilee, whether there was an earthquake or not — we receive conflicting replies, and the conflicts can be harmonized only with an abundant supply of ingenuity and some tampering with the text. Again, the problem is not with Scripture but with our questions. And the problem with such questions is not that they are about history but that they ask a particular kind of question about history, a question Scripture does not intend to address with authority. The Bible is concerned about history, but not the kind of history an historian or "objective observer" would be interested in. History is treated as recital. God has acted in our history, and Scripture proclaims and announces that so we may live in response to God.

Analogously, inquiry concerning morality is certainly appropriate to Scripture, but not necessarily every kind of moral inquiry. The New Testament, as we have observed, consistently intends to shape the character and conduct of its readers; but it is quite unconcerned with providing either a systematic treatise on ethical theory or a comprehensive moral code. It was not and is not concerned with addressing the sorts of moral questions that sometimes seem to monopolize ethical reflection in pluralistic societies, the questions of an impartial morality, an "autonomous" morality, a morality that obliges a person whatever his commitments and causes may be — indeed, in spite of them if need be. To ask Scripture to provide such an ethic is simply inappropriate to Scripture. Both Jack Sanders and J. L. Houlden fault the New Testament for failing to provide an autonomous ethic. But the fault is not with the New Testament; the fault is with the question. The bottom line for New Testament morality is not impartial reason. It is loyalty to the God who raised Jesus from the dead. To ask Scripture to be what it is not is inappropriate; therefore, to ask it to be a systematic treatise or a comprehensive code or an autonomous ethic based on reason alone is inappropriate. To ask Scripture the sort of moral question that presupposes it is any of these things is, therefore, also inappropriate.

2) Questions of Identity and Integrity

Scripture is concerned with precisely the kinds of questions from which an autonomous ethic based on "neutral" and "impartial" reason prescinds, and these are particularly appropriate to Scripture. These are questions of moral identity and integrity. An "autonomous" morality must remain impartial to loyalties and commitments and to their effect on one's moral perspective, dispositions, and intentions. But the New Testament begins there, puts the question of loyalty and commitment to its readers, invites from its readers the question, to whom are my ultimate loyalties due? and answers the question with authority as the veritable Word of God. An "autonomous" ethic, with its stance of neutral rationality, requires alienation from our moral identity, from our own histories and communities, from our own moral interests and projects, in order to adopt the impartial point of view. But the New Testament claims our identity, gives us a community and a history, and requires integrity with that identity in our interests and projects. It invites the questions, who am I as a moral agent? what is the moral community that nurtures and supports my identity? what is the story that sustains and grounds my identity? and how do integrity and truthfulness with such an identity, community, and history form and inform the perspective from which I view situations, the dispositions of my character, and the intentions that determine my conduct? Scripture speaks with authority to these questions. Not, to be sure, in a systematic address to them, but in appealing to such considerations — rather than to a code or to some impartial and autonomous principles and rules — in addressing concrete moral questions.

b. WHAT LEVEL OF INQUIRY IS APPROPRIATE?

The same considerations would suggest that inquiry at both the "post-ethical level" and "ethical-principle level" is appropriate to Scripture. Precisely because Scripture is uninterested in an "autonomous" ethic, it is appropriate to ask the "post-ethical" question, why be moral? The inquiry calls for a profession concerning the nature, intentions, and reliability of the one to whom we are finally responsible. It calls as well for a statement of beliefs concerning the nature and destiny of the reality that provides the context for our responsibilities. Such questions are surely appropriate to the New Testament, and the New Testament replies in ways that can create, sustain, and inform loyalty to God and in ways that create and nurture certain perspectives on our world, our history, and our communities within them.

It is also appropriate to inquire of Scripture at the "ethical-principle" level. At this level we must still be careful about the kind of question we ask, the kind of principle we look for. We may not ask it to provide some autonomous principle or principles, impartial to commitments and loyalties, and resting on reason alone. But to inquire about those dispositions and intentions that cohere with Christian identity and inform Christian integrity is certainly appropriate.

Dispositions and intentions are formed and informed by beliefs and perspectives at the "post-ethical" level, and they form and inform decisions and judgments at the "moral-rule" level. Our decisions and judgments at the "moral-rule" level can and must thus be informed by a loyalty and perspective and by dispositions and intentions that are based on the New Testament writings. However, to inquire of Scripture at the "moral-rule" level is, I judge, inappropriate. To ask the New Testament what one ought to decide or how one ought to judge in a particular concrete case and to expect it to reply with an authoritative prescription or command or rule at the "moral-rule" level is inappropriate to these writings. Of course, the New Testament was concerned with concrete questions of conduct, but with the concrete questions of conduct in the communities they were addressing, not for all times and places. To inquire of Scripture at the "moral-rule" level is to treat Scripture as something it is not and did not intend to be, a moral code. The New Testament must continue to bear on our concrete decisions, not directly, but rather in ways mediated by its responses to inquiries concerning our moral identity, our fundamental loyalty and perspective, and the dispositions and intentions that inhere in that identity.

c. CONCLUSIONS AND BACKING

The conclusions, candidly put, are that movements in argument from Scripture to moral claims 1) are not authorized with respect to claims concerning some autonomous, impartial, and universal ethic; 2) are authorized with respect to claims concerning Christian moral identity and integrity at least at the post-ethical and ethical-principle levels of moral discourse; and 3) are not authorized at the moral-rule level of moral discourse. Such authorizations, which limit and license the use of the New Testament in moral argument, are based on the judgments about the questions appropriate to Scripture that have been articulated. Those judgments, moreover, and the authorizations that depend on them, cohere with what has been said about the nature of Scripture, respect the moral agency of persons and their capacity to give and hear reasons, and are particularly apt to certain features of New Testament ethics itself.

The New Testament does not come to us as a timeless moral code dropped from heaven; to treat it and to inquire of it as though it were would be inappropriate. Nor does it come to us as an autonomous ethic based on reason and impartial to the commitments and loyalties of the moral agent; to treat it and to inquire of it as though it were would be inappropriate. Rather, it comes to us as a part of the tradition, a tradition that bears the moral identity of the community and in which that identity is brought to bear both creatively and faithfully on the concrete moral context of particular communities. To treat it and to inquire of it as such — indeed, as the normative part of the continuing tradition — is certainly appropriate. Such judgments about Scripture cohere, I think, with the set of judgments about the questions appropriate to Scripture above and with the authorizations for the use of Scripture based on them.

These authorizations also respect the moral agency of persons and their capacity to give and hear reasons. The quest for an autonomous ethic, for some impartial principle, based on reason, rejects the "reasons" provided by the moral agent's identity and integrity. It requires alienation from ourselves, from concerns about our identity and integrity, in order to adopt an *impartial* point of view. We are asked by such an approach to treat our moral projects and passions as though we were outside, objective observers, to disown the projects and passions which we take as our own and which give us our moral character — and for the sake of morality.

The New Testament neither sponsors nor responds to such an impartial perspective. It respects the moral agency of actors, the importance of commitment and loyalty, and the requirement of integrity. It may call for repentance, for a revision and renewal of identity, but it does not abstract itself from, ignore, or disown the identity and integrity of moral agents. Respect for such a moral agent's capacity to give and hear reasons for his conduct requires something more than limiting Scripture's use to the post-ethical level and something less than using Scripture to provide a timeless code at the moral rule level. Respect for the agent's reasoning capacity suggests the importance of not only a perspective but moral dispositions and intentions formed and informed by the New Testament writings if the agent is expected to conduct himself intelligently and intelligibly with integrity. Respect for this reasoning capacity suggests, moreover, the inappropriateness of authorizing the formation of a timeless code based on the New Testament that would command unthinking obedience. Such respect suggests the appropriateness, on the other hand, of authorizing continuing appeals to the reasons, the dispositions and intentions, the perspective and commitment that stand behind the New Testament rules and concrete admonitions and judgments.

Finally, these authorizations are particularly apt to certain features of New Testament ethics itself. One may remember the crisis of *Halakah* wrought by Jesus' announcement that the kingdom of God is at hand: the emphasis at the beginning of the Christian moral tradition was shifted to *Haggadah,* to the issues of identity, perspective, dispositions, and intentions, and away from the code with its external commandments. Or one may recall the early church's creative and faithful use of the tradition of Jesus' words and deeds to shape character and conduct, telling and retelling the stories that provided and nurtured their identity and perspective, evoked and sustained certain dispositions and intentions. They shaped and modified the words of Jesus and the catechetical tradition freely and faithfully, bringing them to bear on questions of conduct without allowing them to petrify into a timeless code that would need only to be subsequently applied.

Or one may recall certain features of New Testament ethics themselves. Mark's ethic was ill-disposed to rules and codes, insisting that questions of conduct be dealt with in terms of Christian integrity, faithful to the perspective, dispositions, and intentions that fit the action of God in Christ. Matthew's Gospel, so much more well-disposed to rules, nevertheless focused on a righteousness which exceeded and surpassed codal morality precisely because it claimed the whole person and demanded integrity. Luke proceeded by way of stories — not legislation or rules — to form a community marked by dispositions and intentions to care for the poor and powerless and to respect Christians with other opinions and rules. Paul's "new discernment" brought rules and moral guidelines under the critical and transforming light of God's act in Jesus Christ. That eschatological event had established a reality that has provided identity and perspective and certain fundamental values. The rules — whatever their source — did not govern discernment; rather, discernment was exercised upon them, so that they were made fit instruments for making concrete the shape of Christian integrity in the particular time and place of the first readers of the letters. For us to render Paul's timely admonitions into a timeless code would not be appropriate to Paul's own pattern of discernment. Finally, these authorizations are particularly apt to the New Testament image of the church as "full of goodness, filled with knowledge, and able to instruct one another" (Rom. 15:14). Gifted by the Spirit of God, the church is given a particular identity and perspective, certain dispositions and intentions, and the task of moral discernment. The moral rules of Jewish and Gentile Christians were different, but there was no attempt to impose one timeless and universal or biblical set of rules. Rather, their one fundamental loyalty, the perspective and values they shared in Christian integrity, was the basis of mutual exhortation and discernment.

Today mutual admonition and discernment will be served, I think, by authorizations for the use of Scripture such as those I have suggested. We should refuse to license the movement in argument from the New Testament to either an autonomous principle or a moral rule. We should rather license the movement from the New Testament to claims about the reality within which we must respond, to claims about our moral identity as people loyal to God, and to claims about the dispositions and intentions that mark truthfulness to that reality and integrity with that identity.

3. What Does One Understand When One Understands These Writings?

Our earlier examination of the variety of judgments concerning the message of Scripture and of the ways these judgments served to license and limit appeals to Scripture did not allow any identification of a consensus about the message of Scripture. It did, however, lead to certain limiting recommendations for methodological proposals for Scripture's use in moral argument. First, judgments about the wholeness of Scripture are methodologically necessary; moral discourse would be served by candor about these judgments. Second, these judgments rest not so much on an exegetical demonstration as they do on the experience of Scripture's authority in the context of one's own moral struggles on the one hand and the believing community and its moral tradition on the other. And third, the judgments about the message of Scripture may not be substituted for the writings themselves. They may only be fashioned and exercised in the midst of reverently listening to the canonical text within the believing community.

a. GOD'S RELATIONSHIP TO US IN SCRIPTURE[105]

To build on those limiting recommendations a more constructive proposal for what one understands when one understands Scripture is — on the basis of those recommendations themselves — both difficult and necessary. The fundamental clue in them is that in judgments about the message of Scripture we must give an important priority to the experience of Scripture's authority in the context of one's own moral life. That suggests the possibility of a new examination of God's relationship to Scripture and about God's relationship to the Christian community in and through Scripture.

In the past, God's relationship to Scripture and to the Christian community through Scripture has ordinarily been construed as *revealer simpliciter.* The content of Scripture, therefore, was often identified with revelation, and the task of a theological ethic was to systematize and republish that content. What one understands when one understands Scripture is simply the content of Scripture, which somehow transcends the historical and cultural relativity of other human writings. With such a construal of God's relationship to Scripture and to the Christian community through Scripture, it is little wonder that the temptations to violate the Chalcedonian limits remained so strong.

Neo-orthodoxy attempted to rescue the authority of Scripture from both its detractors and its defenders, but it retained the construal of God's relationship to Scripture and to the Christian community through Scripture as *revealer simpliciter.* The change was neo-orthodoxy's insistence that what was revealed was not the content but God himself. Or, to put it differently, the content of revelation was not some information about God and his will but God himself, God as a "thou" in encounter with us. This enabled neo-orthodoxy to acknowledge fully and freely, on the one hand, the authority of Scripture and, on the other hand, the historical and cultural relativity of Scripture, for it only witnessed to that revelation: it cannot and does not constitute the encounter, it only mediates and enables it.

The task of a theological ethic, then, is not to systematize and republish the content of Scripture, but to facilitate a new revelation, a new encounter, a concrete command of God in that moment. The cost of such a program is to render even "the Word of God" (Barth) or the "Kerygma" (Bultmann) empty ciphers, denoting no specific content at all but pointing toward an event or encounter in which God discloses himself. But this disqualifies such ciphers from methodological significance for authorizing the movement from Scripture to moral claim, or for limiting and licensing in any intelligible way the use of Scripture in moral discourse. When what we understand when we understand Scripture cannot be — may not be — formulated, then it cannot be used as a criterion to test the adequacy of any particular use of Scripture. Moreover, this model seems adequate neither to Christian experience nor to Scripture itself. Which of us, being human, has seen God or directly encountered God? Who has heard or obeyed the direct revelation of some concrete command of God in the moment? The New Testament itself suggests that God's being is revealed only at the end of time.[106]

God's relationship to Scripture and to the Christian community through Scripture should not be construed as *revealer simpliciter.* God's Word is no less purposeful and intentional than are human words, and God's intention — attested by both Christian experience of Scripture's authority in the context of the moral life and by the common purpose of the New Testament writings — is to transform and sanctify human identity, to bring it and the whole creation into coherence with his reign. Therefore, God's relationship to Scripture and to the Christian community through Scripture should be construed as that of sanctifier. In the New Testament writings themselves the human authors were calling and empowering particular communities to live with integrity and truthfulness in the midst of concrete and specific moral crises. God bore to these human authors, to their writings, and to their first recipients the relationship of sanctifier.

In and through these writings God continues to call and empower people to live with integrity and truthfulness in a different time and place, facing different concrete questions. He continues to be sanctifier in his relationship to the church through these human words. What one understands when one understands the New Testament, then, is not a systematic set of doctrines or rules or a systematically indeterminate "Word of God," but the power of God to renew life, to transform identities, to create for himself a people and a world for his own possessing and for their flourishing.

b. THE RESURRECTION AS KEY

The key to such an understanding in the New Testament itself is the resurrection of the crucified Jesus of Nazareth. That event discloses God's power and purpose. It inaugurates and guarantees his eschatological reign. The New Testament does not treat the announcement that God raised Jesus from the dead as one doctrine among many to be brought into systematic coherence with the others. Nor does it treat the resurrection as an arcane and metahistorical "event" or as an expression of the rise of faith in response to the kerygma. The announcement of the resurrection was in the early church and in the New Testament — and it still is in the continuing church — the affirmation of an event by which God lays claim to our world, our history, and our selves and unveils his purpose and his power to renew them.

The affirmation of the resurrection, which stands as the basis and at the center of the New Testament, is not simply a claim about an historical fact — although clearly the truth of the historical claim is of fundamental importance to the appropriateness of other claims. The affirmation of the resurrection was and continues to be the affirmation not only of an event but of God's cause and purpose disclosed in the event as well. And formally, it was and continues to be not merely a proposition but a self-involving utterance equivalent to the acknowledgment of this Jesus as Lord.

The resurrection is an eschatological event, to be sure, disclosing and guaranteeing the final victory of God's cause and purpose. But the cause and purpose are protological, present already and always in creation and providence and in God's dealings with Abraham and his seed. To call it an eschatological event is to admit that it points ahead to what cannot be seen and is not yet fully experienced. The resurrection, after all, is not like the resuscitation of the clinically dead or the revivification of Lazarus; those people are raised to die again. But the resurrection of Jesus is an event in our flesh, our world, and our history that transcends the enclosures of our mortality and evil; it establishes something new, but something from which our flesh, our world, and our history have (happily) no escape. It is something new, but the cause and purpose whose final triumph it discloses and establishes is as old as light. To call that cause and purpose protological is to claim that it was the cause and purpose of God from the very beginning, that it is present in creation and providence and in his making and keeping the covenant. Therefore, the Christian will disown neither creation nor providence nor the Old Testament as sources of moral wisdom, but he will insist that they bear on his character and conduct in ways that cohere with the final revelation, the resurrection. The light they have to shed on identity and behavior must pass through the prism of the resurrection. It is God the Creator, Provider, Judge, and Covenanter who raised Jesus from the dead and who bears toward Scripture and toward us in and through Scripture the relationship of sanctifier.

The affirmation of the resurrection and thus of God's cause and purpose was first made, and continues to be made, in the midst of life under the sign of the cross, in the midst of the apparent power of sin and death. The truth about our world is dripping with blood: poverty and pain, disease and death, wars and rumors of war. And the resurrection of the crucified one neither blinds Christians to this reality nor makes liars of them. The creation does not yet flourish; it is not yet released from its "bondage to decay" (Rom. 8:21). People still die, purchase security at the altar of lesser gods, smite and hate, insult and envy. In such a world, affirming the resurrection and the cause of

God disclosed in it continues to be not just an objective proposition but a self-involving commitment. If the crucified one is raised, then, as the early church said, he is Lord; and if he is Lord, then all of life must be reoriented to the vision of Christ at God's right hand. God's gift of the renewal of life is and must be affirmed; identities are and must be transformed; perspectives are and must be reformed; dispositions and intentions are and must be formed and informed by this eschatological event. To affirm the resurrection in a world like this one is to stand in *spite* of death and evil, to hope for and work for life and its flourishing, to align and identify oneself with the crucified one in the expectation of a resurrection like his, to refuse to allow evil the last word in our lives or in God's world. The God who raised Jesus from the dead and thus established his eschatological reign bears toward us the relationship of sanctifier in the resurrection and in the literature that depends on it and articulates it. This is what one understands when one understands the New Testament.

c. CONCLUSION AND BACKING

This understanding of the New Testament message may not be substituted for the writings themselves. It is fashioned and must be exercised by the believing community in the midst of listening reverently to the whole canonical text. This judgment about the New Testament message enables us to see all of it as exercises in Christian discernment, as faithful and creative attempts to interpret and direct the character and conduct of Christian communities and the individuals within them in the light of God's eschatological act of raising Jesus from the dead. And it requires that we use all of it — and any part of it — in ways coherent with that message today. The God of the resurrection is the sanctifier in these writings, and he enables and requires us to live out of and toward the resurrection through these writings. The authorization I am recommending may be candidly stated as this: If, and only if, the movement from Scripture to moral claims today is coherent with the message that God has already made his eschatological power and purpose felt in the resurrection, is the use of Scripture authorized.

This authorization will allow and require the use of Scripture to call for loyalty to Christ and to the God who raised him. It will allow and require the use of Scripture to explicate the identity and perspective of those who are loyal to the risen Lord and the dispositions and intentions that cohere with loyalty to him. But loyalty to the risen Lord will not permit the simple repetition of the New Testament as normative for us without critical reflection, without passing through the prism of the resurrection, without being authorized by coherence with the eschatological power and purpose of God. To do so would be to assign the living Lord of all creation a slim slice of time and space, neither of which is ours, except by the pretense of playing the role of first-century Christians. To do so would be to construe God's relationship to us as archaizer rather than sanctifier.

There is backing for our authorization in the Gospels. There, in the resurrection conviction that the living Lord continued to address his people in Jesus' words and deeds, the tradition was used both faithfully and creatively so that the living Lord might lead his people by remembering this past to live truthfully and with integrity in a new situation. The authorization backed by the Gospel literature warrants the use of this literature to form and inform our identity and perspective, our dispositions and intentions; for it is Jesus, after all, who was raised, and his story is normatively decisive for our own. Jesus not only promised the inauguration of God's reign but made its power felt in himself. In the narratives of his words and deeds, of his cross and resurrection, we can discern the purpose and power of God's eschatological reign. The Gospels do not pass down the memory of his deeds and words with a biographical interest but with a practical one; and it remains so in the life of the church. The narratives were and must be elucidated by his resurrection, and they render a living Lord who leads his people in the remembrance of this past to live truthfully and with integrity nearly two millennia later in a changed and changing world.

Consider Matthew's Gospel, for example: we are not first-century Jewish Christians recently exiled from the synagogue, and using Matthew's Gospel in ways coherent with this understanding of the New Testament will not require us to pretend that we are. Matthew's *Halakic* rulings may not simply be repeated for the church today; but Matthew's Gospel — even in the rendering of *Halakic* rules — renders the living Lord. To adopt Matthew's *Halakic* rulings for a first-century Jewish Christian community as normative for a twentieth-century Christian community would be to identify God's eschatological reign with his sanctifying governance of that particular community, and thus restrict it. Matthew's Gospel, even in the rendering of rules, provides an agent whose character and intentions are normatively decisive for our own. So it also enables and requires a community capable of discernment and judgment in ways faithful to that Lord and appropriate at once to God's eschatological reign and to their own time and place. In that Lord, God's reign lives and moves and has its origin, and in that Lord, the Christian community lives and moves and has its identity. The memory of Jesus' words and deeds in Matthew's Gospel functions to form and inform our identity and our Christian community — our perspective, dispositions, and intentions.

There is no identity without memory, and there is no community without common memory. Of course, the very manner of telling Jesus' story is influenced by the particular intentions of the specific individuals addressing a concrete audience. The way to tell the story of Jesus was and remains a moral issue precisely because it is so intimately related to the question of what sorts of people and what kind of community its hearers ought to be. The four Gospels and the other traditions of Jesus in the New Testament provide many stories as they tell the one story, and the authorized use of them will not provide one neat, systematic account of Christian identity and character. The phenomenon of four canonical Gospels should be enough to dispel such illusions. Even so, they do tell the one story, and the New Testament's and church's memory of it enables and requires those who affirm the resurrection to make it their own story, to shape their characters to its character and their lives to its narrative. Thus God is our sanctifier in these writings, and thus the living Lord leads us in remembrance of him to live truthfully and with integrity in a changed world.

There is also backing for our authorization in the epistolary literature, particularly in what we have called Paul's "new discernment." There, in the conviction of the resurrection and in response to concrete crises of particular communities, Paul articulates and calls for a Christian identity and perspective, and for virtues, intentions, and principles that cohered with them. He brought moral rules from any source whatever under the critical and transforming illumination of this identity and perspective. Even the use of the Hebrew scriptures and of the tradition of Jesus' words was normed by God's eschatological power and purpose in raising the crucified one from the dead. Paul's discernment never rested on a code but always on the Christian identity provided by participation in Christ's cross and resurrection. How ironic that Paul's advice to specific first-century churches should sometimes be treated as a code in the contemporary Christian community! The authorization backed by Paul's new discernment warrants the use of the Pauline materials to form and inform Christian identity and perspective, to defend certain dispositions, intentions, and principles as coherent with the reign of God inaugurated by Christ's resurrection or, to use Paul's phrase, with "life according to the Spirit." But it will not warrant the use of Paul's concrete admonitions as moral rules for a changed and changing contemporary world. They too must submit to the critical and transforming illuminations of a Christian identity founded in the resurrection of a crucified one. One may pass, for example, from Scripture to moral claims concerning dispositions and intentions appropriate to the eschatological unity of male and female in Christ. One may not, according to the proposed authorization, move directly from Paul's rule concerning the silence of the Corinthian women to action-guiding claims concerning the behavior of women in congregations today. Such a use would be inconsistent with Paul's own discernment and with the authorization proposed. Paul's concrete moral conclusions may still be the right ones today, but they may not be claimed as right simply because they are found in the New Testament. They must be shown to be right by a contemporary calculation of means and consequences under the aegis of the Christian identity and perspective, under the governance of dispositions and intentions and principles that cohere with the reign of God disclosed and guaranteed in the resurrection and are known in and through the New Testament. So God bears toward us — as well as toward the Corinthians, Galatians, and other communities in these writings — the relationship of sanctifier, not archaizer. And so the crucified one claims us for his own and leads us into a manner of life worthy of the gospel in a changed world through these writings.

In the Pastoral Epistles and in some of the Catholic Epistles, to be sure, commonplace morality is increasingly accepted, and the eschatological reign of God is seen as exercised in quite ordinary regulations and in quite mundane activities. While our authorization would not permit the direct appeal to the conventional first-century morality of those Epistles or require a contemporary church order composed of these churches', it would use them, for example, to remind us that the Christian perspective is not a Gnostic one, that Christians are disposed neither to asceticism nor to libertinism, that our intentions include the sanctification — not the dismissal or denial — of mundane and common relationships and responsibilities. Thus the God who raised Jesus from the dead sanctifies this mundane world and this common history.

Even the Apocalypse, finally, provides backing for our proposal. It has a practical interest rather than a calculating one. It reminds the seven churches of their loyalty to the risen Lord, of their identity in his cross and resurrection, of their eschatological perspective, of their dispositions to patient endurance and hope, and of their intentions to live with integrity and truthfulness. It refuses simply to reiterate the advice of the apostles to honor the emperor in a changed world. Rather, standing where the apostles stood, on the foundation of the resurrection, it discerns that the Christian identity and perspective, dispositions and intentions, call for a counter-empire existence. But the authorization backed by Revelation will not warrant the straightforward analogy of Babylon and Rome to any contemporary government any more than it would warrant a direct appeal to Romans 13 to call for mindless obedience to, say, the Third Reich. The analogy *may* be appropriate, but it will need to be shown to be appropriate by a contemporary calculating of the implications of the Christian identity, perspective, dispositions, intentions, and principles — all founded on the resurrection of the crucified one — for one's relationship to any concrete government today. Thus the risen Lord reminds us again of the reign of God and the great reversal it brings and calls us to share in his suffering and in his victory with lives that defend his claim to the earth and its poor. Thus God bears toward us in Revelation too the relationship of sanctifier.

Neither too much nor too little must be made of the claim to find backing within the New Testament for the proposed authorization for the use of the New Testament in moral argument. On the one hand, the particular construal of Scripture that stands behind such an authorization also stands behind the appeal to the New Testament to provide backing for the authorization. There is, I think, no way out of that sort of circularity. On the other hand, the inability to demonstrate coherence between Scripture itself and a proposal for its use would and should count against the proposal. The proposal acknowledges the final test of the Christian community's experience of Scripture's authority in the context of its own moral life. I offer the proposal, indeed, as no final word but as a modest contribution to the church's task of continually rediscovering and recovering a manner of life worthy of its story and its Scripture.

4. What Is the Relevance of Other Sources?

The final methodologically significant question still calls for our attention: what is the relevance of other sources? The consensus identified earlier called for some kind of dialogue between Scripture and other sources, a dialogue in which Scripture was to have the last word at least at the level of Christian identity. To build on that consensus is a complex undertaking, in part because of the variety of sources one might consider: philosophy, sociology, economics, commonplace morality, role responsibilities, our involvement and identification with particular causes and projects, to name only a few. Another part of its complexity has to do with the variety within any one of these sources; within philosophy, for example, there is linguistic analysis, existentialism, phenomenology, Kantianism, Hegelianism, Aristotelianism, Platonism, and so forth. And yet another part of the complexity of this issue is the variety of positions on this question within the New Testament itself. Matthew makes use of the Jewish legal tradition in ways that would be alien to a number of other writers in the New Testament. Revelation situates Christ and the Christian identity over against Roman citizenship and culture, whereas some other literature in the New Testament makes positive use of one's involvement in the project of Rome and of Hellenistic moral commonplaces. I do not intend to treat this issue fully, but, short of that, I feel that the following observations are methodologically significant and coherent with what has gone before.

a. THE MORAL-RULE LEVEL

At the level of moral rules, where the question is, what should I do? the answer is ordinarily arrived at by an analysis of the facts and by application of the community's rules. Other sources play the major role here both in terms of the analysis of the facts and in terms of the community's rules. The doctor, for example, who asks, "What should I do?" will conduct a scientific diagnosis and follow the rules of good medical practice. He will not rely on the New Testament for either scientific information or the rules of "good medical practice." The parent who wonders what to do will try to find out what happened and what is likely to happen and will follow the commonplace rules of "good parenting." The woman who asks what she should do analyzes the situation and may follow the conventional rules assigning rights and duties to women.

At this level, then, the sciences — both the natural sciences and the human sciences — play an important and often critical role in the analysis of the facts of the case. The doctor will use his knowledge of biology and chemistry; the parent may read some psychology; the woman, some sociology. Of course, it may be appropriate to argue that some models of scientific analysis are more coherent than others for a perspective on persons and their societies formed and informed by the New Testament. For example, it may be argued that in psychology the behavioral model is necessarily limited and reductionistic when weighed against the Christian vision, or that in sociology the Marxist model is too pessimistic and deterministic, even though appropriately sensitive to structural ways in which the poor are oppressed and violated, when weighed against the Christian perspective. In this way, even while the New Testament provides neither scientific theory nor scientific analysis, it can provide the last word about whether and how a particular scientific model can be used with Christian integrity as well as scientific integrity. Changes in the model or in the analysis, however, must be argued on scientific grounds, not on biblical grounds.

b. THE ETHICAL-PRINCIPLE LEVEL

"Good medical practice," "good parenting," and "conventional sex roles" in any particular community provide sources of rules, but these rules are not unchallengeable. To challenge the rules, however, is to enter the ethical-principle level. Here the New Testament provides the critical source within the Christian community for the evaluation, criticism, and change of the rules, but other sources are relevant too. The perspectives, dispositions, intentions, and principles appealed to by the particular community to justify its rules in the first place are relevant, and so especially is the commonplace moral wisdom of a culture and moral philosophy.

The relationship of the New Testament — or of the identity, perspective, dispositions, and intentions grounded in the New Testament — to the questioned rules may sometimes be to defend them, adding to them dispositions and intentions that are grounded in God's relationship to them as sanctifier in the resurrection of Jesus. The relationship may sometimes be to criticize them, either critically reconstructing them (transforming them) or rejecting them for some others. The last word about whether to follow a particular community's rules belongs — in principle — to Scripture, not because the movement from Scripture to moral claims about rules is authorized (for, according to our proposal, it is not authorized) but because Scripture does enable and require Christians to have a loyalty and identity, perspective, dispositions, intentions, and principles that govern their character and conduct. They must act in ways that have integrity with their story, that are truthful to the affirmation that God raised Jesus from the dead — and sometimes that integrity and truthfulness may be found *within* the conventional rules of particular communities, but sometimes only by *rejecting* those rules. In practice, of course, the passage from identity, perspective, dispositions, and intentions to judgments about the rules and about what one really ought to do is a long and complex passage. And just as Matthew and Mark reached different conclusions about rabbinical rules, so Christians today can — and often do — reach different conclusions about whether and how to follow "the rules," say, of "good medical practice," "good parenting," and the "conventional role assignments" for women. This variety is partly due to a different ordering and priority of New Testament dispositions, intentions, and principles. It is partly due to the eschatological situation recognized in the New Testament perspective, namely that the world and its people do not yet flourish and that God's reign is not yet unchallenged. In such an eschatological situation, those things considered good can come into conflict not only with evil but with each other — real "goods" can come into real conflict. But finally, the variety is also partly due to the different weighing of other sources by Christians. Even so, concerning the judgment on the rules themselves, the New Testament has, in principle at least, the final word.

Among other sources at this level are moral philosophy and the moral identities, with their attendant perspectives, dispositions, intentions, and principles, which belong to people by virtue of the fact that they belong to other particular communities. To take the second of these first, those moral identities that are inherited along with memberships in other communities are not necessarily disowned as sources of moral wisdom by the New Testament itself, but they are brought under the critical and reconstructive lordship of Jesus Christ. Jews and Gentiles, for example, were not required to cease being Jew and Gentile when they became Christians; but their final allegiance was claimed for the living Lord and the eschatological reign of God. The married were not required to become unmarried, but the eschatological perspective did affect character and conduct also within marriage. Today's world provides other identities and perspectives that need not necessarily be disowned, but today's Christians must bring them too under the critical and transforming power and purpose of God. We must develop a relationship toward them appropriate to their relationship to God the sanctifier and to the Jesus whom he raised. That relationship may sometimes require the criticism of such an identity or indeed the disowning of it, sometimes the affirmation of such an identity within and under Christ's reign, and sometimes — perhaps usually — the critical reconstruction of such an identity. In many instances, of course, all of these relationships will be appropriate to our participation in another community and the complex ways in which that community shapes our perspective, dispositions, and intentions.

The identity of a physician, for example, insofar as it is associated with the intentions to heal, to relieve the suffering of the sick, and to preserve life, is to be affirmed within and under the reign of God who intends human life and its flourishing. The physician's identity has recently been tempted, however, through the great successes of medical science, to form a perspective that looks on humans as the sum total of the physical and chemical mechanisms that operate on them according to scientific laws. He may thus form a disposition to treat them as such. A critical reconstruction of the physician's identity and its attendant attitude toward both technology and patients may then be appropriate to submission to God's eschatological reign. And if the physician's identity should ever assume the character of social management, with the accompanying intention to eliminate the unproductive and troublesome, then that identity — or at least that aspect of the identity — should be rejected and disowned. The appropriate relevance of the doctor's perspective as a source of moral wisdom at this level can itself be a complex question; it may neither be uncritically disowned nor uncritically owned in relation to God the sanctifier. The last word belongs to Scripture's formation of Christian identity, not to the physician's perspective.

A parent's identity and dispositions would seem to be affirmed within the eschatological reign of God, the Father of our Lord Jesus Christ. But that identity and its attendant perspective and dispositions can be affected by the cultural context in which it is assumed. The role and character of "good parenting" has sometimes been construed as bringing a child into young adulthood as a "neutral" agent, unfettered by any familial religious loyalties or fundamental moral values; at other times it has been construed as the effective conditioning and manipulating of the child into the forms of behavior the parent wants. The identity of parent will not necessarily be disowned in these instances, but a critical reconstruction of the meaning of parenting will be required before it is allowed to function as a source of wisdom about the rules to be followed within parenting. It would be a mistake to try to lift these rules from the New Testament, but the New Testament retains in the Christian community the final word at this level and in this dialogue.

Our other example was the conventional role assignments for women. When these provide for women and require of women an identity as sexual object — helpless, childish, and inferior — then they must be criticized and reconstructed even if some might be able to appeal to Scripture at the moral-rule level in an attempt to support such role assignments. When those roles and that identity enable men to view women and to be disposed to treat women as less than equal partners in God's project, then those rules and that identity must be disowned. Of course, one need not cease being male or female; but the meaning and relevance of that identity must be subject to the eschatological reign of God the sanctifier. Women's liberation is a part of God's cause. But if we make the contemporary movement a part of our cause, if we identify with it and allow it to form and inform our perspective and dispositions and to provide a source of moral wisdom when we evaluate conventional role assignments and construct new ones, then it too must finally come under the critical and reconstructive reign of God. One may question whether the New Testament's perspective on freedom is the one generally operative in the women's liberation movement. The risen Christ frees people, including men, for service and fellowship, not for self-serving independence and surely not to license. The last word belongs to Scripture's formation of Christian identity and its attendant perspective, dispositions, and intentions. It does not belong to conventional role assignments for women (even ones found in Scripture), nor to other causes and projects to liberate women from them.

The examples could be multiplied. The point, however, would remain that our other identities and loyalties need not be disowned, but they must be brought captive to the risen Lord. The one who bears toward us the role of sanctifier in Scripture bears that relationship toward us in all our lesser loyalties and communities and identities. The complexity of this relationship of Scripture to these other sources need not be denied in order to render intelligible and methodologically significant the claim that Scripture has the last word in this dialogue.

Moral philosophy provides a different kind of source at this level, a different sort of partner-in-dialogue. Moral philosophy, of course, is a complex enterprise, and its relationship to Scripture is correspondingly complex. A major concern of contemporary moral philosophy has been "meta-ethics," the study of the meaning of moral terms. Another major concern, however, has been the more traditional one of defining, defending, and applying certain fundamental principles. It is the second of these that functions as an important source at the ethical-principle level and interests us here as a partner-in-dialogue with Scripture concerning what rules ought to be obeyed and why. Most contemporary normative theory differs from the sources we have been considering by its intentional abstraction from particular loyalties and identities. Its project is to identify, justify, and apply certain moral principles which hold on the basis of reason alone, independent of the roles or character of persons, and which may serve, therefore, as a standard by which to judge any and all human institutions, rules, and actions.

There are, of course, a wide variety of normative moral theories, and the relationship of the Scripture-grounded identity and perspective to any one of them can only be worked out fully and concretely by considering the individual theory. Even so, a couple of general observations seem possible. In the first place, neo-orthodoxy's "theological veto" on natural morality and moral philosophy may not be allowed to stand. When the veto is based on the radical fallenness of human nature and all of its projects, the cavalier dismissal of arguments based on reason alone strikes me as an *argumentum ad hominem* on the scale of an *argumentum ad humanum*. Such a position is an inappropriate response not only to humans but to their creator and sustainer, the very God who raised Jesus from the dead and is their sanctifier. Moreover, it is quite inappropriate to the New Testament itself, where the natural morality and the ethical theory of the first century were clearly not summarily dismissed.

The second observation, on the other hand, is that natural morality and normative theories, even the best of them, may not be simply identified with the Christian ethic based on Scripture. Precisely because these theories abstract themselves from considerations of loyalty and identity, the Christian will not be able to base his character or his conduct on them alone with any integrity. He will see them as essentially minimal requirements, which threaten to distort the Christian's discernment of the character and conduct worthy of the gospel if — but perhaps only if — their minimalism is not acknowledged.

More specifically, utilitarianism, with its reduction of morality to the utility principle, is ill-suited to recognize the minimal character of the legitimate claims of utility or to acknowledge the moral importance of integrity. If one adds to that the philosophical problems with utilitarianism,[107] one can see that it is not the most auspicious candidate for a partner-in-dialogue with Scripture. Deontological theories are better suited to acknowledge the minimal character of their claims and the moral importance of identity and integrity. The notion of categorical rights and wrongs, either denied or elided into utility by the utilitarians, provides an important source of moral wisdom and restraint. There are varieties of deontological theories, of course, and important differences between them. But the natural morality that knows fairness to be required, promise-keeping to be a duty, and lying and killing to be wrongs — and the moral theories that defend, articulate, and apply such moral principles[108] — are well-suited to be partners-in-dialogue with Scripture both in the church and in the world.

We have already noted the minimal character of the claims of such theories. They tell us not what goods to seek but what constraints to exercise in seeking them. When such theories ignore or deny the minimal character of their claims, they can badly distort the moral enterprise: by reducing role-relationships like husband and wife, teacher and student, and doctor and patient to contractual relationships between autonomous individuals; by undermining the ancient enterprise of answering in theory and in the formation of character and conduct the question of what persons were meant to be and to become; and by reducing morality to autonomy as deftly and devastatingly as the utilitarians reduce it to maximizing happiness. A culture that ignores or denies the minimal character of such claims, as our culture has, will be composed of atomistic individuals, capable of contracts but ignorant of community, marked by a rigid tolerance, prohibiting not only the punishment but the public negative judgment and even the public questioning of autonomous behavior that does not interfere with anyone else's autonomy. In such a culture many moral issues will no longer be considered moral issues at all but either "religious" issues (e.g., abortion) or matters of "preference" (e.g., homosexuality). When the minimal character of the claims of such theories is ignored or denied, neither the theories nor the public morality of a culture informed by them is well-situated to be a partner-in-dialogue with Scripture. The moral identity, perspective, dispositions, and intentions grounded in Scripture will stand in criticism of such reductionism and attempt the critical reconstruction of a fuller account of morality.

When such theories acknowledge the minimal character of their claims, however, they can provide a valuable source alongside Scripture for discernment and judgment of actions and policies. Indeed, sometimes they may provide the last word in the dialogue since the claims of justice are appropriately adamant and the claims of categorical rights and wrongs are by definition categorical. In that dialogue such theories may challenge and judge certain claims made on the basis of Scripture. Scripture has, after all, been used to justify racial and sexual discrimination; it has been used to justify "holy wars," crusades, and inquisitions; it has been used to justify the abuse of power and the violation of the rights and integrity of others in order to pursue what has been taken to be God's cause. Secular moral wisdom, and especially the principle of justice, has sometimes challenged such uses of Scripture and led the church to reconsider particular practices and to repent of them. We must note that it is not the authority of Scripture itself that comes under criticism and review here, but authorizations for the use of Scripture in moral argument and moral claims made employing such authorizations. In the churches Scripture itself has sometimes finally corroborated the judgments of secular morality and been vindicated against both its detractors and its so-called defenders in such cases. The final word belongs to Scripture. Even so, the point is methodologically significant and may be formulated candidly as this: If a moral claim, even one purportedly based on Scripture, is inconsistent with justice, it should not be allowed to stand, and if an authorization for the use of Scripture warrants claims that are inconsistent with justice, it should not be allowed to stand. The candor of that formulation, of course, does not mask its abstractness. There are various formulations of the meaning and requirements of justice and of categorical norms. I would not suggest that authorizations for the use of Scripture be tested for consistency with each novel and fashionable theory of justice that comes along, particularly in a culture tempted to reduce morality to autonomy and public morality to tolerance. Moreover, there are sometimes Christian reasons — reasons based on an identity and perspective grounded in the New Testament — for preferring theories that emphasize equality as well as liberty to theories that simply require liberty.[109]

In the dialogue at this level the Christian identity based on Scripture will urge the construal of justice and of categorical rights and wrongs that coheres with its own perspective and principles; it will criticize any reduction of morality to these minimal principles; but it will acknowledge that the minimal claims of justice are nevertheless overriding, that they may legitimately criticize and judge both claims made on the basis of Scripture and authorizations for the use of Scripture. The one who bears toward us the relationship of sanctifier in Scripture is the very one who created the world and preserves it, restraining the effects of sin on the meaning and value he built into the world by his law. That law is knowable apart from Scripture, confirmed and critically reconstructed by Scripture, but also capable of providing a minimal but critical standard for testing claims based on Scripture and authorizations for the use of Scripture. Natural morality and the normative ethics that articulate it and defend it are valued partners-in-dialogue with Scripture at this level. Such a dialogue will be a complex undertaking: on the one hand, it will protect the independence and autonomy of moral philosophy and its project of articulating and defending principles that hold on the basis of reason alone, independent of the character, identity, and roles of persons; on the other hand, it will be committed to the critical reconstruction of those principles in view of the cosmic sovereignty of the Creator and Preserver who raised Jesus from the dead and who bears toward us in Scripture the relationship of sanctifier.

c. THE POST-ETHICAL LEVEL

At the post-ethical level the question is, *why* be moral? The question can be construed either as an appeal for the justification of the basic moral principle (or principles) or as an explanation of what moves one to be moral and act morally. In justification of the basic moral principles there cannot be any further appeal to moral principle; otherwise the principle one is attempting to justify would not be basic. There can, however, be appeals to sources other than Scripture. One can, I think, justify some minimal but basic principle of respect for persons as implicitly accepted whenever anyone engages in moral discourse. It would be inconsistent to implicitly affirm such principles while explicitly denying them by some moral claim. One can perhaps justify and motivate moral principles on prudential grounds, that being moral and acting moral is finally in one's own interest. And there may be other sources at the post-ethical level. All of them, however, are insignificant and mute when Christians consider questions at this level. Why be moral? Because God is God. Why be moral? Because I am not my own but belong to him. The replies to questions at this level appeal to God's identity, to his integrity, power, and promise, and to the identity of those who trust in him and would be faithful to him. The source for such replies is the Christian tradition, preeminently the normative part of that tradition found in the Scriptures, and within the Scriptures particularly the New Testament, when it is owned as one's own.

In the New Testament God the Creator is the God who raised Jesus from the dead and who bears toward us the relationship of sanctifier. Therefore, no Gnostic dualism releases us from moral responsibility in his world to pursue either libertinism or asceticism. On the contrary, in relationship to the Creator we know ourselves and all creatures to be dependent on him and to require the ordering of the creation according to his will and intention. He has established his own cosmic reign against every contender in raising Jesus from the dead; now, while the powers of sin and death continue to contend against his reign, Christians know that part of their faithful response to God the Creator, part of their trusting dependence, part of God's ordering of the creation is morality and, more concretely, the moral identity, perspective, dispositions, and intentions that cohere with the affirmation that the Creator God raised Jesus from the dead.

God the Covenanter is the God who raised Jesus from the dead and who bears toward us the relationship of sanctifier. Therefore, no arbitrary or whimsical freedom marks his reign. He has established himself on the flourishing of his creation and his people. Christians know, in relation to the Covenanter, that they are covenanted. We discover our freedom in no arbitrary and whimsical neutrality or autonomy but precisely in being bound to him and by him to other persons and the creation's flourishing. He has established his covenant in raising Jesus from the dead; now, while persons and the creation do not yet flourish, being bound to him obliges us to morality and, more concretely, to the identity, perspective, dispositions, and intentions that cohere with the affirmation that the Covenanter raised Jesus from the dead.

Jesus of Nazareth is the one who walked among us doing signs and wonders, who announced that God's reign is at hand, who called for repentance and faith, and who died on a cross. The shape of repentance and faith, therefore, will always be formed and informed by the church's remembrance of this Jesus. His story gives us identity and perspective, and his words and deeds enable and require us to be formed by and to form certain dispositions and intentions. Now, in remembrance of him — "until he comes" — part of repentance and part of faith will always be morality, certainly not the prudential calculations of reciprocity but a peculiar identity as his apprentices with its attendant perspective, dispositions, and intentions.

God the Judge is the God who raised the crucified Jesus from the dead and bears toward us the relationship of sanctifier. Therefore, eschatological watchfulness becomes us, not only the expectant watching for his final victory and his final judgment on all that hinders his creation's flourishing, but earnest watchfulness concerning our own character and conduct, watchfulness concerning our susceptibility to the powers of sin and death, watchfulness concerning the temptations to sloth and pride, watchfulness concerning our identity and perspective, our dispositions and intentions, in sum, our morality.

In all these ways — and more — the New Testament provides the last word for Christians at the post-ethical level. Moreover, in each of them — and in the others — the reasons for being moral form and inform the moral identity and perspective, the dispositions and intentions, of the agent.[110] The reasons for being moral apply not so much to morality-in-general as to the morality which coheres with loyalty to the God who raised Jesus from the dead and who bears toward us in Scripture the relationship of sanctifier.

The reasons for being moral give direction and warrant for the use of Scripture at the ethical-principle level to identify and develop the perspective, dispositions, intentions, and principles that cohere with the Christian identity. At that level the dialogue with other sources is vigorous and complex. One does not necessarily disown other identities and perspectives but brings them into and under the reign of God. The natural morality that acknowledges justice and certain categorical rights and wrongs and the moral theories that articulate and defend such a morality are especially valuable partners-in-dialogue at the ethical-principle level, and their identification of certain duties as obligations irrespective of loyalties may challenge and judge some of the ways in which Scripture has been used to rationalize injustice and wrongs. Scripture retains the last word in the dialogue at this level by corroborating such judgments on certain uses of Scripture and by demanding more than the minimalist account of morality such theories can provide.

By forming and informing Christian identity, as well as the moral perspectives, dispositions, and intentions that constitute it, Scripture also bears on questions at the moral-rule level, however mediately. It is inappropriate to inquire of Scripture at this level, expecting some authoritative, concrete command or rule. Scripture is not a direct source of moral guidance at this level, but all our rules and all our conduct based on them may and must be tested for integrity with the Christian identity, perspective, dispositions, intentions, and principles. In this way, Scripture has the last word also at the moral-rule level, and the God who bears toward us the relationship of sanctifier claims all of our life for his kingdom.

5. Conclusion

Addressing ourselves to the methodologically significant questions has yielded a number of suggestions, but four points that I take to be most important have been formulated candidly as authorizations. These merit repetition here as a kind of summary of the proposal.

1. Only if the use of a Scripture passage is coherent with its intention is that use in moral argument authorized.
2. The use of Scripture in moral argument a) is not authorized with respect to claims concerning an autonomous, impartial, and universal ethic; b) is authorized with respect to claims concerning Christian moral identity and its perspective, dispositions, intentions, and principles at the ethical-principle and post-ethical levels of moral argument; and c) is not authorized with respect to claims at the moral-rule level of moral argument.
3. If and only if the use of Scripture is coherent with the message that God has already made his eschatological power and purpose felt in raising Jesus from the dead, is it authorized.
4. Only if the moral claim is consistent with justice is the movement from Scripture to moral claim authorized.

This modest proposal has provided no recipe for making decisions on the basis of Scripture. It has formulated no neat and tidy Christian ethic that may be identified as *the* New Testament ethic. I do not offer the book either as the last word in New Testament studies or as the last word in Christian ethics. Its ambition is to help bridge the gulfs that have sometimes separated the academic disciplines of New Testament studies from Christian ethics, and both academic disciplines from the common life and common faith of the churches. Only when these gulfs are bridged will Christian ethics have integrity as *Christian* ethics or New Testament studies be able to address not only questions concerning the early church but the questions of the continuing church. More importantly, only when these gulfs are bridged will the continuing church make full use of the gifts God the Sanctifier has given it for the continuing discourse and discernment concerning a "manner of life worthy of the gospel of Christ" (Phil. 1:27).

NOTES

INTRODUCTION

1. An excellent treatment of the church as a community of moral discourse is provided by James M. Gustafson, "The Church: A Community of Moral Discourse," *The Church as Moral Decision-Maker* (Philadelphia: Pilgrim Press, 1970), pp. 83–95. Bruce C. Birch and Larry Rasmussen, *Bible and Ethics in the Christian Life* (Minneapolis: Augsburg, 1976), pp. 125–41, and James B. Nelson, *Moral Nexus: Ethics of Christian Identity and Community* (Philadelphia: Westminster, 1973), are also very good.

2. The examples given are all taken from I Corinthians. See I Cor. 7: 8-10; 11:2-16; 12-14; 16:1-4, and 5. See J. C. Hurd, Jr., *The Origin of I Corinthians* (New York: Seabury, 1965), for an able reconstruction of the correspondence between the Corinthians and Paul.

3. This is not to deny the role of the charismatic prophets in the early churches' moral discernment. Evidently, the prophets had the gift of knowing and making known in plain, intelligible speech the will of God for some concrete problem the community or its members faced. Through them the Spirit spoke. The precise nature of the phenomenon of prophecy is unclear and subject to a wide variety of interpretation. (See Dudley Ford, "Prophecy in the New Testament," *The Reformed Theological Review*, 31 [1972], 10–25). According to Frederick Dale Bruner, *A Theology of the Holy Spirit* (Grand Rapids: Eerdmans, 1970), p. 297, the prophetic gift refers to "the free, helpful discussion of Christians together and their contribution in thoughtful speech to each other." If that is so, then prophecy is virtually identical to the moral discourse we have been describing. But even if it is not, prophecy is still to be tested by the whole congregation (I Thess. 5:20, 21) in the light of their Christian tradition and confession, a task which involves the prophetic gifts of every member of the congregation (I Cor. 14:29) and discourse, reason-giving, and reason-hearing within the worshipping and discerning community. On prophecy, see J. Panagopoulos, *Prophetic Vocation in the New Testament and Today* (Leiden: E. J. Brill, 1977).

4. Martin Dibelius, one of the pioneers in form criticism, has demonstrated and emphasized that the early church made use of the form and content of the ethical materials of Hellenistic Judaism and of other contemporary moralists. But from this he infers that these materials finally controlled moral discernment in the early church (once its initial eschatological enthusiasm waned and it faced the demands of settled life in the world) and in the New Testament. To acknowledge that the early church used the moral commonplaces of its contemporaries, however, is not to say *how* it

used them. Dibelius overlooks the possibility that the convictions and loyalty which made the church a community of moral discourse controlled and determined the use of these traditional materials, adapting and transforming them in the service of a distinctively Christian life. Such, at least, as I hope to show, is what happened in the New Testament. See Martin Dibelius, *Urchristentum und Kultur* (Heidelberg: Carl Winters Universitäts-buchhandlung, 1928), and *An Die Kolosser. Epheser. An Philemon (Handbuch zum Neuen Testament*, 3rd ed., rev. by H. Greeven; Tübingen: J. C. B. Mohr, 1953). For criticism of Dibelius, see especially Victor Paul Furnish, *Theology and Ethics in Paul* (Nashville: Abingdon, 1968), pp. 259–62 et passim, and John Howard Yoder, *The Politics of Jesus* (Grand Rapids: Eerdmans, 1972), pp. 166–92.

5. Indeed, as David Kelsey, *The Uses of Scripture in Recent Theology* (Philadelphia: Fortress, 1975), has shown, "part of what it means to call a text or set of texts 'scripture' is that its use in certain ways in the common life of the Christian community is essential to establishing and preserving the community's identity" (p. 89; see also pp. 90–100). That the Scripture of the church is an authority for the church's common life is, therefore, an analytical judgment (ibid). The locution "Scripture is an authority for the church's moral discernment," then, is not a description of a set of texts in terms of one of its peculiar properties but rather a "performative utterance" committing the speaker to use those texts in certain ways (yet unspecified) in moral discernment and judgment (cf. ibid., pp. 89, 109–12). What those certain ways are, however, *how* Scripture is to be used in moral discernment and judgment, or in other aspects of the church's common life, cannot, according to Kelsey, be known through an analysis of either the concept "Scripture" or the concept "authority."

CHAPTER I

1. For example, I Cor. 7:10-11; I Cor. 9:14. The extent and character of Paul's use of Jesus' moral teachings is debatable; see Victor Paul Furnish, *Theology and Ethics in Paul* (Nashville: Abingdon, 1968), pp. 51–65. See also I Tim. 5:18, where what is evidently a saying of Jesus is joined with a quotation of Deut. 25:4 and appealed to as "Scripture."

2. *The Didache* or *The Teaching of the Twelve Apostles* was a manual which served as a basis for Christian instruction in the early second century. The first part contains moral instruction based on the ancient distinction between "The Two Ways." The second part gives directions concerning rites and roles in the church. See J. B. Lightfoot, *The Apostolic Fathers* (London: Macmillan, 1891), pp. 119–29.

3. Carl F. H. Henry, *Christian Personal Ethics* (Grand Rapids: Eerdmans, 1957), pp. 278–326. Harvey K. McArthur, *Understanding the Sermon on the Mount* (New York: Harper, 1960), pp. 105–48, and Robert T. Stein, *The Method and Message of Jesus' Teachings* (Philadelphia: Westminster, 1978), pp. 89–96, each provide summaries of the various interpretations of Jesus' ethic. See also Richard H. Hiers, *Jesus and Ethics* (Philadelphia: Westminster, 1968), which focuses on the question of eschatology and ethics.

4. For example, Hans Windisch, *The Meaning of the Sermon on the Mount* (Philadelphia: Westminster, 1951); John Knox, *The Ethic of Jesus in the Teaching of the Church* (New York: Abingdon, 1961); Thomas Jefferson, *The Life and Morals of Jesus of Nazareth* (New York: Funk, 1940); and a number of Anabaptist writers.

5. For example, Newman Smyth, *Christian Ethics* (New York: Scribners, 1892); Walter Rauschenbusch, *The Social Principles of Jesus* (New York: Association Press, 1916); T. W. Manson, *The Teaching of Jesus* (Cambridge: Cambridge University Press, 1935 [2nd ed.]); most recently, R.E.O. White, *Biblical Ethics* (Atlanta: John Knox, 1979).

6. For example. L. H. Marshall. *The Challenge of New Testament Ethics* (New York: Macmillan. 1947): Lindsay Dewar, *An Outline of New Testament Ethics* (London: University of London Press, 1949).

7. Rudolf Bultmann, *Jesus and the Word* (New York: Scribners, 1958), p. 66.

8. Besides Bultmann, ibid., see also H. R. Niebuhr, *The Meaning of Revelation* (New York: Macmillan, 1941).

9. S. G. F. Brandon, *Jesus and the Zealots* (New York: Scribners, 1967).

10. For example, Reinhold Niebuhr, *An Interpretation of Christian Ethics* (New York: Harper & Brothers, 1935).

11. For example, a number of monastic texts and Thomas à Kempis, *The Imitation of Christ* (London: S. M. Dent & Sons, 1910).

12. For example, Newman Smyth, *Christian Ethics.*

13. For example, a number of social gospel writers, preeminently Walter Rauschenbusch, *The Social Principles of Jesus.*

14. H. R. Niebuhr, *The Meaning of Revelation.* p. 166.

15. See already *The Didache.* 6 (J. B. Lightfoot, *The Apostolic Fathers.* pp. 125f.); Gerd Thiessen, *The First Followers of Jesus* (London: SCM, 1978), argues that in the first century the "wandering charismatics" obeyed Jesus' teachings in a radical fashion while the "local sympathizers" did not.

16. Martin Luther, "Secular Authority: To What Extent It Should Be Obeyed," *Works of Martin Luther.* Vol. III (Philadelphia: A. J. Holman, 1930), pp. 228–73; cf. also, for example, Henry Cadbury, *The Peril of Modernizing Jesus* (New York: Macmillan, 1937).

17. Albert Schweitzer, *The Quest of the Historical Jesus* (New York: Macmillan, 1961), p. 354. Schweitzer's position has recently been forthrightly restated and defended by Jack T. Sanders, *Ethics in the New Testament* (Philadelphia: Fortress, 1975), pp. 1–29. Richard H. Hiers, *Jesus and Ethics.* pp. 39–78, makes it clear, however, that in spite of his position on Jesus' eschatology, Schweitzer remained concerned about the relevance and authority of Jesus for contemporary life.

18. C. H. Dodd, *Gospel and Law* (New York: Columbia University Press, 1951); see Hiers, *Jesus and Ethics,* pp. 115–32.

19. Amos Wilder, *Eschatology and Ethics in the Teaching of Jesus* (New York: Harper, 1950).

20. For example, Donald G. Barnhouse, *His Own Received Him Not. But . . .* (New York: Revell, 1933), pp. 38, 40.

21. Martin Dibelius, *The Sermon on the Mount* (New York: Scribners, 1945).

22. For example, Reinhold Niebuhr, *An Interpretation of Christian Ethics.*

23. For example, Thomas Jefferson, *The Life and Morals of Jesus of Nazareth.*

24. In his work by that title (*The Peril of Modernizing Jesus*); see also Albert Schweitzer, *The Quest of the Historical Jesus.*

25. The most important and influential form critics have been Martin Dibelius, *From Tradition to Gospel* (London: Nicholson & Watson, 1934); Rudolf Bultmann, *History of the Synoptic Tradition* (New York: Harper & Row, 1963); and (in England) Vincent Taylor, *The Formation of the Gospel Tradition* (London: Macmillan, 1943). To agree with their premise that sayings of Jesus and stories about Jesus first circulated independently and orally is not, of course, necessarily to agree with the historical skepticism of some of the form critics who suppose most of the Gospel material to be creations of the early church. Form criticism is fundamentally a literary, not an historical, discipline. On form criticism, see also Edgar V. McKnight, *What is Form Criticism?* (Philadelphia: Fortress, 1969).

26. Source criticism is concerned with written sources for the Gospels rather than oral sources, although it is often difficult to draw clear distinctions. Even so, it can hardly be doubted that our Gospels used written sources (cf. Lk. 1:1-4). I will be assuming that Matthew and Luke make use of Mark and another source which scholars call Q. This remains a consensus in spite of some spirited (but unsuccessful)

criticism. It also is the case that Mark himself makes use of other early collections of the oral tradition. The question of literary sources for John's Gospel is much debated; I will be assuming that John does not have any *literary* dependence on the Synoptic Gospels. See further William A. Beardslee, *Literary Criticism of the New Testament* (Philadelphia: Fortress, 1970).

27. Redaction criticism is the discipline that focuses on the theological, moral, and pastoral motivations of the author as he collects, arranges, and shapes traditional material. See Norman Perrin, *What is Redaction Criticism?* (Philadelphia: Fortress, 1969), and J. Rohde, *Rediscovering the Teaching of the Evangelists* (Philadelphia: Westminster, 1968).

28. Thus Dibelius, *From Tradition to Gospel.*

29. Mt. 5:20; see Joachim Jeremias, *The Sermon on the Mount* (Philadelphia: Fortress, 1963); Christoph Burchard, "The Theme of the Sermon on the Mount," in Luise Schottorff et al., *Essays on the Love Commandment* (Philadelphia: Fortress, 1978).

30. Ernst Käsemann, "The Problem of the Historical Jesus," in his *Essays on New Testament Themes* (Naperville, Ill.: A. R. Allenson, 1964), p. 37. See also Norman Perrin, *Rediscovering the Teaching of Jesus* (London: SCM, 1967), pp. 39-43.

31. Ethelbert Stauffer, "Der Stand der Neutestamentlichen Forschung," in L. Henning, ed., *Theologie und Liturgie.* p. 93, cited by Nils Alstrup Dahl, "The Problem of the Historical Jesus," in his *The Crucified Messiah* (Minneapolis: Augsburg, 1974), p. 71.

32. T. W. Manson, *Studies in the Gospels and Epistles* (Philadelphia: Westminster, 1962); also his *The Teaching of Jesus.* For a review of this position, see D. E. Nineham, "Eyewitness Testimony and the Gospel Tradition," in *Journal of Theological Studies,* NS 9 (1958), 13-25, 243-52, and 11 (1960), 253-64. Anthony Hanson in turn has responded to Nineham's review and position in "The Quandary of Historical Skepticism," in A. Hanson, ed., *Vindications* (London: SCM, 1966), pp. 74-102. Nineham responds again in ". . . Et hoc genus omne — An Examination of Dr. A. T. Hanson's Strictures on Some Recent Gospel Study," in W. R. Farmer et al., ed., *Christian History and Interpretation: Studies Presented to John Knox* (Cambridge: Cambridge University Press, 1967), pp. 199-222.

33. H. Reisenfeld, *The Gospel Tradition and Its Beginnings* (London: A. R. Mowbray, 1957); B. Gerhardsson, *Memory and Manuscript* (Uppsala: Universitet, 1961). See the review of this position in W. D. Davies, *The Setting of the Sermon on the Mount* (Cambridge: Cambridge University Press, 1964), pp. 464-80.

34. See Jeremias' description of these laws and his use of them to recover the original meaning of the parables of Jesus in his masterful book *The Parables of Jesus* (rev. ed., New York: Scribners, 1963).

35. See his equally masterful *Jerusalem in the Time of Jesus* (Philadelphia: Fortress, 1969).

36. See his treatment of "abba" in *The Prayers of Jesus* (Philadelphia: Fortress, 1978), pp. 11-65.

37. The term is Harvey K. McArthur's in his "A Survey of Recent Gospel Research" in *Interpretation.* 18 (1964), 39-55. The best representative may be C. H. Dodd, *History and the Gospel* (New York: Scribners, 1938).

38. See Nils Alstrup Dahl, "The Problem of the Historical Jesus," in his *The Crucified Messiah.* pp. 48-89. He refers to Julius Schniewind's "Zur Synoptikerexegese," *Theologische Rundschau.* 2 (1930), 129-89, and his discussion of "longitudinal" and "cross-section exegesis."

39. See, e.g., S.G.F. Brandon, *Jesus and the Zealots.*

40. Cf. the motive for the "first quest." See Albert Schweitzer, *The Quest of the Historical Jesus.* p. 4: "The historical investigation of the life of Jesus did not take its rise from a purely historical interest; it turned to the Jesus of history as an ally in the struggle against the tyranny of dogma."

41. Thus Nils Alstrup Dahl, op. cit., pp. 72-74.
42. As Adolf Harnack, *What is Christianity?* (New York: Harper, 1957), p. 51, describes the teaching of Jesus.
43. That it is a secondary formulation may be seen above all in the specifically Christian admonition to "believe the gospel," Bultmann, *History of the Synoptic Tradition* (New York: Harper & Row, 1963), p. 118. C. H. Dodd is to be numbered among those who acknowledge that Mk. 1:14-15 is a summary rather than a verbatim report of a saying of Jesus, but he takes this and other "generalizing summaries" in Mark to be part of an early tradition providing a narrative of the Galilean ministry which Mark uses as a framework for his Gospel. C. H. Dodd, "The Framework of the Gospel Narrative," in his *New Testament Studies* (New York: Scribners, 1954), pp. 1-11. For a critique, see D. E. Nineham, "The Order of Events in St. Mark's Gospel — an Examination of Dr. Dodd's Hypothesis," in D. E. Nineham, ed., *Studies in the Gospels* (Oxford: B. Blackwell, 1955), pp. 223-39.
44. See Joachim Jeremias, *New Testament Theology* (New York: Scribners, 1971), pp. 31-34, for a tabulation of the attestation of Jesus' use of "kingdom" in various sources. He also demonstrates that the apparent emphasis on the "kingdom" cannot be attributed to either the Jewish environment or to early Christianity, that it "comes from Jesus himself" (p. 34). Ibid., pp. 96-97, shows attestation in multiple forms. See also N. Perrin, *Rediscovering the Teaching of Jesus*, pp. 34-63. On "repent," see E. Würthwein and J. Behm, *"metanoéō, metanoia"* in Kittel, ed., *TDNT*, IV (Grand Rapids: Eerdmans, 1967), 975-1008.
45. See Perrin, *The Kingdom of God in the Teaching of Jesus* (Philadelphia: Westminster, 1963), for a history of the interpretation of the concept from Schleiermacher and Ritschl to the early 1960s.
46. This consistent reference to both the present reality of the kingdom and its future consummation is one of the main themes of T. W. Manson, *The Teaching of Jesus* (2nd ed.).
47. Gerhard von Rad, *Old Testament Theology. Vol. II: The Theology of Israel's Prophetic Traditions* (Edinburgh: Oliver & Boyd, 1962), pp. 99-125, esp. p. 117. See Perrin, *The Kingdom of God in the Teaching of Jesus*, pp. 160-62.
48. On apocalypticism in general, see Klaus Koch, *The Rediscovery of Apocalyptic* (London: SCM, 1972); G. E. Ladd, "Apocalyptic Literature," *ISBE* (rev. ed.), I (Grand Rapids: Eerdmans, 1979), 151-61; H. H. Rowley, *The Relevance of Apocalyptic* (London: Lutterworth, 1944); D. S. Russell, *The Method and Message of Jewish Apocalyptic* (Philadelphia: Westminster, 1964); W. Schmithals, *The Apocalyptic Movement* (Nashville: Abingdon, 1975); P. D. Hanson, *Dawn of Apocalyptic* (Philadelphia: Fortress, 1975). Apocalypticism is a very complex phenomenon in its origins, its literary forms, and its characteristic teaching.
49. G. E. Ladd, "Apocalyptic Literature," pp. 155f.
50. W. D. Davies, "Apocalyptic and Pharisaism," in his *Christian Origins and Judaism* (Philadelphia: Westminster, 1962), pp. 19-30.
51. This point, first insisted upon by Schweitzer, *The Quest of the Historical Jesus*, has, after a long and vigorous discussion, become virtually a consensus among New Testament scholars. See Perrin, *The Kingdom of God in the Teaching of Jesus*, especially pp. 158-59; Ulrich Wilkens, "The Understanding of Revelation Within the History of Primitive Christianity," in W. Pannenberg, ed., *Revelation as History* (New York: Macmillan, 1968), p. 72; and many others. This is not to say that the phrase "kingdom of God" is typical of first-century Jewish apocalyptic; see Jeremias, *The Theology of the New Testament*, p. 32. Perrin, *The Kingdom of God in the Teaching of Jesus*, pp. 168-85, demonstrates that, although the use of the phrase "kingdom of God" in apocalyptic literature is rare, where it does appear it refers to "God's decisive intervention in history and human experience" and to "the final state of the redeemed to which his intervention is designed to lead" (p. 184). That the "kingdom of God" and, in Matthew's phrase, "the kingdom of heaven" are synonyms may be

considered a certainty. Matthew uses the phrase "kingdom of heaven" for the same reality Mark and Q refer to as "the kingdom of God" because of his own and his readers' Jewish piety, which conscientiously avoided the name of God. This scrupulous observance of the third commandment of the decalogue is one indicator of the Jewish-Christian character of Matthew's Gospel. There can yet be no absolute certainty about which of the phrases Jesus himself used, although Jeremias, *The Theology of the New Testament*, p. 97, argues quite convincingly that Jesus used "the kingdom of God." He cites both the fact that, although Jesus does frequently avoid the name of God by means of a substitution or circumlocution, he does not consistently avoid reference to "God" and the fact that the term "the kingdom of heaven" appears first in Jewish literature as a substitute for "the kingdom of God" around the time of Matthew's Gospel (in R. Johanan ben Zakkai, *j. Kidd.* 59d 28; see Jeremias, ibid., pp. 9–14).

52. Mk. 1:15, Gk. *eggiken.* On *eggus, eggizein,* see W. G. Kummel, *Promise and Fulfillment* (Naperville, Ill.: A. R. Allenson, 1957), pp. 19–25; see ibid, pp. 19–87, for a demonstration that Jesus expected and announced the kingdom in the imminent future.

53. The Kaddish was:

Exalted and hallowed be his great name in the world which he created according to his will. May he let his kingdom rule in your lifetime and in your days and in the lifetime of the whole house of Israel, speedily and soon. Praised be his great name from eternity to eternity. (Jeremias, *New Testament Theology,* p. 198)

Cf. Luke 11:2, "Hallowed be thy name. Thy kingdom come." Both the Kaddish and the Lord's Prayer petition for the speedy establishment of God's cosmic reign. Both Jeremias, loc. cit., and Perrin, *The Kingdom of God in the Teaching of Jesus*, p. 193, make the point that the Lord's Prayer knows that that future kingdom is already making its power felt. The Matthean version of the prayer (Mt. 6:9-13) is later than Luke's and contains liturgical expansions; at this point it is probably influenced by the church's faith in Christ's enthronement following the resurrection, for the expansion is, "Thy will be done on earth as it is in heaven" (vs. 10). The prayer has undoubtedly been shaped by usage in the church, but it is difficult to take seriously any skepticism about the authenticity of the earliest tradition. It was common practice for Jewish teachers to teach their disciples a prayer (see, e.g., Lk. 11:1). Moreover, the Aramaic original lies just below the surface of the Gospel's rendition of it into Greek (Jeremias, *The Prayers of Jesus,* pp. 89–94, especially p. 94, where he reconstructs the Aramaic original).

54. For Jesus' expectation of a resurrection, see not only the controversy with the Sadducees (Mk. 12:18ff. par.) but also Mt. 12:41f. (par. Lk. 11:31f.); Lk. 14:14, etc. For his expectation of a judgment, see Lk. 10:12 (par. Mt. 10:15); Lk. 10:14 (par. Mt. 11:22); Mt. 12:36; 25:31ff., etc. For his expectation of the destruction and renewal of the world, see Mk. 13:31 (par. Mt. 24:35; Lk. 21:33); Mt. 5:18 (par. Lk. 16:17); Mt. 19:28 (par. Lk. 22:28-30); Mk. 10:30 (par. Mt. 19:29; Lk. 18:29,30), etc.

55. Luke 17:21b, "The kingdom of God is in the midst of you" (RSV; Gk.: *èntòs hymōn estin*; KJV: "The kingdom of God is within you"), has often been used to defend the view that the kingdom of God "*means* the reign of God within each soul living under the divine sovereignty" (R.E.O. White, *Biblical Ethics* [Atlanta: John Knox, 1979], p. 78). '*Entòs hymōn* is indeed ambiguous. It can mean either "within" (Mt. 23:26) or "among," "in the midst of." The Aramaic preposition which lies behind it, according to T. W. Manson, *The Sayings of Jesus* (London: SCM, 1949), pp. 303–4, has the same ambiguity. Since the meaning cannot be settled on linguistic grounds, it is necessary to look at the immediate context. The verse must be understood in terms of the antithesis to the negative clauses that precede it: "The kingdom is not coming with signs to be observed, nor will they say, 'Lo, here it is!' or 'There!' " (17:20b,21a). Here Jesus disowns the apocalypticists' concern for the "signs of the

times" and their attempts to calculate the time and place of God's decisive act. In the similar antitheses in 17:23-24, the positive clause predicts the sudden and universal disclosure of the Son of Man. On that model Luke 17:21b would be making a similar prediction, but the *estin* seems to stand in the way of such an interpretation. In the Aramaic of Jesus, however, there would be no copula, no *estin*. The original time reference, then, must be discerned from the antithetical structure and from the parallel with 17:23-24, both of which point to the future. The contrast in 17:21b is then plain: the time and place of the kingdom cannot be calculated; it "will (suddenly) be in your midst" (so Jeremias, *Theology of the New Testament*, p. 101; see also T. W. Manson, *The Sayings of Jesus*, pp. 303-4). Luke (or some earlier Greek-speaking carrier of the tradition) is responsible for the *estin*; it coheres with Luke's theology which moves in the direction of "realized eschatology." Even in Luke, however, the verse cannot be used as a basis for "spiritualizing" the kingdom, for Luke also provides the context of the question of the Pharisees, and Luke would not have Jesus say the kingdom of God is "within" the hearts of the Pharisees. Within Luke, then, the meaning is that the kingdom of God is (already) "among" them or "in the midst" of them in the person and ministry of Jesus. (Manson, op. cit., allows the possibility of such an interpretation but prefers to take the phrase as a prophecy of the sudden and unexpected coming of the kingdom.) At any rate, there is no basis in Luke 17:21 for construing the kingdom as an inner, spiritual reality.

56. See especially Luke 11:20: "But if it is by the finger of God that I cast out demons, then the kingdom of God has come upon you" (par. Mt. 12:28). This is one of the very few sayings whose authenticity has never been seriously challenged. It is also agreed that Luke's reference to "the finger of God" (cf. Mt.: "spirit of God") preserves the tradition of Q and that it refers to Ex. 8:19 (see T. W. Manson, *The Teaching of Jesus*, pp. 82-83, and Perrin, *Rediscovering the Teaching of Jesus*, pp. 63-67).

The saying — and every source in multiple forms (and indeed the ancient Jewish texts, see J. Klausner, *Jesus of Nazareth* [New York: Macmillan, 1927], pp. 17ff.) — attests to the fact that Jesus' ministry involved exorcisms and other miracles. The saying provides Jesus' interpretation of these events. There is considerable debate about the meaning of Gk. *ephthasen*, whether it means that the kingdom of God has "come near" or "arrived." (See Kummel, *Promise and Fulfillment* [Naperville, Ill.: A. R. Allenson, 1957], pp. 105-9, who argues that it means that the kingdom has arrived.) Neither the linguistic evidence nor the context sustains the interpretation "come near." The point is, apparently, that the future kingdom is already making its power felt, has "arrived," in Jesus' mighty works. The act of God that will destroy the reign of sin and death has already taken effect in the miracles and exorcisms of Jesus. The saying must not be taken to remove the kingdom from the future into the present, however; it remains a future kingdom — but a future kingdom already making its power felt in the present. Far from being allied with the demons, Jesus is allied with the coming kingdom of God, and his exorcisms are the beginnings of God's conflict with the powers of the age and of God's ultimate triumph.

57. See especially the much-overlooked article by James M. Robinson, "The Formal Structure of Jesus' Message," in Klassen and Synder, eds., *Current Issues in New Testament Interpretation* (New York: Harper, 1962), pp. 91-110. It is Robinson's point that even formally Jesus' message is "a proclamation to the present in view of the imminent future" (p. 100). The unbridgeable gulf in apocalyptic thought between "this age" and "the age to come" is being crossed in the formal structure of Jesus' message. Attention might also be directed to Jesus' "but I say unto you," to the fact that he spoke "with authority, and not as the scribes and Pharisees." (See Käsemann, "The Problem of the Historical Jesus," *Essays on New Testament Themes*, pp. 15-47, esp. 37ff.)

58. Albert Schweitzer, *The Quest of the Historical Jesus*, p. 354. The term

Schweitzer used to designate his view is "Konsequente Eschatologie," ibid., pp. 330–97. It is translated as "thoroughgoing eschatology" in Montgomery's translation.

59. See Dodd, *The Parables of the Kingdom* (London: Nisbet, 1935).

60. Perrin, *The Kingdom of God in the Teaching of Jesus*, pp. 74–78 and 83–84, gives convenient summaries of the evidence for the kingdom as present and future in Jesus' ministry. See also Kummel, *Promise and Fulfillment*. The double reference is more and more a consensus among New Testament scholars. For example, on the one hand, C. H. Dodd has shifted from his concept of "realized eschatology" to Jeremias' "sich realisierende Eschatologie" (Dodd, *The Interpretation of the Fourth Gospel* [Cambridge: Cambridge University Press, 1953], p. 447, n. 1). On the other hand, Rudolf Bultmann has shifted from his demythologized version of Schweitzer's "consistent eschatology" (in which the future crisis really expresses that the present is a time of decision) to an emphasis on the breaking-in of God's grace in "the conduct" of Jesus (*ZTK*, 54 [1957], 224, reprinted in *Glauben und Verstehen*, 3 [1960], 176f.) There remain, of course, important differences of emphasis on the present and future and differences of articulating their relationship.

61. See nn. 56 and 57.

62. See n. 55.

63. That eschatological vision is related by the context Luke provides for this fragment to Jesus' performance of exorcisms — and such is almost certainly the case historically. As Jeremias, *The Theology of the New Testament*, p. 95, says, "Jesus' visionary cry of joy leaps over the interval of time before the final crisis and sees in the exorcisms performed by the disciples the dawn of the annihilation of Satan."

64. Cf. also I Thess. 5:2-8; I Pet. 5:1-10; and see P. Minear, *Commands of Christ* (Nashville: Abingdon, 1972), pp. 152–77.

65. J. Jeremias, *Jesus' Promise to the Nations* (Naperville, Ill.: A. R. Allenson, 1958), pp. 41–46.

66. See Norman Perrin, *Rediscovering the Teaching of Jesus*, pp. 102–8, and E. Fuchs, *Das Urchristliche Sacraments Verständnis* (Bad Canstatt: R. Müllerschön, 1958?), both of whom emphasize the importance of table fellowship in Jesus' ministry. The eschatological meal — conventionally reserved for the future and for the righteous — is celebrated already now and with publicans and sinners.

67. On "Repentance," see Behm and Würthwein, *"metanoéō, metanoia,"* *TDNT*, IV, 975–1008. The words "repent" and "repentance" do not often appear on the lips of Jesus in the Gospels. "Repentance" (Gk. *metanoia*) appears on Jesus' lips only in Lk. 15:7 and Lk. 5:32 (where it is obviously secondary, cf. Mk. 2:17); "repent" (Gk. *metanoéō*) appears somewhat more often on Jesus' lips, but again mainly in Luke, where it is often secondary. The call to repent is present in multiple forms and sources, however, even where the words are not used. (Behm, op. cit., p. 1002: "The whole proclamation of Jesus . . . is a proclamation of *metanoia* even when the term is not used.") Along with Mark — and the majority of New Testament scholars — we may allow "repentance" as a summary of Jesus' teaching. Even so, we may hardly infer much from the word; we need to look rather at its cognates in the rest of Jesus' teaching.

68. On this topic see Minear, *Commands of Christ*, pp. 83–97.

69. The saying is surely authentic, as its occurrence in multiple sources and in the midst of multiple forms attests; the settings are probably secondary. On the evangelists' development and application of the saying to a wide variety of new situations by shifts in the narrative context, see below and Minear, *Commands of Christ*, pp. 83–98.

70. See James M. Robinson's description of the form of these sayings, "The Formal Structure of Jesus' Message," *Current Issues in New Testament Interpretation*, ed. William Klassen and Graydon Snyder (New York: Harper, 1962), pp. 91–110, esp. pp. 103–4.

71. On this topic see Minear, *Commands of Christ*, pp. 132–51; Martin Hengel,

Property and Riches in the Early Church (Philadelphia: Fortress, 1974) pp. 22–30; Jeremias, *New Testament Theology,* pp. 221–23; and Richard Batey, *Jesus and the Poor* (New York: Harper & Row, 1972), pp. 5–23.

72. Although the original saying probably contained no explicit reference to the kingdom, the tradition in both Matthew and Luke was "surely right" in adding such references, for the kingdom is an implicit assumption of the original saying; so Minear, *Commands of Christ,* p. 149.

73. See the materials cited in n. 71.

74. Concerning the authenticity of the nucleus of this parable, see Jeremias, *Parables,* pp. 207–9. Moreover, the demands are attested in other ways, in the announcements of the kingdom, Jesus' own behavior, and other sayings.

75. See Jeremias, *Jerusalem in the Time of Jesus,* pp. 126–34.

76. See Jewett, *Man as Male and Female* (Grand Rapids: Eerdmans, 1975), pp. 94–111; Jeremias, *New Testament Theology* (New York: Scribners, 1971), pp. 223–27.

77. On this, see Jewett, *Man as Male and Female,* pp. 86–94; Jeremias, *Jerusalem in the Time of Jesus,* pp. 359–76, and the bibliography there.

78. The protection of women by the prohibition of divorce may be cited (Mk. 10:11 and par.). Mk. 10:12, which prohibits divorce by women, presupposes a Hellenistic situation but rests perhaps on Jesus' implicit attack on the double standard of morality (see, e.g., Mt. 5:28 and also Jn. 7:53–8:11, which some scholars have taken to preserve an authentic memory even though it is not in the earliest copies of John's Gospel).

79. The passage is often taken simply to call attention to the greater importance of spiritual things. But the challenge to the conventional role assignments for women in first-century Palestine may not be overlooked. Martha is described in the saying as "anxious" (Gk. *merimnaō*; cf. Mt. 6:25; Lk. 12:22), a word which often refers to the concerns prompted by the values and standards of the present age. The "good portion" Mary has chosen is, in contrast, the kingdom. The conventional values and standards of the present age led to Martha's urging Mary to resume her role assignment as "woman." The choice of the kingdom and its present effectiveness in Jesus led Mary, in contrast, scandalously to assume a place among the disciples. The contrast is not between "secular" goods and "other-worldly" goods or between practical life and contemplative life. The contrast is between the values and standards of the present age and the kingdom.

80. See Jeremias, *New Testament Theology,* pp. 227–28; Albrecht Oepke, *"pais,* etc.," *TDNT,* V (Grand Rapids: Eerdmans, 1967), 637–52.

81. See Jeremias, *Parables,* pp. 124–46.

82. Indeed in Mt. 21:31, "The tax collectors and the harlots go into the kingdom of God before you," the verb *proagousin* should probably be taken in an exclusive rather than a temporal sense: "The tax collectors and the harlots shall enter the kingdom — and not you!" See Jeremias, *Parables,* p. 125, n. 48. On the authenticity of this verse, see ibid., p. 80.

83. Almost all of the sayings and parables within which the concrete commands to "judge not" and to "forgive" are found call attention to the apocalyptic judgment and forgiveness. See also the petition of the Lord's Prayer, "And forgive us our sins, for we ourselves forgive everyone who is indebted to us," Lk. 11:4; cf. Mt. 6:12.

84. Matthew greatly expands the saying to provide rules for such admonition in the church, Mt. 18:15-17.

85. Jeremias, *New Testament Theology,* pp. 203–18; Schnackenburg, *The Moral Teachings in the New Testament* (London: Herder and Herder, 1965), pp. 56–81; H. Kleinknecht and W. Gutbrod, *"nomos,* etc.," *TDNT,* IV, 1059–65.

86. See Robert J. Banks, *Jesus and the Law in the Synoptic Tradition* (London: Cambridge University Press, 1975), pp. 1–9, for summaries and bibliography of some divergent opinions.

87. Banks, ibid. and below, ch. II.

88. E. Lohse, *New Testament Environment* (Nashville: Abingdon, 1976), pp. 115-20, 167-78; C. K. Barrett, *New Testament Background* (New York: Macmillan, 1957); and George Foot Moore, *Judaism*, I (Cambridge, Mass: Harvard University Press, 1932), 161ff.

89. The oral law, therefore, while its validity rests on its exposition of the written law, is nevertheless its equal in inspiration and authority. The Sadducees, as is well known, were unique among the significant parties in the first century because they did not accept this understanding of the oral law, insisting that the written law alone was authoritative. The Sadducees, however, had no role in the formation of Judaism past the destruction of the Temple in Jerusalem.

The oral law finally achieved written form in the *Mishnah* of R. Judah in the late second century. The *Mishnah* arranges the legal tradition topically, collecting the prescriptions and prohibitions of the rabbis into six "divisions" and sixty-three tractates. The *Mishnah* is the antecedent of the *Talmud*, which arose in the fifth century. The oral tradition also took literary form in *midrashim*, which (in contrast to the *Mishnah*) were organized on the basis of the biblical text, following it verse by verse. The *Mishnah* is mostly legal material (*Halakah*). The *midrashim* may concentrate on either the legal materials or the broader tradition with its edifying and homiletical stories (*Haggadah*).

90. *Tosephta Sanhedrin* 7.11, quoted in Barrett, *The New Testament Background* (New York: Macmillan, 1957), p. 146.

91. On the much-disputed thesis of W. D. Davies, *The Setting of the Sermon on the Mount*, pp. 109-90, that rabbinical Judaism expects a "New Torah" in the new age, see Robert Banks, "The Eschatological Role of Law in Pre- and Post-Christian Jewish Thought" in Banks, ed., *Reconciliation and Hope* (Exeter: Paternoster, 1974), pp. 173-85.

92. Mk. 7:19b, "making all foods clean," at any rate, is surely Mark's interpretation and application of Jesus' teaching for a Gentile Christian audience. Matthew omits this abrogation of kosher regulations. The dissatisfaction with mere observance of *Halakoth*, moreover, is attested in multiple sources and in multiple forms.

93. Joachim Jeremias, *Jesus als Weltvollender, Beiträge zur Forderung Christlicher Theologie*, vol. xxx (Gütersloh: C. Bertelsmann, 1930).

94. Ulrich Wilckens, "The Understanding of Revelation within the History of Primitive Christianity," in Wolfhart Pannenberg, ed., *Revelation as History* (London: Macmillan, 1968), pp. 57-82.

95. Explicit links are made in the tradition between "authority" and the cleansing of the temple (Mk. 11:28-33 par.), his exorcisms (Mk. 1:21-28,39; Lk. 4:31-37), and his forgiving sins (Mk. 2:10, 11; Lk. 7:48).

96. Jeremias, *New Testament Theology*, pp. 35-36, 250-55.

97. Even if the antitheses of Matthew's Gospel are redactional (so Jack Suggs in Luise Schottorff, *Essays on the Love Commandment*); the imperious "I" is itself well attested in the sources. For a defense of the authenticity of the antitheses, see Jeremias, *New Testament Theology*, pp. 251-53.

98. See, e.g., *Eth. Enoch* 37.4; U. Wilckens, "The Understanding of Revelation within the History of Primitive Christianity," in Pannenberg, ed., *Revelation as History*, p. 70.

99. Especially E. Käsemann, "The Problem of the Historical Jesus," *Essays on New Testament Themes* (Naperville, Ill.: A. R. Allenson, 1957), pp. 15-47 (and there especially 42ff.).

100. In contrast, see, e.g., *Aboth. Rabbi Nathan*. 24.

101. Furnish, *The Love Command in the New Testament* (Nashville: Abingdon, 1972), pp. 24-45. T. W. Manson, *The Teaching of Jesus*. pp. 302-8.

102. Judging from the agreements of Matthew and Luke against Mark, the tradition must have been preserved in Q as well.

103. Furnish, *The Love Command in the New Testament.* pp. 25f. Luke makes of them one commandment.
104. See Furnish, *The Love Command in the New Testament*, pp. 74-84.
105. See works cited in n. 101.
106. Luke's order is to be preferred, for Matthew has edited the material in the interest of his antitheses, Mt. 5:21-48, and of the contrast with the righteousness of the scribes.
107. Minear, *Commands of Christ.* pp. 30-46.
108. See Manson, *The Teaching of Jesus.* pp. 315-19.
109. Verhey, "Divorce in the New Testament," *ISBE* (rev. ed.), I, 976-78.
110. *Mishnah Gittin* IX.10 preserves something of this debate. The famous rabbis Hillel and Shammai disagreed about the meaning of "some indecency" in Deut. 24:1ff. Hillel said that the words (Hb. *'erwath dabar*) quite plainly meant "some unseemly thing" and argued accordingly that the Torah permitted a man to divorce his wife for any "unseemly thing," including burning his toast. Shammai's exegesis transposed the words so that he read *dabar 'erwah* (cf. Gk. *logos porneias,* Mt. 5:31), and he argues accordingly that adultery (or at least some unlawful sexual conduct) was the only legitimate reason for divorce. The famous Akiba focused on another part of the text. From "if then she finds no favor in his eyes," Akiba moved to the claim that divorce is permissible even if the man finds another woman more attractive.
111. That the "absolute" prohibition of divorce in Mk. 10 is authentic can be seen in the independent attestation by Paul (I Cor. 7:10-11). And it cannot be explained either in terms of the Jewish heritage or the ethos of the early church.
112. Manson, *The Teaching of Jesus.* pp. 237-43.
113. The inscription on the cross was "The King of the Jews" (Mk. 15:26). Some have doubted the authenticity of the inscription, but to make that title on the cross an invention of the early Christian church is hardly credible.
114. For example, Robert Eisler, *Iēsous Basileus ou basileusas* (Heidelberg: Carl Winter, Vol. I, 1929; Vol. II, 1930), S.G.F. Brandon, *Jesus and the Zealots* (New York: Scribner, 1968).
115. See, for example, Oscar Cullman, *Jesus and the Revolutionaries* (New York: Harper & Row, 1970), Martin Hengel, *Was Jesus a Revolutionist?* (Philadelphia: Fortress, 1971).
116. J. Jeremias, *Jerusalem in the Time of Jesus;* Eduard Lohse, *The New Testament Environment* (Nashville: Abingdon, 1976).
117. Solomon installed Zadok as high priest (I Kings 2:35). In Ezekiel 40-48 the priestly ministry is given to the sons of Zadok (Ezek. 40:46; 43:19; 44:15; 48:11). The old Zadokite dynasty of high priests came to an inglorious end with the Hellenizer Jason. The Hasmoneans took over the high priest's office following the Maccabean revolt. The group of priests who gathered around the Teacher of Righteousness to form the community at Qumran called themselves "Sons of Zadok, the priests who keep the covenant" (IQS V. 2,9). See E. Lohse, *The New Testament Environment.* pp. 74-75.
118. Using Is. 40:3, cited IQS VIII.13-15.
119. See, e.g., *The Psalms of Solomon.* a first-century B.C. writing which originates from within Pharisee circles. It refers to Pompey's entering the Holy of Holies and hopes for a Davidic (not Hasmonean) king to rescue them from the Romans.
120. The thesis of Jacob Neusner, *Politics to Piety* (Englewood Cliffs, N.J.: Prentice Hall, 1972-73), that the Pharisees gradually became a pietistic and nonpolitical movement is, however, probably overstated.
121. The Zealots perhaps have their origin among the Pharisees and at least attracted Pharisees as early supporters. See Hengel, *Was Jesus a Revolutionist?,* p. 12, n. 39 and the literature cited there. Also Brandon, *Jesus and the Zealots,* pp. 37-38. The first to join Judas the Galilean in his organized rebellion was identified by Josephus as a Pharisee, R. Saddok; Josephus, *Jewish Antiquities.* XVIII. 4.

122. *The Jewish War.* II.118 (trans. Thackeray; Loeb ed., *Josephus.* II, 367,369).
123. In A.D. 66, when under the leadership of Menahem the son of Judas the Zealots took control of Jerusalem, they burned the city archives, effectively destroying the records of indebtedness (*The Jewish War.* II.427). Somewhat later, the Zealot leader Simon bar Cochba announced the emancipation of the slaves (*The Jewish War,* IV.508). The radical theocratic vision apparently also led to Menahem's execution by rivals within his own party after he went up to the temple to be crowned king in 66.
124. Jeremias, *Jerusalem in the Time of Jesus.* p. 125.
125. Jeremias, *Jesus' Promise to the Nations*, pp. 41–51.
126. S.G.F. Brandon's treatment of this passage unsuccessfully attempts to hide the anti-Zealot character of such an entry even while he makes much of it as a carefully planned messianic entry. See Brandon, *Jesus and the Zealots.* p. 349, n. 2.
127. See, e.g., the story of the transition from charismatic authority to the monarchy in the "former prophets," I Sam. 8–10.
128. See Verhey, "Humble," *ISBE* (rev. ed.), II (Grand Rapids: Eerdmans, 1982), 775–78.
129. The ironic question in Mt. 11:8 and Lk. 7:25 seems directed in judgment against the luxury at Herod Antipas' court.
130. Even Brandon, who makes much of the cleansing, acknowledges that the act "appears to have been of a more symbolic character" than the seizure of the temple by the Zealots in A.D. 66 (*Jesus and the Zealots.* p. 338). That it was not the act of a Zealot is above all plain from the quotation of Is. 56:7: "My house shall be called a house of prayer for all peoples." That quotation, however, may have been added in the oral tradition. So Bultmann, *The History of the Synoptic Tradition* (New York: Harper & Row, 1963), p. 36.
131. Hengel, *Was Jesus a Revolutionist?*, p. 27. The attempts to portray Jesus as a programmatic pacifist have always stumbled and fallen at the temple-cleansing.
132. See above, pp. 18–19.
133. See Arthur Dyck, *On Human Care* (Nashville: Abingdon, 1977), pp. 82–83. See further Verhey, "In Defense of Theocracy," *Reformed Review.* 34 (1981), 98–107.
134. U. Wilckens, "The Understanding of Revelation Within the History of Primitive Christianity"; W. Pannenberg, *Jesus — God and Man* (Philadelphia: Westminster, 1968), pp. 53–114.

CHAPTER II

1. Thus, at least, Acts would lead one to suppose 2:38, 3:19, 5:31, 8:22, 11:18, 17:30, 20:21, 26:20. The historical reliability of the Luke-Acts treatment of the speeches is, of course, much debated. (See F. F. Bruce, "The Speeches in Acts — Thirty Years Later," in R. Banks, ed., *Reconciliation and Hope* [Grand Rapids: Eerdmans, 1974], pp. 53–68.) And there is no doubt that "repentance" is a special concern of Luke-Acts. But Mk. 6:12 provides independent testimony; the passage, by representing Jesus as charging the disciples to take up his message of repentance, assumes that the exhortation to repentance was part of Christian preaching from the very beginning.
2. Mk. 6:7-13 par. Lk. 10:1-16. The same passages suggest that Gerd Theissen, *The First Followers of Jesus* (London: SCM, 1978) is probably right when he describes the initial bearers of the tradition as "wandering charismatics." He seems, however, to have overstated the case. James, for example, seems not to have been a wandering charismatic (Acts 12:17); and Peter seems not to have been as "homeless" as Theissen supposes (Mk. 1:29 and par.). The contrast between the "wandering charismatics" and "local sympathizers" is suggestive but overdrawn.

3. This against the thesis of B. Gerhardsson and H. Reinsenfeld. See W. D. Davies, *The Setting of the Sermon on the Mount* (London: Cambridge University Press, 1964), pp. 464–80.

4. Oscar Cullmann, "The Tradition," in his *The Early Church* (Philadelphia: Westminster, 1956), p. 62.

5. Perhaps Paul's remark and his careful distinction between his advice and the tradition is peculiarly relevant to the Corinthian situation. It may have been necessary to emphasize these points against the practice of the spiritual enthusiasts of deciding moral questions on the basis of the ecstatic utterances of the prophets. The tradition would then provide an important test for their claims (see, e.g., I Cor. 12:1-4). Even if peculiarly relevant to the Corinthian situation, however, the distinction is presented as one that may be assumed rather than one that demanded a demonstration.

6. For this distinction see David Kelsey, *The Uses of Scripture* (Philadelphia: Fortress, 1975), p. 95.

7. Credit for this observation, of course, belongs to the form critics, especially Dibelius and Bultmann. See the classic work of Martin Dibelius, *From Tradition to Gospel* (London: Nicholson & Watson, 1934), and Rudolf Bultmann, *History of the Synoptic Tradition* (New York: Harper & Row, 1963). See also Vincent Taylor, *The Formation of the Gospel Tradition* (London: Macmillan, 1943). The form critics were very often quite skeptical about the historical reliability and authenticity of the traditions. They emphasized the creative role of the church so much that they sometimes lost sight of the preservative role of the church. The appreciation of their classification of the forms, however, does not entail historical skepticism. The church "bears" the tradition; it does not simply create it. The work of H. Reisenfeld and B. Gerhardsson, while it challenges the historical skepticism of the form critics, seems to me to err on the opposite side, to so emphasize the professional preservation of the tradition that it loses sight of the creative modifications and enlargements of the tradition.

8. Following Bultmann's classification. Dibelius and Taylor give similar classifications.

9. The examples of "controversy dialogues" and "scholastic dialogues" given by Bultmann are:
   a) Occasioned by Jesus' healings: Mk. 3:1-6 par.; Lk. 14:1-6; Lk. 13:10-17; Mk. 3:22-30 par.; Mk. 2:1-12 par.
   b) Otherwise occasioned by the conduct of Jesus or the disciples: Mk. 2:23-28 par.; Mk. 7:1-23 par.; Mk. 2:15-17 par.; Mk. 2:18-22 par.; Mk. 11:27-33 par.; Lk. 7:36-50.
   c) The master is questioned (by the disciples or others): Mk. 10:17-31 par.; Mk. 12:28-34 par.; Lk. 12:13-14; Lk. 13:1-5; Matt. 11:2-19 par.; Mk. 10:35-45 par.; Mk. 9:38-40; Lk. 17:20-21; Mk. 11:20-25 par.; Lk. 9:51-56.
   d) Questions asked by opponents: Mk. 12:13-17; Mk. 12:18-27; Mk. 10:2-12.

10. Examples of the biographical apophthegm cited by Bultmann are: Mk. 1:16-20 par.; 2:14 par.; Lk. 9:57-62 par.; Mk. 3:20f., 31-35 par.; Lk. 11:27-28; Mk. 6:1-6 par.; Mk. 10:13-16 par.; Mk. 12:41-44 par.; Lk. 10:38-42; Lk. 17:11-19; Lk. 19:1-10; Lk. 19:39-40; Mt. 21:15-16; Mt. 17:24-27; Lk. 13:31-33; Mk. 11:15-19 par.; Mk. 13:1-2 par.; Lk. 19:41-44; Mk. 14:3-9; Lk. 23:27-31 (plus Mk. 7:24-31 par.; Mt. 8:5-13 par.).

11. Bultmann, pp. 40–41.

12. Ibid., pp. 60–61.

13. The saying about forgiveness may be an interpolation (so Bultmann, ibid., p. 15), but it nevertheless demonstrates the capacity of the oral tradition to be turned once to a polemical or apologetic purpose and again to a moral or hortatory purpose.

14. Bultmann, p. 61. One might pause to argue that some of the biographical apophthegms can be used for other purposes, as well, for example, to polemical advantage (e.g., the prophecy of the destruction of Jerusalem, Lk. 19:41-44). One

might also challenge Bultmann's hypothesis that the narrative sections are merely "ideal scenes" created in the tradition to make a saying more comprehensible. It need not (and cannot successfully) be argued that this is never the case. Where there is the supplying of an "ideal scene," however, it seems more often the work of the evangelists than the tradition. Moreover, the scene, even if added, may be a genuine memory. The apophthegm of Luke 17:11-19 contains a remembrance of Jesus' teaching his disciples to attend to the religious and moral significance of episodes like those that give the context for Jesus' saying here and in the other apophthegms. See Etienne Trocme, *Jesus as Seen by His Contemporaries* (London: SCM, 1973), pp. 49-50.

15. Stephen Neill, *Interpretation of the New Testament, 1861-1961* (London/New York: Oxford University Press, 1964), pp. 247-48.

16. J. Jeremias, *Infant Baptism in the First Four Centuries* (Philadelphia: Westminster, 1961).

17. Following Bultmann's classification, p. 69. Bultmann's thorough inventory of these sayings need not be repeated here. It is often difficult to know exactly how to classify certain sayings. Are the beatitudes, for example, to be counted among the prophetic sayings or the wisdom sayings? Bultmann's concern to trace the evolution of these groups of sayings is not our concern. It should be observed, however, that the operative assumption is that the tradition here too both preserves and creates, that it preserves more than Bultmann supposes and is more creative than his Scandinavian opponents are willing to grant. Bultmann acknowledges the "possibility" that many of the sayings may go back to the historical Jesus and ascribes certain sayings to Jesus with a "measure of confidence," p. 105. The thesis of Reisenfeld and Gerhardsson stumbles on the simple fact that Jesus is both less and more than a rabbi, and his disciples both less and more than rabbinical students. The resurrection both allows and calls for adaptation, expansion, and selection of the tradition because the living Lord speaks in the tradition. Even so, the rabbinical patterns would suggest a check on lay creativity — and would suggest the likelihood that the sayings would be less plastic than the narratives (on the model of the rabbinic handling of *Halakah* and *Haggadah* respectively).

18. This tradition — and perhaps the whole tradition of "dominical saying" — may well have its origin in the missionary preaching of the itinerant preachers sent out by Jesus; cf. Mk. 6:7-12; Mt. 10; Lk. 9. And see below, p. 213, n. 29.

19. Lk. 12:32 is very likely created by the community. There is, moreover, a creative tendency discernible in this traditional form to focus on the person of Jesus rather than the saying itself. See Bultmann, pp. 150ff.

20. See Bultmann, pp. 102-3, 106-8; Dalman, *Jesus — Jeschua* (New York: Macmillan, 1929), pp. 200-9, for lists of parallels.

21. As I Pet. 4:8b and Eph. 4:26 are often attributed to Jesus in the later Christian tradition.

22. Cf. I Cor. 1:18-30.

23. On "eschatological wisdom," see especially the work of R. A. Edwards and especially his *A Theology of Q: Eschatology, Prophecy, and Wisdom* (Philadelphia: Fortress, 1976). The point here is not to argue that these sayings (or any particular saying) are authentic. W. D. Davies, *The Setting of the Sermon on the Mount*, appendix XI (London: Cambridge University Press, 1964), "Wisdom Sayings of Jesus," does, however, make precisely such a case against Bultmann's skepticism concerning the authenticity of those sayings paralleled in the Jewish wisdom tradition (pp. 457-60). There is, surely, from the very beginning the danger that this wisdom tradition will be torn from its eschatological context and be rendered either secret *gnosis* (as in the *Gospel of Thomas*) or conventional prudence.

24. See James M. Robinson, "The Formal Structure of Jesus' Message," in W. Klassen and G. Snyder, eds., *Current Issues in New Testament Interpretation*

(New York: Harper & Row, 1962), pp. 91-110.
25. Cf. also Lk. 6:20-26; Mt. 5:3-12; Lk. 7:23 par.; Mt. 11:6; Mt. 11:21-24 par. Lk. 10:13-15, etc. The "woes" against the scribes and Pharisees are relevant morally as well as polemically (Mt. 23; Lk. 11:37-54; Mk. 12:38-40).
26. Bultmann, op. cit., pp. 130-49.
27. Cf. Mk. 7:19 with Mt. 15:17, for example.
28. See Bultmann, p. 138 n. 1.
29. H. Schurmann, "Die Vorösterlichen Anfänge der Logientradition. Versuch eines formgeschichten Zugangs zum Leben Jesu," in H. Ristow and K. Matthiae, eds., *Der Historische Jesus und der Kerygmatische Christus* (Berlin: Evangelische Verlagsanstalt, 1961), pp. 342-70, makes the interesting suggestion that these missionary instructions are primitive and that the mission of the disciples during Jesus' lifetime provides the *Sitz im Leben* for the origin of the tradition concerning Jesus. But the concern of this section is not with the authenticity of the sayings but with their use. Even if Schurmann is right, the early churches used and shaped the memory of his words; they did not simply or merely preserve them.
30. This against the position of Dodd and W. D. Davies.
31. Perhaps this can be most clearly seen in what Ernst Käsemann calls "sentences of holy law." The category of law is used both because the *protasis* expresses some "casuistic legal expression" and because the *apodosis* is modeled on the *jus talionis*. The *jus talionis*, however, refers to an eschatological judgment. Käsemann gives a number of examples from Pauline materials, for example, I Cor. 3:17: "If anyone destroys God's temple, God will destroy him." Besides identifying the form, Käsemann claims to be able to identify the *sitz im leben* in which the form, "sentences of holy law," *originated* as the utterances of the early Christian prophets. That claim is, however, unwarranted. The form would, then, hardly have been modeled after Old Testament casuistry. It is much more likely that the prophets and others adopted and adapted the ways in which Jesus brought the coming reign of God to bear upon the present. For example, the form can be seen in Mt. 6:14: "And if you forgive men their trespasses, your heavenly father will also forgive you," and in Mk. 8:38: "For whoever is ashamed of me and of my words in this adulterous and sinful generation, of him will the Son of man also be ashamed, when he comes in the glory of his Father with the holy angels" (see also Mt. 10:32; Mk. 4:24; Mt. 5:19; Mt. 10:41, etc.). The point here is not to judge the authenticity of these sayings but to demonstrate that in the moral tradition of the early church the eschatological ethic creates "law" but cannot be reduced to *Halakah*. In this form the eschatological judgment is already made effective in the present. Such legal judgment is done on the model of Jesus and as authorized by Jesus (Mt. 16:19; 18:18). Ernst Käsemann, "Sentences of Holy Law in the New Testament," *New Testament Questions of Today* (Philadelphia: Fortress, 1969), pp. 66-81. See also his "The Beginnings of Christian Theology," ibid., pp. 82-107. J. M. Robinson, op. cit., p. 277, provides an appreciative but critical response. The use of this category in Sanders, *Ethics in the New Testament* (Philadelphia: Fortress, 1975), seems exaggerated. The eschatological perspective claims conduct along with the total person, but it is not content with a codified set of rules for conduct to be used for *Halakah*.
32. See Bultmann, pp. 150-66.
33. C. H. Dodd, *Parables of the Kingdom* (London: Nisbet, 1935); Jeremias, *The Parables of Jesus* (New York: Scribners, 1963); Bultmann, pp. 166-205.
34. A. Julicher, *Die Gleichnisreden Jesu* (Darmstadt: Wissencraft, 1963 [1910]). To contrast the interpretation of the parables in the early church and in recent scholarship is not to discredit or demean either. There are simply different legitimate intentions. The early church intended to allow the living Lord to address their situation by the way they shaped the tradition of Jesus' parables. It was a living tradition at once being preserved and shaped. Some recent scholarship on the parables, in-

cluding the work of Dodd and Jeremias, as well as Julicher, has attempted to reach behind the Gospel records of the parables to the proclamation of Jesus himself. The legitimacy and importance of such an undertaking is not denied by this contrast, and indeed was shared in the opening chapter of this book.

35. Jeremias, p. 67.

36. Ibid., pp. 70–77.

37. Ibid., pp. 77–79.

38. Other instances where the "moral" is made explicit in an application attached by means of "So . . ." (Gk. *outas*) include Mt. 18:35 (forgiveness), Lk. 17:10 (dutifulness), Mt. 13:49 (moral watchfulness), Lk. 14:33 (renouncing possessions), Mk. 13:29 (watchfulness), Lk. 15:7,10 (welcoming sinners), Lk. 12:21 (disposition toward riches). See Bultmann, p. 184.

39. E.g., Mk. 13:29,35 and Mt. 25:13 (Watch!); Lk. 10:37b (Go and do likewise!); Lk. 16:9 (Make friends for yourself by means of unrighteous mammon!); and Lk. 17:10 (Say, "We are unworthy servants; we have only done what was our duty").

40. E.g., Mt. 20:16 ("The last will be first . . ."); Lk. 14:11; Lk. 10:14b ("Everyone who exalts himself will be humbled . . .").

41. This analysis of the parable is indebted to Jeremias, *The Parable of Jesus*. pp. 176–80, 63–66, 67–69, where it is worked out in considerable detail.

42. Jeremias prefers to call this the "parable of Servant entrusted with Supervision" (p. 55) because the parable only speaks of one servant. It does, however, plainly contrast two kinds of stewardship. On the parable, see Jeremias, pp. 55–58.

43. Cf. Jeremias, pp. 48–63. In the parable of the talents one can see the moral use of the parables in illustrations besides the canonical ones; the Gospel of the Nazarenes has one of the servants squander the money on harlots and flute players (cf. Lk. 15:30; 12:45).

44. Bultmann, pp. 218–44; Dibelius, *From Tradition to Gospel*. pp. 70–103. Once again our interest is not with the authenticity of the miracle stories but with their use in the early church. However, it may be observed that the fact that Jesus did mighty works is attested in multiple sources and forms.

45. Bultmann, pp. 244–317; Dibelius, pp. 104–32.

46. Bultmann, p. 245; Dibelius, p. 104.

47. This presupposes that Mk. 16:1-8 was an original part of the passion narrative. This has been denied by some, notably Bultmann, p. 285. But the preceding story of the burial is quite plainly complementary to this one; they belong together. Together they announce his real death and his real resurrection (cf. I Cor. 15:4).

48. The moral interest is not the only interest affecting and shaping the tradition. Apologetic motifs (e.g., Matthew's story of the guards at the tomb, 27:62-66) including the proof from prophecy (e.g., the birth stories in Matthew), are found, and dogmatic motifs (e.g., Mk. 15:2, Jn. 18:33-37) sometimes shape the story.

49. Bultmann, p. 254, says that "the dialogue between Jesus and the devil reflects Rabbinic disputations." That is so, but the force of that remark does *not* suggest that Jesus overcomes the devil by being a cleverer interpreter of Scripture. He overcomes the devil by his humble submission to God and his will. Not coincidentally, the passages Jesus quotes are all from Deut. (8:3; 6:13; 6:16), when Israel was in the wilderness confronted with the costly path of humble submission to God's will.

50. Contra Bultmann, pp. 254–56.

51. Paul Feine and Johannes Behm, reedited by Werner George Kummel, *Introduction to the New Testament* (Nashville: Abingdon, 1966), pp. 62, 63.

52. On this see P. Achtemeier, "Pre-Markan Miracle Catenae," *JBL*. 89 (1970), 265–91.

53. See Vincent Taylor, *The Gospel according to St. Mark* (London: Macmillan, 1952).

54. Mark was surely *not* merely a "collector, a transmitter of tradition, an editor"

(Dibelius, *From Tradition to Gospel,* p. 3). Redaction criticism has made plain the role of the evangelists as authors.

55. Eduard Schweizer, *The Good News According to Mark* (Richmond: John Knox, 1970), pp. 201ff.

56. On *haustafeln* see David Schroeder, *Die Haustafeln des Neuen Testaments* (Ph.D. dissertation, Heidelberg, 1959) whose work is popularized by John H. Yoder, *The Politics of Jesus* (Grand Rapids: Eerdmans, 1972), pp. 163–92; also see Wolfgang Schrage, "Zur Ethik der Neutestamentliche Haustafeln," *NTS,* 21 (1974), 1–22.

57. E.g., Col. 3:18–4:1; Eph. 5:21–6:1; I Pet. 2:13–3:8; Titus 2:2-10. See below, pp. 67–70.

58. 109:1 in the LXX, which is quoted here. Cf. Acts 2:34-35; Heb. 1:13; Mk. 14:61.

59. The passage is, therefore, still far from a doctrine of "two kingdoms."

60. P. Minear, *Commands of Christ* (Nashville: Abingdon, 1972), pp. 84–87.

61. Most notably, by W. R. Farmer, *The Synoptic Problem: A Critical Analysis* (New York: Macmillan, 1964). See also C. S. Petrie, " 'Q' is Only What You Make It," *NovT,* 3 (1959), 28–33; D. L. Dungan, "Mark — The Abridgement of Matthew and Luke," *Jesus and Man's Hope,* 1, ed. D. Miller (Pittsburgh: Pittsburgh Theological Seminary, 1970), 74–81.

62. A convenient summary of the arguments in favor of the Q hypothesis can be found in Feine, Behm, Kummel, *Introduction to the New Testament* (Nashville: Abingdon, 1966), pp. 50–58.

63. On the question of order see the articles of V. Taylor, "The Order of Q," *Journal of Theological Studies,* IV New Series (April 1953), 27–31, and "The Original Order of Q," in A. J. B. Higgins, ed., *New Testament Essays,* pp. 246–69.

64. T. W. Manson, *The Sayings of Jesus* (London: SCM, 1957), p. 16.

65. A. Harnack, *The Sayings of Jesus* (New York: G. P. Putman's Sons, 1908), pp. 168,229; T. W. Manson, op. cit., p. 15; Dibelius, *From Tradition to Gospel* (London: Nicholson & Watson, 1934), pp. 238ff.; V. Taylor, *The Formation of the Gospel Tradition* (London: Macmillan, 1943), p. 182.

66. W. D. Davies, *The Setting of the Sermon on the Mount,* pp. 366–86.

67. Ibid., pp. 368–80.

68. Ibid., p. 386.

69. Ibid.

70. H. E. Tödt, *The Son of Man in the Synoptic Tradition* (Philadelphia: Westminster, 1965), pp. 241ff.

71. Ibid., p. 246.

72. James M. Robinson, "Logoi Sophon: On the Gattung of Q," in James M. Robinson and Helmut Koester, eds., *Trajectories through Early Christianity* (Philadelphia: Fortress, 1971), pp. 71–113.; P. Hoffmann, *Studien zur Theologie der Logienquelle* (NT Abh 8; Munster: Aschendorff, 1972) and "Die Versuchsgeshichte und der Logienquelle," *Biblische Zeitschrift,* 13 (1969), 207–23; D. Luhrmann, *Die Redaktion der Logienquelle* (WMANT, 33, 1969); R. A. Edwards, "The Eschatological Correlative as a Gattung in the New Testament," *ZNW,* 60 (1969), 9–20; *The Sign of Jonah: In the Theology of the Evangelists and Q* (1971); E. Bammel, "Das Ende von Q," *Verborum Veritatis* (1970), pp. 39–50; Graham N. Stanton, "On the Christology of Q" in B. Lindars and S. S. Smalley, eds., *Christ and Spirit in the New Testament,* pp. 27–42. For surveys of some of the recent literature, see R. D. Worden, "Redaction Criticism of Q: A Survey," *JBL,* 94 (1975), 532–46. Most recently R. A. Edwards, *A Theology of Q: Eschatology, Prophecy, and Wisdom* (Philadelphia: Fortress, 1976) has provided a compelling account of the intentions and character of Q. It is to this work by Edwards, especially, that the treatment here is indebted, although the judgments about order here are more confident than Edwards thinks possible (see above, n. 63).

73. Even Graham Stanton, op. cit., who comes closest to defending a catechetical

purpose of Q, does so by synthesizing the position of Tödt et al. that Q has a kerygmatic purpose with the earlier position. He says: "There is no reason to regard Q either as solely kerygmatic material or solely didactic material — for the customary division is often both artificial and misleading" (p. 41).

74. See especially James M. Robinson, "Logoi Sophōn," and R. A. Edwards, *A Theology of Q,* pp. 58-79.

75. Note, for example, the joining of Solomon and Jonah in Lk. 11:31-32=Mt. 12:41-42. See Edwards, *A Theology of Q,* passim.

76. Edwards, ibid., p. 93.

77. On the apocryphal gospels, see Edgar Henneke and Wilhelm Schneemelcher, *New Testament Apocrypha,* Vol. I (Philadelphia: Westminster, 1963); Helmut Koester, "Apocryphal and Canonical Gospels," *Harvard Theological Review,* 73:1-2 (1980), 105-30; Elaine Pagels, *The Gnostic Gospels* (Philadelphia: Fortress, 1975).

78. P. Carrington, *Primitive Christian Catechism* (Cambridge: Cambridge University Press, 1940); E. G. Selwyn, *The First Epistle of St. Peter* (London: Macmillan, 1947), Essay II, pp. 365-466.

79. On the question of "the apostolic decree," see Hans Conzelmann, *History of Primitive Christianity* (Nashville: Abingdon, 1973), pp. 88-90.

80. It is ironic that Rudolf Bultmann's *Theology of the New Testament* (New York: Scribners, 1951), which is so extraordinarily cautious and skeptical about "The Message of Jesus," is so imaginatively credulous in reconstructing "The Kerygma of the Hellenistic Church Aside from Paul" (pp. 63-183).

81. Consider, for example, the opponents of Paul in the Corinthian church. These spiritualists were arrogant about their tolerance of immorality (I Cor. 5:2); they made slogans like "All things are lawful" (I Cor. 6:12; 10:23); "every . . . sin which a man commits is outside the body" (I Cor. 6:18, following the Greek text and omitting the "other" of the RSV); "all of us possess knowledge" ([Gk. *gnōsis*] I Cor. 8:1). At the same time they (or at least some of their group) were ascetic: "It is good for a man not to touch a woman" (I Cor. 7:1). See J. C. Hurd, Jr., *The Origin of I Corinthians* (New York: Seabury, 1965).

82. Following Selwyn and Carrington, op. cit.

83. Selwyn, op. cit., pp. 369-75; especially Table I, pp. 370-71. Also see Robert Hodgson, Jr., "Testimony Hypothesis," *JBL,* 98 (Sept. 1979), 376-78.

84. Selwyn, ibid., pp. 372-74. Selwyn's additional argument on the basis of these parallels that Silvanus acted as amanuensis is unnecessary and unlikely; see Ernest Best, *A Commentary on the First and Second Epistles to the Thessalonians* (New York: Harper & Row, 1972), pp. 178-79.

85. See Best, pp. 158-70.

86. Selwyn, op. cit., pp. 375-84; especially Table II, pp. 376-78.

87. As Best does, op. cit., pp. 215ff.

88. Selwyn, op. cit., pp. 393-400; especially Table VI, pp. 394-95. The passages are I Pet. 2:1,2; 4:1; Jas. 1:21; Rom. 13:12,14; Col. 3:8,9,10,12 (also perhaps 3:5-7); Eph. 4:22,24,25,26,29,31,32 (also perhaps 4:17-19); Heb. 12:1; Gal. 3:27; also I Clement 13:1; 57:2; II Clement 1:6; Herm. Mand. I:2; II:3; V:2, 8 et passim.

89. W. D. Davies, *Paul and Rabbinic Judaism* (New York: Harper & Row, 1948), p. 129; Carrington, *Primitive Christian Catechism,* pp. 81ff.

90. Selwyn, op. cit., pp. 389-93, identifies four main metaphors for this change in identity associated with baptism, rebirth (I Peter, James, John), a new creation, the contrast of the old and new man (Pauline materials), and the contrast of light and darkness.

91. Selwyn takes the armor of God material to belong to a persecution tradition.

92. Selwyn, p. 400, notes that "abstain" (Gk. *apechesthai*) appears regularly in the LXX with the sense it has in the tradition, but "cast off" (Gk. *apotithesthai*) never does; that the "abstain" tradition alludes to the Holiness Code (at least Lev. 19:2 and 18); and that the "abstain" tradition is related to "the apostolic decree" in

which Jewish Christians provided a *modus vivendi* for Gentile converts to follow for fellowship with them.

93. Selwyn. pp. 406 – 19; especially Tables VIII A, pp. 408 – 10, and VIII C, p. 416. There is a related set of passages in Col. 3:12-15 and Eph. 4:1-3, 32; 5:2, but the form is quite different; see Selwyn, ibid., Table VIII B, p. 411.

94. In I Peter the tradition is developed by appeals to Ps. 34 (I Pet. 3:10-12) and to the cross of Christ (3:18) and applied to the issue of persecution.

95. See David Daube, "Participle and Imperative in I Peter," an "Appended Note" in Selwyn, pp. 467 – 88, for the paraenetic use of such a form.

96. *Haustafeln* seems to have been used first by Luther as a title for the domestic duties which he appended to his shorter catechism.

97. The broader codes may be entitled *gemeindetafeln*. See Col. 3:18-4:1; Eph. 5:21–6:9; I Tim. 2:1-15; 6:1,2; Titus 2:4-10; 3:1; I Pet. 2:13–3:8; 5:5,6; Rom. 13:1-7. See also Didache IV. 9-11; Barnabus XIX. 5,7; I Clement i. 3; xxi. 6-9; Polycarp, Phil. iv, v. See Selwyn, pp. 419–39 and relevant tables; John H. Yoder, *The Politics of Jesus* (Grand Rapids: Eerdmans, 1972), 163–92: K. Weidinger, *Die Haustafeln*; W. Schrage, "Zur Ethik der Neutestamentliche Haustafeln," *NTS*, 21 (1974), 1–22.

98. M. Dibelius, *An die Kolosser. Epheser. An Philemon. HZNT.* XII (3rd ed.; Tubingen: Mohr, 1953), pp. 48 – 49.

99. John Yoder's otherwise splendid treatment of the *Haustafeln* (*The Politics of Jesus*. pp. 163 – 92) is marred by his tendentious refusal to acknowledge the likelihood that the tradition is "borrowed" from the common morality. The emphasis on roles is not initiated by the Christian tradition, but it is transformed. Yoder presupposes a "Christ against Culture" model, but this tradition at least is better seen in the light of a "Christ transforming Culture" model.

100. On the transvaluation of *tapeinos* in the Christian tradition compared to conventional Greek morality, see Verhey, "Humble," *ISBE.* II, 775 – 78.

101. Victor Paul Furnish, *The Moral Teachings of Paul* (Nashville: Abingdon, 1979), pp. 120 – 22. The Christian tradition is also indebted to the Jewish codes for the regularity of "fear" in these instructions and, probably, for the use of the participle with imperatival force.

102. Contrast the position of Jack T. Sanders, *Ethics in the New Testament* (Philadelphia: Fortress, 1975), pp. 73 – 75, 83 – 88.

103. I Thess. 1:6; 2:4,14,17; 3:2-5,8,13; 5:1-11,18; II Thess. 1:4-10; 2:15,17; 3:3; I Pet. 1:6,7,10,11,13,21; 2:4,5,8,9,12,20,21,24; 3:14,15; 4:3,5,7,12,13,17-19; 5:4,8-10,12; Heb. 10:23,30,32,33; Acts. 1:7; 20:28; Js. 4:7; 5:8; II Pet. 3:10; Rev. 16:15; Rom. 2:5-11; 5:2; 12:12; 13:11,13,14; I Cor. 1:7,8,9; 7:29; 15:1; 16:13; Phil. 1:27,28; 4:1; Col. 4:2,3,12; Eph. 1:14; 4:27; 6:11,13-18. See Selwyn, Table XIV, pp. 442 – 49, and the treatment of these parallels, pp. 439 – 59.

104. Carrington, *Primitive Christian Catechism*. ch. IV, esp. pp. 51 – 54.

105. The passages here would be: for "watch" (Gk. *gregorēsate*), I Thess. 5:4-11; I Pet. 1:13,21; 2:4,5,8,9,21,24; 4:3,7; 5:8; Eph. 6:18; Col. 4:2,3; Rom. 13:13,14; I Cor. 16:13; for "Stand" (Gk. *stēkete*), I Thess. 3:8; II Thess. 2:15,17; 3:3; I Pet. 4:19; 5:8-12; Eph. 6:11,13,14; Col. 4:12; I Cor. 15:1; 16:13; Phil. 4:1; Js. 4:7.

CHAPTER III

1. This point is made by virtually every analysis of New Testament ethics, e.g., R.E.O. White, *Biblical Ethics* (Atlanta: John Knox, 1979), p. 228. For J. L. Houlden, *Ethics and the New Testament* (Harmondsworth: Penguin, 1975), pp. 1 – 24, and Jack Sanders, *Ethics in the New Testament* (Philadelphia: Fortress, 1975), passim, the lack of an autonomous ethic is a great difficulty with New Testament ethics. There are, of course, some passages that at least hint at the possibility of an "autonomous"

ethic, that is, moral knowledge which is independent of religious loyalties (e.g., Rom. 1 and 2). But the New Testament is not concerned with the formulation and defense of a natural law position. It is rather concerned with the formation of character and conduct according to the loyalty to the God who raised Jesus from the dead.

2. See the article by Hans-Georg Geyer, "The Resurrection of Jesus Christ: A Survey of the Debate in Present Day Theology" in C.F.D. Moule, ed., *The Significance of the Message of the Resurrection for Faith in Jesus Christ* (Naperville, Ill.: A. R. Allenson, 1968).

3. The topical approach is found in, e.g., William Lillie, *Studies in New Testament Ethics* (Edinburgh: Oliver & Boyd, 1961), and John Murray, *Principles of Conduct* (Grand Rapids: Eerdmans, 1957).

4. Thus Rudolf Schnackenburg, *The Moral Teaching of the New Testament* (New York: Herder and Herder, 1967); White, *Biblical Ethics;* Houlden, *Ethics and the New Testament;* and Sanders, *Ethics in the New Testament.*

5. Thus Amos Wilder, *The Language of the Gospel: Early Christian Rhetoric* (New York: Harper & Row, 1964), p. 36. Mark evidently introduces the word "gospel" (Gk. *euangelion*) into the traditional material (1:1,14,15; 8:35; 10:29; 13:10; 14:9) and, moreover, uses the term as a "title" for his whole work (1:1); see W. Marxsen, *Mark the Evangelist* (Nashville: Abingdon, 1969), pp. 117-50.

6. Marxsen, pp. 117-50. His analysis cannot be repeated here, but we may at least call attention to the fact that "gospel" is used for Jesus' proclamation in 1:14,15 and for Mark's work in 1:1 (Marxsen, p. 118). The number of historical present tenses is also striking. See also Gerhard Friedrich, *"euangelizomai*. etc.," *TDNT.* II, 707-37, esp. 727-29.

7. The traditional identification is well argued in V. Taylor, *Commentary on Mark's Gospel.* A number of excellent scholars, however, have begun to challenge the traditional view, arguing for Galilee (Marxsen, *Mark the Evangelist.* pp. 54-95, following Lohmeyer, *Galiläa und Jerusalem* [Gottingen: Vandenhoeck & Ruprecht, 1936] and R. H. Lightfoot, *Locality and Doctrine in the Gospels* [New York: Harper & Bros., 1938]) or southern Syria (Howard Clark Kee, *Community of the New Age* [Philadelphia: Westminster, 1977], pp. 100-5, and against Galilee!). Whatever the precise locality — and Rome still seems the likeliest candidate — the characteristics of confronting Roman and Jewish claims from a position of estrangement and powerlessness are clear.

8. So also Sanders, p. 32. See also Ernest Best, "Discipleship in Mark: Mark 8:22-10:52," *Scottish Journal of Theology.* 23 (1970), 327-31.

9. Paul Minear, *Commands of Christ* (Nashville: Abingdon, 1972), pp. 153-64.

10. See Howard Clark Kee, *Community of the New Age.* pp. 146ff.

11. Sanders, p. 33.

12. Houlden, p. 41.

13. Ibid., p. 46.

14. Sanders, p. 33.

15. Raymond Anderson, "The Minimal Ethic Phenomenon in the Gospels," an unpublished paper.

16. Victor Paul Furnish, *The Love Command in the New Testament* (Nashville: Abingdon, 1972), pp. 25-30.

17. Kee, p. 158.

18. It should not be overlooked that in the list of things "left . . . for my sake and the gospel" (Mk. 10:29-30), husbands and wives are conspicuously absent; cf. I Cor. 7:12-16.

19. In 10:28, however, to boast of generosity or to use it as a claim to entitlement seems to be rebuked. To use even generosity as a *basis* for confidence rather than God is subtly to fall back into the old patterns.

20. For the justification of this position, see Minear, pp. 83-89, and above, p. 53.

21. Of Mark's 661 verses, over 600 are used again in Matthew. A. Wikenhauser, *New Testament Introduction* (New York: Herder & Herder, 1958), p. 223.

22. On questions of introduction, see Feine, Behm, Kummel, *Introduction to the New Testament.*

23. On these "battle-fronts," see Gerhard Barth, "Matthew's Understanding of the Law," in Gunther Bornkamm, Barth, and H. J. Held, eds., *Tradition and Interpretation in Matthew's Gospel* (Philadelphia: Westminster, 1963), pp. 58–164.

24. On this passage, see G. Barth, "Matthew's Understanding of the Law," pp. 64–73, and J. P. Meier, *Law and History in Matthew's Gospel* (Rome: Biblical Institute Press, 1976). "Fulfill" does not mean to change or modify or cleanse: it stands in contrast here to abolish and means "to establish." The law holds, and Jesus brings it to its eschatological fruition when the will of God is wholly done. Cf. Mt. 3:15.

25. Consider also Mt. 11:13, where the author modifies the Q tradition to protect the continuing validity and eschatological fulfillment of the law. The contrast still found in Luke 16:16 between the time of the law and the prophets and the time of John and Jesus is elided into the theme of the fulfillment of the prophets and the law (Mt. 11:13). See Barth, "Matthew's Understanding of the Law," pp. 63–64.

26. Matthew's concern certainly includes the defense of Jesus against charges brought by the Jewish synagogue. The apologetic motive is operative here as well as in Matthew's additions in 3:14-15, where he responds to the charge that Jesus testified against himself when he underwent John's baptism of repentance; and in 27:62-66, 28:11-15, where with the story of the guards he responds to the accusation that Jesus' disciples had stolen the body (28:15!). But Matthew's motive is also polemical: he re-presents the story over against both the synagogue and the antinomians within the Christian community.

27. And see G. Barth, "Matthew's Understanding of the Law," pp. 91–92.

28. See G. Barth, pp. 86–90.

29. See above, p. 209, n. 110.

30. The specific reference of Gk. *porneía* in Matthew's "concession" is much debated. J. Bonsirven (*Le divorce dans le Nouveau Testament*, 1948) surveys plausible references and finally favors a reference to illegal marriages, marriages forbidden by Jewish law (see, e.g., Lev. 18:6-18). In I Cor. 5:1, the word does apparently refer to incest. But such a restricted reference is unusual and, in our passages, unnecessary and unwarranted. Such a restriction would make the saying too obvious to require special mention: invalid marriages may be dissolved. Others also have insisted on the distinction between Gk. *moicheía* and Gk. *porneía*, but have suggested on that basis only that some other form of sexual immorality than adultery (Gk. *moicheía*) is meant, usually premarital sexual intercourse (see, e.g., E. J. Mally, *Jerome Biblical Commentary*). In apparent support of such a distinction is the fact that the Old Testament punishment for adultery — death (e.g., Lev. 20:10; Deut. 22:22) — would seem to make the permission of divorce superfluous. But the death penalty for adultery is formally dismissed around A.D. 30 (*b. Sanh.* 41a), and probably had been little used for some time before. Gk. *porneía* seems to be the broader of the two terms; it can refer to a variety of sexual infidelities, including adultery (Ecclesiasticus 23:22,23). Gk. *moicheía* is a narrower term. On the basis of this, Matthew's legal concession should not be understood as referring only to either marriage within prohibited degrees or premarital fornication but, like Shammai, to the range of sexual immoralities covered by the Hb. 'erwâ. Gk. *porneía*, or RSV "unchastity," including adultery.

31. It is a "scholastic dialogue" in Mark's Gospel.

32. G. Barth, "Matthew's Understanding of the Law," p. 77.

33. One might compare Hillel's famous response to the proselyte, "What is hateful

to you do not do to your fellow: that is the whole law; the rest is its explanation; go and learn." *Shabbath* 31a, quoted by Claude G. Montefiore, *Rabbinic Anthology* (London: Macmillan, 1938), p. 200 (539).

34. So also G. Barth, p. 77; Furnish, *The Love Command,* p. 33.

35. So also Bornkamm, "Das Dopplegebot der Liebe," *NT Studien für Rudolf Bultmann,* p. 93; Barth, pp. 75-78, and Furnish, pp. 33-34. For all of these, however, the love command becomes *the* key for the interpretation of the whole law, but other clues to its meaning are also used, e.g., Hosea 6:6, the narrative of creation, the "golden rule"; and it will not do to reduce these to the love commandment or to identify them with it. Nor will it do to say that the love commandment *constitutes* the law for Matthew, as — in an apparent slip — Furnish does, p. 34.

36. That the pattern was self-conscious may be seen in the concluding formula which stands at the end of each of the discourses (Mt. 7:28; 11:1; 13:53; 19:1; 26:1).

37. The literature on the Sermon on the Mount, of course, is enormous, but see especially Harvey McArthur, *Understanding the Sermon on the Mount* (New York: Harper, 1960), Joachim Jeremias, *The Sermon on the Mount* (Philadelphia: Fortress, 1963), and W. D. Davies, *The Setting of the Sermon on the Mount* (London: Cambridge University Press, 1966).

38. Jeremias, *The Sermon on the Mount.* p. 23.

39. On the beatitudes, see Robert Guelich, "The Matthean Beatitudes: 'Entrance Requirements' or Eschatological Blessings," *JBL.* 95 (1976), 415-34; Willis De Boer, "Beatitudes," *ISBE.* I, 443-44.

40. See Verhey, "Humble," *ISBE.* II, 775-78.

41. Mt. 5:4, "Blessed are they that mourn" (cf. Lk. 6:21b), is the exception: it reflects the announcement of the reversal effected by the kingdom rather than any exhortation to respond to it morally. Matthew probably keeps it because of its relationship to Old Testament promises, e.g., Is. 61:2.

42. B. W. Bacon, "Jesus and the Law," *JBL.* 47 (1928), 223, and G. D. Kilpatrick, *Origins of Matthew's Gospel* (Oxford: Clarendon Press, 1946), p. 107 describe Matthew as a *nova lex.* Against them, see Barth, pp. 153-59. To Barth's treatment I would only add that Matthew omitted Mk. 1:27, which indeed described Jesus' teachings as "a new teaching."

43. G. Barth, p. 94, takes the law, "An eye for an eye and a tooth for a tooth" (Mt. 5:38), to be "completely overthrown" in "a complete abolition." But the law is not to be understood as prescriptive but as restrictive; it does not demand an eye for an eye, but restricts revenge. The law may be rendered unnecessary, but it will not do to say it is abolished or overthrown.

44. Implicit in this freedom *from* anxiety is the freedom *for* generosity, made explicit in Lk. 12:33.

45. G. Barth, p. 73.

46. So G. Barth, pp. 73-75.

47. Sanders, *Ethics in the New Testament,* p. 44; see Käsemann, "Sentences of Holy Law in the New Testament," *New Testament Questions of Today* (Philadelphia: Fortress, 1969), pp. 66-81.

48. The passage, of course, has been subject to a great deal of study. See O. Cullmann, *Peter* (Philadelphia: Westminster, 1953), for a careful analysis.

49. Davies, *The Setting of the Sermon on the Mount.* p. 225.

50. Matthew's handling of Mark is artful here (cf. Mk. 9:33-50). By omitting the reference to the quarreling of the disciples, the question "who is the greatest?" becomes an honest inquiry about rank within the community. And by immediately introducing the episode with the little child, the question of rank is answered in terms of priorities in pastoral care. The little ones, the insignificant ones, the ones most easily overlooked and looked down on are the first priority for pastoral care. Mark's rebuke of quarreling leaders has become a rule for governance in the church. The parable of the lost sheep (Mt. 18:11-14; cf. Lk. 15:3-10) is modified from the same perspective.

51. Most recently Sanders, *Ethics in the New Testament,* pp. 44. See also Hans Windish, *The Meaning of the Sermon on the Mount* (Philadelphia: Westminster, 1956).

52. The fulfillment of prophecy is a central motif in Matthew (1:22; 2:5,15,17,23; 3:3; 4:14; 8:17, etc.).

53. On this parable, see Jeremias, *Parables,* pp. 187–89.

54. Note the contrast to the self-confident boast of the dead in the Egyptian Book of the Dead, cited in Jeremias, p. 208.

55. Jeremias, p. 209.

56. Luke and Acts belong together as two volumes of a single work even though they are separated in the New Testament.

57. The traditional identification of the author of the book of Luke with Luke, the physician and companion of Paul, has been vigorously challenged recently. For the case against the tradition, see Feine, Behm, Kummel, pp. 102–5. A convincing defense of the tradition has recently been given by E. E. Ellis, *The Gospel of Luke* (London: Nelson, 1966), pp. 40–51. "It is," as Eric Franklin said, "perhaps only Paul, the complete existentialist, and Luke, the out-and-out purveyor of salvation history to the exclusion of eschatology, who could never have been companions"; *Christ the Lord* (Philadelphia: Westminster, 1975), p. 119; see also pp. 179–85.

58. The modification is not inspired by a concern for historical accuracy; in 4:23 the Capernaum miracles (cf. Mk. 1:21-38) have already occurred. The modification is made because of the significance of this episode to Luke.

59. One of the things Luke accomplishes with this device is to shift the emphasis away from the imminence of the kingdom (Mk. 1:15) to "today" (4:21, the Gk. *sémeron* has emphatic position). "Today" the "acceptable year of the Lord" has come — and remains (the Gk. *peplérōtai* is a perfect tense). This eschatological shift of emphasis is typical of Luke. The shift is noted grandly, but its significance is exaggerated, in Conzelmann's epochal study *The Theology of St. Luke* (London: Faber and Faber, 1960). See Franklin, *Christ the Lord,* for a response to Conzelmann which notes the same shift without exaggerating its significance.

60. Jeremias, *Jesus' Promise to the Nations* (Naperville, Ill.: A. R. Allenson, 1958), pp. 44–46.

61. It contains the "great insertion" of Q materials and special Lucan materials into the order of Mark.

62. Franklin, *Christ the Lord,* p. 171. Luke often represents Jesus as the guest of the wealthy (e.g., 19:5,8), hardly evidence of a "social prejudice" against the rich.

63. Compare the bracketing of the proclamation of the resurrection by the reports of the community of goods in Acts 4:32-35.

64. The cross is not treated as the saving event by Luke. This has been observed by many and used to contrast Luke and Paul (P. Vielhauer, "On the 'Paulinism' of Acts," in L. E. Keck and J. L. Martyn, eds., *Studies in Luke-Acts* [London: SPCK, 1968], pp. 33–50). Luke knows (something, at least) of Paul's theology on this point and attributes it to him in his speech to the Ephesian elders (20:28) without disagreeing with it. That the author chooses another treatment of the cross does not seem to me to prove that he could not have been a companion or that he must have been a postapostolic admirer and imitator. Indeed, such theological independence could hardly be expected of a later admirer and imitator. We are, nevertheless, indebted to Vielhauer et al., for now the question is posed why Luke, the companion of Paul, would choose not to express in narrative fashion Paul's theology of the cross. A part of the answer, I suggest, is the intimate relationship between portrayal of the reversal of cross and resurrection and the announcement of an eschatological reversal in response to which he calls upon his audience to respond with solicitude for the poor and oppressed.

65. Sanders, *Ethics in the New Testament,* pp. 36f.

66. Sanders, p. 37.

67. On the metaphorical use of possessions in Luke's gospel, see further Luke T. Johnson, *The Literary Function of Possessions in Luke-Acts* (Missoula, Montana: Scholars Press, 1977), pp. 126–71: "Luke sees possessions as a primary symbol of human existence, the immediate exteriorization of and manifestation of the self" (p. 221).

68. See John H. Yoder, *The Politics of Jesus,* pp. 26–77, and Robert B. Sloan, Jr., *The Favorable Year of the Lord: A Study of Jubilary Theology in the Gospel of Luke* (Austin, Texas: Schola Press, 1977).

69. Contrast the community of goods among the Essenes; see 1QS (Manual of Discipline) 1.11ff.; Martin Hengel, *Property and Riches in the Early Church* (Philadelphia: Fortress, 1971), pp. 32f.; Richard Batey, *Jesus and the Poor* (New York: Harper & Row, 1972), pp. 44–49.

70. Hengel, p. 32. Organization was, of course, necessary (see, e.g., Acts 6:1-6), but Luke is relatively unconcerned about the organization. The tension between the picture of the conduct of missionaries in Lk. 9:3-4 and 10:4-9 and the picture of Paul's conduct in Acts stands against any reading of Luke as providing legal rulings. There is also some tension between alms-giving, sabbatical legislation, and the community of goods as policies.

71. Sanders, p. 37.

72. See Paul K. Jewett, *Man as Male and Female* (Grand Rapids: Eerdmans, 1975), pp. 86–94.

73. Albrecht Oepke, *"gunē," TDNT,* I, 777–80.

74. H. J. Cadbury, *The Making of Luke-Acts* (New York: Macmillan, 1927), p. 263; Sanders, p. 36, n. 19.

75. It must be noted that Luke does not look down on reproduction. Indeed, he enunciates the reversal theme with respect to Elizabeth precisely in that the barren one is pregnant (1:7,24,25,36). But Luke rejects the reduction of women to their reproductive roles.

76. Cadbury, p. 264.

77. Hans Conzelmann, *The Theology of St. Luke* (London: Faber and Faber, 1960), p. 31; Jacob Jervell, *Luke and the People of God* (Minneapolis: Augsburg, 1972), p. 119f.

78. Conzelmann, pp. 68ff., attempts to show that Jesus stays out of Samaritan territory in Luke, an impossible task (9:51-56; 17:11-19). But the Samaritans are not Gentiles for Luke (compare Acts 8 and 10) but heterodox Jews. See Jervell, pp. 113–32.

79. See further Jervell, pp. 41–74; also pp. 75–112, 113–32; Donald Juel, *New Testament Literature* (Nashville: Abingdon, 1978), pp. 215–35.

80. All the Gospels have the Baptist cite Is. 40, but only Luke cites it down to this fifth verse.

81. On this section, see especially Jervell, pp. 133–51.

82. Jervell, p. 137.

83. Against Conzelmann, *Theology of St. Luke*, pp. 145ff., 212f.; see Jervell, p. 145.

84. Cf. Gal. 2:6; it seems likely that the decree was developed after the council to facilitate fellowship between Jewish and Gentile Christians.

85. Ernst Haenchen, *The Acts of the Apostles* (Philadelphia: Westminster, 1971), p. 469.

86. Haenchen, p. 449.

87. Later copiests rendered the ritual commands into a summary of morality; the Western text may be translated "refrain from idolatry and fornication and blood (shed) and whatever you would not have your neighbor do to you."

88. Jervell, pp. 153–83.

89. And he says nothing about any resignation from office — as one would expect if John Yoder's representation of the "politics of Jesus" were correct ("The function exercised by government is not the function to be exercised by Christians," *The Politics of Jesus,* p. 199).

90. Jervell, pp. 153–83.
91. Especially the Ebionites. See Wayne Meeks, ed., *The Writings of St. Paul* (New York: Norton, 1972), pp. 176–84.
92. See, e.g., Elaine Pagels' study of the way the second-century Valentinian Gnostics claimed Paul and represented his teachings, *The Gnostic Paul* (Philadelphia: Fortress, 1975).
93. On the introductory questions, see Feine, Behm, Kummel. E. E. Ellis, *Paul and His Recent Interpreters* (Grand Rapids: Eerdmans, 1961) has made a valiant attempt (but finally unsuccessful in my view) to defend the Pauline authorship of the Pastorals. I am convinced that Paul is the author of Colossians, Ephesians, and II Thessalonians, but in view of the critical questions and in view of the somewhat different moral emphasis, it seems best, nevertheless, to treat them separately.
94. See William Doty, *Letters in Primitive Christianity* (Philadelphia: Fortress, 1973).
95. Along with personal ambassadors like Timothy and Titus.
96. See Paul Schubert, "The Apostolic *Parousia*: Form and Significance," in W. R. Farmer, C. F. D. Moule, and R. R. Niebuhr, eds., *Christian History and Interpretation* (London: Cambridge University Press, 1967), pp. 249–68.
97. Furnish, *Theology and Ethics in Paul* (Nashville: Abingdon, 1968), has masterfully demonstrated this point.
98. In Rom. 5:1-5, the hortatory use of the indicative induced some copiests to write the hortatory subjunctive, Gk. *exōmen*, for the indicative, Gk. *exomen*.
99. Paul Schubert, *Form and Function of the Pauline Thanksgivings* (Berlin: Alfred Töpelmann, 1939), p. 89. Philem. 4-7 gives thanks for Philemon's "love," his "sharing" (Gk. *koinōnia*), and "because the hearts of the saints have been refreshed" through him. These indicatives are rendered imperatives in the subsequent exhortations on the basis of love (9) and partnership (17, Gk. *koinōnos*) to "refresh my heart (i.e., Onesimus, vs. 12) in Christ" (vs. 20). The "comfort" (Gk. *paraklēsis*, vs. 7) Paul has in Philemon is intimately related to the appeal (Gk. *parakalō*, vs. 9) he makes to Philemon.
100. Note also Philemon 7 and 9; see above, n. 99.
101. Furnish, *Theology and Ethics in Paul*, p. 109.
102. See Leander E. Keck, *Paul and His Letters* (Philadelphia: Fortress, 1979), pp. 66–73.
103. On the relationship of indicative and imperative, see further Furnish, *Theology and Ethics in Paul*, pp. 224–27.
104. Käsemann, "Sentences of Holy Law in the New Testament," *New Testament Questions of Today*, pp. 66–81. The form of such expressions is a conditional sentence with a casuistic legal expression in the *protasis* and a statement of eschatological judgment in the *apodosis*; e.g., I Cor. 3:17; 14:38; 16:22; Gal. 1:9; II Cor. 9:6, etc. See above, p. 213 n. 31.
105. Sanders, *Ethics in the New Testament*, p. 48.
106. These three elements are identified by James Gustafson in a number of pieces, but with typical acumen in "Moral Discernment in the Christian Life," in Gene Outka and Paul Ramsey, eds., *Norm and Context in Christian Ethics* (New York: Scribners, 1968), pp. 17–36.
107. Furnish, *Theology and Ethics in Paul*, p. 176.
108. See Lewis Smedes, *All Things Made New* (Grand Rapids: Eerdmans, 1970).
109. J. Louis Martyn, "Epistemology at the Turn of the Ages: II Cor. 5:16," in Farmer, Moule, and Niebuhr, eds., *Christian History and Interpretation*, pp. 269–88.
110. Cf. Moule, "The Influence of Circumstances on the Use of Eschatological Terms," *Journal of Theological Studies*, 15 (1964), 1ff.
111. Robin Scroggs, *Paul for a New Day* (Philadelphia: Fortress, 1977), p. 70. Against such a view, Wolfgang Schrage has issued the definitive reply, *Die konkreten Einzelgebote in der paulinischen Paränese* (Gütersloh: Gütersloher Verlagshaus, 1961).

112. On freedom in Paul, see Peter Richardson, *Paul's Ethic of Freedom* (Philadelphia: Westminster, 1979).

113. On love in Paul, see Furnish, *The Love Command in the New Testament*, pp. 91–118.

114. This central section of Paul's encomium to love uses verbs, not predicate adjectives (as do most English translations), to describe the *works* of love.

115. Furnish, *Theology and Ethics in Paul*, pp. 25–92, gives the outstanding account of Paul's use of traditional material.

116. Explicitly in I Cor. 7:10-11 and 9:14 (and in nonmoral contexts, I Cor. 11:23-24; I Thess. 4:16-17; I Cor. 14:37), implicitly in allusions to Jesus' words (e.g., Rom. 12:14; 14:13,14; I Thess. 5:2; I Cor. 13:2). The extent of these allusions is debated; Furnish, pp. 56–59, is perhaps overly cautious in reaction to Resch and Davies. See also Scroggs, pp. 64–65.

117. Davies, *Paul and Rabbinic Judaism*, p. 144.

118. When Paul exhorted his hearers to the "imitation of Christ" (e.g., I Cor. 11:1; I Thess. 1:6), the focus is not on the "earthly Jesus" but on the cross; see Furnish, *Theology and Ethics in Paul*, pp. 218–24.

119. See above, ch. II, section B.

120. As Furnish has shown, *Theology and Ethics in Paul*, pp. 42–68. See especially his treatment of the vice lists, pp. 84–86.

121. The literature on Paul's use of the law is enormous. See, e.g., C.E.B. Cranfield, "St. Paul and the Law," in Richard Batey, ed., *New Testament Issues* (New York: Harper & Row, 1970), pp. 148–72; H. Kleinknecht and W. Gutbrod, *"nomos,"* *TDNT*, IV, 1022–85.

122. M. S. Enslin, *The Ethics of Paul* (New York: Harper & Bros., 1930), pp. 17–44, 90–106, et passim, gives a helpful analysis of Paul's relationship to Stoicism.

123. In a diatribe the speaker or writer makes use of an imaginary interlocutor who asks questions or raises objections. The best treatment is still Rudolf Bultmann, *Der Stil der paulinischen Predigt und die kynisch-stoische Diatribe* (Göttingen: Vandenhoeck & Ruprecht, 1910).

124. *Dissertations*, II. xix.24.

125. C. H. Dodd, *"ENNOMOS CHRISTOU,"* *Studia Paulina in honorem Johannis de Zwaan* (Haarlem: Bohn, 1953), pp. 96–110.

126. Davies, *Paul and Rabbinic Judaism*, pp. 142–46; also *The Setting of the Sermon on the Mount*, pp. 352–66, esp. 353.

127. Dodd, p. 107.

128. Davies, *Paul and Rabbinic Judaism*, p. 144.

129. Furnish, *Theology and Ethics in Paul*, pp. 60–63.

130. Ibid., p. 64. This tradition finds expression (in different ways) in Calvin, *Comm. ad loc.*, in Rudolf Bultmann, *Theology of the New Testament*, Vol. I (New York: Scribners, 1951), p. 268, and others.

131. The text and context of I Cor. 9:21 has also to do with questions of identity: Jewish identity "under the law," Gentile identity "outside the law," and Christian identity in Christ (Gk. *ennomos Xristou*).

132. Minear, *The Obedience of Faith* (Naperville, Ill.: A. R. Allenson, 1971).

133. Cf. the interesting work of Krister Stendahl, *Paul among Jews and Christians* (Philadelphia: Fortress, 1976), esp. pp. 78–96, "Paul and the Introspective Conscience of the West." See also Dahl, *Studies in Paul* (Minneapolis: Augsburg, 1977), 95–120.

134. Minear shows how the theological sections of Paul's letter to the Romans are related to the exhortations in chapters 14 and 15.

135. On the collection, see K. F. Nickle, *The Collection* (SBT 48; London: SCM Press, 1966).

136. Steve Bartchy, *First Century Slavery and I Corinthians 7:21* (SBLDS 11; Missoula: Scholars Press, 1973).

137. Leaving aside the intriguing proposals of Knox that Philemon is the overseer of the churches and that Aristarchus is the owner of Onesimus and the one in whose home the church meets (Knox, *Philemon among the Letters of Paul* [New York: Abingdon, 1959]).

138. See Theo Preis, "Life in Christ and Social Ethics in the Epistle to Philemon," *Life in Christ* (London: SCM, 1954), pp. 32–42.

139. Stendahl, *The Bible and the Role of Women* (Philadelphia: Fortress, 1966), p. 32.

140. The word for "deacon" is Gk. *diakonos*. The masculine form is used, and it is better translated "deacon" or "minister" than the RSV's "deaconess"; cf. I Cor. 3:5; II Cor. 3:6; 6:4. The word for "helper" is Gk. *prostatis*. Etymologically, the word is formed from the words "to stand" and "before." The word itself, when applied to women, is a symptom that the subjection (compounded of "thrown" and "under") of women is overcome.

141. On this passage, see further Furnish, *Moral Teaching of Paul* (Nashville: Abingdon, 1979), pp. 95–102.

142. Furnish, ibid., pp. 91–92; Robin Scroggs, "Paul and the Eschatological Woman," *Journal of American Academy of Religion*, 40 (1972), 283–303; Conzelmann, *I Corinthians* (Philadelphia: Fortress, 1975).

143. Furnish, ibid., p. 91.

144. Richard and Catherine Clark Kroeger, "Pandemonium and Silence at Corinth," *Reformed Journal*, June 1978, pp. 6–11.

145. See further Verhey, "The Second Epistle to Philemon," *Reformed Journal*, Feb. 1978, pp. 7–10.

146. The RSV helpfully identifies "all things are lawful" as a Corinthian slogan by putting it in quotation marks; it similarly identifies 6:13a. In 6:18, however, "Every sin which a man commits is outside his own body" ought also to be identified as a slogan which Paul qualifies. 7:1a, "It is well for a man not to touch a woman," is another slogan, but among the ascetics of the Corinthian enthusiasts. See also 1:12; 8:1,4; 10:23, and Hurd, *The Origin of I Corinthians* (New York: Seabury, 1965).

147. The apparent priority of this reason for marriage here is relative to the context, a response to the eschatological assumptions of the Corinthians. That Paul does not consider this the fundamental ground for marriage is plain from I Thess. 4:5, where Christians are instructed to marry "in holiness and honor, not in the passion of lust like heathen who do not know God."

148. The equality of husband and wife in marriage is assumed in the parallel advice given to them throughout I Cor. 7. See I Cor. 7:10 and 11, 12 and 13, 14a and 14b, 16a and 16b, 32-33 and 34.

149. Dahl, "Paul and Possessions," *Studies in Paul* (Minneapolis: Augsburg, 1977), pp. 23,25; M. Hengel, *Property and Riches in the Early Church* (Philadelphia: Fortress, 1974), pp. 54–59.

150. Dahl, p. 35.

151. Paul can also use fund-raising techniques that have become almost conventional. He tells the Corinthians about the generosity of the Macedonians (II Cor. 8:1-5); he had already encouraged the Macedonians by boasting about the Corinthians (9:2); and now he warns the Corinthians that *they* may be embarrassed if their generosity does not match Paul's boast (9:3-5).

152. See especially Philo's *Embassy to Gaius*. Furnish, *Moral Teachings of Paul*, discusses this and other parallels in his helpful and interesting treatment of Rom. 13, pp. 117–36.

153. We cannot here entertain the complex and much-debated question about whether the *exousia* (Rom. 13:1) are to be understood Christologically as the "powers" over whom Christ has won the victory on the cross. See Clinton Morrison, *The Powers That Be* (Naperville, Ill.: Allenson, 1960), for a fine review of this discussion.

154. For a careful defense of Paul's authorship of both epistles, see Ernst Percy, *Die Probleme der Kolosser und Epheserbriefe* (Lund: Gleerup, 1946). Against Pauline authorship, see Edward Lohse, *Colossians and Philemon* (Philadelphia: Fortress, 1971).

155. On the Colossian opponents, see Moule, *The Epistles to the Colossians and to Philemon* (Cambridge: University Press, 1962), pp. 29–34.

156. John Reumann, "Excursus: The 'Christ Hymn' of Col. 1 in Recent Discussion," *Creation and New Creation* (Minneapolis: Augsburg, 1973), pp. 42–56.

157. That some of these passages are indebted to an eschatologically oriented tradition is irrelevant, for the author of Colossians was no mere transcriber of traditions.

158. Contrast the opinion of Sanders, *Ethics in the New Testament*, pp. 68–70. It must be granted that Colossians has little concern with the imminence of the end, but then Paul's "concern" with imminence has been greatly exaggerated.

159. Sanders, p. 79.

160. Ibid.

161. Furnish, *The Love Command*, p. 120. Contrast Sanders, for whom it has a "purely formal" presence in Colossians (p. 68) and "has lost its cutting edge" (p. 69).

162. See further Verhey, "Humble, Humility," *ISBE*, II, 775–78.

163. See above, pp. 67–70.

164. Contrast Frances W. Beare's comment that there is a "fading of the eschatological expectation" in this passage, *The Interpreter's Bible*, II (New York: Abingdon, 1955), 227.

165. C. H. Dodd, "Christianity and the Reconciliation of the Nations," in his *Christ and the New Humanity* (Philadelphia: Fortress, 1965), pp. 11–13.

166. See further F. F. Bruce, *The Spreading Flame* (Grand Rapids: Eerdmans, 1958), pp. 267–71.

167. On "the dividing wall of hostility," see Verhey, "Hostility, Dividing Wall of," *ISBE*, II, 768.

168. On these "powers," see Hendrikus Berkhof, *Christ and the Powers* (London: SPCK, 1966); G. B. Caird, *Principalities and Powers* (Oxford: Clarendon Press, 1956); Clinton Morrison, *The Powers that Be*; Richard Mouw, *Politics and the Biblical Drama* (Grand Rapids: Eerdmans, 1976), pp. 85–115.

169. Morrison, p. 99.

170. The political aspect of "the powers" is not absent from other writings, e.g., I Cor. 2:8; the mention of the angels in I Cor. 6:3 in connection with litigation; the beast of Rev. 13; and perhaps even the Gk. *exousiae* of Rom. 13:1.

171. The best defense of Pauline authorship is E. E. Ellis, *Paul and His Recent Interpreters* (Grand Rapids: Eerdmans, 1961).

172. Gk. *didaskalia*, "doctrine" or "teaching," occurs fifteen times in the Pastorals as compared with six in the rest of the New Testament. Gk. *hugiēs, hugiainō*, "sound," appears in connection with doctrine only in the Pastorals.

173. Eduard Schweizer, "Two New Testament Creeds Compared," in Klassen and Snyder, eds., *Current Issues in New Testament Interpretation*, pp. 166–77.

174. See Easton, "Ethical Lists" in *The Pastoral Epistles* (New York: Scribners, 1947), pp. 197–202; Barrett, *The Pastoral Epistles* (Oxford: Clarendon Press, 1963), pp. 25–28.

175. I Tim. 2:15, RSV: "Yet woman will be saved through bearing children. . . ." may better be translated "woman will be brought safely through childbearing." *Dià* with the genitive can be used in this way (cf. I Pet. 3:20). If so, it suggests that the curse on Eve (Gen. 3:16) had been lifted and would balance the appeal to submit. Notice, in confirmation, the singular "woman."

176. *Eusebia* was a common Greek word in moral literature; it meant "loyalty, respect, reverence" as well as "piety." It appears in the Pastorals thirteen times, in Acts three times, in II Pet. five times, and nowhere else in the New Testament. The

main reference in the Pastorals is "piety," or "godliness" (but see the use of *eusebeō* in I Tim. 5:4).

177. We will postpone analysis of the Johannine letters until the next section, which deals with the Johannine literature.

178. A. Harnack, "Probabilia über die Adresse und den Verfasser des Herbräerbriefs," *ZNW,* 1 (1900), 16ff., argued that the most likely author was Priscilla.

179. The plural is noteworthy in contrast to Paul's use of the singular "sin." Paul was interested in the "power" of sin which reigned in the old age and still exerts itself. Hebrews is more interested in the forgiveness of the guilt which attaches to individual immoral acts.

180. The influence of Platonic idealism on Hebrews has been suggested by many (e.g., J. Hering, "Eschatologie biblique et Idealisme platonicien" in W. D. Davies and D. Daube, eds., *The Background of the New Testament and its Eschatology* [Cambridge: University Press, 1964], pp. 450–54, and James W. Thompson, "Hebrews 9 and Hellenistic Concepts of Sacrifice," *JBL,* 98 [1979], 567–78). For Plato and his followers, of course, material and visible objects are not the ultimate realities; they are merely copies of "ideas" which exist eternally in heaven and which can be known only by reason, not by the senses. Some Platonic influence need not be ruled out, but it is radically wrong to interpret Hebrews in terms of a timeless eternity. Hebrews clearly refers to a heavenly world, but the comparisons and contrasts are basically eschatological rather than idealistic. The heavenly world is the world God has "prepared" (e.g., 11:16); it is established in the once-for-all work of Christ, and it awaits the consummation of his victory (e.g., 9:28). A fine discussion of "The Eschatology of the Epistle to the Hebrews" is given by C. K. Barrett in *The Background of the New Testament and its Eschatology,* pp. 363–93. On the question of the use of the Old Testament see Markus Barth, "The Old Testament in Hebrews," in Klassen and Snyder, *Current Issues in New Testament Interpretation,* pp. 53–78.

181. See most recent commentaries on Heb. 13. As Sanders correctly observes (*Ethics in the New Testament,* p. 109), the justifications offered in the chapter for the admonitions were apparently part of the tradition and cannot always be correlated to the theological concerns of the rest of the Epistle.

182. Tertullian, *On Modesty,* 20.

183. Dibelius, *James,* rev. by Heinrich Greeven; tr. M. A. Williams (Philadelphia: Fortress, 1976), pp. 1–11, treats James form critically and identifies it as paraenesis.

184. Dibelius has shown quite thoroughly and convincingly the eclecticism of the author, p. 5 et passim. This renders quite improbable the cases of those like A. Meyer, *Das Ratsel des Jk,* who claimed James was a Christian revision of a Jewish writing, a "Testament of the Patriarch Jacob"; and like M. H. Shepherd, "The Epistle of James and the Gospel of Matthew," *JBL,* 75 (1956), 40ff., who argues for a literary dependence of James on Matthew. James draws on the paraenetic traditions of Hellenism, Judaism, and early Christianity, including the sayings of Jesus.

185. Especially noteworthy are Jas. 1:22 (cf. Mt. 7:20,24); 2:5 (cf. Mt. 5:3); 3:12 (cf. Mt. 7:16); 3:18 (cf. Mt. 5:9); 4:10 (cf. Mt. 23:12); 4:11 (cf. Mt. 7:1); 4:13 (cf. Lk. 12:16ff.); 5:2; (cf. Mt. 6:19); 5:12 (cf. Mt. 5:34-37).

186. See, e.g., 1:7-8; 2:12-13; 4:4; 5:1,9.

187. See Dibelius, pp. 39–45, 47–50.

188. See the bibliography in Dibelius, p. 174.

189. Dibelius, pp. 174–80.

190. See Dibelius, pp. 168–74.

191. E.g., both James and Paul—and *only* they—use the Gk. phrase *ek pisteōs* connected with justification; Sanders, p. 120.

192. Sanders, p. 119.

193. See Willi Marxsen, *Der 'Frühkatholizismus' in Neuen Testament* (Neukirchen: Neukirchener Verlag, 1958), pp. 22–38; and his *Introduction to the New Testament* (Philadelphia: Fortress, 1968), pp. 193–98.

194. See further Georg Eichholz, *Jakobus und Paulus* (Munich, 1953).

195. The demand that one "keep oneself unstained from the world" (1:27) can be read in the sense of a demand for ritual cleanliness. But if James intended it in such a sense, it is at least curious that he nowhere else makes such ritual purity a matter of instruction. It is far better to understand "unstained" in an ethical sense, referring to moral purity. See James 4:4; see also Dibelius, pp. 120–23.

196. See Dibelius, pp. 116–20.

197. Dan Via, "The Right Strawy Epistle Reconsidered: A Study in Biblical Ethics and Hermeneutic," *JR*, 49 (1969), 262. Via says James fails to do this "consistently or successfully."

198. Against Dibelius, who claims that "the expression refers to *the* law," p. 142.

199. Dibelius, p. 142.

200. See Dibelius, pp. 144–46, for an excursus on this argument.

201. The inference may rely on the "as yourself," that is, "as one who is like you," or perhaps Lev. 19:15 had influenced the interpretation of Lev. 19:18 in Jewish paraenesis. At any rate, the argument does not treat the law as a code.

202. Sanders' characterization of this illustration as "an arbitrary example of the test of faith" (p. 125) will not do precisely because of the repetition of this concern in other instructions within James. One need not claim that the illustration is arbitrary in order to deny that caring for the needy is *the* theme of James.

203. See Dibelius, loc. cit.

204. I remain unconvinced by arguments against attributing I Peter to Peter and Silvanus. But the question of authorship may for our purposes be bracketed.

205. See Feine, Behm, Kummel, pp. 294–96.

206. 1:3,12,23; 2:2,10,25; 3:18-22.

207. See Selwyn, pp. 253–58. See the tabulation of occurrences on p. 253 for evidence that this word group is significantly more frequent in I Peter.

208. It is striking and Christologically significant that in the early Christian tradition *doxa* becomes an attribute not only of God but of Christ.

209. Furnish, *The Love Command*, pp. 161–62.

210. Each one is gifted and each one is exhorted to use his or her gift for the sake of others; cf. I Cor. 12.

211. For I Peter's reliance on the paraenetic tradition, see Selwyn, passim, but especially pp. 363–466.

212. The advice about adornment and submission were commonplace in both the Jewish and Hellenistic paraenetic traditions; cf. I Tim. 2:9ff.

213. To designate women "the weaker sex" was already a stock phrase; cf. Plato, *Republic*, V.455D, V.457A.

214. Or, if Peter is the author, in the midst of their expectation of civil persecution and their endurance of petty but ubiquitous persecution. See Selwyn, pp. 52–56.

215. The resemblance is clearest in Jude 4-16 and II Pet. 2:1-18 but is also plain in Jude 17-18 and II Pet. 3:1-3 and other places. The likeliest explanation seems to be that II Peter used Jude as a source. See Feine, Behm, Kummel, p. 303.

216. The comparison between the two is interesting here. II Peter puts the catalogue in chronological order; he adds reminders of God's kindness to go along with the examples of God's severity (Noah, 2:5; Lot, 2:7); and he avoids quoting the apocryphal book *I Enoch* (Jude 14-16) and even alluding to The Assumption of Moses (Jude 10; cf. II Pet. 2:11). See J. N. D. Kelly, *Epistles of Peter and Jude* (London: A&C Black, 1969), p. 226.

217. It is possible that this word is chosen in criticism of the *gnosis* of the libertines II Peter opposed.

218. On the question of authorship and other introductory questions, see Feine, Behm, Kummel, pp. 165–74, 310–12, 315–16, 329–31.

219. For example, in John's Gospel Jesus does not proclaim the kingdom of God, but himself; he does not use short and aphoristic sayings but extended and complex

discourses; the miracles or "signs" in John are mostly unique and intended to produce faith rather than provided as a response to faith; in John Jesus' ministry begins and focuses in Judea, not Galilee; etc.

220. John's Gospel is the only major New Testament book in which this term does *not* occur.

221. Contrast the Synoptic record where Gentiles are continually pressing their way into the narrative.

222. Note the contrast in John's and Paul's treatment of the vine, an old image for Israel (Jn. 15:1-8; Rom. 11:17-24). John is uninterested in the grafting in of "wild branches," or Gentiles.

223. Note the contrast in the handling of the common miracle tradition in Jn. 4:46-54; Mt. 8:5-13 par. Lk. 7:1-10. In John one is not even led to suspect that the "nobleman" is a Gentile, and there is no mention of the exemplary faith of a Gentile (as in Mt. 5:10; Lk. 7:9).

224. J. A. T. Robinson, "The Destination and Purpose of St. John's Gospel," in Richard Batey, ed., *New Testament Issues,* pp. 191–209.

225. In John's Gospel it is Jesus, not John the Baptist, who is "the prophet"; see also 1:21,25.

226. On this commandment, see Furnish, *The Love Command,* pp. 132–48.

227. E.g., Sanders, pp. 92–100; Ernst Käsemann, *The Testament of Jesus* (Philadelphia: Fortress, 1966), pp. 59–70.

228. E.g., *Hymns,* XIV; *Manual of Discipline,* IX, 15–22.

229. Käsemann, p. 68.

230. R. Schnackenburg, *The Moral Teaching of the New Testament,* p. 328; see also Furnish, *The Love Command,* pp. 146–48.

231. Käsemann, pp. 59–60, takes John 3:16 to be only a traditional formula and uninstructive for John's own position. But besides this classic text, other texts in John point to the same frontier. Jesus is "the savior of the world" (4:42) and "the light of the world" (8:12; 9:5; 12:46). Cf. also 3:17; 6:33; 12:47. Käsemann treats such texts quite cavalierly.

232. Käsemann acknowledges that "John cannot conceive of love without selfless service and surrender" (p. 61), but he takes this too to be due to primitive tradition and, curiously, not characteristic of John's manner of speaking about love. In general, he minimizes the significance of the texts which make Christ's death the fundamental clue to the nature of love.

233. "No one who abides in him sins" (I Jn. 3:6; cf. also 3:9; 5:18) seems to contradict John's position in 1:8,10. I take this sentence (and 3:9; 5:18) to have the force of an imperative. Indeed "abide" is earlier used as an imperative (2:24,27,28). The construction is like one used at our dinner table occasionally; when my thirteen-year-old simply grabs what he wants without waiting for it to be passed, I say, "That is not done at this table." My literalist ten-year-old sometimes discloses that she has not understood by remarking, "Yes, it is; he just did it." I intended the remark as reminder and as a rebuke, as an exhortation. John also exhorts his readers by this construction to abide in Christ and not to sin. He does not intend to claim that they are in fact sinless.

234. Consider also the parallel structure of I Jn. 1:5 and 3:11. In the first, the Christian tradition is summarized in a theological affirmation; in the second, in the command to love one another.

235. Rudolf Bultmann, *The Johannine Epistles* (Philadelphia: Fortress, 1973), p. 28; see also Schnackenburg, p. 328.

236. Sanders, p. 93.

237. Against Käsemann and Sanders, et al., who emphasize 2:15-17 with its instruction, "Do not love the world," this missionary frontier is especially important. In 2:15-17, "the world" signifies the reign of lust and pride. To hold oneself aloof from lust and pride, from this world in the sense of 2:15-17, does not entail holding

oneself aloof from the persons of this world; else Christ would not have been sent to this world or have died to save it.

238. Described above, pp. 12–13.

239. Revelation was probably written during the reign of Domitian (81–96). Under Domitian the imperial cult was vigorously promoted and enforced. Most of the cities of Asia Minor addressed were centers of Roman civil religion. Moreover, having been put out of the synagogues, Christians could not claim the status of *religia licita*. See Elizabeth Schüssler Fiorenza, *Invitation to the Book of Revelation* (Garden City, N.Y.: Image Books, 1981), pp. 61–67.

240. Collins, "The Political Perspective of the Revelation to John," *JBL,* 96 (1977), 242. See further Frank M. Cross, Jr., *Canaanite Myth and Hebrew Epic* (Cambridge, Mass.: Harvard University Press, 1973), esp. 105–6; Patrick D. Miller, *The Divine Warrior in Early Israel* (Cambridge, Mass.: Harvard University Press, 1973), esp. pp. 64–65.

241. See further Minear, "Sovereignties in Conflict" in *I Saw a New Earth* (Washington: Corpus Books, 1968), pp. 228–34.

242. See Minear, *I Saw a New Earth,* pp. 34–62, for an outstanding analysis of the literary form of these letters. Fiorenza, pp. 56–67, is more helpful in her analysis of the concrete theological and moral issues addressed in them.

243. Sanders, p. 114.

244. "Jezebel" was a woman "prophet." It is noteworthy that in his trenchant attack on her (2:20-23), the author never denounces her as a *woman* claiming office and leadership in the church.

245. Fiorenza, pp. 28–30, 64–66.

246. Ibid., p. 65.

247. Ibid., p. 76.

248. Ibid., p. 84.

249. The curious and difficult characterization of those who "follow the lamb wherever he goes" as "those who have not defiled themselves with women, for they are chaste [Gk. virgins]" (14:4) should probably not be read as a requirement of celibacy. Revelation nowhere else hints at such an ascetic stance. At a number of places, however, sexual offenses are a mark of the life of imperial Rome (e.g., esp. ch. 17) and a symbol of unfaithful collaboration with Rome (e.g., 3:22; 17:8). So here at 14:4, I take it, the point is not to require celibacy but to exhort the community to a faithful counter-empire existence.

250. The commandments are not identified, but as in the rest of the Johannine writings, we can only assume that the law and the teachings of Jesus were to guide conduct in ways that were familiar to the Christian conventicles recently exiled from the synagogue.

251. It should be observed that the merchants' slave-trade is especially singled out for rebuke, 18:13.

252. Sanders, p. 114.

CHAPTER IV

1. One may plausibly suggest that the history of Christian ethics could be written in terms of the history of the interpretation of Scripture. Eric Osborn, *Ethical Patterns in Early Christian Thought* (Cambridge: Cambridge University Press, 1976), is one attempt to do that for the first four centuries; Osborn distills from the New Testament four ethical "patterns" — righteousness, discipleship, faith, and love — and examines their function and development in Clement of Alexandria, Basil the Great, John Chrysostom, and Augustine of Hippo.

2. There are, of course, occasionally dissenting voices. In 1970 Robin Scroggs

made the suggestion that there is "a widespread intuitive acceptance" of the "affirmation" that "the New Testament and the creeds are no longer in any way authoritative or canonical for us" ("Tradition, Freedom, and the Abyss," *New Theology No. 8*, Martin E. Marty and Dean G. Peerman, eds. [New York: Macmillan, 1971], pp. 84-101, esp. p. 85). Whether this quite negative "affirmation" is accepted within the churches either widely or intuitively is doubtful, but Scroggs for one declares his agreement. He proceeds, however, to insist on "the necessity of a dialectic between tradition and contemporary creativity" (p. 92) and even to suggest a couple of guidelines for the movement from tradition to contemporary reflection (pp. 95ff.). But to urge that "necessity" is surely to suggest that Scripture is in some way authoritative. What Scroggs actually opposes is not the authority of Scripture but rather certain ways of using Scripture (and he says as much, p. 92). But to say that Scripture has authority is to express precisely the necessity of reference to it in contemporary Christian moral reflection, it is not to declare what authorizes certain moves from the tradition to contemporary creativity and not others. Conversely, to deny the authority of Scripture would be to deny the necessity of reference to it; it would surely not either open or settle the question of what authorizes certain moves from tradition to contemporary creativity and not others.

3. The World Council of Churches' study reports published under that title, *From the Bible to the Modern World* (Geneva: World Council of Churches, 1949), are a part of the recent history of our question. The attempt to formulate an adequate basis for social criticism and construction had led to the debate between the advocates of some kind of natural law ethic and the advocates of "an ethic of inspiration." The "ethic of inspiration" apparently triumphed, for in 1946-1949, study conferences were convened with the convictions that the Bible gave them unity and that the Bible's unity would give them a foundation for social thought and action. Within these conferences new debates emerged. Karl Barth's emphasis on gospel and Anders Nygren's advocacy of law was only one such debate. The participants did succeed in hammering out some final theses about the authority of Scripture (Alan Richardson and Wolfgang Schweitzer, eds., *Biblical Authority for Today* [London: SCM, 1951], pp. 240-44), but the conclusion observes the variety of modes of applying Scripture and explains, "Interpreters diverge because of differing doctrinal and ecclesiastical traditions, differing ethical, political, and sociological situations, differing temperaments and gifts" (p. 243). See further Edward Duff, S. J., *The Social Thought of the World Council of Churches* (New York: Association Press, 1956).

The consensus that had been reached began to dissolve with the decline of the Biblical Theology Movement (see Brevard Childs, *Biblical Theology in Crisis* [Philadelphia: Westminster, 1970]), and in 1967 the meeting of the Faith and Order Commission at Bristol called for the initiation of a new study of biblical authority more attentive to and appreciative of the diversity of the biblical materials, more realistic about our temporal distance from the biblical situation, and more sensitive to other "authorities" (James Barr, "The Authority of the Bible: A Study Outline," *Ecumenical Review*, 21 [1969], 135-51). A new report was adopted in 1971 ("The Authority of the Bible," in *Faith and Order: Louvain, 1971*, Faith and Order Paper No. 59 [Geneva: World Council of Churches, 1971]; also in *Ecumenical Review*, 23 [1971], 419-37).

4. David H. Kelsey, "Appeals to Scripture in Theology," *Journal of Religion*, 48 (1968), 1-21, and *The Uses of Scripture in Recent Theology* (Philadelphia: Fortress, 1975), has made this point very well. See also Allen Verhey, "The Use of Scripture in Moral Discourse: A Case Study of Walter Rauschenbusch," unpublished Ph.D. dissertation, Yale University, 1975, pp. 1-8.

5. James M. Gustafson, "The Place of Scripture in Christian Ethics: A Methodological Study," *Interpretation*, 24 (1970), 430-55; reprinted in his *Theology and Christian Ethics* (Philadelphia: Pilgrim Press, 1974).

6. Ibid., p. 444.

7. Ibid., pp. 454-55.

8. Edward Leroy Long, Jr., "The Use of the Bible in Christian Ethics: A Look at Basic Options," *Interpretation,* 19 (1965), 149-62. See also his *A Survey of Christian Ethics* (New York: Oxford University Press, 1967).

9. Henry David Aiken, "The Levels of Moral Discourse," in his *Reason and Conduct* (New York: Knopf, 1962), pp. 65-87. Aiken distinguishes four levels of moral discourse: the emotive, moral, ethical, and post-ethical levels. (1) At the "emotive" level, we simply express, without reflection, our emotive responses to certain actions or states of affairs. (2) At the "moral" level we become reflective about what we ought to do. The question is "what ought I do?" We appeal here to data about the situation and to relevant moral rules. (3) When — as is sometimes necessary — these moral rules are challenged, we move to the critical assessment of the rules themselves. This takes place at the "ethical" level. The question now is "which rules should I follow and why?" Here more general ethical principles are used to test whether a moral rule still makes a legitimate claim on us or not. (4) Finally, at the "post-ethical" level, the question becomes "why be moral?" Here one tries to justify the basic ethical principle(s) when there is no more general ethical principle to which to appeal and/or to motivate the person to do what he knows he ought to do. (Aiken's prescriptivism states that "decision is king" at this level, but one need not be a prescriptivist to notice the different levels of discourse.)

10. Wolfgang Schweitzer, "Biblical Theology and Ethics Today: A Survey of the World Position," in Alan Richardson and Wolfgang Schweitzer, eds., *Biblical Authority for Today* (London: SCM, 1951), pp. 127-54.

11. Ibid., p. 138. Zvi Kurzweil, "Three Views on Revelation and Law," in Robert Gordis and Ruth B. Waxman, eds., *Faith and Reason: Essays in Judaism* (New York: KTAV, 1973), pp. 186-96, describes the variety of the use of Scripture in Jewish ethics from a similar perspective. He demonstrates how the differing judgments of S. R. Hirsch, Franz Rosenzweig, and Martin Buber about the relation of Scripture and revelation affect their use of Scripture in discernment and judgment. Kurzweil does not claim that this typology is exhaustive, but he does relate the positions of Hirsch, Rosenzweig, and Buber to Orthodox, Conservative, and Liberal Judaism. See also Rabbi Arthur Gilbert, "Jewish Attitudes Toward the Bible," in P. Benoit et al., *How Does the Christian Confront the Old Testament?, Concilium,* 30.

12. Schweitzer, p. 151.

13. A matter, of course, concerning which there is also a great diversity of opinion. Schweitzer acknowledges this in pointing to the methodological significance of the question "Who was, or who is, Jesus Christ?" (p. 150). See James M. Gustafson, *Christ and the Moral Life* (New York: Harper & Row, 1968).

14. At the beginning of his perceptive book, *The Uses of Scripture in Recent Theology,* David Kelsey also describes and orders the diverse uses of Scripture in theology focusing on these questions. He discerns a pattern in the ways in which Scripture is "construed" as propositional content, as conceptual content, as a narrative of the acts of God, as a narrative in which Christ is the primary agent, as images of a cosmic process, as images of a self-understanding, or as images of the self-world relation. This pattern could also be used to describe the diversity among ethicists. Kelsey's description is not intended to be exhaustive either (and he refuses to call it a "typology"), but he does show how a decision about how to construe the text is dependent on a decision about the "wholeness" of Scripture.

15. C. Freeman Sleeper, "Ethics as a Context for Biblical Interpretation," *Interpretation,* 22 (1968), 443-60. See also his *Black Power and Christian Responsibility* (Nashville: Abingdon, 1969), pp. 19-20.

16. Charles E. Curran, "Dialogue with the Scriptures: The Role and Function of Scriptures in Moral Theology," *Catholic Moral Theology in Dialogue* (Notre Dame: Fides, 1972), pp. 24-64. See also James Barr, "The Authority of the Bible: A Study Outline," *Ecumenical Review,* 21 (1969), 135-51.

17. Verhey, "The Use of Scripture in Moral Discourse: A Case Study of Walter Rauschenbusch."

18. See n. 9.

19. Stephen Toulmin, *The Uses of Argument* (Cambridge: University Press, 1968). Toulmin's categories of nonformal logic are claim, datum, warrant, qualifier, condition of rebuttal, and backing. If a claim is challenged, a datum may be offered in support. Then it is possible to challenge either the datum itself, which effectively renders it the claim of a new argument, or the relevance of the datum to the particular claim. If the challenge is to the inference from datum to claim, a warrant (or inference-license) will have to be produced. These warrants can have different stringencies, sometimes insisting that the inference is a necessary one, sometimes acknowledging that the inference is a probable one. Such is the linguistic task of the qualifier. The conditions of rebuttal state exceptions to the inference-license. The backing provides support for the warrant. So, to use Toulmin's example, if one challenges the *claim* "Harry is a British citizen," it is possible to state the *datum* that "Harry was born in Bermuda." The inference is licensed by a *warrant* "if a person is born in Bermuda, he will probably be a British citizen." The "probably" in that warrant is the *qualifier*, and a *condition of rebuttal* would be "unless both his parents were aliens." *Backing* for the warrant might include certain legal statutes. The relation of backing to warrant can also be analyzed as a separate argument in which the first warrant would be the claim, supported then by data and a second warrant.

Toulmin's categories are used very advantageously by David Kelsey, *The Fabric of Paul Tillich's Theology* (New Haven: Yale, 1967); "Appeals to Scripture in Theology," *Journal of Religion,* 48 (1968), 1–21; and *Uses of Scripture in Recent Theology.*

20. Kelsey, *Uses of Scripture,* pp. 89–113.

21. Immanuel Jacobowitz's response in *The Condition of Jewish Belief,* compiled by the editors of *Commentary* magazine (New York: Macmillan, 1966), pp. 109–16, esp. p. 110.

22. E.g., Shemaryahu Talmon, "The Bible in Contemporary Israeli Humanism," *Judaism,* 21 (1972), 79–83.

23. Louis Jacobs, *Principles of the Jewish Faith: An Analytical Study* (New York: Basic Books, 1964).

24. See, e.g., Marvin Fox, "Judaism, Secularism and Textual Interpretation," in Marvin Fox, ed., *Modern Jewish Ethics: Theory and Practice* (Columbus: Ohio State University Press, 1975), pp. 3–26, and Seymour Siegel, response in *The Condition of Jewish Belief,* pp. 223–28.

25. Harold Lindsell, *The Battle for the Bible* (Grand Rapids: Zondervan, 1976).

26. Harold Lindsell, *The World, the Flesh, and the Devil* (Washington, D.C.: Canon, 1973).

27. Verhey, "The Use of Scripture in Moral Discourse," shows what other warrants and conditions of rebuttal for the movement in argument from Scripture to moral claim are operative in Carl F. H. Henry's more perceptive and sophisticated work from a similar perspective (Henry, *Christian Personal Ethics* [Grand Rapids: Eerdmans, 1957]).

28. Jack T. Sanders, *Ethics in the New Testament.* See my review of this work in *Reformed Review,* 29 (1976), 186–89.

29. Sanders, p. 130.

30. Bruce Birch and Larry Rasmussen, *Bible and Ethics in the Christian Life* (Minneapolis: Augsburg, 1976), pp. 45–46. See also Sanders, pp. 143–54; Curran, op. cit.; Schweitzer, op. cit.; Gustafson, "The Place of Scripture."

31. Chalcedon (451) did not issue a positive statement as much as a series of negative ones: the conjunction of the divine and human natures of Jesus Christ is made *asynkytōs, atreptōs, adiairetōs,* and *achoristōs.*

32. See especially Rudolf Bultmann, "Is Exegesis Without Presuppositions Possible?" in Schubert Ogden, ed., *Existence and Faith: Shorter Writings of Rudolf*

Bultmann (New York: Meridian, 1960), pp. 289–96, and "The Problem of Hermeneutics" in *Essays, Philosophical and Theological* (London: SCM, 1955), pp. 234–61. For criticism of the effects of Bultmann's hermeneutic on Christian ethics, see Thomas C. Oden, *Radical Obedience: The Ethics of Rudolf Bultmann* (Philadelphia: Westminster, 1964); Heinz-Horst Schrey, "The Consequences of Bultmann's Theology for Ethics," in Charles W. Kegley, ed., *The Theology of Rudolf Bultmann* (New York: Harper & Row, 1966), pp. 183–201; Richard M. Hiers, *Jesus and Ethics: Four Interpretations*; C. Freeman Sleeper, "Ethics as a Context for Biblical Interpretation"; Max L. Stackhouse, "Editor's Introduction," in Walter Rauschenbusch, *The Righteousness of the Kingdom* (Nashville: Abingdon, 1968), pp. 13–69.

33. Jacobowitz, op. cit.; see also his *Jewish Medical Ethics* (New York: Bloch, 1975).

34. Gerald Blidstein, *Honor Thy Father and Mother* (New York: KTAV, 1976).

35. Jacobowitz, "Review of Recent Halakhic Periodical Literature," *Tradition,* 4 (1962), 257–70.

36. Solomon Freehof, *Reform Responsa* (New York: Hebrew Union College Press, 1960), p. 22.

37. "Death and Burial in the Jewish Tradition," in Daniel J. Silver, ed., *Judaism and Ethics* (New York: KTAV, 1970), pp. 199–212.

38. Hans Jonas, "Contemporary Problems in Ethics from a Jewish Perspective," in ibid., pp. 29–48.

39. See Martin Buber, "The Man of Today and the Jewish Bible," in *Israel and the World* (New York: Schocken, 1948), pp. 89–102.

40. Brevard Childs, *Biblical Theology in Crisis* (Philadelphia: Westminster, 1970).

41. Richard Mouw, "Commands for Grown-ups," *World View,* 15 (1972), 38–42.

42. James Childress, "Scripture and Christian Ethics," *Interpretation,* 34 (1980), 371–80.

43. James Sellars, *Theological Ethics* (New York: Macmillan, 1966), p. 101. See also J. L. Houlden, *Ethics and the New Testament* (Harmondsworth: Penguin, 1973), pp. 115–25.

44. E.g., Robert E. Fitch, *Of Love and Of Suffering* (Philadelphia: Westminster, 1970); and Coenraad A.J. Van Ouwerkerk, "Gospel Morality and Human Compromise," *Moral Problems and Christian Personalism, Concilium* 5, 7–21; and especially the fine study by Gene Outka, "On Harming Others," *Interpretation* 34 (1980), 381–93.

45. E.g., John Reumann and William Lazareth, *Righteousness and Society: Ecumenical Dialogue in a Revolutionary Age* (Philadelphia: Fortress, 1967).

46. H. Richard Niebuhr, *The Meaning of Revelation* (New York: Macmillan, 1941), pp. 156–75. On H. R. Niebuhr's use of Scripture see James M. Gustafson's "Introduction" to H. R. Niebuhr, *The Responsible Self* (New York: Harper & Row, 1963), pp. 19–25.

47. E.g., Rudolf Bultmann, *Jesus and the Word* (New York: Scribners, 1934). See above, n. 32.

48. E.g., Curran, op. cit.; Sleeper, op. cit.; Hendrik Kraemer, *The Bible and Social Ethics* (Philadelphia: Fortress, 1965); H. Edward Everding and Dana W. Wilbanks, *Decision-Making and the Bible* (Valley Forge, Pa.: Judson, 1975); Gijs Bouwman, "Can We Base our Spiritual Life Today on the Bible?", *Spirituality and Secularization. Concilium,* 49, 23–35.

49. E.g., James H. Cone, *Black Theology and Black Power* (Marynoll, N.Y.: Orbis Books, 1979); Jürgen Moltmann, *Theology of Hope* (New York: Harper, 1967); Paul Lehmann, *Ethics in a Christian Context* (New York: Harper & Row, 1963); Marcus Barth and Verne Fletcher, *Acquittal by Resurrection* (New York: Holt, Rinehart and Winston, 1964).

50. Wolfhart Pannenberg, *Theology and the Kingdom of God* (Philadelphia: Westminster, 1969).

51. Reumann and Lazareth, *Righteousness and Society* (Philadelphia: Fortress, 1967).
52. William R. Baird, *The Corinthian Church: A Biblical Approach to Urban Culture* (New York: Abingdon, 1964).
53. Pannenberg, p. 115.
54. Baird, op. cit.; see also Bruce D. Rahtjen, *Scripture and Social Action* (Nashville: Abingdon, 1966).
55. Mehl, "The Basis of Christian Social Ethics," in John C. Bennett, ed., *Christian Social Ethics in a Changing World* (New York: Association Press, 1966).
56. John H. Yoder, *The Politics of Jesus*, p. 23.
57. Jürgen Moltmann, "Toward a Political Hermeneutic of the Gospel," in *Religion, Revolution, and the Future* (New York, Scribners, 1968), p. 100.
58. H. Richard Niebuhr, *The Responsible Self* (New York: Harper and Row, 1963).
59. See Stanley Hauerwas' skillful use of "story" as a way to construe Scripture's authority in "The Moral Authority of Scripture: The Politics and Ethics of Remembering," *A Community of Character* (Notre Dame: Notre Dame Press, 1981), pp. 53-71.
60. Childress, "Scripture and Christian Ethics," *Interpretation*, 34 (1980), 371-80.
61. Sleeper, "Ethics as a Context for Biblical Interpretation," *Interpretation*, 22 (1962), 443-60.
62. Sleeper, "Language and Ethics in Biblical Interpretation," *Journal of Religion*, 22 (1968), 443-60.
63. Stackhouse, op. cit.
64. Mouw, op. cit., p. 40.
65. Ellul, *To Will and To Do* (Philadelphia: Pilgrim Press, 1969).
66. This move is quite similar to Karl Barth, *Church Dogmatics*, III/4 (Edinburgh: T.&T. Clark, 1961), where, after having insisted on the theological character of revelation, he uses Scripture to provide "formed references," which while not quite "moral law" are quite close to it in practice.
67. St. Augustine, *On Christian Doctrine*, I, xxxvi.
68. Alan Richardson and Wolfgang Schweitzer, eds., *Biblical Authority for Today* (Philadelphia: Westminster, 1951), p. 240.
69. Kraemer, op. cit., p. 30.
70. Ibid., pp. 30,31.
71. A similar emphasis on the transhistorical Christ can be found in Jacques Ellul, for whom the narratives present a Jesus Christ who transcends moral distinctions, who is deliverer and yet commander; see, e.g., *The Judgment of Jonah* (Grand Rapids: Eerdmans, 1971) and *The Politics of God and the Politics of Man* (Grand Rapids: Eerdmans, 1972). On Ellul's use of Scripture see Vernard Eller, "How Jacques Ellul Reads the Bible," *Christian Century*, Nov. 29, 1972, pp. 1212-15.
72. Amos Wilder, *Kerygma, Eschatology, and Social Ethics* (Philadelphia: Fortress Press, 1966).
73. Gutiérrez, *A Theology of Liberation* (Marynoll, N.Y.: Orbis Books, 1973).
74. E.g., Hugo Assmann, *Theology for a Nomad Church* (Marynoll, N.Y.: Orbis Books, 1975).
75. E.g., James H. Cone, op. cit., and *A Black Theology of Liberation* (New York: Lippincott, 1970).
76. E.g., Rosemary Ruether, *Liberation Theology* (Ramsey, N.J.: Paulist, 1972).
77. E.g., J. Verkuyl, *The Message of Liberation in Our Age* (Grand Rapids: Eerdmans, 1970).
78. J. Deotis Roberts, *Liberation and Reconciliation* (Philadelphia: Westminster, 1971).
79. Yoder, *The Politics of Jesus*, p. 250.
80. Richard Mouw, *Politics and the Biblical Drama*.

81. William Stringfellow, *An Ethic for Christians and Other Aliens in a Strange Land* (Waco: Word, 1973).

82. Sellars, *Theological Ethics.*

83. Colin Morris, *Unyoung, Uncolored, Unpoor* (Nashville: Abingdon, 1969).

84. S. G. F. Brandon, *Jesus and the Zealots.*

85. James Douglas, *The Non-Violent Cross: A Theology of Revolution and Peace* (New York: Macmillan, 1968).

86. Henry, *Christian Personal Ethics,* p. 346.

87. See Verhey, "The Use of Scripture in Moral Argument."

88. Brevard Childs, *Biblical Theology in Crisis* (Philadelphia: Westminster, 1970), p. 136. Childs' recommendation is an important corrective, and he uses it brilliantly in a chapter on sexuality, but an implicit judgment about what one understands when one understands the canon is operative and should be made explicit; see my review of Childs' book in *Reflection,* 70, 14–15.

89. Gustafson, "The Place of Scripture in Christian Ethics," p. 444. See also his "The Relation of the Gospels to the Moral Life," in *Jesus and Man's Hope, II,* ed. Donald Miller and D. Y. Hadidian (Pittsburgh: Pittsburgh Theological Seminary, 1971), pp. 103–17.

90. Birch and Rasmussen, op. cit., p. 194.

91. Jewish thinkers seldom write about the message of Scripture. Leo Baeck's insistence that the message of Scripture is its "ethical monotheism" (*The Essence of Judaism* [New York: Schocken, 1948]) seems to have little continuing influence. There are a few more echoes (e.g., Barbara Ann Swyhart, "Reconstructionism: Hokhma as an Ethical Principle," *Judaism,* 24, 436–46) of M. M. Kaplan's suggestion (e.g., his response in *The Condition of Jewish Belief*) that Scripture is really *about* the covenant as the concept of Jewish community which stands as a prototype for the world community. Martin Buber's existential reading of the literature as a report and elicitation of an encounter with the Eternal Thou (e.g., op. cit.) seems to have been more influential among Christian ethicists than Jewish, but some continuing influence can surely be seen (Arthur A. Cohen, "Revelation and Law," in *Faith and Reason: Essays in Judaism,* ed. Robert Gordis and Ruth Waxman [New York: KTAV, 1973], pp. 273–79; and Emil Fackenheim, *Quest for Past and Future: Essays in Jewish Theology* [Bloomington: Indiana University Press, 1968], are influenced by Buber but allow a much larger place for the law). Eric Gutkind, *Choose Life: The Biblical Call to Revolt* (New York: Henry Schumann, 1952), judges the message of Scripture to be resistance to the inequities of the status quo inspired by a vision of the messianic social hope. Representatives of Reform Judaism sometimes still identify the message of Scripture with some prophetic summary like Micah 6:8 (e.g., Milton Himmelfarb, "Introduction," in *The Condition of Jewish Belief,* p. 4). Many Jewish writers, however, simply insist that what one understands when one understands the Scripture is the Torah, the laws of Moses. Even within orthodox Judaism, however, that judgment can be nuanced differently with important methodological effects. Norman Lamm, for example, agrees that what one understands when one understands the Scripture is Torah, but he quite rightly insists that "Torah" is more than "nomos," that it "includes the full spectrum of spiritual edification: theological and ethical, mystical and rhapsodic" (his response in *The Condition of Jewish Belief,* p. 125). While this judgment neither relativizes nor limits the use of Scripture to provide moral laws interpreted and applied by rabbis, it does license and emphasize a much broader and more "haggadic" use of Scripture concerned with disposition and perspective alongside an "halakic" use (*Faith and Doubt: Studies in Traditional Jewish Thought* [New York: KTAV, 1971]).

92. H. D. Lewis, *Morals and Revelation* (London: George Allen & Unwin, 1951), severely criticizes this feature of Emil Brunner's ethic.

93. Kraemer, op. cit. There was, from the first, opposition to this position within the WCC, first by William Temple and later by others: Alan Richardson, "An An-

glican Contribution," in *Biblical Authority for Today,* ed. Richardson and Wolfgang Schweitzer, pp. 112–26, is noteworthy. In "The Authority of the Bible," *Faith and Order: Louvain, 1971* (Faith and Order Paper No. 59) this theological veto itself seems finally to be candidly overridden.

94. See Ellul, *To Will and To Do.*

95. Paul Lehmann, *Ethics in a Christian Context.*

96. Yoder, *The Politics of Jesus,* pp. 19–22.

97. See Jacobowitz's response in *The Condition of Jewish Belief,* pp. 109–16.

98. Sanders, *Ethics in the New Testament,* p. 130.

99. Again Jewish discussions provide instructive parallels. Ernst Fisch, "A Response to Ernst Simon," *Modern Jewish Ethics: Theory and Practice,* ed. Marvin Fox, pp. 57–61, for example, charges Ernst Simon with surrendering Jewish identity when he gives control to nonbiblical sources of moral insight. Simon, "The Neighbor (*Re'a*) Whom We shall Love," ibid., pp. 29–56, had said that the neighbor whom the Jew is to love (Lev. 19:18) is exegetically and historically limited to the fellow Jew; that interpretation, however, is to be discarded for an extra-*Halakic* ethical norm of universal neighbor-love because it violates "moral sense." Fisch, however, insists that the Jew stick with Torah, and his concern is that the Jewish moral tradition and identity not be surrendered for "ethical humanism."

100. Jewish reflection is also instructive here. Eugene B. Korn, "Ethics and Jewish Law," *Judaism,* 24, 201–14, comes close to affirming a wholly autonomous morality, and struggles with the implications. He argues for the autonomy of the moral law, for the independence of moral statements from their source in Torah or even in God. "One cannot claim moral justification by citing a Biblical verse or *Halakic* exegesis" (p. 210). The ritual laws, however, different in kind from moral laws, are binding on the Jews precisely because they are found in Torah. Moreover, the position Korn seems to adopt here, a position that would add biblical duty (ritual) to an independent natural morality, quickly shades into a position that places biblical ethics and natural ethics and natural morality in paradoxical tension when Korn insists that the halakic Jew must submit simultaneously to two authorities when deciding what to do (p. 208). This simultaneous submission to the Torah and autonomous morality will allow neither the theological veto's suspension of the ethical nor a wholly autonomous dismissal of halakah. Agreement between these sources cannot be demonstrated, but is an assumption made in faith. The simultaneous submission to two authorities, Torah and natural moral wisdom, has been suggested by a number of other Jewish writers. Some of these have emphasized that within traditional halakic interpretation of Torah the rabbis have used other sources as well (Yitzchak D. Gilat, "The Halakah and Its Relationship to Social Reality," *Tradition,* 13/4, 68–87; Marvin Fox, "Judaism, Secularism, and Textual Interpretation" in *Modern Jewish Ethics-Theory and Practice,* ed. Marvin Fox, pp. 3–26; Eugene Borowitz, "Subjectivity and the Halachic Process," *Judaism,* 13/2, 211–19; Borowitz, "Authentic Judaism and the Halachah," *Judaism,* 19/1, 66–76; Jakob Petuchowski, "Plural Models within the Halakah," *Judaism,* 19/1, 77–89.) Others have emphasized the mutual influence of the Bible and other sources on contemporary Jews (Samuel Hugo Bergmann, "Expansion and Contraction in Jewish Ethics," *The Quality of Faith: Essay on Judaism and Morality* [Jerusalem: World Zionist Organization, 1970]). The recommendations for dialogue are consistently unclear about whether the Bible or natural morality has "the last word." The suggestion of Borowitz, "Authentic Judaism and the Halakah," *Judaism,* 19/1, 66–76, however, is methodologically clearer than most: the Torah has been and is to be applied in terms of criteria that allow and demand use of other sources, the criteria of practical feasibility, economic viability, ethical significance, and spiritual meaningfulness.

101. Among the clearest and most candid are Birch and Rasmussen, *Bible and Ethics in the Christian Life;* Sellars, *Theological Ethics;* and Curran, "Dialogue with the Scriptures: The Role and Function of Scriptures in Moral Theology."

102. See my review of Birch and Rasmussen in the *Union Seminary Quarterly Review*, 34/1, 50–52, where I suggest that their canon criterion and church criterion are necessary for testing proposals for the use of Scripture rather than sufficient as a discrete proposal.

103. James Mackey, *Tradition and Change in the Church* (Dayton, Ohio: Pflaum, 1968), pp. 42f., cited by Stanley Hauerwas, "The Moral Authority of Scripture," *A Community of Character*, p. 61.

104. *Riggs* v. *Palmer*, 115 New York 506, 22 N.E. 188 (1889), excerpts reprinted in Phillip E. Davis, ed., *Moral Duty and Legal Responsibility, A Philosophical-Legal Casebook* (New York: Appleton-Century-Crofts, 1966), pp. 22–33. I am indebted for this reference to my friend Chris Hackler.

105. This section is indebted to David H. Kelsey, "The Bible and Christian Theology," *The Journal of the American Academy of Religion*, 48/3, 385–402.

106. See, e.g., James Barr, *Old and New in Interpretation* (London: SCM, 1966); Wolfhart Pannenberg, ed., *Revelation as History* (London: Macmillan, 1968).

107. See, for example, W. D. Ross, *The Right and the Good* (Oxford: Clarendon Press, 1930), and Bernard Williams, "A Critique of Utilitarianism," in J. C. C. Smart and Bernard Williams, *Utilitarianism: For & Against* (London: Cambridge University Press, 1973), pp. 75–150.

108. See, for example, John Rawls, *A Theory of Justice* (Cambridge, Mass.: Harvard University Press, 1971), and Charles Fried, *Right and Wrong* (Cambridge, Mass.: Harvard University Press, 1978).

109. Or, more concretely, for preferring John Rawls' *A Theory of Justice* to Robert Nozick's *Anarchy, State, and Utopia* (New York: Basic Books, 1974).

110. This is much more carefully and analytically worked out in James M. Gustafson, *Can Ethics be Christian?* (Chicago: University of Chicago Press, 1975), pp. 82–116.

INDEXES

BIBLICAL REFERENCES

Note: Passages have been used in this index rather than individual texts. A reference may be to either the passage or texts within it or both.

SUBJECTS

AUTHORS